C000277025

RICHARD II

RICHARD II
A TRUE KING'S FALL

KATHRYN WARNER

AMBERLEY

Dedicated to the memory of John Alan Lamb, who died on
10 January 2017. Always remembered, always loved.

First published 2017

Amberley Publishing
The Hill, Stroud
Gloucestershire, GL5 4EP

www.amberley-books.com

Copyright © Kathryn Warner, 2017

The right of Kathryn Warner to be identified as the Author of this work has been asserted
in accordance with the Copyrights, Designs and Patents Act 1988.

All rights reserved. No part of this book may be reprinted or reproduced or utilised in any
form or by any electronic, mechanical or other means, now known or hereafter invented,
including photocopying and recording, or in any information storage or retrieval system,
without the permission in writing from the Publishers.

British Library Cataloguing in Publication Data.
A catalogue record for this book is available from the British Library.

ISBN 978 1 4456 6278 7 (hardback)
ISBN 978 1 4456 6279 4 (ebook)

Family trees by Thomas Bohm, User design.
Typesetting and Origination by Amberley Publishing.
Printed in the UK.

Henry of Bolingbroke: Go, some of you convey him to the Tower.
King Richard II: 'O good! convey? conveyors are you all,
That rise thus nimbly by a true king's fall.

Shakespeare, *Richard II*, Act 4 Scene 1

Contents

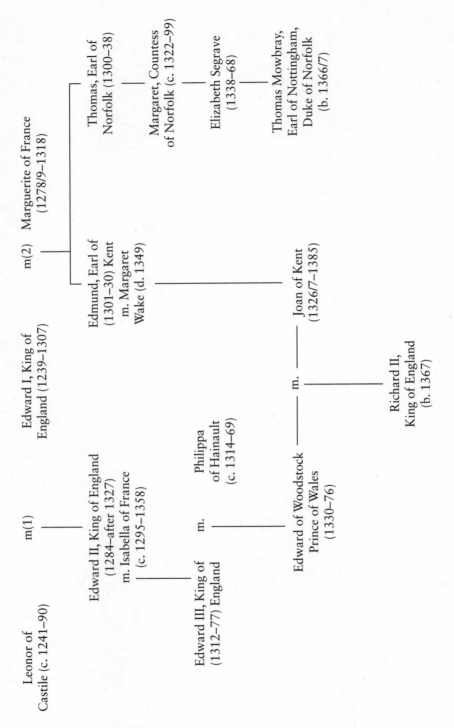

Richard's paternal and maternal descent.

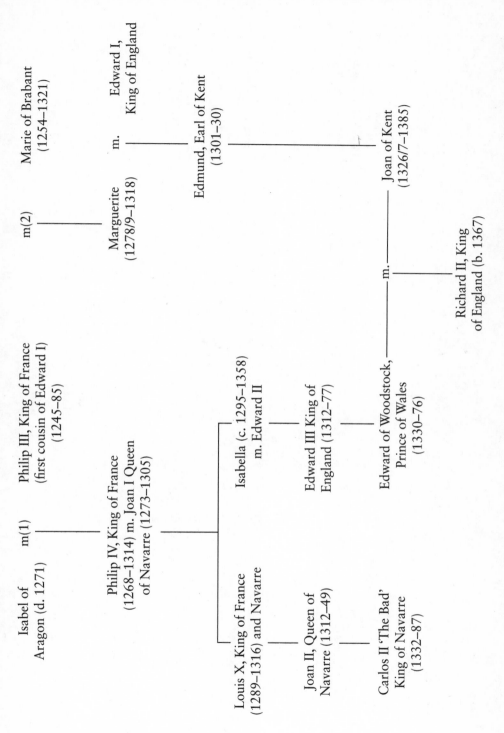

Richard's French descent.

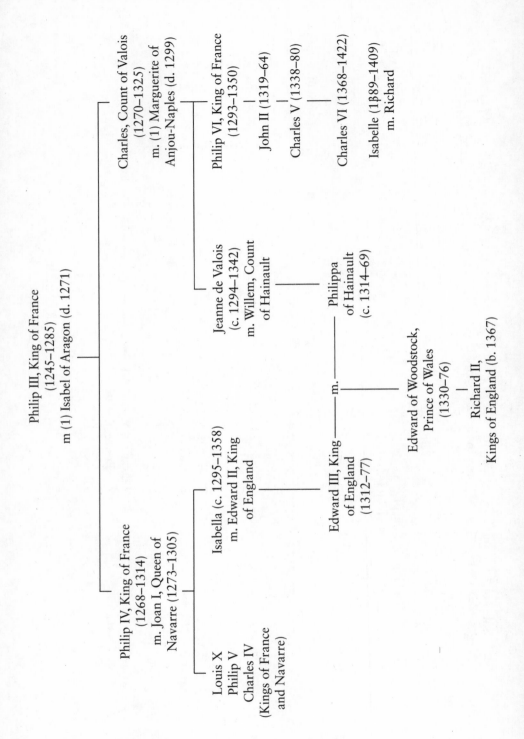

The French royal family and connections to Richard.

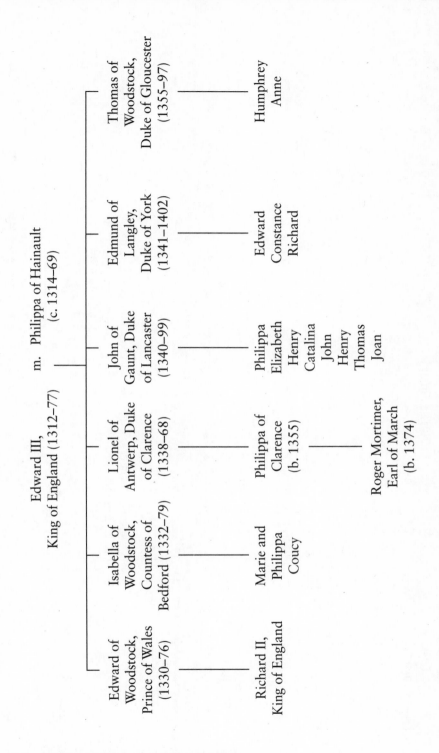

Edward III's children and grandchildren.

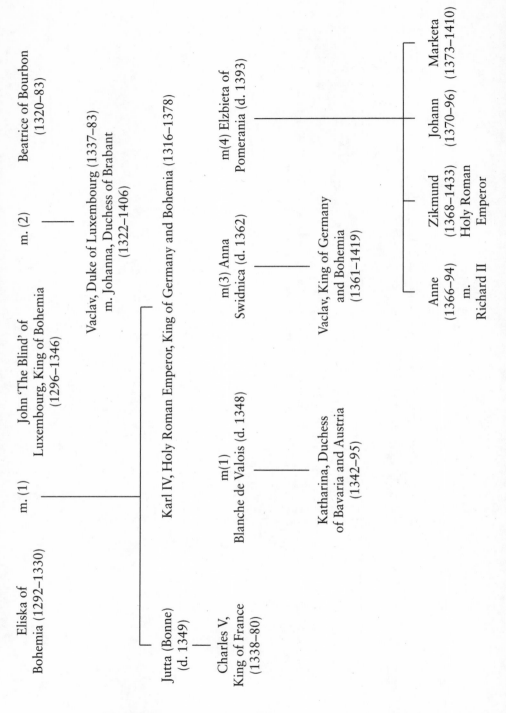

Descent of Richard's queen Anne of Bohemia.

Who's Who: English and European Royalty and Nobility in the Late Fourteenth Century

Richard II, known as Richard of Bordeaux after his birthplace in Aquitaine, France: king of England, lord of Ireland, prince of Wales, duke of Aquitaine and Cornwall, earl of Chester; born 6 January 1367

Anne of Bohemia, also sometimes called Anne of Luxembourg, queen of England (b. 1366): daughter of Karl IV, Holy Roman Emperor and king of Bohemia, and his fourth wife Elżbieta of Pomerania; marries Richard II in 1382

Isabelle of France, also called Isabelle de Valois, queen of England (b. 1389): eldest daughter of Charles VI, king of France, and Isabeau of Bavaria; marries Richard II in 1396

Edward of Woodstock (b. 1330), prince of Wales and Aquitaine, duke of Cornwall, earl of Chester: father of Richard II; eldest son of Edward III and Philippa of Hainault; 200 years after his death, begins to be known as the 'Black Prince'

Joan of Kent (b. 1326/7), princess of Wales and Aquitaine; countess of Kent in her own right: mother of Richard II; granddaughter of Edward I, king of England

Edward III, king of England (b. 1312): eldest child of Edward II and Isabella of France; becomes king in 1327; Richard II's paternal grandfather

Philippa of Hainault, queen of England (b. *c*. 1314): wife of Edward III; daughter of Willem, count of Hainault and Holland, and niece of Philip VI of France; Richard II's paternal grandmother

Edmund of Woodstock, earl of Kent (1301–1330): youngest son of Edward I and his second wife Marguerite of France, half-brother of Edward II and uncle of Edward III; father of Joan of Kent and maternal grandfather of Richard II

Margaret Wake, countess of Kent (*c*. mid to late 1290s–1349): daughter of John, Lord Wake, and Joan Fiennes; widow of Sir John Comyn; Richard II's maternal grandmother

Edward II, king of England (1284–after 1327), son of Edward I and his first wife Leonor of Castile, and **Isabella of France**, queen of England (*c*. 1295–1358), daughter of Philip IV, king of France and Jeanne I, queen of Navarre: parents of Edward III, and Richard II's great-grandparents

Marguerite of France, queen of England (1278/9–1318): daughter of Philip III of France and half-sister of Philip IV; second wife of Edward I, stepmother of Edward II, and mother of Edmund of Woodstock, earl of Kent; Richard's great-grandmother

Edward I (1239–1307), king of England from 1272: married firstly to Leonor of Castile (d. 1290), Edward II's mother, and secondly to Marguerite of France (d. 1318), Edmund of Woodstock's mother: Richard's great-great-grandfather on his father's side and his great-grandfather on his mother's

Lionel of Antwerp, duke of Clarence, earl of Ulster (b. 1338): second son of Edward III and Philippa of Hainault; uncle of Richard II; married to Elizabeth de Burgh and secondly to Violante Visconti

Elizabeth de Burgh, duchess of Clarence, countess of Ulster (1332–1363): first wife of Lionel of Antwerp; niece via her mother Maud of Lancaster of Henry, duke of Lancaster; first cousin of Blanche of Lancaster, Henry Percy, earl of Northumberland, and Richard Fitzalan, earl of Arundel; a descendant of Edward I

Philippa of Clarence, countess of March (b. 1355): only child and heir of Lionel of Antwerp and Elizabeth de Burgh; granddaughter of Edward III and first cousin of Richard II; marries **Edmund Mortimer, earl of March** (b. 1352)

Roger Mortimer, earl of March (b. 1374): elder son and heir of Edmund Mortimer and Philippa of Clarence, and heir of his grandparents Lionel of Antwerp and Elizabeth de Burgh; great-grandson of Edward III. Marries Richard II's half-niece Alianore Holland in 1388; their son and heir **Edmund Mortimer** is born in 1391

John of Gaunt, duke of Lancaster (b. 1340): third son of Edward III, and Richard II's uncle; married firstly to Blanche of Lancaster, then Constanza of Castile and thirdly Katherine Swynford

Blanche of Lancaster, duchess of Lancaster (b. *c.* 1342): younger daughter of Henry, duke of Lancaster (*c.* 1310–1361), and becomes her father's sole heir when her sister Maud dies childless in 1362; marries John of Gaunt in 1359; Richard's aunt by marriage

Henry of Lancaster (often known as Henry of Bolingbroke, his birthplace in Lincolnshire), earl of Derby, duke of Hereford, later duke of Lancaster (b. 1367): son and heir of John of Gaunt and Blanche of Lancaster; Richard II's first cousin; married to Mary de Bohun, younger daughter and co-heir of the earl of Hereford; becomes King Henry IV in 1399

Philippa of Lancaster, queen of Portugal (b. 1360): elder daughter of John of Gaunt and Blanche of Lancaster; marries King João I of Portugal in 1387 and is the mother of the 'Illustrious Generation'

Elizabeth of Lancaster (b. 1363/4), duchess of Exeter, countess of Huntingdon: younger daughter of John of Gaunt and Blanche of Lancaster; marries firstly John Hastings, earl of Pembroke (b. 1372; marriage annulled before consummation) then Richard II's half-brother John Holland

Constanza of Castile, rightful queen of Castile in her own right, duchess of Lancaster (b. *c.* 1354): elder daughter and heir of King Pedro 'the Cruel' of Castile and his mistress Maria de Padilla; marries John of Gaunt in 1371 as his second wife; Richard's aunt by marriage

Catalina (Katherine) of Lancaster, queen of Castile (b. 1372/73): only child of John of Gaunt and Constanza of Castile, and Constanza's heir; Richard's first cousin; half-sister of Henry, Philippa and Elizabeth of Lancaster; marries Enrique III of Castile and mother of Juan II

Katherine Swynford, duchess of Lancaster (b. *c.* 1345/50): long-term mistress of John of Gaunt and becomes his third wife in 1396; mother of his four illegitimate children the Beauforts, who are legitimised in 1397

John Beaufort (b. *c.* 1373), earl of Somerset and marquis of Dorset; **Henry Beaufort** (b. *c.* 1375), bishop of Lincoln, later a cardinal; **Thomas Beaufort** (b. *c.* 1377), later duke of Exeter; and **Joan Beaufort** (b. *c.* 1379), countess of Westmorland: children of John of Gaunt and Katherine Swynford, born illegitimate, legitimised in 1397; Richard's first cousins

Edmund of Langley, earl of Cambridge, duke of York (b. 1341): fourth son of Edward III, Richard II's uncle; married to Isabel of Castile, then to Richard's half-niece Joan Holland

Isabel of Castile, duchess of York (b. *c.* 1355): younger daughter of King Pedro 'the Cruel', and sister of Constanza, duchess of Lancaster; marries Edmund in 1372

Edward of York, earl of Rutland, duke of Albemarle, later duke of York (b. 1373/4): elder son and heir of Edmund of Langley and Isabel of Castile; Richard II's first cousin; marries or betrothed to Beatriz of Portugal, daughter of King Fernando, as a child, then Philippa Mohun, sister of the countess of Salisbury

Constance of York (b. 1374/6): only daughter of Edmund of Langley and Isabel; marries Thomas, Lord Despenser, later earl of Gloucester; later has an illegitimate daughter with Edmund Holland, earl of Kent

Richard of Conisbrough (b. *c.* 1375 or 1385): younger son of Edmund of Langley and Isabel; later earl of Cambridge; Richard II's godson; marries Anne Mortimer (b. 1390), daughter of Roger Mortimer, earl of March (b. 1374); father of Richard, duke of York, and grandfather of Edward IV and Richard III

Thomas of Woodstock, earl of Buckingham, duke of Gloucester (b. 1355): fifth and youngest son of Edward III, and Richard II's uncle; married to Eleanor de Bohun, elder daughter and co-heir of the earl of Hereford

Eleanor de Bohun (b. *c.* 1366), countess of Buckingham and duchess of Gloucester, and **Mary de Bohun** (b. *c.* 1368/70), countess of Derby: daughters and co-heirs of Humphrey de Bohun, earl of Hereford, and descendants of Edward I; Mary's eldest son (b. 1386) is King Henry V

Humphrey of Gloucester (b. 1382): only son of Thomas of Woodstock and Eleanor de Bohun; Richard II's first cousin; dies as a teenager in 1399 and never marries

Anne of Gloucester (b. 1383): eldest daughter and ultimate heir of Thomas of Woodstock and Eleanor de Bohun; marries Edmund Stafford, earl of Stafford

Isabella of Woodstock, countess of Bedford (b. 1332): eldest daughter of Edward III and Queen Philippa, and the only one who lives past adolescence; Richard II's aunt; marries Enguerrand (or Ingelram) Coucy in 1365

Philippa Coucy, countess of Oxford, duchess of Ireland (b. *c.* 1367): younger daughter of Isabella of Woodstock and Enguerrand Coucy; granddaughter of Edward III and first cousin of Richard II; married to Robert de Vere, earl of Oxford and duke of Ireland

Thomas Holland, earl of Kent (b. 1350/51): elder son of Joan of Kent and her first husband Sir Thomas Holland (d. 1360); half-brother of Richard II; marries Alice Fitzalan, sister of the earl of Arundel

Thomas Holland, earl of Kent and duke of Surrey (b. 1374): son and heir of above; Richard II's nephew; marries Joan Stafford, daughter of Hugh, earl of Stafford; childless

Alianore Holland, countess of March (b. *c.* 1373): eldest daughter of Thomas Holland the elder, and Richard's niece; marries Roger Mortimer, earl of March (b. 1374)

Joan Holland, duchess of York (b. *c.* 1380): daughter of Thomas Holland the elder, and Richard's niece; marries the king's widowed uncle Edmund of Langley, duke of York, in 1393

Edmund Holland, earl of Kent (b. 1383/84): younger son of Thomas Holland the elder, his brother Thomas's heir, and Richard II's nephew; marries Lucia Visconti of Milan; has an illegitimate daughter with Constance of York

Margaret Holland, countess of Somerset (b. *c.* 1385): daughter of Thomas Holland the elder, and Richard's niece; marries Richard's first cousin John Beaufort; mother of Joan Beaufort, queen of Scotland, and great-grandmother of Henry VII

John Holland, duke of Exeter and earl of Huntingdon (b. *c.* 1352/55): second son of Joan of Kent, and Richard II's other half-brother; married to Richard's first cousin Elizabeth of Lancaster; his heir is his second son John, b. *c.* 1395

Charles V, king of France (b. 1338): eldest son of John II (d. 1364) and Jutta/Bonne of Bohemia (d. 1349); first cousin of Richard's queen Anne of Bohemia; grandson of Philip VI and the third Valois king of France; married to Jeanne de Bourbon

Charles VI, king of France (b. 1368): son of Charles V and Jeanne de Bourbon; marries Isabelle or Isabeau of Bavaria in 1385; father of Richard's second queen Isabelle de Valois and of Katherine de Valois, queen of Henry V of England

Louis, duke of Anjou (b. 1339); **John**, duke of Berry (b. 1340); **Philip** 'the Bold', duke of Burgundy (b. 1342): brothers of Charles V and uncles of Charles VI; and **Louis**, duke of Bourbon (b. 1337): brother of Jeanne de Bourbon and also Charles VI's uncle

Louis, duke of Orléans (b. 1372), younger son of Charles V and brother of Charles VI; married to his first cousin Valentina Visconti of Milan; his son and heir is **Charles** (b. 1394), who marries Richard II's widow Isabelle

Carlos II 'the Bad', king of Navarre (b. 1332), great-grandson of Philip IV of France, and second cousin of Edward of Woodstock; possibly Richard's godfather; married to Jeanne de Valois, daughter of John II of France and sister of Charles V; his son and heir is **Carlos III** (b. 1361)

Fernando I, king of Portugal (b. 1345), son and heir of **Pedro I** (d. 1367); Fernando's daughter **Beatriz** (b. *c.* 1373), who briefly marries or is betrothed to Edward of York; and Fernando's half-brother and successor **João I** (b. 1357), who marries Philippa of Lancaster

Pedro I 'the Cruel', king of Castile (b. 1334), probably Richard's godfather; marries Charles V of France's sister-in-law Blanche de Bourbon but repudiates and imprisons her; he and his mistress Maria de Padilla are parents of Constanza, duchess of Lancaster, and Isabel, duchess of York

Enrique II of Trastámara, king of Castile (b. 1334), half-brother, usurper and murderer of King Pedro; his son and successor **Juan I** (b. 1358); and Juan's son **Enrique III** (b. 1379), who marries Catalina of Lancaster

Pedro IV, king of Aragon (b. 1319), and his sons **Juan I** (b. 1350) and **Martin I** (b. 1356), both from his third marriage to Eleanor of Sicily; Juan I's daughter **Yolande**, b. *c.* 1381, is put forward as Richard's bride in 1395

Jaime IV, king of Majorca (b. *c.* 1336), nephew of Pedro IV of Aragon; Richard's godfather; marries Giovanna I, queen of Naples

Giovanna I, queen of Naples (b. 1328); married to 1) András of Hungary (d. 1345), 2) Louis of Taranto (d. 1362), 3) Jaime IV, king of Majorca (d. 1375) and 4) Otto, duke of Brunswick (d. 1398)

Gosdantin (Constantine) IV, king of Armenia, known as Richard in western Europe, possibly Richard II's godfather; and his distant cousin and successor **Levon (Leo) V** (b. 1342)

Václav (in Czech, or **Wenzel** in German), king of Germany and Bohemia (b. 1361): son of the Holy Roman Emperor Karl IV and his third wife Anna Świdnica; half-brother of Anne of Bohemia and Richard II's brother-in-law; married to Johanna of Bavaria, then Sophia of Bavaria

Zikmund (or Sigismund), Holy Roman Emperor, king of Germany, Bohemia, Italy, Hungary and Croatia (b. 1368): full brother of Anne of Bohemia and Richard II's brother-in-law; married to Maria of Hungary, then Barbara of Celje

Karl (Charles) IV, Holy Roman Emperor, king of Germany, Bohemia and Italy (b. 1316): son and heir of John 'the Blind' and Eliška Přemyslovna, king and queen of Bohemia; crowned emperor in 1355; marries 1) Blanche de Valois 2) Anna of the Palatinate 3) Anna Świdnica and 4) Elżbieta of Pomerania; father of Anne of Bohemia

Elżbieta of Pomerania, Holy Roman Empress (b. *c.* 1346/47): marries Karl IV in 1363; daughter of Bogislaw, duke of Pomerania, and granddaughter of Kazimierz III, king of Poland; mother of Anne of Bohemia, Zikmund, Johann von Görlitz and Markéta; Richard's mother-in-law

The English Nobility in the Late Fourteenth Century

Henry of Grosmont, first duke of Lancaster (*c.* 1310–1361): only son and heir of Henry, earl of Lancaster (d. 1345); great-grandson of Henry III; father of Blanche of Lancaster and father-in-law of John of Gaunt; maternal grandfather of Henry of Lancaster, later King Henry IV (b. 1367)

Robert de Vere, earl of Oxford, marquis of Dublin and duke of Ireland (b. 1362), married to Richard II's first cousin Philippa Coucy; son of Thomas de Vere, earl of Oxford, and Maud Ufford; his heir is his uncle Aubrey de Vere

Maud de Vere, *née* Ufford, countess of Oxford (b. *c.* 1345): mother of Robert de Vere and widow of Thomas de Vere, earl of Oxford (d. 1371); half-sister of Elizabeth de Burgh, duchess of Clarence (1332–1363); niece of Henry, duke of Lancaster

Maud of Lancaster, countess of Ulster (b. *c.* 1312): sister of Henry, duke of Lancaster; mother of Elizabeth de Burgh, duchess of Clarence, and Maud Ufford, countess of Oxford; grandmother of Philippa of Clarence and Robert de Vere; great-grandmother of Roger Mortimer, earl of March (b. 1374)

Blanche of Lancaster, Lady Wake (b. *c.* 1302/05): eldest sister of Henry, duke of Lancaster; widow of Thomas, Lord Wake (d. 1349), uncle of Joan of Kent; Richard II's great-aunt; has no children

Edmund Mortimer, third earl of March (b. 1352): son and heir of Roger Mortimer (1328–1360), second earl of March, and Philippa Montacute, sister of the earl of Salisbury; marries Edward III's granddaughter Philippa of Clarence

Richard Fitzalan, earl of Arundel and Surrey (b. *c.* 1346): son and heir of Richard Fitzalan, earl of Arundel (*c.* 1313–1376) and Eleanor of Lancaster (*c.* 1318–1372), sister of Henry, duke of Lancaster; first cousin of Elizabeth de Burgh, Maud Ufford, Blanche of Lancaster and Henry Percy, earl of Northumberland; married to Elizabeth de Bohun, sister of the earl of Hereford, and secondly to Philippa Mortimer, second daughter of Edmund Mortimer and Philippa of Clarence; his son and heir is Thomas (b. 1381)

Elizabeth Fitzalan, *née* de Bohun, countess of Arundel (b. *c.* 1340s/1350): sister of Humphrey de Bohun, earl of Hereford, and half-sister of Roger Mortimer, second earl of March (1328–1360); marries Richard Fitzalan, earl of Arundel

Elizabeth Mowbray, *née* Fitzalan, countess of Nottingham and Countess Marshal, later duchess of Norfolk (b. *c.* 1366): daughter of Richard Fitzalan, earl of Arundel, and Elizabeth de Bohun; first cousin of Eleanor and Mary de Bohun, and of Edmund Mortimer, third earl of March; marries Thomas Mowbray, earl of Nottingham and duke of Norfolk

Thomas Fitzalan, later earl of Arundel (b. 1381): eldest son and heir of Richard Fitzalan, earl of Arundel, and Elizabeth de Bohun; brother-in-law of Thomas Mowbray, earl of Nottingham; marries Beatriz, illegitimate daughter of King João of Portugal

Alice Holland, *née* Fitzalan, countess of Kent (b. *c.* late 1340s/early 1350s); sister of Richard Fitzalan, earl of Arundel; married to Richard II's half-brother Thomas Holland; mother of Alianore, countess of March, Joan, duchess of York, Thomas, duke of Surrey, and others

Joan de Bohun, *née* Fitzalan, countess of Hereford (b. *c.* late 1340s/early 1350s); the earl of Arundel's other sister; married to Humphrey de Bohun, earl of Hereford (1342–1373); her daughters Eleanor and Mary are married to Richard II's uncle Thomas of Woodstock (b. 1355) and his cousin Henry of Lancaster (b. 1367)

Humphrey de Bohun, earl of Hereford and Northampton (1342–1373): half-brother of Roger Mortimer, second earl of March (1328–1360) and uncle of Edmund Mortimer, third earl of March (b. 1352); great-grandson of Edward I and grandfather of Henry V

Thomas Beauchamp, earl of Warwick (b. 1338/9): son of Thomas Beauchamp, earl of Warwick (1314–1369) and Katherine Mortimer; first cousin of Roger Mortimer, second earl of March (1328–1360); married to Margaret Ferrers, a descendant of Edward I; his son and heir is Richard, b. 1381

Marie de St Pol, countess of Pembroke (b. *c.* 1303): daughter of Guy, count of St Pol; great-granddaughter of Henry III; marries Aymer de Valence, earl of Pembroke, in 1321, and widowed in 1324

Margaret of Norfolk, sometimes known as Margaret Marshall or Margaret of Brotherton (b. *c.* 1322): countess and later duchess of Norfolk in her own right; daughter and heir of Thomas of Brotherton, earl of Norfolk and Earl Marshal (1300–1338), son of Edward I, half-brother of Edward II and uncle of Edward III. Margaret is a first cousin of Edward III and Joan of Kent; married firstly to John, Lord Segrave (d. 1353) and secondly to Walter, Lord Manny (d. 1372)

Elizabeth Segrave (1338–1368), married to John, Lord Mowbray (1340–1368), nephew of Henry, duke of Lancaster; and **Anne Manny** (1355–1384), married to John Hastings, earl of Pembroke (1347–1375): daughters and co-heirs of Margaret of Norfolk

Thomas Mowbray (b. 1366/7), earl of Nottingham, Earl Marshal, later duke of Norfolk; grandson and heir of Margaret of Norfolk via his mother Elizabeth Segrave; also a grandson of Joan of Lancaster, one of the six sisters of Henry, duke of Lancaster; married to

Elizabeth Fitzalan, daughter of the earl of Arundel and niece of the earl of Hereford; his elder brother **John Mowbray** dies childless in 1383

John Hastings, earl of Pembroke (b. 1372): another grandson of Margaret of Norfolk via his mother Anne Manny; married as a child to John of Gaunt's daughter Elizabeth of Lancaster and secondly to Philippa Mortimer, daughter of Philippa of Clarence and Edmund Mortimer, earl of March

Margaret Courtenay, *née* de Bohun, countess of Devon (b. 1311): granddaughter of Edward I; first cousin of Edward III, Joan of Kent and Margaret of Norfolk; aunt of Humphrey de Bohun, earl of Hereford (1342–1373); married to Hugh Courtenay, earl of Devon (1303–1377)

Edward Courtenay, earl of Devon (b. *c.* 1357): grandson and heir of Hugh Courtenay (d. 1377), earl of Devon, and Margaret de Bohun; married to Maud Camoys

William Montacute, earl of Salisbury (b. 1328), first or second husband of Joan of Kent; later marries Elizabeth Mohun; uncle of Edmund Mortimer, third earl of March; his heir until 1382 is his son William, thereafter his nephew **John Montacute** (b. *c.* 1350), a descendant of Edward I

Philippa Mortimer, *née* Montacute, countess of March (b. *c.* 1332): sister of William Montacute, earl of Salisbury; married to Roger Mortimer, second earl of March (1328–1360); mother of Edmund Mortimer, third earl of March (b. 1352) and grandmother of Roger, fourth earl of March (b. 1374)

William Ufford, earl of Suffolk (b. *c.* 1330): first cousin of Maud de Vere, *née* Ufford, countess of Oxford; married to Joan Montacute, first cousin of the earl of Salisbury

Hugh Stafford, earl of Stafford (b. *c.* 1343): descendant of Edward I; married to Philippa Beauchamp, sister of Thomas Beauchamp, earl of Warwick; their eldest son is **Ralph,** b. *c.* mid-1360s, and their ultimate heir, their fourth son **Edmund,** earl of Stafford, marries the duke of Gloucester's daughter and heir Anne of Gloucester

Thomas Despenser, earl of Gloucester (b. 1373): son and heir of Edward, Lord Despenser (d. 1375) and nephew of the bishop of Norwich; a descendant of Edward I; married to Richard II's first cousin Constance of York

Henry Percy, earl of Northumberland (b. 1341); nephew of Henry, duke of Lancaster, via his mother Mary of Lancaster; a descendant of Henry III; married to Margaret Neville

Thomas Percy, earl of Worcester (b. 1343): brother of the earl of Northumberland; never marries

Henry Percy (b. 1364): son and heir of the earl of Northumberland and known as 'Hotspur'; married to **Elizabeth Mortimer** (b. 1371), elder daughter of Edmund Mortimer and Philippa of Clarence and Edward III's eldest great-grandchild

Philippa Hastings, *née* **Mortimer,** countess of Pembroke and Arundel (b. 1375): younger daughter of Edmund Mortimer and Philippa of Clarence; married firstly to John Hastings, earl of Pembroke (b. 1372) and secondly to Richard Fitzalan, earl of Arundel (b. *c.* 1346)

Michael de la Pole, earl of Suffolk (b. *c.* 1330): son of a wool merchant of Hull, raised to the peerage by Richard II, and also chancellor of England; married to Katherine Wingfield; his son and heir is **Michael,** also earl of Suffolk, b. 1367, married to Katherine, daughter of Hugh, earl of Stafford

Guichard d'Angle, earl of Huntingdon: a nobleman of Poitou in France, enemy then ally of Edward of Woodstock, and Richard's tutor

Enguerrand Coucy, earl of Bedford (b. *c.* 1340): a nobleman of France, and hostage in England for King John II after the battle of Poitiers; marries Richard's aunt Isabella of Woodstock in 1365; father of Richard's cousins **Marie,** countess of Bar and Soissons, and **Philippa,** countess of Oxford

William Scrope, earl of Wiltshire (b. *c.* 1350): son of Richard Scrope, lord of Bolton in Yorkshire; first cousin of Michael de la Pole; married to Isabel Russell

Ralph Neville, earl of Westmorland (b. *c.* 1364): son of John Neville, lord of Raby, and Maud Percy; first cousin of Henry and Thomas Percy, earls of Northumberland and Worcester; married to Margaret Stafford, daughter of Hugh, earl of Stafford, and secondly to Richard II's first cousin Joan Beaufort; grandfather of Edward IV and Richard III via his youngest child Cecily

The Rome Popes

Urban VI, born Bartolomeo Prignano, pope from April 1378 to October 1389

Boniface IX, born Piero Tomacelli, pope from November 1389 to October 1404

The Avignon Popes (or Anti-Popes)

Clement VII, born Robert of Geneva, pope from September 1378 to September 1394

Benedict XIII, born Pedro Martínez de Luna y Pérez de Gotor, pope from September 1394 to March 1403

Introduction: 'My Large Kingdom for a Little Grave'[1]

'My God, what a wonderful land this is, and fickle, which has exiled, slain, destroyed and ruined so many kings, so many rulers, so many great men, and which never ceases to be riven and worn down by dissensions and discords and envy.'[2] These words, spoken by Richard of Bordeaux on 21 September 1399 while imprisoned in the Tower of London after his downfall and recorded (in Latin) by the eyewitness and chronicler Adam Usk, inspired William Shakespeare 200 years later to write his famous 'For God's sake let us sit upon the ground, and tell sad stories of the death of kings' soliloquy in his play about Richard. Adam Usk watched Richard dining at the Tower, and later saw him put on a barge to be taken to distant Pontefract Castle in Yorkshire. Here, only a few months later, the former king was murdered, probably by being slowly starved to death, after the failure of a plot by some of his supporters to free him and restore him to the throne. His first cousin Henry of Lancaster, exiled from England by Richard in October 1398 and deprived of all of his enormous inheritance by the king some months later, had returned to the kingdom with an army to claim his rights. Richard's support quickly fell apart, and in late September 1399 he was forced by parliament to abdicate in favour of his cousin. Henry of Lancaster took over the throne, and his reign as Henry IV began on 30 September 1399. Richard II, now simply Sir Richard of Bordeaux, was imprisoned for some weeks at the Tower of London before being sent to the more remote Pontefract Castle, where he died on or around 14 February 1400, weeks after his thirty-third birthday. The forced abdication and death of Richard II led indirectly, a few decades later, to the long series of armed conflicts between different branches of the English royal family which much later became known as the Wars of the Roses. Richard had no children and no legitimate brothers or sisters born to the same father: he was the only surviving legitimate offspring of Edward III's eldest son Edward of Woodstock. The second son Lionel left only one daughter, and Richard's usurper and murderer Henry IV was the son and heir of the third son. The Wars of the Roses, to put it simply, were the struggles between the descendants of Edward III's third son, in the male line, and the descendants of his second son, in the female line.

Richard II was only the second king of England to be forced to abdicate his throne, after his great-grandfather Edward II in 1327. Richard was devoted to Edward's memory and made strenuous though ultimately futile attempts to have him canonised as a saint, and there were some eerie parallels between the end of his reign and the end of his great-grandfather's. Edward II's reign came to a close in 1326 with him wandering hopelessly around Wales with Hugh Despenser the Younger, his chamberlain and perhaps lover – certainly his close political ally. Richard II's reign came to an end in 1399 with him wandering hopelessly around Wales with Hugh Despenser the Younger's great-grandson Thomas Despenser. Both Hugh and Thomas Despenser were executed for their association with the fallen king, and both tried to flee from South Wales.

Edward II had also had enormous problems with a Lancastrian first cousin, Thomas, earl of Lancaster, though in this case Edward won that particular battle and had Thomas of Lancaster beheaded in March 1322. Richard II lost his own struggle with his Lancastrian first cousin Henry, great-grandson of Thomas's brother Henry. Adam Usk says that one of the causes of Richard's deposition was his sodomy, something else he had in common with Edward II.[3] The saying that 'history is written by the victors' has become a tired old cliché, but it is true that the vast majority of the chronicles of the reigns of both Edward II and Richard II were necessarily affected by the writers' awareness of the two kings' downfalls; hindsight can therefore be an issue of which historians should be aware, and some chronicles were edited in the light of Richard II's deposition at the hands of his Lancastrian cousin and his subsequent disgrace and death at the age of only thirty-three. Richard died young and was king of England for only twenty-two years, yet his reign and his character have proved fascinating to many generations of later writers, historians and researchers, not least William Shakespeare.

As with my previous biography of Edward II, this biography of Richard is intended to be more a portrait of an individual than a thorough account of all the politics of the reign. This is the life of Richard of Bordeaux.

'We Were Not Born to Sue, but to Command': Early Life in Aquitaine, 1367–1371

At the time of Richard II's birth, he was third in line to the English throne behind his almost two-year-old brother Edward of Angoulême and his father Edward of Woodstock, prince of Wales and Aquitaine, duke of Cornwall and earl of Chester, eldest of the five sons of King Edward III. Richard was born in the part of southern France then ruled by the English Crown – more specifically by his father – in the middle of the afternoon on Wednesday 6 January 1367, in the archbishop's palace in the duchy of Aquitaine's capital of Bordeaux.[1] His father was thirty-six at the time of his birth, having been born on 15 June 1330, and his mother, Joan of Kent, was forty or almost, born on or shortly before 29 September 1326 or on the same date in 1327. Richard II is often known to history as Richard of Bordeaux, and his brother Edward of Angoulême was also named after his birthplace, as was usual for the English royal family in the fourteenth century: Angoulême is an inland town about ninety miles north-east of Bordeaux.

In the Christian calendar, Richard's birthday of 6 January is the feast of the Epiphany, also known as the feast of the Three Kings. Several contemporary chroniclers report that Richard's baptism at the abbey of St André in Bordeaux two days after his birth was, by a rather remarkable coincidence, attended by three kings who happened to be visiting his father's court at the time, though their identities are not entirely clear. The chronicle of the Canterbury monk

William Thorne names the king of Portugal as one of the three, but as Pedro I of Portugal died on 18 January 1367, only ten days after Richard's baptism, in the Portuguese town of Estremoz 650 miles from Bordeaux, he is most unlikely to have been present.[2] King Pedro I of Portugal is sometimes known to history as 'the Cruel', as is his nephew Pedro I of Castile, who almost certainly was present in Bordeaux in January 1367, and the two men have often been confused.

The three kings are likely to have been Pedro I of Castile (the largest and most powerful of the Spanish kingdoms), Jaime IV, titular ruler of the Spanish island kingdom of Majorca, and Carlos II 'the Bad', king of Navarre, a small realm between Spain and France close to Edward of Woodstock's duchy of Aquitaine. Pedro of Castile and Carlos of Navarre were certainly in Aquitaine in September 1366, and Pedro at least was still there some months later; Carlos may have been as well.[3] It is also possible that King Gosdantin or Constantine IV of Armenia, who was known as Richard in western European sources (and is also sometimes numbered as Gosdantin V), was one of the three kings present in Bordeaux in January 1367 and one of Richard of Bordeaux's godfathers: the St Albans chronicler Thomas Walsingham thought that he was.[4] Jaime IV of Majorca was Richard of Bordeaux's main sponsor, or godfather, and lifted him from the font during his baptism on 8 January.[5] Jaime was about thirty at the start of 1367, and was king of Majorca in name only, as he never actually ruled the island. He was the third husband of Giovanna I, queen of Naples in her own right, who had been put on trial (and acquitted) when she was still only a teenager in 1345 for the murder of her first husband, András of Hungary. Jaime himself had been taken prisoner and kept in an iron cage in Barcelona by his own uncle King Pedro IV of Aragon for fourteen years before escaping in 1362 and fleeing to Naples, where he married Queen Giovanna.

As for the other kings, Pedro of Castile had come to Bordeaux to ask for the help of Richard's father Edward of Woodstock in regaining his kingdom, from which he had been expelled in 1366 by his illegitimate half-brother Enrique of Trastámara. Edward of Woodstock's kinsman Carlos II 'the Bad' had inherited the small kingdom of Navarre from his mother Jeanne II, the only surviving child of Louis X of France and Navarre, in 1349. Carlos the Bad was sometimes an ally of Edward III and Edward of Woodstock in their ongoing war against France, which began in the 1330s when Edward III claimed the French throne as the only surviving grandson of Philip IV, and sometimes an enemy.

As the grandson of Edward III's uncle Louis X of France, Philip IV's eldest son (which made him Edward of Woodstock's second cousin), Carlos the Bad had a good claim to the French throne himself. And yet another king had been present when Richard's older brother Edward was born in Angoulême in January 1365, and attended the celebrations: Peter de Lusignan, king of Cyprus, who was travelling around Europe promoting a crusade.[6]

Having three kings attend one's baptism was rather extraordinary, though the fact that two of them may have been Carlos the Bad and Pedro the Cruel, hardly the most pleasant of nicknames, might be considered not altogether an advantage. Neither were the lives and deaths of the kings in question even remotely auspicious. Gosdantin/ Richard of Armenia, born as the son of a Cypriot serf, was a usurper on the throne and was assassinated by his own barons in 1373; Pedro of Castile was stabbed to death by his half-brother, who subsequently took his throne; Jaime IV of Majorca spent much of his life imprisoned in an iron cage, was reportedly insane, and never gained control of his kingdom; and Carlos II of Navarre, after a lifetime making himself grossly unpopular with his constant side-switching between England and France, burned to death in his own palace.

Also present in Bordeaux at the time of Richard's birth was the chronicler Jean Froissart, who would meet Richard again in England in the mid-1390s. Just three months before Richard was born, Froissart had been at Berkeley Castle in Gloucestershire in the south-west of England, trying – and failing – to find out exactly what had happened to Richard's great-grandfather Edward II, who had supposedly been murdered at the castle in 1327. Froissart wrote many years later that he was sitting in a hall at Edward of Woodstock's court on 6 January 1367 when the marshal of the duchy of Aquitaine entered and declared to him, 'Froissart, write down and commit to memory that my lady the princess [of Wales] has given birth to a fine son!'[7] Richard's formal and public baptism was conducted by Hélie de Salignac, archbishop of Bordeaux, and Jean Froissart says that the bishop of Agen was also present. He had been hastily baptised by midwives shortly after his birth as they feared he would not survive, which perhaps indicates that he was premature or that Joan of Kent had had a difficult birth. They gave him the name John.[8]

His father, or his parents jointly, decided to change his name to Richard, which by 1367 had become a very rare name in the English royal family. The only previous king of England to bear the name was Richard Lionheart, who had been born 210 years earlier in 1157 and died in 1199, and the last English royal with the name was the Lionheart's nephew Richard, earl of Cornwall, younger son of King John and brother of Henry III. Richard of Cornwall died in 1272, and for the next ninety-five years the name was not used again in the English royal family.[9] It would have been more conventional to name the boy Edmund after his maternal grandfather Edmund, earl of Kent, and his paternal uncle Edmund of Langley, or to have stuck with the original John chosen by the midwives, the name of another of his paternal uncles and his grandfather Edward III's brother John of Eltham. Richard may have been named after King Gosdantin or Richard of Armenia, assuming Gosdantin actually was present in Bordeaux, or perhaps in memory of the long-dead Richard Lionheart, who, although born in Oxford, spent most of his early life in Aquitaine. In later years, Richard II was aware of his namesake predecessor: in December 1385, when he was eighteen, he asked the abbot and convent of Waltham Holy Cross to celebrate mass on the anniversary of his own death after he died, and on the anniversary of the death of Richard Lionheart.[10]

At the time of Richard's birth, his paternal grandfather Edward III had sat on the English throne for almost exactly forty years, since 25 January 1327, and was now fifty-four years old. Richard's grandmother Queen Philippa was also still alive when he was born, but his other grandparents were both dead. His maternal grandfather was the uncle of his paternal grandfather: he was Edmund of Woodstock, earl of Kent, the youngest son of King Edward I. Kent was executed in March 1330 (when he was only twenty-eight years old) on the orders of Richard's great-grandmother Queen Isabella, widow of Edward II and then ruling the kingdom in the name of her underage son Edward III. Edmund, earl of Kent, was the son of Queen Marguerite, daughter of King Philip III of France and younger half-sister of Philip IV. In Richard II's confusingly tangled family tree, Marguerite's niece Isabella, Philip IV's daughter, married Edward II and was Edward III's mother and Richard's great-grandmother. Marguerite was also Richard's great-grandmother, and Edward I was Richard's great-grandfather on his mother's side and his great-great-grandfather on his father's. Marguerite of France married Edward I on 8 September 1299 when he was sixty and she twenty; he had been widowed from his first queen, Edward II's Spanish mother Leonor of Castile, for nine years. Their first son Thomas of Brotherton, earl of Norfolk, was born on 1 June 1300 (a week short of nine months after his parents' wedding), and Edmund of Woodstock followed on 5 August 1301, when Edward I was sixty-two. Edmund was not yet six when his father died on 7 July 1307, and grew up during the turbulent reign of his half-brother Edward II, born in April 1284 and seventeen years his senior. Edward II gave him the earldom of Kent on 28 July 1321, a few days before his twentieth birthday.[11] Richard II's mother was, and is, always known as Joan of Kent after her father's title, which she inherited.

Around mid-December 1325 when he was twenty-four, Edmund, earl of Kent, married a widow named Margaret Wake, Richard II's maternal grandmother, in what was surely a love or lust match. Although she was descended from Llywelyn ab Iorwerth, prince of North Wales, and his wife Joan, illegitimate daughter of King John of England, Margaret came from a fairly minor baronial house and was thus not a very illustrious match for a man who was son and brother of kings of England, grandson and nephew of kings of France. Margaret's date of birth is not known, but her brother Thomas, Lord Wake was born in 1298, and she must have been some years older than Edmund, earl of Kent. She was married first to the Scottish nobleman Sir John Comyn, whose father John 'the Red Comyn', lord of Badenoch, was stabbed to death by his great rival Robert Bruce a few weeks before Bruce had himself crowned king of Scotland in 1306. The younger John Comyn fought for Edward II against Bruce at the battle of Bannockburn on 24 June 1314, but was killed during the English king's heavy defeat. Margaret Wake gave birth to their son Aymer Comyn, named after her husband's maternal uncle Aymer de Valence, earl of Pembroke, sometime before 16 August 1314 (possibly as much as several years before). The little boy, who was Richard II's half-uncle, was dead by 25 October 1316.[12] As Margaret was old enough to be married and to have given birth by the time of the battle of Bannockburn in June 1314, when her future second husband Edmund was not yet thirteen years old, she must have been some years older than he. Margaret Wake remained a widow for eleven and a half years after John Comyn's death, and married Edmund in Paris near the end of 1325, where both of them were attending Edward II's queen, Edmund's sister-in-law and first cousin Isabella of France. Isabella was then refusing to return to England and to her husband Edward, and thus precipitated the crisis which led to Edward II's deposition and Edward III's accession in January 1327.[13]

Edmund, earl of Kent, and Countess Margaret had three or four children: sons Edmund and John and daughters Joan and possibly Margaret, though the latter, if she existed at all, is extremely obscure and must have died young and childless.[14] If Joan of Kent was born in September 1326 she was the couple's eldest child, born just over nine months after their wedding and at the same time as her father was taking part in his sister-in-law Queen Isabella's invasion of England (the invasion force sailed from Dordrecht in Holland on 21 or 22 September 1326 and arrived in Suffolk on 24 September). This raises an interesting question as to where Joan of Kent was born: perhaps in Hainault or Holland, as her heavily pregnant mother would hardly have risked taking part in the invasion of England at her husband's side if she knew she was about to give birth at any time. If Joan's birth occurred in September 1327, she was born, almost certainly in England, mere days after the alleged murder of her uncle Edward II at Berkeley Castle, Gloucestershire, on 21 September that year.[15]

Of her two brothers, Edmund of Kent was the elder son of Earl Edmund and Margaret Wake and was born sometime in the late 1320s, and John was born posthumously on 7 April 1330, nineteen days after their father's beheading on the orders of his sister-in-law Queen Isabella. John of Kent was probably named after their maternal grandfather John, Lord Wake, and was the youngest grandchild of Edward I; the eldest, Gilbert de Clare, earl of Gloucester, had been born all the way back in May 1291, thirty-nine years previously. Joan and Edmund of Kent were two of the three godparents of their brother John, and lifted him from the font during his baptism at Arundel Castle in Sussex on the day of his birth. It is not impossible that Joan and Edmund were twins, though this is only speculation.[16] The heavily pregnant Countess Margaret, with her children Joan and Edmund and perhaps the obscure Margaret (assuming she existed), was ordered to be imprisoned at Salisbury Castle with only two attendants on 14 March 1330. This was five days before her husband's beheading for the odd crime of attempting to free his supposedly dead half-brother Edward II from captivity, despite the fact that he had attended his funeral more than two years previously.[17]

After he took over the governance of his own kingdom a few months later, Edward III gave his uncle Edmund, earl of Kent, a posthumous pardon and restored his elder son Edmund the younger to his rightful inheritance, but the boy died before 13 October 1331, still a young child.[18] John of Kent succeeded to his father's earldom and married Elisabeth of Jülich, a niece of Edward III's queen Philippa, but died childless on 27 December 1352, aged twenty-two. This left his elder sister Joan as his heir to the earldom of Kent. Joan was also the heir of her childless uncle Thomas, Lord Wake, who died on 30 May 1349 perhaps of the plague which was then ravaging the country, and inherited lands in Cumberland, Lincolnshire, Yorkshire and other counties from him. Her mother Margaret, dowager countess of Kent, did not long outlive her brother, and died on 29 September 1349.

Like Edmund of Kent, Richard II's father was younger than his wife. He was a legend in his own lifetime, a great warrior who fought in the vanguard at the battle of Crécy in 1346 when he was only sixteen years old and captured King John II of France during his victory at the battle of Poitiers ten years later. Edward of Woodstock was born at the royal palace of Woodstock near Oxford on 15 June 1330, the first child of King Edward III (then seventeen) and his queen Philippa of Hainault (then probably fifteen or sixteen). Edward III had succeeded to the throne on the forced abdication of his father Edward II three and a half years earlier in January 1327, when he was only fourteen. At the time of Edward of Woodstock's birth, the kingdom was being ruled by his grandmother the dowager queen Isabella of France and her ally Roger Mortimer, who had created the grandiose earldom of March, or earl of all the English–Welsh borderlands, for himself in late 1328. Edward III married Philippa of Hainault in York on 24 or 25 January 1328, his parents' twentieth wedding anniversary (Edward II and Isabella of France married in Boulogne, northern France, on 25 January 1308).

Philippa was the third or fourth daughter of Willem, count of Hainault and Holland, and was also, via her mother Jeanne de Valois, the niece of Philip de Valois. Philip became King Philip VI of France on 1 April 1328 following the death of his cousin Charles IV – Charles, like his older brothers Louis X and Philip V, left only daughters – who was Queen Isabella's brother and Edward III's uncle. Philippa of Hainault was born into a vast network of powerful relatives stretching across Europe. Like her husband, who was her second cousin, she was the great-grandchild of Philip III of France and his half-Spanish, half-Hungarian queen Isabel of Aragon. Her father's first cousin Henry of Luxembourg was elected Holy Roman Emperor in 1308, and another of his first cousins, Matilda of Hainault, succeeded her mother as princess of Achaea in Greece.

Philippa's eldest sister Margareta married Henry of Luxembourg's successor as Holy Roman Emperor, Ludwig of Bavaria, and was also queen of Germany and Italy; her niece Beatrix was queen of Sweden; and her aunt Catherine de Valois was titular empress of the Latin empire of Constantinople in her own right. One of Queen Philippa's great-great-grandmothers was Erzsébet (or Elizabeth) the Cuman, born into a nomadic people of the Eurasian steppe who practised shamanism and who fled into Hungary in the 1230s and 1240s to escape the invasions of the Mongols and settled there. Erzsébet was the daughter of the Cumans' khan or chieftain, whose name was probably either Seyhan or Köten, and converted to Christianity before her marriage to István (or Stephen) V, king of Hungary and Croatia. The blood of the Cumans, a Turkic people who inhabited a vast area of modern-day Russia, Ukraine and Kazakhstan, thus ran in the veins of Philippa's descendants, including Richard II. Richard was also descended from emperors of Byzantium and Nicaea, grand princes of Kiev in modern-day Ukraine, princes of North Wales, and kings of England, France, Germany, Jerusalem, Hungary, Croatia, Naples, Castile, Aragon, Navarre and Leon.

Philippa of Hainault was about thirteen or fourteen when she married the fifteen-year-old Edward III in January 1328. Her powerful mother-in-law Isabella of France, keen to remain the real queen in the country, did not grant Philippa a household, lands or income for many months, and only allowed Philippa to be crowned as queen of England on 18 February 1330 when she was already five months pregnant with Richard II's father Edward of Woodstock. On 19 October 1330, four months after the birth of his first son, Edward III arrested Roger Mortimer at Nottingham Castle and had him hanged at Tyburn a few weeks later, removed his mother from power and confiscated the numerous lands and vast income she had granted herself, and took over the governance of his own kingdom.

Edward III, though, was not a man to bear a grudge: decades later he arranged the marriage of his eldest granddaughter Philippa of Clarence to Roger Mortimer's great-grandson Edmund Mortimer, which in Richard II's reign was to bring the Mortimers close to the throne. On 13 November 1330, the young king turned eighteen. Queen Philippa, about sixteen, gained her rightful position as queen at last, nearly three years after her wedding. Her motto, '*ich wrude muche*' either means 'I work hard' or 'I rejoice much', and either seems appropriate. The queen accompanied her husband on military campaigns and was a loyal and supportive wife to him for decades, her chaplain founded Queen's College, Oxford in her honour in 1341, and she took an active interest in English industry: she opened up coal mines and lead mines, and helped to reorganise the wool industry in East Anglia. A vastly different kind of person from her mother-in-law Isabella of France, who rebelled against her own husband after he confiscated her lands in 1324 and allowed his powerful chamberlain and favourite Hugh Despenser the Younger to oust her from her rightful position at his side, Queen Philippa was nevertheless in her own way a strong and capable personality.

Edward III and Philippa of Hainault produced many more children after Edward of Woodstock. Half of their dozen offspring died in infancy or in early adulthood: two sons named William after Philippa's father Count Willem of Hainault, and daughters Joan, Blanche, Mary and Margaret. Four sons and one daughter besides Edward of Woodstock lived past their teens, and their birthplaces became part of their names: the eldest daughter Isabella of Woodstock, born in 1332 and named, as convention demanded, after her paternal grandmother Isabella of France; Lionel of Antwerp (in modern-day Belgium), born in 1338; John of Gaunt (i.e. Ghent, also in modern-day Belgium), born in 1340 and named after his godfather and kinsman Duke John III of Brabant; Edmund of Langley, born in 1341; and Thomas of Woodstock, by far the youngest, born in 1355 and a full quarter of a century younger than his eldest brother.

Edward of Woodstock, very curiously given that he was one of the most eligible bachelors in Europe, did not marry until 1361 when he was almost thirty-one. Two of his younger brothers married before he did: Lionel married Elizabeth de Burgh, a great heiress six and a half years his senior, when he was still a child, and nineteen-year-old John of Gaunt married the even greater heiress Blanche of Lancaster in 1359. Various marriages were proposed for Edward of Woodstock throughout his childhood and adolescence and into adulthood. When he was only a little over a year old in July 1331, a marriage was proposed for him with a daughter of Philip VI of France. On 3 May 1340, Edward III put forward Edward of Woodstock's second cousin Margarethe, second daughter of Duke John III of Brabant (the territory of Brabant is now in Belgium and the Netherlands), who was born in 1323 and was seven years the boy's senior, as his son and heir's bride. The king even granted the rights to his eldest son's marriage to Duke John and promised that if the marriage to Margarethe did not go ahead he would repay her dowry twofold.

In 1344, however, the pope refused to grant a dispensation for the two to wed on the grounds that Edward of Woodstock's marriage into the French royal family would be more useful to make 'peace between the two crowns'.[19] Margarethe of Brabant instead married Louis, count of Flanders, in 1347, and her daughter was later proposed as a bride for Edward of Woodstock's younger brother Edmund of Langley. In November 1345, and again in July 1347, another unsuccessful attempt was made to provide the teenage Edward of Woodstock with a royal bride, this time Leonor, youngest daughter of King Afonso IV of Portugal. Matters had advanced far enough on the second occasion that the English envoys were instructed to discuss with Afonso a time and place for Leonor to arrive in England and proceed to her wedding with Edward, but because of delays in communications and travel, the envoys arrived in Portugal in November 1347 to find that they were too late and the young woman had just married Pedro IV of Aragon (and was to die of the plague less than a year later).[20] English history would be considerably different if Edward III's envoys had arrived in Portugal as planned some months earlier and Leonor of Portugal had married Edward of Woodstock and borne children.

Richard II's mother Joan of Kent, on the other hand, had a colourful marital history which seemingly involved being married to two men at the same time when she was only thirteen or fourteen. According to her later testimony, in or around the spring of 1340 she secretly married Sir Thomas Holland, who although a knight of the royal household was far beneath her in status. He was the second son of Sir Robert Holland, a knight of Lancashire and a close friend and ally of Edward II's powerful cousin Thomas, earl of Lancaster (after whom Thomas Holland was named and who was probably Holland's godfather), though Robert went over to the king's side when Lancaster rebelled against Edward in 1321/22. Edward II subsequently had Lancaster beheaded and Robert Holland imprisoned. Holland was waylaid in a wood in Essex and himself beheaded in 1328 by Lancastrian supporters infuriated at his betrayal of the earl; they sent his severed head to Thomas of Lancaster's brother and heir Henry. Thomas Holland was a good few years Joan of Kent's senior, born in about 1314 or 1315 and thus in his mid-twenties in 1340. Evidently, though, she found him extremely appealing, and they married clandestinely and consummated the marriage, or so they later claimed. Holland's sister Isabella also lived in an unconventional relationship: she was the mistress of the much older John de Warenne, earl of Surrey, and was left items in his will when he died aged sixty in 1347. Surrey named Isabella Holland in the will as his *compaigne*, a word which usually only referred to wives, though he had been unhappily married to Edward II's niece Joan of Bar for forty-one years. Thomas Holland was one of the earl's executors.[21]

Joan of Kent cannot have been more than thirteen and a half at the time of her supposed marriage in the spring of 1340, and would only have been twelve if she was born in September 1327. Thomas Holland was twice her age, a gap which makes their supposed love-match seem less romantic and more creepy and abusive to modern sensibilities (though contemporary opinion would have held an earl's daughter and king's granddaughter marrying a man so far beneath her in rank as a far worse misdemeanour).[22] Holland left England not long afterwards, taking part in a crusade in Prussia until the summer of 1341 or later. In the meantime, Joan's mother Margaret, dowager countess of Kent, either unaware of Joan's existing marriage or believing that Thomas Holland was dead, went ahead with another marriage for her in early 1341. Joan's groom on this occasion was William Montacute or Montague, son and heir of Edward III's close friend the earl of Salisbury and born in June 1328. His father died in January 1344 and William succeeded him as earl in 1349 when he turned twenty-one, and because of his high rank was deemed to be a far more suitable match for Joan than a mere knight such as Thomas Holland, who was a second son and not even his father's heir. Joan claimed later that she did not dare tell anyone that she was already married for fear of what they might say or do.

Thomas Holland returned to England and in 1344, bizarrely, became the steward of the young earl of Salisbury and his wife, who was really Holland's wife. Neither Joan nor Holland said anything about their 1340 marriage for a few years, not until Holland had acquired a large sum of money from Edward III for fighting during the Crécy campaign of 1346/47 and capturing the count of Eu. With this money, Holland may have felt that he could keep Joan in the style to which she was accustomed, and began proceedings at the papal court in Avignon in about late 1347 to reclaim her as his wife. William Montacute refused to let her go and supposedly kept her prisoner against her will, but finally in November 1349 the pope declared that Joan's marriage to him was invalid and that her first marriage to Thomas Holland should be repeated officially and publicly.[23] Joan's first child with Holland, Thomas Holland the younger, was born in 1350 or 1351 (he was nine or ten when his father died at the end of 1360).[24]

The whole situation is peculiar and not easily explicable, and there really seems no good reason why Holland and Joan would have kept quiet about their marriage for so many years. It may in fact be that they fell in love or lust when Joan was already married to William Montacute, and began an affair in or after 1344 when Holland became Joan and Montacute's steward. Perhaps they concocted the story of a previous marriage so that Joan's marriage to Montacute could be annulled (divorce in the modern sense was impossible and a pre-existing impediment to her Montacute marriage would be the only reason for the pope to grant an annulment of it). Thomas Holland's becoming Montacute's steward in 1344 would have given them opportunity to meet and get to know each other.[25] After the annulment was granted in 1349, William Montacute married Elizabeth Mohun, one of the three daughters and co-heirs of John, Lord Mohun in Somerset. Elizabeth cannot have been more than a child at the time of her wedding: she lived until 1415, and her sister Philippa (who was a full sister with the same mother, not a much younger half-sister) married Richard II's first cousin Edward of York, who was born in the early 1370s, as her third husband in the late 1390s.

The chronicler Jean Froissart called Joan of Kent 'the most beautiful and the most amorous woman in England', and the *Chronique des quatre premiers Valois* called her 'one of the beautiful women of the world'.[26] Countess of Kent and Lady Wake in her own right, the granddaughter and niece of English kings and great-granddaughter of the French king Philip III, Joan was well off, well connected and self-confident. She had several children with Thomas Holland, who were Richard II's older half-siblings: Thomas Holland the younger; John Holland, born in or after *c.* 1352; Joan, who married John IV, duke of Brittany; and Maud, who married Waleran of Luxembourg, count of Ligny and St Pol in France. Joan of Kent, thanks to her irregular early marriages, was known sarcastically to one contemporary English chronicler as the 'Virgin of Kent'.[27] She is often known nowadays as the Fair Maid of Kent, but this is a later nickname not used in her own lifetime, as is her husband's famous nickname, the 'Black Prince', which first appeared in a book published in the sixteenth century almost 200 years after his death. Joan probably grew up in the household of Queen Philippa, wife of her first cousin Edward III. She had only been two or three years old when her father was judicially murdered for the 'crime' mentioned earlier, when he allegedly tried to free a dead man from unlawful captivity. Joan's mother Margaret Wake lived until 1349, when Joan was in her early twenties, and must have told her daughter what had happened in 1329/30.

Although Earl Edmund attended his half-brother Edward II's funeral in December 1327, he later became convinced that Edward was still alive, and tried to free him from captivity. Numerous influential people joined him, including the archbishop of York (who wrote a letter in January 1330 declaring that Edward II was alive and in good health, and ordering numerous provisions for him), the bishop, mayor and sheriff of London, the earls of Buchan and Mar in Scotland, and a long list of lords, knights and sheriffs, as well as many lower-ranking men and former members of Edward II's household.[28] When the plot came to light, the earl of Kent had been executed, and some of his adherents were imprisoned and had their lands and goods confiscated. Others fled the country, including Kent's brother-in-law and Joan's uncle Thomas, Lord Wake (who had played an important role in Edward II's downfall and deposition in 1326/27 at the side of his first cousin Roger Mortimer), and were only invited back some months later when Edward III overthrew his mother and Mortimer and took over the governance of his own realm. As an adult Richard II would become fascinated by his great-grandfather Edward II, and it is likely that Joan of Kent or others told him the dramatic story of how his grandfather had tried to rescue Edward years after his official death. It was part of Richard's family history, and the fact that his paternal grandmother Queen Philippa was pregnant with his father when his maternal grandfather was executed on the orders of his great-grandmother Isabella of France, Edward II's queen, may have increased his interest in the story. Queen Isabella lived until as late as August 1358, only a few years before he was born, and his father and probably his mother knew her well; the story of Edward II's murder or survival and his wife's possible involvement in it was not ancient irrelevant history to Richard.

Edward of Woodstock and Joan of Kent married in secret in the spring or early summer of 1361, only some months after Sir Thomas Holland's death in late December 1360. Edward was close to thirty-one, an advanced age for a member of the royal family to be getting married, especially one who was prince of Wales, duke of Cornwall and earl of

Chester and the heir to the English throne. The archbishop of Canterbury declared their marriage invalid on the grounds of consanguinity: not only were the couple first cousins once removed – Joan was the granddaughter of Edward I and Edward was his great-grandson – but Edward of Woodstock was also the godfather of Joan's two Holland sons, which created a spiritual affinity and impediment to marriage. By the summer of 1361, King Edward III had come round sufficiently to petition the pope for a dispensation, which was granted on 7 September 1361. The wedding of Edward of Woodstock and Joan of Kent took place again publicly at Windsor on 10 October in the presence of most of the royal family. And yet their irregular and clandestine marriage, and Joan's previous bigamy, was to continue to cause problems.

Joan's first (or second) husband William Montacute, earl of Salisbury, was still alive when she married Edward; he lived, in fact, until June 1397, and outlived Edward, Joan and all but two of Joan's half-dozen children. In 1370, the pope reputedly put pressure on Edward of Woodstock not to execute the bishop of Limoges by threatening to declare his children illegitimate.[29] To make matters even worse, the dispensation belatedly granting them permission to marry was not correctly formulated, and a year later had to be reissued by the new pope.[30] There is evidence that Richard II fretted about the legality of his parents' union, and he kept a safe-box of seventeen documents relating to it and other documents about the dissolution of his mother's marriage to William Montacute.[31] Joan's colourful marital history was used as a weapon against her son: at the time of Richard's birth it was rumoured in Bordeaux that he was Joan's son by a French lover, though there is no reason at all to take this seriously, and not the slightest hint that Edward of Woodstock or anyone of importance believed that Richard was not his son. The rumour was used against Richard by his cousin, enemy and murderer Henry IV in 1399, but then of course it was a political weapon used in the service of Richard's deposition, and does not mean that Henry or anyone else necessarily believed it.[32] Chronicler Adam of Usk muttered darkly on the topic of 'unsavoury things' he had heard about Richard's birth: that 'he was not born of a father of the royal line, but of a mother given to slippery ways,' and, rather mysteriously, 'to say nothing of many other things I have heard.'[33] It was even rumoured, almost certainly spuriously, that Joan had once been the mistress of her father-in-law and first cousin the king, and that Edward III was opposed to the marriage on these grounds.[34]

It was an unusual marriage for other reasons: kings and prospective kings of England had married foreign women, but not English women, for many generations. King John had married an English noblewoman, Hawise of Gloucester, in 1189, but had the marriage annulled when he came to the throne ten years later and married the French heiress Isabelle of Angoulême instead. Since then, English kings and heirs to the throne had married French women for the most part. The queen of King John's son Henry III, Eleanor of Provence, was the daughter of the count of Provence and granddaughter of the count of Savoy. Edward I married firstly Leonor of Castile, daughter of the king of Castile in Spain and half-French on her mother Joan of Ponthieu's side, and secondly Marguerite, daughter of Philip III of France and half-sister of Philip IV. Edward II married Philip IV's daughter Isabella, and Edward III married Philippa of Hainault, granddaughter of Philip IV's brother Charles de Valois and niece of Philip VI.

The reasons for Edward of Woodstock's long bachelorhood are not entirely clear. It would be tempting to think that he was in love with Joan of Kent for a long time and waiting for her, but he could hardly have guessed that Thomas Holland would die in his mid-forties and leave Joan a widow at only thirty-three or thirty-four. Then again, Edward's marriage to Joan brought him lands and income in England but no powerful allies and kinsmen and no diplomatic benefits in another country, so perhaps it was a love match after all. He had other consolations during his long years as a bachelor: a mistress, Edith Willesford, who at some point almost certainly before he married Joan bore him a son named Roger Clarendon, who was knighted and to whom Edward left items in his will. Roger may have been born at the royal manor of Clarendon in Wiltshire. The prince of Wales also fathered a son called Edward, for whom he bought a pony called Lyard Hobyn in 1349, though this is the only known mention of the boy and he seems not to have survived his father or to have been known to his much younger half-brother Richard II.[35] The prince was only in his late teens at the end of the 1340s, a young age to have fathered an illegitimate child old enough to have a pony bought for him, so apparently Edward had been sexually precocious (perhaps not surprising for a young man who commanded the vanguard of his father's army when he was only sixteen). Edward's sister Isabella of Woodstock also married late, in July 1365 when she was thirty-three; Edward III was indulgent of his two eldest children and allowed

Isabella to turn down numerous suitable husbands before she settled on Enguerrand Coucy, a French nobleman and hostage in England after the battle of Poitiers who was a few years younger than she.

At any rate, Edward of Woodstock and Joan of Kent's marriage was evidently a happy, loving one, and in 1367, the year of their son Richard's birth, Edward called Joan his 'very dear and very loyal heart, beloved consort' (in the French original, *trescher et tresentier coer, bien ame compaigne*).[36] In 1348, long before they married, he had referred to her as Jeannette, an affectionate diminutive of her name; Edward and Joan must have known each other all their lives.[37] The marriage of Richard's maternal grandparents Edmund, earl of Kent, and Margaret Wake seems also to have been a love match, and that of his paternal grandparents, although arranged, was a loving and affectionate partnership which lasted for over forty years. Edward of Windsor, the future Edward III, and Philippa of Hainault were betrothed in August 1326, when Edward was not yet fourteen and Philippa probably about twelve.

Queen Philippa many years later told the chronicler Jean Froissart that when she and Edward spent time together in Hainault in the late summer of 1326, Edward felt more affection and liking for her than for her sisters, and chose her as his future bride in preference to them. Although this tale has been repeated numerous times as if it is certainly true, Philippa was wearing rose-tinted spectacles and indulging in romanticising of the highest order. Her older sisters Margareta and Johanna were already married by 1326 and her younger sister Isabella was probably only a toddler or baby, so Edward preferring her over them meant very little. Besides, Philippa's betrothal was arranged in order to provide ships and mercenaries for her future mother-in-law Isabella to invade the sovereign nation of England and depose her own husband, and was unlawful as well. Edward of Windsor was at the time officially engaged to another girl (King Alfonso XI of Castile's sister Leonor) and his legal guardian, his father Edward II, stood in firm opposition to his marrying Philippa and thus did not consent to their betrothal. The circumstances could hardly have been less romantic and appealing, and the situation had nothing whatsoever to do with the whims and feelings of two adolescents. Nevertheless, it is not at all improbable that Edward and Philippa did like each other very much when they met, and the idealistic version that the future king of England fell in love with his bride and chose her over her sisters was probably a family story that Richard heard when he was growing up. Certainly he knew of the immense affection between Edward and Philippa during the long years of their marriage (at least, until the king began his flagrant affair with his notorious mistress Alice Perrers in the 1360s). Richard thus had the devoted marriages of his parents and both sets of grandparents as examples, and his own marriage to Anne of Bohemia would also prove to be a most successful and close one.

Edward III formally appointed Edward of Woodstock as prince of Aquitaine in July 1362. He and Joan moved there and set up court in Bordeaux, where they lived splendidly: Edward held numerous jousts and revels in Aquitaine, as did his father in England, and hosted more than eighty knights at his table every day.[38] The *Anonimalle* chronicle says that as the prince of Aquitaine, Edward of Woodstock was so high and mighty that he kept Aquitanian lords waiting for four or five days to see him, and when he finally deigned to admit them into his presence he made them kneel before him for many hours before finally permitting them to rise – behaviour which his son Richard probably later copied.[39] Not everyone approved of Edward and Joan's style of living as prince and princess of Aquitaine. In November 1363, the marshal of Brittany complained that Joan and the ladies of her court wore furred gowns with slit coats and great fringes, which, he said reprovingly, were copied from the fashions worn by the mistresses of English freebooters and did Joan's reputation no good whatsoever.[40] Joan of Kent's extravagance was notorious even by the standards of medieval royalty: in early 1362 she spent the huge sum of £200 on a single set of jewelled buttons, at a time when most people in England earned something in the region of 4*d* or 5*d* a day.[41] Not to be outdone, her son Richard II once paid the staggering amount of more than £850 on a set of buttons in the shape of eagles enriched with gems and pearls, which seems an almost impossibly large sum to spend on mere buttons.[42]

Edward of Woodstock and Joan of Kent's elder son, inevitably and confusingly named Edward, was born in the town of Angoulême in the duchy of Aquitaine on 27 January 1365; Joan wrote a letter to the mayor and aldermen of London telling them her good news on 4 February.[43] In England, the birth of the next heir to the throne was celebrated with ten days of feasts and jousting tournaments, and the king rewarded the messenger who had brought him 'the pleasing news' of Edward of Angoulême's birth with a very generous income of £40 a year.[44] Edward of Woodstock held the greatest jousting tournament of his period of rule over Aquitaine in Angoulême in late April 1365 to celebrate the birth of his son and heir, and in May sent his father a gift of a lion and a leopard, which presumably were intended to join the menagerie in the Tower of London.[45] Richard of Bordeaux was born when his brother was not quite two years old; in the month of Richard's birth, his grandfather the king of England, nearly as extravagant as his daughter-in-law Joan of Kent, spent £20 on a velvet garment 'embroidered with pelicans, images and tabernacles of gold' and received a gift of thirty wild boar from Charles V of France.[46] The prince of Wales and Aquitaine, and all his and his father's subjects, must have rejoiced at the news of Richard's birth: the succession to the English throne seemed well assured, with a fit, healthy, enormously popular warrior in his thirties and his two sons to follow Edward III. Yet fate was about to intervene, and it did so soon after Richard's birth and after yet another of Edward of Woodstock's great military triumphs.

England had long been allied with Castile, the largest and most powerful of the Spanish kingdoms. Edward I had married Leonor of Castile back in November 1254 when they were both teenagers, and she was the mother of Edward II and grandmother of Edward III. Edward II arranged the marriages of two of his four children into Castile in the mid-1320s, though these did not go ahead because of his deposition in early 1327, and Edward III's second daughter, Edward of Woodstock's sister Joan, died on her way to marry Pedro, heir to the throne of Castile. Alfonso XI of Castile – who in the 1320s had been betrothed to Edward II's daughter Eleanor of Woodstock – died of a fever in March 1350, leaving his fifteen-year-old son Pedro to succeed him. Pedro's mother was Maria of Portugal, queen of Castile, who was Alfonso XI's first cousin on both sides (his father and her mother were siblings, and his mother and her father were siblings). Perhaps because he felt little sexual attraction to a woman he was so closely related to, Alfonso much preferred the company of his mistress Leonor Guzman. He gave her lands and titles and a prominent position at court, and had ten children with her; their eldest surviving son was Enrique of Trastámara, sometimes known as the Bastard of Trastámara, who was born in January 1334 and was seven months older than his legitimate half-brother Pedro. After Pedro succeeded to the Castilian throne he had Leonor Guzman killed, but he soon proved himself little better than his father in marital affairs.

With Joan of England having died on her way to marry him, in 1353 Pedro wed the fourteen-year-old French noblewoman Blanche de Bourbon, whose mother was a half-sister of Philip VI of France. Her elder sister Jeanne de Bourbon had married their cousin the future Charles V of France (Philip VI's grandson) some years before. Pedro imprisoned Blanche within days of their wedding and went off with his mistress Maria de Padilla, whom he may have married in secret before going through a wedding ceremony with Blanche. The unfortunate Blanche, queen of Castile in name at least, remained in prison for eight years and died there in 1361. Pedro and Maria de Padilla, meanwhile, had several children together, of whom two daughters survived infancy: Constanza, born in about 1354 and Pedro's heir, and Isabel, born in about 1355. Pedro's appalling treatment of Blanche de Bourbon made him a bad enemy: her brother-in-law and cousin the future Charles V, who succeeded his father John II as king of France in 1364.

In Castile, Enrique of Trastámara yearned for revenge on the half-brother who had killed his mother, and he found a willing ally in Charles V, who saw a chance to detach England from its long-term ally and weaken the English position in the Iberian peninsula, and thus strengthen his own position. Charles V and Pedro IV of Aragon, another enemy of Pedro of Castile, helped Enrique lead an invasion of the kingdom in 1366. Pedro fled and went to Edward of Woodstock in Aquitaine for help, while Enrique of Trastámara was proclaimed king of Castile. Pedro and Edward were distantly related via common descent from Fernando III, king of Castile and Leon (d. 1252), and Edward decided that he simply had to help a king and kinsman in need. In addition, it may be that Pedro had promised to make him or his son Edward of Angoulême king of Galicia, a region of Castile, in return for his aid, and certainly the Castilian king pledged a great deal of money to the prince of Wales and Aquitaine as payment. Jaime IV of Majorca accompanied Edward of Woodstock, and only a few weeks after Richard of Bordeaux's birth his father yet again proved his mettle as a great military commander. Edward, Pedro of Castile, Jaime IV and Edward's brother John of Gaunt, duke of Lancaster, met Enrique of Trastámara and his forces at Nájera in northern Spain on 3 April 1367 and defeated him. King Pedro was once more in charge of his kingdom; Enrique of Trastámara fled back to France, while his brother Don Sancho was captured. Edward of Woodstock took possession of a horse which had belonged to Enrique, and sent it to his father in England.[47]

Pedro was keen to take revenge on his vanquished enemies, but Edward of Woodstock persuaded him to show them mercy and leniency. This would have dire consequences two years later. Enrique of Trastámara returned to Castile in September 1368 and was reunited with his allies, and on 14 March 1369 defeated his half-brother at the battle of Montiel. Nine days later he stabbed Pedro to death, and soon afterwards made himself king of Castile. Only thirty-four at the time of his murder, King Pedro left his teenage daughter and heir Constanza and her younger sister Isabel from his relationship with his mistress Maria de Padilla (in 1362, the year after the death of the unfortunate Blanche de Bourbon, queen in name only, the Cortes of Castile had declared the girls legitimate).[48] They married two of Richard II's uncles; English involvement in the turbulent affairs of the kingdom of Castile was far from over. For the time being, though, with Charles V's ally King Enrique II of the house of Trastámara firmly on the throne of the half-brother he had murdered, England's long-term ally Castile had become its enemy. Edward of Woodstock's forces had spent many months in Spain in 1367 while Pedro tried to raise money to pay the prince for his support. Dysentery spread like wildfire, and Edward's men were short of food and water and suffered in the baking heat of the Spanish summer; malaria also stalked their camps. Jaime IV of Majorca became so ill and weak that he had to be left behind when Edward finally returned to Bordeaux; he was soon captured by Enrique of Trastámara, and Edward himself had come down with a slow, lingering illness which would leave him little more than an invalid for the rest of his life and would kill him nine years later. This may have been recurring bouts of malaria, or of dysentery.[49] No more children would be born to Edward of Woodstock and Joan of Kent.

A few days after the battle of Nájera, probably on Maundy Thursday (which fell on 15 April in 1367), Richard of Bordeaux's cousin and nemesis Henry of Lancaster, who is usually known to history as Henry of Bolingbroke after his birthplace in Lincolnshire, was born.[50] On 1 June 1367, Henry's grandfather Edward III gave £5 to the messenger, Ingelram Falconer, who brought him news of the birth.[51] Henry was the only surviving son of the king's third son John of Gaunt – then in Spain with his elder brother the prince of Wales and Aquitaine – and John's first wife Blanche of Lancaster, and was named after his maternal grandfather Henry of Grosmont, first duke of Lancaster, one of the great men of the fourteenth century. Duke Henry was courteous, chivalrous, kind, sensual and pious, a warrior and a larger-than-life personality who in 1354 wrote a book in French called

The Book of Holy Medicines, in which he declared that he loved the company of women and tried to impress them by stretching out his legs in his stirrups during jousting tournaments so they would admire his calves, and who also loved dancing, getting drunk, eating salmon with rich sauces, the sound of nightingale song and of barking hounds, the sight and feel of rings on his fingers, and the smell of flowers. He was hugely wealthy and influential, and also royal: his father Henry, earl of Lancaster (d. 1345), was a grandson of King Henry III and first cousin of Edward II, and was also the younger half-brother of Queen Joan I of Navarre and the uncle of Edward II's queen Isabella of France.

Duke Henry's death in 1361 at the age of about fifty came as a heavy blow to his cousin the king and the rest of the royal family. His elder daughter Maud made a most unhappy marriage to Queen Philippa's nephew Willem, count of Hainault and Holland, who became insane and was confined for more than thirty years, and died in her early twenties in 1362. The vast Lancastrian inheritance, which included the earldoms of Lancaster, Leicester, Derby and Lincoln, thus passed entirely to Henry's younger daughter Blanche and her husband John of Gaunt. Blanche, who married John in 1359 – the wedding was attended by the kings of France and Scotland as well as John's father the king of England – was as attractive and appealing a person as her remarkable father, and the great poet Geoffrey Chaucer wrote his first long poem about her shortly after her early death: *The Book of the Duchess*. As John and Blanche's only surviving son Henry of Lancaster became heir to the Lancastrian fortune, and as the grandson of the king he was as royal as Richard of Bordeaux. Henry and his older sisters Philippa and Elizabeth grew up in the care of their great-aunt Blanche, Lady Wake, the eldest sister of Duke Henry of Lancaster and the widow of Joan of Kent's uncle Thomas, Lord Wake.

Edward of Woodstock returned to Aquitaine from Spain bedridden in late September 1367, and was met outside Bordeaux by his wife and their two-year-old son Edward of Angoulême. Richard, still only a few months old, can only ever have known his father as an invalid. The prince of Wales and Aquitaine intended to return to England in March 1368, but this was postponed because of his poor health, and Richard was to remain in the land of his birth for three more years.[52] Edward of Woodstock's last military action took place in the French town of Limoges in September 1370 after the inhabitants surrendered to the dukes of Berry and Bourbon (brother and brother-in-law of

Charles V), and he and his brother John of Gaunt besieged the town and recaptured it, an action which later gained notoriety when the chronicler Jean Froissart drastically overestimated the number of men, women and children killed during the siege and its aftermath as 3,000 – in truth the number was closer to 300.[53] Too ill to continue, Edward resigned his position as the king's lieutenant in Aquitaine on 5 October 1372.[54] By then, he, Joan of Kent and Richard had returned to England.

In his infancy Richard was looked after by a nurse named Mundina Danos or Danes or Denys, an Aquitanian woman, aided by another Aquitanian named Reymunda de Berce or Bourk. Mundina was replaced at some point by Eleanor Savage, the wife of one of Edward of Windsor's retainers, but moved to England, perhaps when Richard himself did, and settled in Surrey. On 1 February 1378, Richard, or rather someone acting on his behalf as he was still only eleven, granted Mundina an income of £30 a year, and in January 1386 he granted her a tun of wine every year. She married Walter Rauf or Ralph, King Richard's tailor, sometime before 12 March 1381, having previously been married to a man called Rolland Danos, who was still alive in March 1379.[55] Mundina Danos and Walter Rauf were still alive and of 'great age and debility' in 1405, when Richard's cousin and successor Henry IV confirmed Richard's grants of lands, manors and income to them.[56] In 1380, Richard acknowledged Eleanor Savage's 'good service in nursing the king during infancy'.[57] There are also references to 'the king's nurse Agnes Corby', who was still alive in April 1399 and who served as a damsel in the households of Richard's mother Joan of Kent and his second queen Isabelle de Valois, and in August 1394 Richard granted an income of ten marks (£6 13s 4d) a year to his 'rocker' (i.e. the woman who rocked his cradle), Eliona of France.[58]

As Richard spent his early years in France with a French nurse, it seems likely that French was the first language he heard around him and perhaps spoke, but it is also certain that he could speak fluent English, and it is sometimes thought that he was the first king of England since before the Norman Conquest in 1066 who was a native speaker of the language. It has been pointed out that although Richard was born in France he was 'more thoroughly English than any of his forebears', being the first king of England since the Norman Conquest of wholly English parentage, and after Richard left Aquitaine as a small child he rarely showed any further interest in visiting France.[59] (He did, briefly, visit the far north of the country in 1396 on the occasion of his second marriage.) Jean Froissart, who met Richard in the mid-1390s, comments that the king spoke and wrote French very well, which he would hardly have said if Richard's native or preferred everyday language was French. Probably Richard was effortlessly bilingual.

By the late fourteenth century the English royalty and nobility were using the English language more and more often, though they still often spoke, wrote and read in French as well, and it is unclear when they began to speak English as their first and preferred language. Duke Henry of Lancaster, father-in-law of Richard's uncle John of Gaunt, claimed in his *Book of Holy Medicines* in the mid-1350s that as he was English he had not had much experience with French and asked to be excused if his use of the language was not good, though as the book was written in fluent and cultured French this claim cannot be taken entirely seriously.[60] At the time of his grandson's accession to the throne in September 1399, the younger Henry of Lancaster's 'mother tongue' was said to be English.[61] Edward III, half-French via his mother Isabella, probably spoke French as his first language, though issued some of the mottoes of his jousting tournaments in English. Richard's great-grandfather Edward II also apparently spoke French as a matter of preference, though presumably was also fluent in English as he spent much time with his lowborn subjects such as fishermen, carpenters, shipwrights and blacksmiths, who would not have spoken or understood French.[62] Richard II's first cousin Edward of York, also a grandson of Edward III and about six or seven years Richard's junior, wrote a book in English about hunting in the early fifteenth century.

In the 1380s, John Trevisa, chaplain of Thomas, Lord Berkeley at Berkeley Castle in Gloucestershire, translated Latin works into English for his master, who was born in 1353; Berkeley's grandfather, born in the 1290s, and perhaps even his father (who died in 1368), would never have commissioned reading material in English. English in the late fourteenth century became more popular as a language for reading and writing among the nobility, though they still owned more books in French and Latin than in English. Richard of Bordeaux was certainly taught Latin as well as French and English, and may have learnt some German after his 1382 marriage to Anne of Bohemia: one of his books contained the German sentence *ich bin dyn*, 'I am yours'.[63] It is probable that the multilingual Anne of Bohemia continued to speak Czech, her other main language besides German, with members of her

Bohemian retinue who remained with her in England, and therefore also possible that Richard heard this language around him on occasion and perhaps came to understand some of it.[64] Several members of Queen Anne's household in England came from Poland, the homeland of Anne's mother, and Polish may have been yet another language spoken at the English court in the 1380s and 1390s.

Richard could read and write, and an example of his signature still exists. He owned several books in French and Latin, and knew the works of the contemporary poets Geoffrey Chaucer (who wrote in English) and John Gower (who wrote in English, Latin and French). His reign is something of a golden age of English literature. John Gower wrote around 1390 that he had met Richard on the Thames, and that the king recognised him and had the poet brought aboard his barge. Richard asked Gower to write 'some new thing' about love for him, and thus Gower wrote his *Confessio Amantis*, 'Confessions of a Lover'. Gower later rewrote his prologue to the *Confessio* to remove the reference to Richard after the king was overthrown by his cousin Henry. The most famous of all medieval English poets, Geoffrey Chaucer, wrote his greatest works during Richard's reign and was certainly well known to the king, yet there are no indications that Richard patronised Chaucer or commissioned any of his works.

Another great poet of Richard's era was William Langland, who wrote the masterpiece *The Vision of Piers Plowman* in the 1370s and died in about 1386, and the 'Pearl Poet' wrote the poems *Pearl*, *Gawain and the Green Knight* and others in the late 1300s; *Pearl* and *Gawain* are still widely read and studied today. There was also the anchoress and mystic Julian of Norwich, who was about a quarter of a century older than Richard II and who wrote *Revelations of Divine Love*, the first book in English known to have been written by a woman, in the 1390s. Margery Kempe, born in Norfolk in the early 1370s and only about five or six years younger than Richard, wrote (via scribes, not by her own hand as she was illiterate) what is often considered the first autobiography in English, the *Book of Margery Kempe*, in the 1420s. Less happily, a fifteenth-century alliterative poem called *Richard the Redeless* – the last an archaic word meaning 'without counsel' – took Richard II to task for his failures as a leader.[65] Richard's cousin and usurper Henry of Lancaster, however, showed a far greater interest in books than Richard, to the point of being a bookworm: in 1406 when he was king, Henry spent a long time sitting in an abbey library reading, and was able to read and write in English, French and Latin.[66] Richard's uncle Thomas of Woodstock, duke of Gloucester, also had a larger and more varied book collection than the king: at the time of his murder in 1397 he owned more than eighty books, including several Bibles and religious meditations, law books, and books on English history. Only three of these books were in English, the rest being in French or Latin.[67]

When Richard was thirteen he paid the large sum of £28 for romances in French and for a Bible also in French, and kept books in his private closet which suggests that he could and did read them; nineteen were rebound in the late 1380s.[68] He was described by one chronicler as 'an inquisitive searcher of antiquities relating to his royal ancestors', and most unusually for a medieval king showed a deep interest in history.[69] Richard was well aware of his royal ancestors and the names of former queens-consort of England: in July 1392, for example, he asked a chaplain at the church of St John the Baptist in Devizes, Wiltshire to say prayers for the souls of King Henry I of England and Henry's first wife Maud (*née* Edith) of Scotland, who had died in 1135 and 1118 respectively and who were his seventh great-grandparents.[70] As previously noted, Richard was aware of the anniversary of the death of King Richard I 'Lionheart', who died in France on 6 April 1199 and who was the older brother of his fourth great-grandfather King John. The chronicler Adam Usk states that when Richard was imprisoned in the Tower of London after his deposition in 1399, he was able to recount the names and histories of the kings who had suffered at the hands of their subjects since the settlement of England. Richard was even something of a numismatist. On 4 May 1386, when he was nineteen, he heard that £11 18*s* in 'old sterling' had been found under the high altar at the chapel of St Hilda in York, and he allowed the chapel to keep the money, but ordered that at first the coins were 'to be brought to the king that he may look at them.'[71] Richard II was, in many ways, most unusual for a Plantagenet king.

2

'This Royal Throne of Kings, This Sceptr'd Isle': Arrival in England, 1372–1376

Until he was almost four, Richard had the company of his older brother Edward of Angoulême, who was a little under two years his senior. Sadly, Edward died young, probably on or around 29 September 1370, when he was five years old, according to the Wigmore chronicle.[1] Rather curiously given that he was so close to the English throne, and given the joyful celebrations in England for ten days after his birth in 1365, the date of Edward of Angoulême's death is not certainly recorded except by one English chronicler (and the boy never set foot in England), and it is also possible that he died in early 1371, around the time that he turned six and Richard of Bordeaux turned four. Richard can barely have remembered his brother, yet in later years honoured his memory: in April 1391 he paid £100 for a marble tomb to be made over Edward's body at Langley Priory in Hertfordshire, which had been founded by their great-grandfather Edward II in 1308.[2] Possibly Richard's childhood was somewhat isolated. He may have known his half-brother Roger Clarendon, though Roger's date of birth is uncertain and he was probably quite a few years older than Richard. Richard also had his half-siblings the Hollands, Thomas, John, Maud and Joan, but they were also much his senior, born in the 1350s, and can hardly have been his companions in youth. Richard's later companions and friends in England included Robert de Vere, earl of Oxford, who was five years his senior, John Mowbray, grandson and heir of Joan of Kent's first cousin Margaret of Norfolk, who was eighteen months his senior, and Ralph Stafford, eldest son of the earl of Stafford, who was around his own age or a little older. There was also John Mowbray's younger brother Thomas, who was almost exactly Richard's age, and Richard's cousin Henry of Lancaster, three months his junior. Richard's other male relatives were too distant in age to be true companions in childhood and adolescence, such as his first cousin Edward of York, born in about 1373 or 1374, and his half-nephew Thomas Holland and his first cousin once removed Roger Mortimer, who were both born in 1374. His illegitimate cousins the Beaufort brothers were also born in the 1370s, and another first cousin, Humphrey of Gloucester, was not born until the early 1380s.

Richard's first tutor, when he was about six or seven, was Sir Richard Abberbury, who later became the chamberlain of Richard's queen Anne of Bohemia.[3] His second was a Frenchman named Guichard d'Angle who was captured at the battle of Poitiers in 1356 and who later became a close friend and ally of Edward of Woodstock and fought with him at Nájera, and whom Richard later made earl of Huntingdon.[4] The third, and last, was Sir Simon Burley, an intelligent and competent man who later became Richard's chamberlain and who, because of his influence over and close association with the young king, was destined to suffer an unpleasant fate at the hands of Richard's uncle and enemy Thomas of Woodstock. It is highly likely that Richard wished to bestow Guichard d'Angle's old earldom of Huntingdon on Burley in the 1380s, but Burley had made so many enemies that this was not to be. Abberbury, d'Angle and Burley would have taught Richard how to ride and how to use arms, and also social and table manners.[5]

Like his great-grandfather Edward II, but most unlike his father and grandfather Edward III who both loved the sport, Richard rarely if ever took part personally in a jousting tournament (though he may have participated in March 1386 and at the great Smithfield tournament in October 1390).[6] As with Edward II, this was not because Richard was a weakling. In Edward II's case, it was probably because he was his father's only surviving son for many years and Edward I did not wish his heir to risk his life competing in a dangerous sport, and this may have been the case for Richard II as well; or perhaps, with his exalted sense of his own royalty and separateness from everyone else, he preferred to keep a distance from his subjects and not compete at their level.[7] The king did enjoy watching jousting tournaments, however: he held Christmas jousts every year, and also every April as part of the Knight of the Garter ceremonies. He also held tournaments at Westminster in 1385, Smithfield in 1386 and twice each in 1390 and 1397, and at Windsor in 1399.[8] Conventionally, Richard did very much enjoy the sports of hunting and falconry, and every summer of his reign participated in hunts at one or another royal forest in the south of England; he also spent a lot of money on falcons, for example £78 in 1399, the last year of his reign.[9]

An examination of Richard II's remains in Westminster Abbey in 1871 revealed that he stood six feet tall. His grandfather Edward III's life-size effigy measured five feet ten and a half inches (and chronicler Thomas Walsingham described the king as 'not overly tall'), his great-grandfather Edward II was said by contemporaries to have been tall, and his great-great-grandfather Edward I, who was also his great-grandfather on his mother's side, was nicknamed Longshanks because of his great height. When Edward I's skeleton in Westminster Abbey was examined centuries after his death, he was found to have been six feet two inches. The *Historia Vitae et Regni Ricardi Secundi* or *History of the Life and Reign of Richard II* says that Richard 'was of the common stature, his hair yellowish, his face fair, round and feminine and sometimes flushed, abrupt and stammering in his speech, capricious in his manners' – an acute observation, though the statement that Richard was 'of the common stature' seems rather unlikely given his height.[10] Jean Froissart, who met Richard in the mid-1390s, also refers to his frequent changes of colour, at the Salisbury parliament of 1384 Richard is said to have gone white with rage, and the writer Jean Creton recorded that in 1399 Richard turned pale with anger; he seems to have been a person whose changes of mood could clearly be seen in his face, and it is also interesting to read that he was 'abrupt and stammering' in speech.[11]

The king was a very physically attractive man: the royal clerk Adam of Usk called him 'fair among men as another Absalom', *si secundus Apsalon pulcherimus*, and Richard of Maidstone called him 'as gracious as Absalom' and 'as handsome as Paris'.[12] (Absalom was one of the Biblical sons of King David, and 2 Samuel 14:25 says of him, 'But in all Israel there was none to be so much praised as Absalom for his beauty: from the sole of his foot even to the crown of his head there was no blemish in him.' Paris was the man who fell in love with Helen of Troy in Homer's epic.) The poet John Gower declared that Richard early in his reign was 'the most beautiful of kings and flower of boys' when he actually was a boy, and Richard of Maidstone wrote that in beauty he had no equal among kings.[13] The archbishop of Canterbury Thomas Arundel, certainly no friend of Richard, called him a beautiful man, albeit a false one.[14] Portraits of Richard reveal that he had smooth, fair skin, arched eyebrows, languid eyes, a straight nose, high cheekbones, golden wavy hair, and, later in life, a thin moustache and a rather curious small goatee beard with double tufts.[15] The famous portrait of him in the mid-1390s which hangs to this day in Westminster Abbey (though it has been heavily restored), and which is the earliest realistic portrait of an English king, shows that he also had elegant hands with long, tapering fingers.

There is perhaps something of the feminine in the contemporary or near-contemporary descriptions of Richard, and he was seemingly beautiful rather than handsome, tending more towards the gracile end of the spectrum rather than the burly, well-built end. In 2005, Christopher Fletcher pointed out that 'Richard II enjoys, with the dishonourable exception of Edward II, perhaps the most unmanly reputation of the later Middle Ages' among English kings and has an unfair posthumous 'reputation for unwarlike effeminacy', and also that his critics condemned him for being immature and childish.[16] It is apparent that Richard was healthy, fit and strong, not weak and soft, and he was certainly no physical coward. As his biographer Nigel Saul has stated, the reason for Richard not leading any great military campaigns in France as his father and grandfather had is not because he was physically unable to, but because he did not want to.[17] Christopher Fletcher also comments how peculiar it is that Richard II has gained a reputation for being fundamentally opposed to military action when he led two expeditions to Ireland and one to Scotland.[18] Then again, the son and grandson of two of the greatest warriors of the era preferred to find peaceful solutions for the long-standing war with France started by his grandfather, and this did not please all his contemporaries. The acid-tongued chronicler Thomas Walsingham, a monk of St Albans, declared that Richard's knights were more devoted to the goddess of love Venus than to the god of war Mars, more at home in the bedchamber than in the field of battle or on the jousting field, and more likely to use words than lances in defence.[19]

Richard of Bordeaux was a very different man to his father in other ways, too. He is often said to have been an aesthete rather than a warrior, refined and artistic, and was personally fastidious and enjoyed being clean and well turned-out.[20] He had the bath-houses of his palaces at Sheen in Surrey, Eltham in Kent and Langley in Hertfordshire rebuilt in luxurious style, and is famous for inventing the pocket handkerchief, specifically for having small pieces of cloth cut for the sole purpose of cleaning his nose: records of his tailor Walter Rauf show that Rauf made *parvis peciis factis ad liberandum domino regi ad portandum in manu suo pro naso suo tergendo et mundando*, 'small pieces [of linen] made for giving to the lord king to carry in his hand for wiping and cleaning his nose'.[21] George Stow has pointed out that no earlier references to such pieces of cloth have been found in England or France, and that the long-winded way of describing the cloth indicates that there was as yet no single word for them and that therefore it is not unreasonable to assume that Richard did invent them or was the first person to use them.[22] Richard took a great interest in his appearance and his clothing, and had a servant named Bendenell de Beek whose specific job was 'worker of the king's gold cloths'; Beek received a very generous income of 12*d* a day.[23] Early in his reign, Richard's personal *broderer* or embroiderer and 'linen furnisher' was called John de Scrowesburgh, later replaced by William Sauston, Stephen Vyve and Robert Ashcombe.[24]

Richard's paternal grandmother Philippa of Hainault died on 15 August 1369. She was in her mid-fifties and had been married to Edward III for forty-one and a half years, and was buried at Westminster Abbey on 9 January 1370, three days after the third birthday of the grandson in Aquitaine she never saw. The king paid a stonemason named John Orchard £5 for making 'diverse images in the likeness of angels' and six angels made of copper for her tomb, and images of alabaster 'upon a small marble tomb for an infant son and daughter of the queen'.[25] This was Philippa's third daughter Blanche, who was born and died in 1342, and her sixth son William of Windsor, born and died in 1348. The queen outlived seven of her twelve children, and had not seen her eldest child Edward of Woodstock for a few years at the time of her death. Her tomb, which the king had had made in the month of Richard's birth by a Frenchman named Hawkin Liege at a cost of 200 marks (£133), and alabaster effigy still exist in Westminster Abbey.[26] Unlike other royal effigies of the thirteenth and fourteenth centuries, it is not a stylised image of a queen but an attempt at a genuine portrait, which shows that at the end of her life Philippa tended to plumpness (hardly surprising after a dozen children) and had a kindly face which, although it may not have been conventionally beautiful or even pretty, was nevertheless the face of the woman the king had loved for four decades.

Another close relative who died in Richard's infancy was his uncle Lionel of Antwerp, duke of Clarence, the third but second surviving son of Edward III and Queen Philippa, born in November 1338 and almost eight and a half years Edward of Woodstock's junior. Lionel was still a child when he married the heiress Elizabeth de Burgh, who was six and a half years older than he and a niece of Duke Henry of Lancaster, and their only daughter Philippa of Clarence (Edward III's eldest legitimate grandchild) was born in August 1355. The widowed Lionel married his second wife Violante Visconti in May 1368, but died only five months afterwards, not quite thirty years old. Rumour had it that he was poisoned by his new father-in-law Galeazzo Visconti, lord of Milan, though a more prosaic explanation of food poisoning or a sudden infection or illness is more probable. The poet Geoffrey Chaucer, who had been a member of the household of Lionel's first wife Elizabeth de Burgh, may have attended his wedding to Violante in Milan. Lionel became a father at sixteen in August 1355, and his daughter Philippa of Clarence bore her first child when she was only fifteen: Elizabeth Mortimer, later Lady Percy, born in January 1371 and the eldest great-grandchild of Edward III. Richard of Bordeaux's aunt by marriage Blanche, duchess of Lancaster, also died in September 1368 at the age of only twenty-six, leaving her children Philippa, Elizabeth and Henry of Lancaster, Richard's first cousins.[27] Of Blanche's three surviving children, one was a king of England and another a queen-consort of Portugal, and her son Henry was less than eighteen months old when she died and cannot have remembered his mother at all.

Lionel of Antwerp's death left Richard with three uncles, all on his father's side; his mother's brothers Edmund and John of Kent had died in 1331 and 1352, and her much older half-brother Aymer Comyn as early as 1316. The eldest uncle was John of Gaunt, duke of Lancaster, born in early March 1340 and Blanche of Lancaster's widower. Edmund of Langley, fourth surviving son of Edward III and Philippa of Hainault, was very close in age to his brother John: he was born in June 1341, and was made earl of Cambridge in November 1362 when his father celebrated his fiftieth birthday. In or shortly before November 1365, John of Gaunt travelled to Flanders 'respecting the nuptials' of Edmund and Margaret of Flanders, daughter and heir of Louis, count of Flanders, Nevers and Rethel, a grandson of Edward III's uncle King Philip V of France.[28] Margaret was born in April 1350, and was widowed from her first husband Philip, duke of Burgundy, when she was only eleven in 1361. (Philip of Burgundy, like his wife Margaret, was a great-grandchild of Philip V, and thus also had a claim to the French throne.) The proposed marriage failed when the pope, under pressure from France, refused to issue a dispensation for the two to marry, and in 1369 Margaret married Philip the Bold, later duke of Burgundy, the youngest son of John II of France and brother of Charles V; Edmund of Langley would have to wait a while longer to find a bride.

Finally, Thomas of Woodstock, Edward III and Philippa of Hainault's youngest child, was born on 7 January 1355. He was their seventh son and the fifth to survive into adulthood, and given the long gap following the births of his much older siblings, Queen Philippa's pregnancy in 1354 probably came as something of a surprise to herself and Edward III. In December 1366, shortly before Richard of Bordeaux was born, Thomas's father the king was paying a tutor called Edward Palmer to instruct eleven-year-old Thomas 'in the science of grammar'.[29] Only a dozen years older than his nephew Richard, a full quarter of a century younger than his eldest brother Edward of Woodstock, almost seven years younger than his nearest sibling (William of Windsor, who died as a baby) and thirteen and a half years younger than his nearest surviving sibling (Edmund of Langley), Thomas was born too late to take part in his father and brother's great military campaigns. Edmund of Langley was a mild and politically ineffective character – chronicler Jean Froissart called him *mol et simple et paisible*, 'indolent, guileless and peaceable' – but Thomas was aggressive and hostile, and Richard would have an extremely difficult and tense relationship with him which ultimately resulted in murder.[30]

At the beginning of 1371, just after Richard's fourth birthday, he and his parents travelled to England, leaving Richard's brother Edward of Angoulême buried in Bordeaux (Richard later had the body moved to England). Richard would never see Aquitaine – whose governance was left in the hands of his uncle John of Gaunt – again. The family sailed from Bordeaux to Plymouth, and evidently it was a rough and unpleasant journey which left Richard's father so exhausted and ill that they had to remain in Plymouth for some weeks until the prince regained enough strength to travel on to London.[31] Richard and his parents lived mostly at Edward of Woodstock's favourite manors of Kennington in Surrey and Berkhamsted in Hertfordshire.[32] On 9 October 1371 Edward III pardoned a man named John Norton for murder and for escaping from prison, supposedly at his four-year-old grandson Richard's request.[33] In November that year, Richard's uncle John of Gaunt returned to England with his new bride, whom he had married near Mont-de-Marsan in the south of France that September. She was Constanza of Castile, elder daughter and heir of the murdered King Pedro 'the Cruel', and her younger sister Isabel would marry John's brother Edmund of Langley, earl of Cambridge, on 11 July 1372.[34] This marriage, intended to strengthen the ties between England and the deposed Castilian line, brought Edmund of Langley himself no benefit whatsoever – no lands, income, powerful in-laws or diplomatic advantages – and apparently Isabel found her husband staid and boring. It says a great deal about Edmund's character that he obeyed his father's request to marry King Pedro's younger daughter despite the complete lack of advantage the union brought him and even though he and Isabel were not personally compatible, something his four more spirited brothers might not have done.[35] Edmund was about fourteen years Isabel's senior and already at the beginning of his thirties when they married.

Constanza of Castile gave birth to her and John of Gaunt's only surviving child, Katherine or Catalina of Lancaster, yet another of Richard II's first cousins, before 31 March 1373, when a payment of twenty marks (£13 6s 8d) is recorded from her grandfather Edward III to Katherine Swynford for bringing him news of the child's birth.[36] Katherine Swynford was John of Gaunt's long-term mistress, and bore him an illegitimate son, John Beaufort, the first of four children they were to have together, sometime in 1372 or 1373; John was very close in age to his legitimate half-sister Catalina. Catalina of Lancaster was presumably named after her father's mistress, unless she was born on or around the feast day of Saint Katherine, 25 November, and named in the saint's honour. Duchess Constanza sending her husband's mistress to inform her father-in-law of her child's birth in the knowledge that the king would reward Katherine Swynford financially for doing so, and perhaps naming her daughter after her, raises some interesting points about relations between the two women; it hardly seems as though they were hostile to each other. In various letters of 1374/75,

John of Gaunt referred to Catalina of Lancaster as 'our very dear and beloved daughter Kateryne' (*nostre tres chere et tres ame file Kateryne* in the French original) and to Constanza as 'our very dear and beloved companion the queen [of Castile], Lady Constanza'. On 15 May 1372, Gaunt wrote a letter confirming a grant of twenty marks a year to Katherine Swynford 'for the good and pleasant service which she gives and has given to our very dear companion [Constanza] … and for the very great affection which our said companion has towards the said Katherine'.[37] Catalina of Lancaster was her mother Constanza's heir, and inherited her claim to the throne of Castile usurped by Constanza's illegitimate half-uncle Enrique of Trastámara.

For all the drama and turbulence of her early life in southern Spain – born as the illegitimate child of a king while his wife languished in prison, a king who had his father's mistress assassinated and was later killed by his half-brother in revenge – Constanza of Castile was a rather quiet and retiring figure who made little impression on English history. On 9 February 1372 she made a ceremonial entry into London as queen of Castile, accompanied by numerous lords and knights and the city mayor. Her husband had formally and publicly proclaimed himself the rightful king of Castile some days before, and thereafter was generally addressed as *monseignour d'Espaigne*, 'my lord of Spain', which in fourteenth-century usage meant the kingdom of Castile, not the entire country of Spain. Constanza's brother-in-law Edward of Woodstock hosted the ceremony, which probably means that five-year-old Richard of Bordeaux was also present.[38] Constanza and Isabel, Richard's aunts by marriage from 1372 onwards, had been living in Woodstock's custody since before Richard was born, and he had probably known them all his life.

The *Anonimalle* chronicle described Constanza in 1371 as 'a very beautiful young lady' (*une tresbele damosel*), and the Spanish chronicler Pedro Lopez de Ayala also called her mother Maria de Padilla a beautiful and intelligent woman and stated that her father King Pedro was tall and thin but muscular with very light blond hair, fair skin, and blue eyes. Pedro's father Alfonso XI, who died in his late thirties in 1350 and who was to cause so many problems for his son because of his attachment to his mistress Leonor Guzman and their children, was also pale, blond and blue-eyed. Catalina of Lancaster was described much later in life as 'white, pink and blonde, she was tall and very heavy of body. In the size and thunderousness of her flesh she seemed to be as much of a man as a woman', and Catalina's son Juan II of Castile was said to be 'fair-skinned and slightly ruddy' with hair of 'a very mature hazelnut' and eyes somewhere between green and blue.[39] The writer of the *Anonimalle* says that in February 1372 many inhabitants of London, ladies and damsels came 'to see the beauty of the said young lady', i.e. Constanza. The same chronicler also refers to Constanza in 1381 as a 'woman of great beauty' (*feme de graunde beaute*); he seems to have been very taken with her.[40] Given the descriptions of her grandfather, father and daughter, it seems likely that Constanza was blonde-haired, blue-eyed and fair-skinned and thus matched fourteenth-century English standards of beauty very well, though may, like her daughter, have had a tendency to put on weight later in life. The remains of Constanza's sister Isabel, countess of Cambridge and later duchess of York, were examined in the nineteenth century and she was found to have been extremely short, little more than four feet eight inches, even though her father King Pedro was tall enough for the fact to be commented on, and her niece Catalina was also described as tall. Unfortunately it is impossible to know whether Constanza was of equally small stature. There is often an assumption that Catalina of Lancaster and her descendants, who included Henry VIII's first queen Katherine of Aragon (a great-granddaughter of Catalina and probably named after her), were fair-haired and fair-skinned as a result of their descent from John of Gaunt and the English royal family, but as we see from the contemporary descriptions of the very blond and pale King Pedro the Cruel and his father Alfonso XI – who were both of entirely Spanish and Portuguese origin – this is not necessarily the case.[41]

The procession of 9 February 1372 rode along Cheapside and left John of Gaunt and Constanza at their London home, the luxurious Savoy Palace, which Gaunt had inherited from his first father-in-law Duke Henry of Lancaster. Duchess Constanza appears to have had a close relationship with her young stepson Henry of Lancaster, Duke Henry's grandson, who was only four years old when she married his father: for many years both she and John of Gaunt gave Henry material for clothes, lent him their servants and craftsmen when necessary, and paid for some of his alms and presents.[42] Edward III gave his daughter-in-law Constanza a golden crown encrusted with emeralds, rubies and pearls, probably at the Christmas party held at the royal manor of Woodstock in 1373, which Richard of Bordeaux may also have attended.[43]

On 31 August 1372, Edward III appointed five-year-old Richard as keeper of the realm when he left the country to lead his last expedition to France.[44] The boy was chosen in preference to his seventeen-year-old uncle Thomas of Woodstock, who also remained behind in England, which probably means that the king was publicly acknowledging that Richard was heir to his throne after his father Edward of Woodstock. The military expedition was a response to increasing Castilian and French hostilities in the Bay of Biscay, which led to the capture of John Hastings, earl of Pembroke (widower of the king's daughter Margaret and now married to his cousin Anne Manny) by King Enrique II of Trastámara. The harsh imprisonment imposed on Pembroke killed the young earl in 1375, though Edward of Woodstock's friend and Richard's tutor Guichard d'Angle was released from his Castilian jail still in good health.[45] The king, now almost sixty and accompanied by his three surviving eldest sons Edward of Woodstock, John of Gaunt and Edmund of Langley, achieved absolutely nothing: his ship bobbed around the coast near Winchelsea for a few weeks, unable to sail south because of the winds, until in despair he called off the campaign.[46]

The worsening health of Edward of Woodstock, prince of Wales, was giving the king and everyone else cause for concern, and it was becoming clear that if the prince outlived his father at all, it would not be for long. Richard of Bordeaux would almost certainly become king of England while still a young boy. And Edward III, whose reign until the 1360s had been so glorious, who in the 1350s held the kings of both France and Scotland in captivity, who had restored the prestige of the monarchy after the disastrous reign of his father Edward II and blazed England's name across Europe with his famous military victories, was growing ever more senile and becoming more and more dependent on his notorious mistress Alice Perrers. In August 1373 he even gave Perrers some jewels which had been Queen Philippa's, and at least one of his three children with her was born a few years before the queen's death in 1369.[47] In 1375 the king allowed Perrers to play the role of Lady of the Sun during a jousting tournament, which was probably witnessed by the eight-year-old Richard. Contemporaries were disgusted at the king's very public, preferential treatment of his mistress. For his part, Richard's father came down with a serious and permanent illness mere months after Richard was born, and the boy's memories of him can only have been as an invalid in frequent pain and discomfort, not as the great warrior of the past. It must have seemed to Richard as he was growing up that the days of glory were long gone, only tales he had heard but never experienced. Even his mother, famously the most beautiful woman in England (at least, according to Jean Froissart), who had been married to two men at once and who caught the attention of the most eligible bachelor in Europe, was already forty when he was born. For all his talent as a battle commander, Edward of Woodstock never really shone as a politician and for much of the time was infirm anyway, and in the absence of any real control and direction from him and his father in the early to mid-1370s, the earliest years Richard of Bordeaux would be able to remember, English politics descended ever more into factionalism and discontent.

John of Gaunt, duke of Lancaster, by virtue of being the king's eldest son still capable of leadership and because of the immense wealth and influence he held by his wife Blanche's inheritance, came to dominate politics. In strong opposition to Lancaster stood Edmund Mortimer, the young earl of March (born in 1352), who was married to Lancaster's niece Philippa of Clarence, only child of Edward III's late second son Lionel, and who was the great-grandson of Roger Mortimer, the man Edward III had had executed for treason in 1330. England in the 1370s was in a fairly pitiful state. Bankrupt, riven by factions and dogged by a corrupt Church leadership, its inhabitants suffered from the after-effects of decades-long lavish expenditure on foreign wars which had brought temporary glory but little if any long-term gain. A massive outbreak of the Black Death in 1348/49 and smaller ones in 1361 and 1369 reduced the population by a third or even as much as half. When Edward III died in 1377, Charles V of France was threatening an invasion of England, and Edward's military victories in Scotland and the capture of his brother-in-law David II ultimately came to nothing either. The great poet William Langland wrote a searing indictment of the state in which England found itself in the 1370s in his *Vision of Piers Plowman*. Richard of Bordeaux's inheritance was a most difficult one.

It had all begun so promisingly. Edward III succeeded to the throne in 1327, and proved that unlike his father Edward II, he knew how to be a king and how to rule. In the 1330s Edward claimed the throne of France via his mother Isabella, fourth and youngest child of King Philip IV (d. 1314). Isabella's three brothers Louis X, Philip V and Charles IV died without surviving sons, though all of them left daughters; Louis X's only child Queen Jeanne II of Navarre was the mother of Carlos II 'the Bad' of Navarre and of other children, and two of Philip V's four daughters had descendants. When Charles IV's widow Jeanne of Evreux gave birth to his posthumous daughter Blanche on 1 April 1328 two months after his death, Charles's first cousin Philip, count of Valois (son of Philip IV's brother Charles de Valois) succeeded to the throne as the late king's nearest male relative, and became Philip VI. He was the first king of the Valois dynasty which was to rule France until 1589. Charles IV's sister Isabella of France, in 1328 ruling England in the name of her underage son Edward III, claimed the French throne on Edward's behalf on her brother's death.

Some years afterwards Edward III claimed the throne himself, and began what much later became known as the Hundred Years War. It was a family affair: Philip VI was the son of Edward III's great-uncle Charles de Valois, and was also his wife Philippa of Hainault's maternal uncle. Edward won great victories over Philip at the naval battle of Sluys in 1340 and at the battle of Crécy in northern France in 1346, when Richard of Bordeaux's then sixteen-year-old father Edward of Woodstock commanded the vanguard. One of the men who fell on the French side at Crécy was the king of Bohemia, John 'the Blind', whose granddaughter Anne would become Richard's first queen. The greatest victory of all came at Poitiers in 1356, when Edward of Woodstock captured the king of France himself, Philip VI's son John II, who died at the Savoy Palace in London in April 1364. By the time Richard II was born, however, these glory days of victories over France were a distant memory.

Sixty-year-old Edward III, though slipping ever further into senility and dependence on the rapacious Alice Perrers, bestirred himself sufficiently on 16 June 1373 to make a treaty of 'permanent peace' with King Fernando of Portugal, son of Pedro I who had died in Estremoz a few days after Richard of Bordeaux's birth.[48] (The treaty is still in force today, making it the oldest active peace treaty in the world.) The treaty would be reinforced a few years later when Edward III's granddaughter Philippa of Lancaster married Fernando's half-brother and successor João I. Richard of Bordeaux's godfather Jaime IV, the titular king of Majorca, died at Soria in Castile on 20 January 1375, eight years after he had lifted Richard from the font in Bordeaux. His wife Queen Giovanna of Naples and Sicily paid for his ransom after he was taken prisoner by Enrique of Trastámara in 1367, and he returned to Naples but shortly afterwards went back to Castile to aid Enrique in his war against his former ally Pedro IV of Aragon. Pedro IV was Jaime's uncle who had imprisoned him in a cage for fourteen years. Enrique of Trastámara and Pedro IV made a truce, brokered by John of Gaunt, and Jaime died soon afterwards without ever regaining his lost kingdom of Majorca. The following year, Queen Giovanna married her fourth husband, a German prince: Otto, duke of Brunswick, who had once been challenged to a duel by John of Gaunt's father-in-law Henry, duke of Lancaster before John II of France stepped in to prevent it. Childless, Queen Giovanna adopted John II's son and Charles V's younger brother Louis, duke of Anjou, as her son, and made him heir to her throne but was murdered in 1382 by her cousin Charles of Durazzo. On 6 February 1385 Richard II sent three men, including the mercenary Sir John Hawkwood, to treat for peace with Charles of Durazzo, who was himself murdered a year later.[49] Occupying a European throne in the fourteenth century was frequently a dangerous proposition, as Richard II himself would find out.

3

'I Take My Leave before I Have Begun': The Heir, 1376–1377

Edward of Woodstock, prince of Wales and Aquitaine, duke of Cornwall and earl of Chester, 'the flower of chivalry' as Jean Froissart calls him, died at Westminster on Trinity Sunday, 8 June 1376, a week before his forty-sixth birthday. The date would have pleased him; he was devoted to the Trinity, and was buried according to his own wishes in the church of Canterbury Cathedral in Kent, which was dedicated to the Trinity, in early October. The grieving king took his grandson Richard under the protection of the royal household and ordered him a suit of black clothes as a sign of mourning.[1]

In his will, written the day before he died, Edward of Woodstock left a silk bed to Sir Roger Clarendon, who was his illegitimate son though not named as such in the will, and 'a great bed of red camoca [a kind of silk] embroidered with our arms at each corner' to his confessor Robert de Walsham. The prince left his only surviving legitimate son Richard several items: 'the blue clothing with golden roses and ostrich feathers' and a bed in the same colours which had been given to him by his father the king, another brand-new bed striped with brocade and red camoca with all its hangings, a 'great bed' embroidered with angels and all its pillows, hangings and sheets, and hangings for his chamber including one embroidered with 'mermen of the sea' and one of the great twelfth-century Muslim general Saladin, respected adversary of Richard Lionheart. The prince added, 'We charge our son Richard upon our blessing to keep and confirm to everyone as much as we have so given them, and as far as God has given us power over our said son we give him our curse if he hinder or suffer to be hindered as much as is our said gift' – strong words for nine-year-old Richard to hear from his father. The prince's beloved brother John of Gaunt was one of his executors.[2]

The archbishop of Canterbury, Simon Sudbury, told parliament some months later that although Edward of Woodstock had left them, in effect he still remained among them, 'because he had left behind him such a noble and fine son, who is his exact image and true likeness'.[3] Richard may well have closely resembled his father physically; he could hardly have been more different in character and outlook in most ways, however. On 25 June 1376, Richard was taken into parliament 'so that the lords and commons of the realm could see and honour [him] as the true heir apparent'.[4] Thomas Walsingham wrote rather melodramatically that when Edward of Woodstock died, 'all the hopes of the English died with him'.[5] Edward of Woodstock was born in 1330 as heir to the English throne, and for four and a half decades both he and the people of England had expected that one day he would become their king, but now nine-year-old Richard of Bordeaux was heir to the throne of his aged and ailing grandfather.

In October 1376 a week after Edward of Woodstock's funeral, a meeting was held at the royal manor of Havering-atte-Bower to discuss the succession to the throne, a vital issue given that Richard of Bordeaux was still a child and would not be able to father a child and heir for some years.[6] It was confirmed that Richard was next in line to the throne, and decided that if he were to die without heirs of his body, the throne would pass to Edward III's third son John of Gaunt and then to Gaunt's heirs male, which at that time meant his only legitimate son Henry of Lancaster, followed by the king's fourth son Edmund of Langley and his heirs male (Edmund by then had an infant son, Edward of York, with his wife Isabel of Castile) and then the fifth son Thomas of Woodstock and his heirs male (Thomas's son Humphrey was born six years later in the early 1380s). The king's granddaughter Philippa of Clarence, only child of his second son Lionel, and her two-year-old son and the heir to the earldom of March, Roger Mortimer, were thus excluded, even though there were historical precedents for the succession to the English throne to pass through a female. Henry II had become king of England in 1154 via his mother Empress Maud, only surviving legitimate child of Henry I, and his predecessor King Stephen was the son of Henry I's sister Adele. Edward I in 1290 had set out his wish that if his then six-year-old son the future Edward II died childless, the throne should pass to the king's eldest daughter Eleanor in preference to his younger brother Edmund of Lancaster and Edmund's sons Thomas and Henry.[7] And Edward III himself had claimed the throne of France in the 1330s via his mother Isabella, daughter of Philip IV.

It was extremely important to set out precisely the order of succession to the English throne, especially as the heir was only nine years old. Edward III's great-grandfather Henry III had succeeded to the throne also as a child of nine in 1216, but was unquestionably the son of the previous king, John. Likewise, the fourteen-year-old Edward III in 1327 was unquestionably the son of the previous (albeit deposed and still alive) king Edward II. Richard of Bordeaux's father Edward of Woodstock, however, died before his father and never became king, so the situation was not quite the same. In 1199 on the death of King Richard Lionheart, his youngest brother King John succeeded him to the throne in preference to Arthur of Brittany, twelve-year-old son of John's late elder brother Geoffrey, duke of Brittany.[8] This set a precedent whereby it might be claimed in 1376 that John of Gaunt, as an adult younger son of a king, should have precedence over the underage child of his elder brother who had never been king himself.

Another issue revolved around the governance of the realm during Richard's minority; as he would be too young to rule the kingdom himself for a few years, who would govern in his name? The most powerful figure in England in the 1370s, with his eldest brother an invalid and his father not expected to live much longer, was John of Gaunt, who was almost a king himself at least in name, possessor of the vast Lancastrian inheritance and of an enormous retinue. His niece Philippa of Clarence might also be said to have a good claim to the throne, as the daughter of Edward III's late second son Lionel, and her husband Edmund Mortimer, earl of March, was Gaunt's greatest rival among the magnates in 1376.[9] It seems peculiar that Edward III in October 1376 was willing to set aside his own granddaughter, which might point to John of Gaunt exercising influence over his infirm father and pushing his and his son's claim to the throne at his niece's expense. Given that the king himself had claimed the French throne for decades via his mother Isabella, it seems a little odd that he would decide that his granddaughter and her son did not belong in the line of succession simply because she was female. Then again, there are really no grounds for believing that the entail was anything other than Edward III's own decision, though also no real grounds for assuming that the Havering discussions were intended to be legally binding.[10]

John of Gaunt was even suspected – unfairly and inaccurately, as it turned out – of wishing to declare Richard of Bordeaux illegitimate and make himself king instead when his father died. King Carlos II 'the Bad' of Navarre told the count of Flanders this story sometime between 1372 and 1376, so there were rumours to this effect even outside England, and at the highest levels of society.[11] In the end, despite these rumours, Gaunt remained completely loyal to his nephew for the rest of his life. The question of the succession to the throne after Richard of Bordeaux, and whether or not it would exclude Philippa of Clarence and her Mortimer children, was to become a vital issue over the next few years, especially when Richard failed to father any heirs of his body.

Edward III made his will on 7 October 1376. He bequeathed to 'our future heir Richard' a bed 'marked with the arms of France and England, now in our palace at Westminster', and left his daughter-in-law Joan of Kent 1,000 marks, or £666.[12] A few weeks later, on 20 November, the king made Richard prince of Wales, duke of Cornwall and earl of Chester.[13] This was publicly acknowledging Richard as the heir to the throne. The boy was living with his mother Joan of Kent, who on 20 December 1376 received £200 for his expenses from the king.[14] According to Jean Froissart, at Christmas 1376 Edward III made Richard 'sit at his table above all his own children in great estate, representing that he should be king after his decease'.[15] Richard was summoned to parliament, to be held at Westminster in January 1377, for the first time on 1 December 1376, and on 10 May 1377 the king ordered that he should be paid 200 marks annually, in two instalments at Easter and Michaelmas.[16]

Richard of Bordeaux probably attended his grandfather's Christmas courts in the 1370s, and the annual feast for the order of the Knights of the Garter held at Windsor on 23 April, the feast day of St George.[17] On 23 April 1377 he was knighted and made a Knight of the Garter himself, as the sixty-first member; his cousin Henry of Lancaster, who was three months Richard's junior and had just turned ten, was knighted and also made a Knight of the Garter at the same time. Richard's father had been the first member when his grandfather Edward III founded the order in 1348, Henry of Lancaster's grandfather Duke Henry the second, and Richard's half-brother Sir Thomas Holland the fifty-eighth. Also knighted on 23 April 1377 was Richard's uncle Thomas of Woodstock, now twenty-two, though for some reason he was not made a Knight of the Garter at this time; neither did his father grant him an earldom, and it was left to Richard to do so and to create Thomas a Knight of the Garter, which he duly did in 1380.

Another new knight in 1377 was Richard's later great friend Robert de Vere, then fifteen and heir to the earldom of Oxford. This was perhaps the first occasion the two boys had spent time together, although Richard had presumably been present, with his grandfather the king, at Robert's wedding to his nine-year-old first cousin Philippa Coucy in the late summer or early autumn of 1376, some months after Edward of Woodstock's death.[18] The other boys and young men knighted in April 1377 were John Mowbray, grandson and heir of the countess of Norfolk; three Percys, members of a great noble family from the north of England; and Richard's illegitimate half-uncle John Southeray, son of the king and his mistress Alice Perrers, and only two or three years older than Richard himself. Richard was related to all these young men: John Mowbray's maternal grandmother Margaret, countess of Norfolk, was a granddaughter of Edward I and first cousin of Joan of Kent; Robert de Vere was descended from King Henry III and was a great-nephew of Duke Henry of Lancaster (which made him the second cousin of Henry of Lancaster); and the Percys were also half-Lancastrian via their mother, Duke Henry's youngest sister Mary of Lancaster, and were thus also kinsmen of the king and Richard of Bordeaux.

Around seven in the evening of Sunday 21 June 1377, a long era came to an end: King Edward III of England died at his palace of Sheen, west of London, after a series of strokes.[19] He was sixty-four years old and had been king for a little over fifty years, since the forced abdication of his father Edward II in January 1327. According to the chronicler Thomas Walsingham, who was gossipy and often quite vicious, the king was abandoned at his death by almost everyone including his own family and household. Walsingham also claims that Edward's mistress Alice Perrers, seeing that he was dying, stripped the rings from his fingers and fled, leaving him to die alone. Jean Froissart, on the other hand, gives a completely different version of events and says that the king died surrounded by his family: his three surviving sons John of Gaunt, Edmund of Langley and Thomas of Woodstock; his only surviving daughter Isabella of Woodstock, countess of Bedford; his son-in-law Duke John IV of Brittany (widower of Edward's daughter Mary, now married to Richard of Bordeaux's half-sister Joan Holland); and his grandson-in-law Edmund Mortimer, earl of March.[20] This seems far more probable; it is hard to imagine that the king of England was abandoned by everyone as he lay dying, let alone that his body was robbed of its finery by his mistress.

Richard of Bordeaux, now Richard II of England, was probably at Kennington with his mother Joan of Kent when he became king, and travelled the few miles to Sheen on 22 June.[21] He was the first boy king of England since his great-great-great-grandfather Henry III succeeded to the throne at the age of nine in 1216, though Edward III had been only fourteen in 1327. At Vespers, or sunset – which would have been around 9.30 p.m. in the south of England at this time of year – on 22 June, an important ceremony took place in the young king's chamber at Sheen. The keepers of Edward III's great seal formally handed it over into Richard in a purse of white leather in the presence of the archbishop of Canterbury and the bishop of Worcester, Richard's uncle John of Gaunt, duke of Lancaster, his brother-in-law John, duke of Brittany, Thomas Beauchamp, earl of Warwick, and his cousin Philippa's husband Edmund Mortimer, earl of March.[22] Richard's uncles and everyone else would now have bowed and knelt to him as their liege lord, an important moment in the life of the ten-year-old as he realised that he was now different and set apart from ordinary mortals, even his royally born uncles. If there had been doubt in anyone's mind as to what John of Gaunt would do, whether he would attempt to seize the throne, these doubts soon vanished. Gaunt showed nothing but the utmost loyalty to Richard as his liege lord, now and for the rest of his life. On 1 July 1377, Richard asked the two archbishops and all the bishops of England, and the universities of Oxford and Cambridge, to pray for himself and his realm, and on the 11th, mindful of the dignified respect owed to his royal forebears, ordered the wax around the body of his great-great-grandfather Edward I to be renewed.[23]

Two great English noblewomen also died in 1377. The first was Maud of Lancaster, countess of Ulster, one of the six sisters of Duke Henry of Lancaster, mother-in-law of Richard's late uncle Lionel of Antwerp, and grandmother of Richard's first cousin Philippa of Clarence and of his great friend Robert de Vere, earl of Oxford. The second was Marie de St Pol, countess of Pembroke, who founded Pembroke College at the university of Cambridge in 1347 and who had outlived her much older husband Aymer de Valence by a remarkable fifty-three years. Marie was a link to the distant past: her husband Aymer was the son of one of the half-brothers of King Henry III, Richard II's great-great-great-grandfather, and had been born in the 1270s, and Aymer's nephew John Comyn had once been married to Richard's maternal grandmother Margaret Wake, countess of Kent. Edward III's funeral took place at Westminster Abbey on 5 July 1377, two weeks after his death, which was much sooner than was generally the case with fourteenth-century royal burials: Edward I died on 7 July 1307 and was buried on 27 October; Edward II (supposedly) died on 21 September 1327 and was buried on 20 December; Edward III's mother Isabella of France died on 22 August 1358 and was buried on 27 November; Queen Philippa died on 15 August 1369 and was buried on 9 January 1370. Edward's death mask still exists at Westminster Abbey, the oldest extant death mask of an English king, and shows that he died of a stroke – the mouth is turned down at one side.

The funeral cortege left Sheen on 3 July and crossed London Bridge the same day, and the king's body lay for one night at St Paul's Cathedral before being taken to Westminster on Saturday 4 July. A massive procession of people accompanied the royal body through London, including the late king's three surviving sons, his son-in-law the duke of Brittany and his grandson-in-law the earl of March: apart from Richard, these men were the senior male members of the royal family. Richard of Bordeaux appears not to have taken part in the public ceremonies so as to cede precedence to his late grandfather, though probably attended the funeral itself in Westminster Abbey. Black cloths were hung on the abbey walls, and the king's embalmed body was lowered into the ground wrapped in red samite (a kind of silk) with a cross of white silk placed over it.[24] Previous kings had attended the funerals of their predecessors – Edward III attended Edward II's in 1327, and Edward II attended Edward I's in 1307 – though in later centuries etiquette began to demand that kings of England did not take part in funerals. Edward III was laid to rest next to his beloved wife Queen Philippa. He died while Charles V of France was threatening an invasion of England and the English-ruled parts of France; it was a sad end to a long and dramatic life which had seen great military victories over France and Scotland.

4

'My Crown I Am': Coronation of a Young King, 1377–1378

Richard II's coronation as king of England took place at Westminster Abbey on Thursday 16 July 1377, only eleven days after Edward III's funeral. It was the first coronation in England for half a century, Edward III's having taken place on 1 February 1327 beyond living memory for the majority of the young king's subjects, and understandably generated enormous excitement and enthusiasm. Women, the wives of earls and barons, attended the coronation for the only the third time in English history (they had been invited for the first time to the joint coronation of Richard's great-grandparents Edward II and Isabella of France in February 1308). Edward II had also been the first king to take his coronation oath in French instead of Latin, as Richard also did. Numerous people worked hard to ensure that everything was ready in time: tentmakers in London and Middlesex set up pavilions around the palace of Westminster for the guests and as venues for the forthcoming festivities; stonemasons, carpenters, labourers, plumbers 'and other workers in lead' were hired 'wherever found' (and were liable be arrested and imprisoned if they refused to work); stone and timber were ordered in quantity; and 1,000 barrels of ale were purchased in Hull and Grimsby and transported by ship to London.[1]

The authors of the *Anonimalle* chronicle and the *Chronicon Anglie* wrote long descriptions of the coronation of 'Richard of Bordeaux, the young prince of England' (*Richard de Burdews le iune prince Dengleterre*). On Wednesday 15 July, the day before the coronation, all the lords of the realm present in the capital, with the mayor and aldermen of the city, rode to the Tower of London where Richard was staying. Richard came out dressed in white clothes, well and honourably dressed as befitted his high rank, with his household knights. A great procession then rode from the Tower to Westminster: firstly the London commons, also all dressed in white, then the squires, then the knights, then the aldermen and the mayor, then the two city sheriffs, dressed in white. Then came Richard's uncles John, Edmund and Thomas. A long way behind them, riding on his own in solitary splendour, came Richard, and after another long interval rode the earls, barons and lords. The entire procession, which according to the *Chronicon Angliae* also included a contingent of German mercenaries (*stipendiarii*) and a delegation from Richard's duchy of Aquitaine, rode along Cheapside towards Westminster Palace; the streets were so packed with spectators that the duke of Lancaster had to cut a path through them.[2]

At Cheapside a tower had been constructed, its framework of timber covered with painted canvas, with four turrets. Inside the turrets were 'very beautiful' and well-dressed girls who scattered gold coins over Richard, and there was a small bell-tower on which was displayed an angel wearing a gold crown. Also at Cheapside, a brightly painted conduit was built to provide red and white wine for people to refresh themselves in the midsummer heat (the *Anonimalle* makes a point of commenting how hot the day was). Richard and the rest of the procession then rode along Fleet Street to Westminster Palace where the king would relax and spend the night, while the lords returned to London and others went home.[3]

The night before the coronation Richard took a ceremonial bath, and in the morning was awoken by his servants and dressed in new clothes. Simon Sudbury, archbishop of Canterbury, plus numerous bishops, abbots and priors and the monks of Westminster went in procession from the abbey to the hall of the palace, and some of the temporal lords accompanied Richard through the Painted Chamber of the palace and delivered him to the archbishop and the clergy. In the procession, the duke of Lancaster carried the first sword, Curtana, the earl of March the second sword, and the earl of Warwick the third; the earl of Cambridge (or the earl of Suffolk, according to other evidence) carried the golden sceptre, and the new earl of Buckingham the royal rod. The *Anonimalle* chronicle says that the earls of Stafford, Arundel and Suffolk carried the boy king on their shoulders, while the barons of the Cinque Ports bore a cloth of gold above him. Richard sat on a throne placed on a high scaffold in the middle of the abbey church, and the ceremony began. He swore his coronation oath on the sacrament, and the most important part of the proceedings, at least as far as Richard was concerned, came when he was screened from view by a golden cloth and anointed with holy oil on the chest, shoulders, head and hands by the archbishop of Canterbury. This was the moment that made him a king, God's chosen and anointed on earth, and set him apart from ordinary mortals.

After the ceremony, the king's tutor Sir Simon Burley, now his chamberlain (or unspecified 'lords', says the *Anonimalle*), carried Richard out of the abbey on his shoulders into Westminster Hall, where the post-coronation banquet was to be held. Somewhere in the middle of the hall, one of Richard's shoes fell off and was lost.[4] In retrospect at least, this was interpreted as a bad omen, though the author of the *Anonimalle* prosaically attributed the loss to the shoes being too big for the ten-year-old boy. Richard, who for the rest of his life demonstrated a fascination with his coronation regalia and who sometimes went into Westminster Abbey just to look at it, replaced the shoe in March 1390 with one embroidered with fleurs-de-lis and blessed by Pope Urban VI.[5] Chronicler Adam Usk, who was much attached to prophecies and signs, also narrates the story of Richard's lost shoe and comments that as a result 'the commons who rose up against him hated him ever after, all his long [*sic*] life'. Usk states that there were two more unfavourable signs on the day of the coronation: one of Richard's golden spurs also came off and therefore 'the soldiery opposed him in rebellion', and 'at the banquet a sudden gust of wind carried away the crown from his head', as a result of which he was supplanted by his cousin Henry.[6] This latter point is extremely dubious; it would have taken a wind of hurricane force blowing inside Westminster Hall to remove Richard's extremely heavy crown from his head.

At this point in the proceedings Richard knighted eleven men and boys, including his cousin Edward of York, son of his uncle Edmund of Langley, earl of Cambridge – Edward was only about three or four years old at the time – and the sons of the lords Ros, Talbot and Furnival. He also created four earls. The king's youngest uncle, Thomas of Woodstock, then aged twenty-two, became earl of Buckingham and was also constable of England, and on 17 July was granted an income of £1,000 a year. John Mowbray, grandson and heir of Margaret, countess of Norfolk, and not quite twelve years old, became earl of Nottingham (he was to die at the age of seventeen, leaving his brother Thomas as his and their grandmother's heir). Henry Percy, scion of a great northern family and latest in a long line of lords named Henry Percy, then in his mid-thirties, became the first earl of Northumberland. Richard's former tutor Guichard d'Angle became earl of Huntingdon, though he died in 1380 and so did not have very long to enjoy the honour. Finally, the *Anonimalle* claims that the newly knighted Edward of York, barely more than a toddler, became earl of Colchester, though there is no other confirmation of this appointment and it seems to be the chronicler's own invention or misunderstanding.[7] Also on the day of the coronation, Sir Simon Burley was appointed as master of the king's falcons and keeper of the royal mews at 'Charrying by Westminster', at wages of 12*d* daily; he was confirmed in this role on 23 August 1382. The entry on the Patent Roll gives the usual price paid for falcons in the late fourteenth century, including 20*s* for a falcon-gentle, 13*s* 4*d* both for a goshawk and for a gerfalcon-tercel, and 26*s* 8*d* for a gerfalcon.[8]

During the coronation banquet, Richard sat on a throne with a golden cloth held above him and Edmund Mortimer, earl of March, held his crown above his head so that he could have dinner as it was too heavy for him to be able to eat comfortably while wearing it. (As March was holding the crown it could not have been blown off the young king's head, as Adam Usk states.) Richard's cousin Henry of Lancaster stood in front of the king holding the sword of mercy, Curtana, which responsibility had been delegated to him by his father.[9] Duke John IV of Brittany, who was married to Richard's half-sister Joan Holland, assisted him at meat.[10] The young king's uncle John of Gaunt, titular king of Castile by right of his wife Constanza, duke of Lancaster and earl of Leicester and Lincoln, claimed various privileges at the coronation: to be granted the office of steward of England as earl of Leicester, to carry the sword Curtana during the ceremony as duke of Lancaster, and to 'cut and carve that day before the king' as earl of Lincoln.

Other members of the nobility and officials petitioned to be allowed to perform varying roles during the coronation and the banquet: serving the king was considered a great honour. Margaret, countess of Norfolk in her own right, daughter and heir of Edward I's son Thomas of Brotherton, earl of Norfolk and Earl Marshal of England, asked to perform the office of marshal, but it was given to the new earl of Northumberland Henry Percy instead. This role involved 'appeasing debates in the king's house, assigning lodgings, guarding the door of the king's chamber, and taking of every baron and earl that was made a knight one palfrey and saddle'. Margaret of Norfolk was about fifty-five years old and was Joan of Kent's first cousin; these two and the recently widowed Margaret Courtenay, *née* de Bohun, countess of Devon, were the last remaining grandchildren of Edward I, who had died exactly seventy years earlier in July 1307. Edward III himself had been the fourth-last survivor. Margaret of Norfolk's grandson John Hastings, only son and heir of the late earl of Pembroke, asked to carry the silver-gilt boot spurs during the procession, but as he was not yet five years old he was deemed too young, and Edmund Mortimer, earl of March, was given permission to carry them instead (though according to other evidence, March carried the second sword, not the spurs).

John Hastings' mother Anne Manny, Margaret of Norfolk's only surviving child, was naperer, i.e. in charge of the table linen, and kept the cloths used as her fee; Richard Fitzalan, earl of Arundel and Surrey, served as butler; Thomas Beauchamp, earl of Warwick, carried the third sword and was in charge of dispensing bread, and took the salts, knives and spoons set before the king as his fee; and William, Lord Furnivall was to find a glove for the king's right hand and to hold Richard's right arm as long as he held the rod which English kings always carried during their coronations (in their other hand they held an orb). The mayor of London was granted permission to serve the king from his gold cup 'as well at dinner in hall as after dinner at the spices', and the barons of the Cinque Ports carried a cloth of gold over the king's head 'upon four lances covered with silver, and at the four corners thereof four bells of silver-gilt'. A citizen of London named John Wiltshire was given the responsibility of handing a towel to the king when he washed his hands before eating, and a knight called John Argenthem, who at the last coronation in 1327 had been eight years old and a ward of the new king Edward III, served Richard from a silver cup. Finally, the fifteen-year-old heir to the earldom of Oxford, Robert de Vere, was allowed to perform the office of chamberlain, and also served the king with water 'before and after meat' and removed his basins and towels. The most dramatic role in the coronation was given to Sir John Dymmok, who rode one of the king's great destriers (warhorses) before Richard in the procession, armed, crying out three times that if anyone denied Richard's right, he would defend the king in personal combat.[11] The whole ceremony and the subsequent banquet was a highly choreographed and ritualised event which can only have made a profound impression on the mind of the young boy who sat at the centre of it all.

Although only ten years old, as the new king of England Richard II was an immensely desirable bachelor, and marriage proposals from other European royal families came flooding in both before and after his accession. Charles V of France offered one of his daughters, either Marie, who died aged seven in June 1377, or Isabelle, who died in February 1378 aged four. On 16 January 1378 three men were commissioned to negotiate a marriage between Richard and a daughter of Charles V, though ultimately nothing came of it.[12] (Of all Charles V and Jeanne de Bourbon's children, only Charles VI and his brother Louis of Orléans survived childhood.) Carlos II 'the Bad' of Navarre also offered one of his daughters, presumably either Bonne, who was a little older than Richard, or Juana, who was a little younger and who later married Duke John IV of Brittany and secondly Richard's cousin and successor Henry IV. Robert II of Scotland, first king of the house of Stewart, who had succeeded his half-uncle David II Bruce on the throne in 1371, also put forward one of his many daughters as a bride for Richard.[13]

One final candidate of early 1378 was at first also rejected: the Holy Roman Emperor Karl IV, ruler and overlord of much of modern-day Germany, northern Italy, the Low Countries, southern and eastern France, Austria, Switzerland, Poland and the Czech Republic, proposed his daughter Anne. Richard's counsellors, however, showed little interest. English foreign policy in the Middle Ages tended to revolve around France, so that English kings married French women when they were allied with France, and sought brides from the Spanish kingdoms or the patchwork of counties and duchies in the Low Countries when they were not. Alliance with the Holy Roman Emperor, although he was the powerful ruler of a vast territory, seemed to offer little political advantage to England. And yet within a couple of years this would change, and Richard II ultimately would marry Anne, however unlikely this might have seemed in 1377/78.

Richard's counsellors briefly considered another German marriage for the king in 1380: on 12 June that year, three men including

Sir Simon Burley were appointed 'to treat for a contract of marriage between our person [Richard] and Lady Katherine, daughter of Ludwig, late emperor of the Romans, of celebrated memory'.[14] This can only mean Ludwig of Bavaria, Holy Roman Emperor, who died in 1347 and was the predecessor of Karl IV. The emperor Ludwig had no daughter called Katherine, and she would have been far too old for Richard II even if he had, so this must mean a granddaughter. Ludwig's son Albrecht I, duke of Lower Bavaria and count of Hainault and Holland, did have a daughter called Katharina, presumably the lady intended here, who was born in about 1361 and was Richard's second cousin; Albrecht of Bavaria's mother Margareta of Hainault was the sister of Richard's grandmother Queen Philippa. Katharina of Bavaria had in fact married Wilhelm, duke of Jülich and Guelders, some months before Burley and the others were instructed to negotiate Richard's possible marriage with her, but apparently this news had not yet reached England. Duchess Katharina would be made a Lady of the Garter in 1399, the last year of Richard II's reign.

No official regent was appointed to rule for the underage king, though a council was chosen on 20 July 1377, which was to discharge most royal business.[15] The first council consisted of William Courtenay, bishop of London (a cousin of the king and future archbishop of Canterbury); Ralph Ergham, bishop of Salisbury (John of Gaunt's chancellor and therefore representing the duke's interests); William, Lord Latimer; John, Lord Cobham; and the knights Roger Beauchamp, Richard Stafford, John Knyvet, Ralph Ferrers, John Devereux and Hugh Segrave. A meeting which had taken place earlier in 1377 had ended acrimoniously, and led to John of Gaunt threatening to drag William Courtenay out by his hair; no love was lost between these two men. A series of continual councils held office between 1377 and 1380. The obvious person to have acted as regent would have been John of Gaunt, but he was unpopular and mistrusted. In England there was no precedent for appointing the king's mother as regent: Isabelle of Angoulême had not been allowed any power whatsoever during the early reign of her son Henry III in and after 1216, and even Richard II's great-grandmother Isabella of France, who did wield power between late 1326 and late 1330 for her son Edward III, was never officially appointed regent or even as a member of the regency council. Joan of Kent therefore had probably not expected to hold a position of power during her son's minority, though did enjoy some influence behind the scenes. From June 1377 until her death eight years later, a large number of petitions and grants recorded in the chancery rolls are recorded as having been awarded 'at the request of the king's mother'. The same applies to Richard's uncles John, Edmund and Thomas.[16] Members of Richard's household, especially his tutor Sir Simon Burley and Sir Aubrey de Vere, uncle of the young earl of Oxford, exercised considerable influence in the early years of the reign, dealing with petitions and controlling much of the flow of patronage.

In early August 1377, one of Richard's clerks took possession of an amount of silverware owned by Edward III and kept by him in the chapel of St Stephen in Westminster Palace, which now rightfully belonged to Richard and was to be used in his household. It included fifty-four candlesticks, thirty-eight silver pots, four dozen dishes and seven basins of white silver, 194 other dishes, and thirty-five silver spoons.[17] The young king inherited many splendid items from his grandfather, including five sceptres, three of which were topped with a bird and two with a cross; a spice-plate of jasper; a great *nef* or dish for alms fashioned in the shape of a ship; cups made of ostrich egg or coconut; and stands for drinking vessels, some shaped like dragons and one like a butterfly. Religious items and holy relics were also among the possessions inherited by Richard II, such as a small gold tabernacle said to contain a piece of the tunic Christ wore at the Crucifixion, and a spectacular crucifix with Christ's hands, feet and crown set with diamonds, sapphires, rubies and large pearls.[18]

Richard's first parliament as king was held in the Painted Chamber of Westminster Palace, beginning on Tuesday 13 October 1377 and lasting for six weeks. Simon Sudbury, archbishop of Canterbury, opened proceedings by announcing in Latin and then in French 'Your king comes to you' (*Vostre roy vient a toy*). He went on to state that Richard 'comes before you as your rightful liege lord, and your good and whole-hearted friend ... our said lord the king comes to visit and comfort you in the great troubles, losses and adversities which you have recently suffered', referring to the deaths of Richard's father and grandfather and the French invasion of English territories. Sudbury also remarked, rather pointedly, that God had granted them Richard as their liege lord 'not by election nor by any other such a way, but solely by rightful succession to an inheritance.'[19] There could be no doubt in anyone's mind as to Richard's right to be king, even as a ten-year-old whose father had not been king and who had three adult uncles, who were the sons of a king, still living.

John of Gaunt knelt before his nephew and asked for Richard's attention to be drawn to some terrible slurs aimed at himself, which amounted to accusations of treason, and even his enemies defended him.[20] Rumours had been rife for a while that Gaunt wished to take the throne himself, and also, strangely, that he was a changeling and not the son of Edward III and Philippa of Hainault, but that as a baby he had been accidentally smothered in his cradle and secretly replaced with a peasant boy, and was in fact the son of a Flemish butcher. The dowager princess of Wales, Richard's mother Joan of Kent, managed to achieve reconciliation between her brother-in-law Gaunt and the citizens of London, on the surface at least. In the early years of Richard's reign, almost 22,000 pearls worth almost £500 were seized from Alice Perrers, formerly Edward III's mistress, and given to Joan.[21]

As well as John of Gaunt and his younger brothers Edmund of Langley and Thomas of Woodstock, and their nephew-in-law Edmund Mortimer, earl of March, other important English noblemen in 1377 included Richard Fitzalan, earl of Arundel and Surrey, who was in his early thirties and extremely wealthy, having inherited one earldom from his father and another from his maternal uncle; Thomas Beauchamp, earl of Warwick; William Ufford, earl of Suffolk; Henry Percy, the new earl of Northumberland; and Hugh Stafford, earl of Stafford – these men were all born in the late 1330s or early 1340s. There was also Robert de Vere, born in 1362 and heir to the ancient earldom of Oxford (it had belonged to the de Vere family since 1141, though the Oxfords were probably the least wealthy and influential of all the English earls). Robert's uncle Aubrey de Vere, who much later succeeded him as earl of Oxford, was another important man early in Richard II's reign. Richard did not only allow noblemen to exercise influence, however. In the early 1380s he appointed Michael de la Pole, son of a wool merchant of Hull, as chancellor of England, and later raised him to the peerage when he gave him the earldom of Suffolk after the death of the childless William Ufford. Sir Simon Burley was another man whom Richard trusted absolutely; he was hugely fond of him and often sent him on vital diplomatic missions abroad. Finally, there was a younger generation of noblemen at court in the late 1370s and early 1380s. Robert de Vere became the king's dearest friend. The Mowbray brothers John and Thomas, descendants of Edward I, enjoyed Richard's friendship, as did Ralph Stafford, eldest son and heir of the earl of Stafford and, as another descendant of Edward I, also a kinsman of the king. Richard II's biographer Nigel Saul states that Ralph Stafford was the king's greatest friend in the first few years of his reign, and first in his affections.[22]

There was also Richard's first cousin Henry of Lancaster, son and heir of his uncle John of Gaunt. The two boys were almost exactly the same age, born just three months apart in 1367, and most likely in 1377 when he was knighted Henry began to be known as earl of Derby, one of his father's many titles.[23] Richard and his cousin were very different in character and outlook, however: Henry took part in his first joust in January 1382 when he was still three months away from his fifteenth birthday, while Richard, always conscious of his royal dignity, may never have taken part in one.[24] There are few if any documents that would illuminate the nature of the two boys' relationship so early in Richard's reign, but given later events there is little reason to suppose that they ever felt much affection or liking for one another. There may have been some envy on both sides: on Henry's part because, although he was as much a grandson of Edward III as Richard was, he was the son of the third son, not the eldest son; on Richard's because Henry much more closely personified the fourteenth-century ideal of the 'brave knight' than he ever would, and because Henry's maternal family background was considerably less embarrassing than Richard's was, with a mother who had once been married to two men at once and a grandfather executed for treason. In December 1377, Richard visited St Albans Abbey in Hertfordshire with Henry of Lancaster and Robert de Vere, and spent the first Christmas of his reign at the royal palace of Sheen where his grandfather had died in June. The end of 1377 was spent at the royal castle of Windsor, where Edward III had been born in 1312.[25]

Meanwhile, a truce negotiated between England and France in Bruges in 1375 had officially ended on 24 June 1377, the feast of the Nativity of St John the Baptist – one of Richard II's favourite saints – and just three days after Edward III's death. The French, aided by their ally Castile, immediately attacked much of the south coast of England: Rye was burned on 29 June, and the French and Castilian forces attacked other towns and occupied the Isle of Wight in August and September. They extracted a ransom of 1,000 marks from the population of the Isle of Wight. The bishop, mayor and bailiffs of

Exeter in the south-west were ordered on 27 June, on the grounds that the French were shortly planning to attack the town, to repair the walls and ditches protecting the town and were given powers to compel the residents of Exeter to help and to arrest and imprison those who refused.[26] A fleet under the command of Richard's youngest uncle, Thomas of Woodstock, was sent to disperse a large French-Castilian fleet anchored off Sluys in Flanders, and another royal uncle, Edmund of Langley, was appointed to defend the south coast against the invaders, 'the king understanding that they have landed in great force'.[27] By the end of 1377, however, the worst of the attack was over, and on 16 January 1378 three men including the Frenchman Guichard d'Angle were appointed to make a truce with France. On the same day they were also ordered to discuss a marriage between Richard and a daughter of Charles V as a way of cementing the truce.[28] Castilian ships were being used to harry the English coastline and English ships; the king of Castile, Enrique of Trastámara, was aiding his ally France. Also in 1377, Castile suddenly attacked its northern neighbour the small kingdom of Navarre, ruled by Carlos II 'the Bad'.[29]

Another French invasion of England was expected on 14 July 1378, and that December the town of Melcombe in Dorset was said to have been 'burnt by the king's enemies'.[30] In February 1378 orders were sent to the mayor and bailiffs of Winchester and Salisbury, 'notwithstanding the opposition of some evil-minded persons', to repair their walls, turrets, gates and dykes, which were 'so dilapidated and out of repair as to imperil the city if the French landed, as they recently did'.[31] To secure the northern border and to ensure that their neighbour did not join France in attacking England in a two-pronged attack, Richard's councillors reached out to Scotland, and on 22 October 1378 men were appointed to treat for peace with King Robert II of the house of Stewart. Robert gave England 4,000 marks in June 1378 in part payment of the ransom of his predecessor, David Bruce, who had been captured in battle against his brother-in-law Edward III in 1346 and spent years in captivity in England.[32] Even so, an invasion of the north of England was feared in February 1379 and numerous men in Cumberland, Northumberland, Westmorland and Yorkshire were appointed to 'resist hostile invasion and the destruction of the English tongue', though why anyone thought that a Scottish invasion of England might result in the English language being destroyed was not explained.[33]

A royal Spanish visitor arrived in England and northern France in the summer of 1378: Carloto de Beaumont, illegitimate nephew of King Carlos II 'the Bad' of Navarre. Carloto was about sixteen and was given permission to 'arrest traitors' in the town of Cherbourg in Normandy, which belonged to King Carlos himself. A safe conduct was issued for Carlos to come to England on 31 May 1378 and the chronicler Jean Froissart says that the king of Navarre did indeed visit England that June and was welcomed by Richard at Windsor, though it is not entirely clear if he did or not, as no other evidence exists for his visit. Carlos II, now in his mid-forties, had most probably been in Bordeaux when Richard was born there at the beginning of 1367 and attended his baptism, and the two kings were also related via common descent from Philip IV of France.[34] If he did visit England in 1378, it would have been the first time he and Richard had met since Richard was an infant in Bordeaux. On 12 June 1278 the English Exchequer paid 1,000 marks for provisions and equipment to defend and fortify Cherbourg, and a further £300 for eighty men acting as Carloto de Beaumont's bodyguards.[35] This was because King Carlos had agreed to lease Cherbourg to Richard for three years, and in return Richard promised to send 500 archers and 500 men-at-arms to aid Carlos in his war against Enrique of Trastámara, king of Castile since his murder of his half-brother King Pedro nine years before.

On 1 August 1378, Richard ordered Sir John Neville, his lieutenant in Gascony, to send the promised 1,000 men, commenting that Enrique 'occupies the kingdom of Spain [i.e. Castile]'.[36] The force, in the end, did not set out until late October and numbered far fewer men than it should have. Carlos II's war against his more powerful neighbour Enrique of Trastámara went badly, and in March 1379 Carlos was forced to promise that no child of his would marry an English prince.[37] On 20 June 1381 Richard deferred the return of Cherbourg to Carlos, while promising that he would fulfil all his obligations to him.[38] Enrique of Trastámara, meanwhile, had died on 29 May 1379 and was succeeded as king by his twenty-year-old son Juan I, although in England John of Gaunt and his wife Constanza, Juan's cousin, were still formally recognised and always addressed as king and queen of Castile.[39] Richard II, for his part, always appended 'king of France' to his official titles, 'king of England and France, lord of Ireland, duke of Aquitaine'.

King Fernando of Portugal saw an opportunity in the late 1370s and allied with England to make war on Castile: Richard II's uncle

Edmund of Langley, earl of Cambridge, was dispatched to Portugal in May 1381 to aid the kingdom against the frequent raids by the kingdom of Castile, and to try to conquer Castile for John of Gaunt and Constanza. It was arranged that Edmund's son Edward of York would marry King Fernando's daughter Beatriz, his only surviving legitimate child. An envoy was sent from England to King Fernando and Queen Leonora on 23 May 1380, and on 5 July 1380 the Portuguese royal couple renewed the 1373 treaty with Edward III in a document written in Spanish and Latin.[40] The marriage to Beatriz would have eventually made Edward of York joint ruler of Portugal, but the union of the two children – they were both born in about 1373/4 – ended up being annulled in 1382.

In the end, the earl of Cambridge's campaign in Portugal ended ignominiously, the English troops went out of control and caused absolute mayhem in Portugal which is remembered in that country to this day, and King Fernando went behind Cambridge's back and made peace with Castile.[41] John of Gaunt made preparations to leave England in the spring of 1378 and to sail from Southampton.[42] These preparations went on for months, though Gaunt's only legitimate son and heir, Henry, likely remained with his cousin the king. Throughout the 1370s and throughout Gaunt's marriage to Constanza of Castile, his mistress Katherine Swynford regularly gave birth to Henry of Lancaster's half-siblings the Beauforts, named after one of Gaunt's castles in France which he had inherited from his first wife Blanche of Lancaster and her father Duke Henry. The young Henry of Lancaster received robes, cloaks and shoes for the hunting and hawking seasons from Richard in the early years of the reign, such as a grey fur-trimmed cloak, three coats of blue silk brocade and stockings, slippers, boots and spurs.[43]

In 1377 Richard's council decided to try to make an alliance with Aragon, the second-largest Spanish kingdom and then ruled by King Pedro IV, as it had been since 1336. Pedro was the man who had imprisoned his nephew Jaime IV of Majorca, Richard's late godfather, in an iron cage for fourteen years. Still, the demands of realpolitik required amicable relations with Aragon, neighbour of the powerful kingdom of Castile which was now an ally of France and enemy of England. Richard, or rather his council, dealt with the ongoing imprisonment of the Aragonese count of Denia on 4 August 1377 and again on 28 October. He was Alfonso, a great nobleman and first cousin of King Pedro IV, and had been captured by squires called

Robert Hawley and John Shakell at the battle of Nájera, fought in Castile three months after Richard's birth. Over ten years later the count was still officially a prisoner, though he had returned to Spain, leaving his son Alfonso the younger behind as a hostage, and two knights of Aragon, Berengarius de Pan and 'Peter March' (as English scribes spelt and anglicised his name), came to England in 1377 with regards to the ransom he owed.[44]

Richard's government was keen to maintain good relations with Aragon, but the two squires who had captured Alfonso were demanding a very high ransom for him, not unreasonably, and refused all requests to set it at a lower level or to release the count's son into the custody of the royal council. They were imprisoned in the Tower of London in October 1377, but a few months later dramatically escaped and sought sanctuary in Westminster Abbey. On 11 August 1378, the constable of the Tower broke sanctuary – shockingly – and entered the abbey with a group of armed men. They managed to grab John Shakell, but Robert Hawley eluded capture and hid in the choir, where the monks were celebrating mass. In the ensuing fight, Hawley was killed on the steps of the high altar. A sacristan who tried to help him also lost his life. Westminster Abbey had been desecrated, and all the people involved were excommunicated by the bishop of London William Courtenay, with the exception of Richard II, his mother Joan of Kent and his uncle John of Gaunt. It was a particularly embarrassing and unpleasant episode for all concerned.[45] Nor did this violence solve the issue. Count Alfonso's son was once again said to be under the control of the squire John Shakell in October 1380 and April and June 1381, and the legal battles of Robert Hawley's sister and heir Maud to claim a share of the count's ransom on the grounds of its 'unjust seizure' from her brother dragged on for more than thirty years until 1412.[46]

Another noble prisoner in England early in Richard II's reign was Waleran of Luxembourg, the French count of St Pol and Ligny, captured fighting against English forces in 1374. On 16 June 1379, Waleran was given permission to send his messenger Janekin Granmont to France on his business, and was released on 18 July that year for a payment of 100,000 francs or £16,666 and given permission to marry the 'lady de Courtenay'.[47] This was none other than King Richard's half-sister Maud, *née* Holland, with whom Waleran had, romantically, fallen in love while held in comfortable captivity at Windsor Castle. Maud had previously been married to Hugh Courtenay, who was the eldest grandson and heir of the long-lived Hugh Courtenay, earl of Devon, but died in 1374 before his grandfather. Waleran and Maud married in March 1380 at Windsor and the union produced one daughter, Joan, presumably named after Richard II and Maud's mother Joan of Kent, who married Duke Antoine of Brabant. Richard's cousin Henry of Lancaster attended the wedding, and gave the couple a gilded silver goblet which cost 60s and was paid for by his father John of Gaunt.[48] In exchange for being allowed to marry the king of England's half-sister, Waleran renounced his homage to the king of France and swore to keep his many castles at the English government's disposal. For this reason he was banished from the realm of France until after the death of Charles V, though as this occurred only six months after Waleran's wedding it can hardly have been a major imposition.[49] Richard II apparently showed little interest in his older half-sisters Joan and Maud, though their brothers Thomas and John were a different proposition. Thomas, the elder brother, was made marshal of England on 13 March 1380 and later that year was allowed the earldom of Kent, while the younger brother, John, was made justice of Chester.[50]

On 23 April 1378, the annual Knight of the Garter festivities took place at Windsor in the presence of the young king. Robes of scarlet cloth embroidered with blue garters were ordered for twenty-four knights, including John of Gaunt and his son Henry of Lancaster, earl of Derby, Richard's brother-in-law the duke of Brittany, and the earls of Cambridge, Warwick, Salisbury, Stafford, Suffolk, Northumberland and Huntingdon. Eight women, all of them close relatives of Richard, were made Ladies of the Garter at this time. Only two women had previously had this honour bestowed on them: Richard's grandmother Queen Philippa in 1358, and his aunt Isabella of Woodstock, countess of Bedford, in 1376. The new Ladies of the Garter in 1378 were Richard's mother Joan of Kent, dowager princess of Wales; his aunts by marriage Constanza and Isabel of Castile, duchess of Lancaster and countess of Cambridge; his cousin Philippa Coucy, Isabella of Woodstock's daughter and Robert de Vere's wife; his half-sister Maud, Lady Courtenay, future countess of St Pol; and his cousins Philippa and Elizabeth of Lancaster, daughters of John of Gaunt and his late first wife Blanche. Richard II made thirty-six Ladies of the Garter throughout his reign, well over half of all the ladies thus ennobled in the entire Middle Ages.[51] It seems that he enjoyed the company of women and to have allowed certain women considerable influence over him.

Richard marked the first anniversary of his grandfather Edward III's death on 21 June 1378 with considerable ceremony, and a service of remembrance was held at Westminster Abbey which cost almost £30. This included a payment of 13s 4d to forty 'poor persons' for carrying torches, over £14 for 'two wax lights' to be left constantly burning on the tomb, and 18s for another four wax lights, weighing 80 lbs each, to be burned during the service. And on the first anniversary of his coronation, 16 July 1378, Richard attended the wedding of Anne Wake and his second cousin Sir Philip Courtenay, son of the late earl of Devon and a great-grandson of Edward I, and gave them two silver cups and two silver-gilt ewers as a gift, at a cost of over £22. A few weeks later, Richard rather mysteriously sent his servant John of Nottingham to the area around the town of Buckingham to 'search for certain money under ground, or treasure hidden in the earth'.[52] It was also in 1378 that Richard remembered his first nurse Mundina Danos and settled an income on her, and sometime before 1381 arranged her marriage to his tailor Walter Rauf following the death of her first husband Rolland Danos after 1 March 1379.[53] On 14 September 1378 Richard gave a house in 'Alhalwenstrete the litel' or Little All Hallows Street in the London parish of the same name, which had once belonged to his grandfather's mistress Alice Perrers, to his Aquitanian damsel Reymunda de Bourk or Berce of Bourg-Charente 90 miles from Bordeaux. This was on account of 'her service about the king's body after his birth'.[54] This year the king also remembered his grandmother Queen Philippa's damsel Philippa Chaucer, who was married to the poet Geoffrey Chaucer and who was the sister of his uncle John of Gaunt's mistress Katherine Swynford, and on 26 March 1378 gave her an income of 10 marks a year from the Exchequer.[55]

Parliament was held in Gloucester between 22 October and 14 November 1378, most unusually; this was the first time parliament had taken place outside London and Westminster for forty years. Richard II stayed partly at St Peter's Abbey in Gloucester, now Gloucester Cathedral and the burial place of his great-grandfather Edward II, and partly at Tewkesbury Abbey 10 miles away, where Edward II's last great 'favourite', Hugh Despenser the Younger, lord of Glamorgan, and many of his family and his wife's family the de Clares were buried.[56] Despenser's grandson Edward, Lord Despenser, had also been buried at Tewkesbury Abbey in 1375. Edward's son and heir Thomas, born in 1373, married Richard's first cousin Constance of

York in or before November 1379 when they were both still children (Thomas was only six at this time and Constance even younger). The abbey in Gloucester was so full of people attending parliament in late 1378 that one monk remarked that the place resembled a commercial venue rather than a religious one, and that the grass of the cloister was so trampled by wrestlers and ball-players entertaining the crowds that by the end no grass was left.[57]

In 1379, Richard lost his paternal aunt Isabella of Woodstock, countess of Bedford. Born in 1332 and named after her paternal grandmother Isabella of France, she was the eldest daughter of Edward III and Queen Philippa and the only one who lived past her teens. In 1365, at the advanced (by the royal standards of the time) age of thirty-three, Isabella married the French lord Enguerrand de Coucy, in England as a hostage and a few years younger than she. Edward III paid the very large sum of £100 to the minstrels who entertained the guests at their wedding.[58] The couple had two children, Richard II's first cousins Marie, countess of Bar and Soissons, and Philippa, who married Richard's great friend Robert de Vere, earl of Oxford, in 1376 when he was fifteen and she about nine.

On 8 September and again on 15 October 1379, the lord marshal of England, Sir John Arundel, brother of the earl of Arundel and the countesses of Hereford and Kent, was ordered to go to Brittany with his men.[59] According to the *Anonimalle* chronicle, this was in order to aid the duke of Brittany, Richard II's brother-in-law John IV, against his internal enemies. The *Anonimalle* chronicle, Jean Froissart and Thomas Walsingham all give a curious and highly unpleasant story about Arundel: that on their way to the coast, he and his men robbed poor people and raped numerous women, and therefore were 'greatly cursed' and excommunicated. On 6 December 1379, the feast of St Nicholas, they disembarked from the coast of southern England, when 'there arose a tempest so horrible and hideous that it was phenomenal'; it lasted nine days and destroyed seventeen ships of John Arundel's fleet. The survivors were driven towards the coast of Ireland and tried to land there, but 'because God did not wish to forgive them their wickedness ... the devil was seen in that same ship pulling a monstrous face to make the ship founder'. And so Sir John Arundel and all his men drowned.[60]

To what extent the story of Arundel's permitting rape and theft is unclear, but he certainly did drown off the coast of Ireland. Thomas

Walsingham adds the detail that Arundel and his men looted a convent and set off to sea with women, nuns, they had captured, and goods they had ransacked. When the storm came, Walsingham says that the unfortunate nuns, around sixty of them, were cast overboard in order to lighten the load on Arundel's boats. It was a particularly revolting episode which cast something of a shadow over the early years of Richard II's reign. John Arundel's youngest brother Thomas Arundel had already been made bishop of Ely near Cambridge in 1372 when he was only about twenty, and would later be promoted to archbishop of York and then archbishop of Canterbury, as well as being chancellor of England. Thomas Arundel and Richard II came to dislike each other intensely: Arundel called Richard a 'false' man, while Richard for his part stated that Arundel was 'untrustworthy and vengeful' and exiled him from England.[61]

Generally, the late 1370s, the first few years of the boy king's reign, were reasonably quiet both in England and in Europe, the French and Castilian raids on the south coast of England notwithstanding. This was soon to change, with an almighty schism in the Church and a great rebellion which would break out in the south of England.

5

'For Jesu Christ in Glorious Christian Field': The Great Schism, 1378–1380

Since 1305 the popes had resided in Avignon in southern France, not in Rome, though the Avignon papacy ended in 1377 when Gregory XI finally returned to Rome. Gregory died on 27 March 1378, and on 8 April the cardinals, confronted with a Roman mob demanding that an Italian be chosen and that the new pope should remain in Rome, elected Bartolomeo Prignano, archbishop of Bari, as Pope Urban VI. Some months later a group of cardinals met again in a town between Rome and Naples, and, offended by Urban's behaviour and declaring that their initial election had been invalid because of the pressure put on them by the Roman crowd, elected instead their fellow cardinal Robert of Geneva. Robert took the name Clement VII on 20 September 1378 and returned to Avignon. Urban VI refused to resign, and thereafter two popes existed in strict opposition to each other, one in Rome and the other in Avignon, each convinced that the other was the antipope and even the Antichrist. In later centuries, the Avignon popes of 1378 to 1417 – a period known as the Great Schism – officially began to be considered antipopes by the Catholic Church.

The next pontiff to take the name Clement, Guilio de' Medici in 1523, was also, confusingly, known as Clement VII, the existence of the fourteenth-century Avignon pope Clement VII being ignored. The pope or antipope Clement VII or Robert of Geneva thundered in 1378 that the cardinals 'were, by the violence of the city [Rome] and the terrible uproar of the people, compelled to intrude into the holy apostolic see a certain Bartholomew [Prignano] ... who presumes to call himself pope', but Richard II and the people of England took no notice and adhered to the Roman Urban VI.[1] An Aquitanian clerk living in England was imprisoned in the Tower of London for 'adherence to Robert of Geneva, the antipope', and in May 1383 Richard's kinsman Henry Despenser, bishop of Norwich, set out on crusade against Robert/Clement with more than £6,000 from Richard to pay for 2,500 men-at-arms and 2,500 archers.[2] Francis, prior of Montacute, was accused in Court Christian of being a 'schismatic, heretic and adherent of Robert of Geneva, the antipope', though was pardoned in July 1383 when he stated that he was in fact a follower of Pope Urban.[3]

Between February 1385 and February 1386, Richard II sent letters on behalf of Urban VI to the kings Carlos II of Navarre, Pedro IV of Aragon and James I of Cyprus, calling Urban 'our very holy father' and the 'true vicar of Jesus Christ', and referring to Clement VII as 'the antipope, this Genevan' who had been elected, Richard said, to destroy the unity of Holy Church and 'against the wishes of all good Christians'.[4] The Great Schism of 1378 to 1417 divided Europe along pre-existing political lines: England, Portugal, the rulers of some Italian states and a few others supported Urban VI, the Rome pope; France and its allies, including the Spanish kingdom of Castile, supported Clement VII. Rather curiously, the unprecedented situation of two pontiffs was to bring Richard II a wife.

The proposed marriages in 1377/8 with daughters of the French, Navarrese and Scottish royal families had failed, but a wife still needed to be found for Richard. His advisors strongly considered the possibility of arranging a match with the wealthy Visconti family, lords of Milan and Pavia in northern Italy. Richard's uncle Lionel of Antwerp had in 1368 been briefly married to Violante Visconti, daughter of Galeazzo – or 'Galiache' as an English scribe rendered it – who died in 1378 and was succeeded as lord of Milan by his brother Bernabo (who was himself overthrown in a surprise attack in 1385, imprisoned and killed by his nephew, Galeazzo's son and Lionel of Antwerp's brother-in-law Gian Galeazzo Visconti). In the late 1370s Bernabo Visconti proposed Caterina, one of his almost forty legitimate and illegitimate children, as Richard's bride, and promised to send a large dowry to England with her. Caterina was born in about 1361 and was thus some years older than Richard. An English party was commissioned to discuss the marriage on 18 March 1379 and probably set out for Italy not long afterwards, but nothing came of it, almost certainly because events were overtaken by the Great Schism and its effects.[5]

In 1380 Caterina Visconti married instead her first cousin Gian Galeazzo Visconti, who had previously been married to Isabelle, daughter of King John II of France and Bonne of Bohemia. Gian Galeazzo became the first duke of Milan in 1395. Bernabo Visconti was hardly a father-in-law Richard would have been delighted to have: he was excessively cruel even by the standards of medieval Italy, much given to torturing and inflicting atrocities on his unfortunate subjects, and may have been insane. Another of his daughters, Lucia, was later put forward as a possible bride for Richard's cousin Henry of Lancaster and ultimately married Richard's half-nephew Edmund Holland, earl of Kent, and his eldest, Taddea, married Duke Stephan of Bavaria and was the maternal grandmother of Richard's much younger second queen Isabelle de Valois. Poet Geoffrey Chaucer, who saw the Visconti family up close in their lordships of Milan and Pavia, referred to them in his *Canterbury Tales* as the 'tyrants of Lombardy'.

The Holy Roman Emperor and ruler of a great part of Europe, Karl IV, died in late 1378 a few months after proposing his daughter Anne as Richard's bride and queen of England. Karl divided his vast territories among his sons, and was succeeded as king of Germany and Bohemia by his eldest surviving son, seventeen-year-old Václav (the name in German is Wenzel, or Wenceslas in English). The new king of Germany and Bohemia wrote to Richard II in 1379 about the Great Schism, pointing out that Christendom should unite behind the one true pope. Václav stood on the same side of the divide as England, in favour of the Roman Urban VI, and Richard's advisors thus saw a useful opportunity to detach the young king from his family's long-term ally, France. The emperor Karl IV's father John 'the Blind', king of Bohemia, had been killed at the 1346 battle of Crécy fighting for Philip VI of France against Richard's father Edward of Woodstock and grandfather Edward III; Karl IV himself had grown up at the French court as the godson of Charles IV and married Philip VI's half-sister as the first of his four wives; and his sister Jutta, who took the name Bonne after her marriage, married Philip VI's son the future John II and was the mother of Charles V. Two of Richard's envoys, Sir Simon Burley and Sir Michael de la Pole, chancellor of England, originally sent to Italy to negotiate a marriage with the Visconti rulers of Milan, were sent instead to Germany to meet Václav in the autumn of 1379.[6]

Misfortune struck when both men were taken prisoner and had to pay a ransom to gain their liberty.[7] Václav's half-sister Anna or Anne, who was some months Richard's senior, was still available for marriage (his other young half-sister Markéta, born in September 1373, was, despite her youth, already betrothed to the burgrave of Nuremberg). Matters progressed, discussions were held at John of Gaunt's Savoy Palace in London in May 1380, and on 26 December that year Richard II sent three men to negotiate a marriage with Anne of Bohemia. They were his half-brother Thomas Holland, earl of Kent, his steward Sir Hugh Segrave, who had been previously served his father and been an executor of the prince's will, and his chamberlain and former tutor Sir Simon Burley, released from his recent captivity.

In January 1381, Anne of Bohemia and her mother Elżbieta of Pomerania, the dowager empress and widow of Karl IV, appointed three men as their deputies for contracting Anne's marriage with Richard: Przemylaus, duke of Cieszyn (or Teschen in German, a region now in southern Poland close to the Czech border), Konrad Kreyger and Peter Wartenberg. The men were given safe conducts to travel to England.[8] In English Richard's queen is almost always known as Anne of Bohemia, but in German as Anna von Luxemburg: she came from the house of Luxembourg and her grandfather John 'the Blind' had become king of Bohemia by marriage to Eliška Přemyslovna, daughter of King Václav II. Her great-grandfather Henry of Luxembourg had also been Holy Roman Emperor. The negotiations between England and Germany/Bohemia were greeted with some alarm at the French court, and Charles V offered his daughter Catherine as a bride for Richard – yet another of the French king's children who was to die young – and his son the future Charles VI as a groom for Anne of Bohemia. This offer failed to disrupt the talks between Richard and Václav even though the French king offered the county of Angoulême as Catherine's dowry, and Charles V died not long afterwards.[9]

In the meantime, Richard amused himself on Monday 12 March 1380, the week before Easter, by enjoying the performance of one John Katerine of Venice, described as a dancing-master, who 'played and danced in the presence of the king' and received the generous sum of ten marks from Richard.[10] The same month, Richard paid £28 for a Bible written in Welsh (a language he was presumably unable to understand or read), the poem the *Romance of the Rose* and a book containing the romances of Gawain and Percival, the latter three in two leather cases.[11] The leading London goldsmith Nicholas Twyford delivered a statuette of St John the Baptist and St John the Evangelist to the king's chapel on 23 June 1380, the eve of the Nativity of the Baptist.[12] In July 1380 Richard heard of the death of the aged Blanche of Lancaster, Lady Wake, widow of his great-uncle Thomas Wake and the eldest and last surviving sister of Henry, duke of Lancaster (d. 1361). Blanche of Lancaster, a great-granddaughter of Henry III, was in her mid or late seventies when she died, was born in the reign of Richard's great-great-grandfather Edward I, and had married Thomas Wake as far back as 1316. And Charles V of France died in his early forties on 16 September 1380, leaving his son Charles VI, not yet twelve years old (born on 3 December 1368), to succeed him. As Richard II also did, Charles VI had three paternal uncles, his father's younger brothers, to contend with: Louis, duke of Anjou, John, duke of Berry, and Philip, duke of Burgundy. There was also his mother Queen Jeanne's brother Louis, duke of Bourbon; Charles VI was even more plagued with uncles than his English counterpart. In 1385, Charles married a German woman, Elisabeth or Isabelle of Bavaria, usually known to history as Isabeau. She was the daughter of Duke Stephan III of Bavaria and Taddea Visconti of Milan, whose younger sister Caterina had been proposed as a bride for Richard in the late 1370s. Although they were slightly younger than he, Charles VI and Queen Isabeau would become Richard II's parents-in-law in 1396 when he married his second wife.

On or a little before 1 June 1374, Richard's nineteen-year-old uncle Thomas of Woodstock had married Eleanor de Bohun, who was then probably only about eight years old or even younger. Her new brother-in-law John of Gaunt gave a goblet and a silver ewer to 'the lady of Woodstock on the day of her marriage'.[13] Eleanor was the elder daughter and co-heir of Humphrey de Bohun (d. 1373), earl of Hereford and Northampton, a great-grandson of Edward I and the younger half-brother of Roger Mortimer, second earl of March (d. 1360). It appears that Thomas of Woodstock, who was his sister-in-law's legal guardian, and his new wife Eleanor were hoping that her younger sister Mary de Bohun would take the veil as a nun and were attempting to coach her to this end, as this would leave Eleanor as sole heir to the two earldoms and wealth of their late father.

According to the chronicler Jean Froissart, sometime in 1380 or perhaps in early 1381 Thomas's brother John of Gaunt, duke of Lancaster, abducted Mary from Thomas's Essex castle of Pleshey and married her to his son Henry of Lancaster.[14] To what extent the story of the abduction is true is unclear, but at any rate Henry certainly married Mary, and Thomas of Woodstock and his wife were forced to share her inheritance with his nephew and her younger sister. Gaunt paid the king 5,000 marks for Mary's marriage.[15] Henry of Lancaster and Mary de Bohun were to have six children together, the first born in 1386 when they were both still in their teens; they included a king of England, a queen of Sweden, Denmark and Norway, and an electress palatine of the Rhine. Their wedding took place almost certainly on 5 February 1381 and definitely before the 10th, and the guests were entertained by ten minstrels sent by King Richard and four by his and Henry's uncle Edmund of Langley, earl of Cambridge.[16] Mary's mother Joan de Bohun, *née* Fitzalan, dowager countess of Hereford and sister of the earl of Arundel – still only in her early thirties or so – played an important role in her younger daughter's marriage to Henry of Lancaster, which took place at her manor of Rochford in Essex.[17]

Although it is often stated that Mary gave birth to a son in April 1382 who died young, when she was still only a child herself (she was born in or a little before 1370), this child was in fact her nephew Humphrey of Gloucester, son of her elder sister Eleanor and Thomas of Woodstock. Mary de Bohun and Henry of Lancaster's first child was the future King Henry V, born in Monmouth, Wales in September 1386.[18] Mary de Bohun was specifically said to be still living in the custody of her mother on 6 February 1382 a year after her wedding, which makes it apparent that she was then considered too young to live with her husband and for their marriage to have been consummated. Mary's mother Joan, the dowager countess of Hereford, was given an allowance of £40 a year from Richard II on this date to look after her daughter, and John of Gaunt also gave Joan 100 marks a year for Mary's maintenance.[19] If there was ever any bad feeling between Gaunt and his much younger brother Thomas over John's supposed abduction of Mary de Bohun, it had apparently dissipated by May 1383, when John attended the christening of Thomas's daughter Anne – his and Eleanor de Bohun's second child – at Pleshey in Essex and bought lavish gifts for the little girl and for her attendants.[20] Richard II's first cousin Elizabeth of Lancaster, Henry's sister and John of Gaunt's younger daughter with his first wife Blanche, had also married the previous summer: her groom was the young John Hastings, heir to the earldom of Pembroke and a descendant of Edward I (his mother Anne Manny was the younger daughter and co-heir of Edward I's granddaughter Margaret, countess of Norfolk). Elizabeth was sixteen or seventeen at the time of the wedding, while her little husband John, born in October 1372, was not yet eight. Perhaps not surprisingly, the marriage did not work out, was never consummated and some years later was annulled.

In 1381, two important members of the English nobility died. One was Richard's first cousin by marriage Edmund Mortimer, the twenty-nine-year-old earl of March and Ulster, widower of Philippa of Clarence. March died in Ireland on 27 December 1381, the feast of St John the Evangelist. His early death robbed England of an energetic and able politician, and had March lived a few more years the history of Richard II's reign might look rather different. A few months before her son's death, March's mother Philippa Mortimer, *née* Montacute, sister of William Montacute, earl of Salisbury, also passed away. Philippa had thus been the sister-in-law of Richard's mother Joan of Kent for a few years in the 1340s. The earl of March left as his heir his seven-year-old son Roger Mortimer, who was also the heir of his late mother Philippa of Clarence and of his grandfather Lionel of Antwerp, and who had a good claim to the English throne after Richard II as the senior descendant (with his younger brother Edmund and his sisters Elizabeth and Philippa after him) of Edward III's second son. Richard II became the official guardian of Roger Mortimer; the huge revenues of the important Mortimer inheritance, including the earldoms of March and Ulster and a third of the old earldom of Gloucester, would thus enrich the king's coffers until Roger came of age.

In 1388 the rights to Roger Mortimer's marriage were granted to the king's half-brother Thomas Holland, earl of Kent, and in the same year fourteen-year-old Roger married Kent's eldest daughter Alianore or Eleanor. Their first child Anne Mortimer was born in 1390 when Roger was sixteen; she would become the paternal grandmother of Edward IV and Richard III. On 28 January 1382, when he was still only seven, Roger Mortimer was appointed the king's lieutenant of Ireland, succeeding his father, but of course the appointment was purely nominal and the boy was shipped to Ireland from England on 6 August that year.[21] Also in 1382, Mortimer was addressed as 'the earl of March' despite his youth and was ordered to hold a parliament in Ireland, though generally he was not given this title.[22] As a special favour, Richard would grant Mortimer his lands in Ireland on 18 June 1393, though he was not yet of age (twenty-one), and by early 1394 he had begun to be addressed regularly as the earl of March.[23] March would not have long to enjoy his rich inheritance; he was dead at the age of twenty-four.

Before the death in late 1381 of Roger's father Edmund, earl of March, however, one of the most dramatic events in the country's history took place. In late May that year, the greatest uprising which had ever occurred in England began.

6

'In Rage Deaf as the Sea, Hasty as Fire': The Great Uprising, 1381

It began with the imposition of a poll tax, an unfair tax which fell most heavily on the poor. In fact, it had begun much earlier, with a decades-long and ruinously expensive war that left numerous men maimed and unable to work, with the deadliest outbreak of plague in European history in the late 1340s and further epidemics in the 1360s, and with Edward III and his government passing the Statute of Labourers in 1351 which forbade workers from benefiting from the sudden mass shortages of labour and which pegged wages at pre-plague levels. By the 1370s England boiled with discontent, and when the parliament of November 1380 decided to tax everyone over the age of fourteen at a flat rate, a ludicrous and unjust idea, they inadvertently lit the fuse to a powder keg.

Throughout the early months of 1381, tax collectors had extraordinary difficulties in gathering the due payments – in London they declined even to try to collect the tax for fear of inciting mass unrest. Hundreds of thousands of people contrived to disappear from a register which had been taken in 1377 when it was taken again. In Essex on 30 May, a commissioner newly appointed to oversee the work of the tax collectors was set upon and assaulted, and told by villagers that they would not pay more than they already had.[1] Resentment and anger raged throughout the country, and the two main targets of hostility were Simon Sudbury, archbishop of Canterbury and chancellor of England since January 1380, and Sir Robert Hales, the new (since 1 February 1381) treasurer of England and the prior of the wealthy Knights Hospitaller, an international order of crusading monks. The third target of hatred and rage was Richard II's uncle John of Gaunt, duke of Lancaster, the wealthiest man in the country and deemed responsible, whether fairly or not, for the government's military failings and for the unfair imposition of the poll tax.

This widespread though as yet unfocused rage, and those who felt it, needed a leader, and they found one in Walter 'Wat' Tyler, who probably lived in Maidstone in Kent and originally came from Colchester in Essex. It was he who co-ordinated bands of protestors from these two areas, the main centres of disaffection and rebellion.[2] London and the counties around it was then, and still is, the wealthiest and most economically active region of the country. One might expect inhabitants of the distant and far poorer north of England to rebel; that the focus of rebellion was the Home Counties came as a great shock to those in power. Wat Tyler's name has become synonymous with the great uprising of 1381, and its other main star was the preacher John Ball, who supposedly gave a sermon at Blackheath in front of 200,000 people (says Thomas Walsingham) which included the famous line 'When Adam delved and Eve span, who was then the gentleman?'[3] What was meant by this was that God had created all people equal, and had not divided His creation into serfs and lords. The rebels of 1381 promoted an agenda astonishingly radical for the fourteenth century: the abolition of serfdom and the recognition of a man's right to work for whom he wished, at the wages he wished. Their slogan was 'King Richard and the True Commons'. What they had in mind was a benign monarchy, with the nobility to be abolished, and they did not seek the downfall of Richard II himself (though the *Historia Vitae et Regni Ricardi Secundi* claimed they proposed that 'all of noble blood of either sex be destroyed and killed, and finally the king himself').[4]

Very soon after the initial attack in Essex on 30 May, people all over Essex and Kent began committing acts of disobedience and protest, and destroyed property belonging to tax collectors, office holders and local gentry.[5] They also burned rolls of court and other old legal documents.[6] Within an astonishingly short space of time, a huge group of people had gathered and began to march together towards London. The Essex rebels gathered at Mile End, and others at Blackheath, on or about 9 June, which was Trinity Sunday and thus the fifth anniversary of the death of the king's father.[7] Richard II was then at Windsor on the other side of the city, and as early as Tuesday 11 June 1381 his advisers thought it wisest to seek refuge in the strong fortification of the Tower of London. With the young king in the Tower was his cousin Henry of Lancaster, also only fourteen and the son and heir of the detested John of Gaunt, whose head the rebels wanted on a spike. The duke of Lancaster himself, fortuitously, was far away in the north and thus well beyond the rebels' reach; on hearing of the rebellion, Gaunt sought temporary refuge in Scotland. Richard II's other companions in the Tower included his mother's former husband William Montacute, earl of Salisbury; his half-brothers Thomas and John Holland, the other sons of Joan of Kent; Thomas Beauchamp, earl of Warwick; Robert de Vere, earl of Oxford; Sir Thomas Percy, brother of the earl of Northumberland and future earl of Worcester; and William Walworth, the mayor of London. Some chroniclers include Richard's youngest uncle Thomas of Woodstock, earl of Buckingham. This does not seem terribly likely, as he was a brother of John of Gaunt and thus would also have been a target of the rebels' anger, though Thomas's whereabouts during this period are not clear.[8]

The earl of Salisbury was in his fifties, the earl of Warwick in his forties and Thomas Percy also close to forty, and therefore the young king had experienced men around him. Also present were the chancellor and treasurer Simon Sudbury and Robert Hales, hated targets of the rebels' wrath. The king's mother Joan of Kent, according to chroniclers Froissart and Walsingham, was returning from a pilgrimage to the shrine of Thomas Becket at Canterbury on her way to her son in the Tower when she encountered the rebels heading for London. They treated her disrespectfully, joking around with her and even asking her to kiss them. The *Chronicon Angliae* also says that the mob left Joan unharmed but that the ringleaders invited her to kiss them. Unused to such behaviour, Joan fainted. Walsingham, always judgemental, refers to such men as having 'rough, filthy hands', and as well as calling the rebels 'riff-raff' sneers at them as 'bare-legged rascals' and 'wastrels' who were guilty of 'wickedness'. The northern Kirkstall chronicle also says that the rebels 'were like madmen in the greatest wickedness', the Canterbury chronicler William Thorne calls them 'a turbulent crowd of wicked men', and, continuing the popular theme, the *Vitae et Regni* calls their leaders the 'wickedest criminals'.[9]

Richard and his council sent an envoy to the leaders of the crowd of rebels, which had swollen into the thousands and must have taken on the alarming appearance of an army, asking what they were doing and what they wished for. A meeting between the king and the rebel leaders was arranged for 7 a.m. on Thursday 13 June at Blackheath, which was then just outside the boundaries of the city. When those waiting saw Richard coming, accompanied by the earls of Salisbury, Warwick and Oxford, they rushed towards him, and Simon Sudbury and Robert Hales anxiously advised him to retreat to safety in the Tower. Whether he really wanted to or not, Richard did so, to a chorus of 'Treason! Treason!' Clearly, travelling towards a group of discontented and armed rebels was deemed dangerous for the king's person, so when another attempt was made to meet the rebel leaders, Richard sailed across the Thames by barge. Between Rotherhithe and Greenwich, still on the water, he heard what they had to say. Two main demands were made: Richard must surrender Simon Sudbury, Robert Hales, John of Gaunt and other alleged traitors to be beheaded; and abolish serfdom and agree to a standard rent for land at 4*d* per acre.[10]

During the night of 12 June, mayor William Walworth and the aldermen had tried to close the gates of London, but were forcibly prevented from doing so by some of the inhabitants, so that the 'riff-raff', as Walsingham calls them, had free entrance to the city all night. In the afternoon of the 13th, following the failed negotiations with the king and his councillors, the number of rebels entering the capital increased dramatically.[11] Two aldermen were charged in November 1382 with admitting the Kent rebels over London Bridge, and a third with opening Aldgate to the men from Essex.[12] Men known to be city officials and royal officials, and their property, were attacked in London. Among numerous other examples, a man called Paul Salesbury was pardoned on 22 July 1381 for acts committed on 14 June. One of these acts was that he and others forced an alderman of London called William Baret, his wife and servants out of their home, and Salesbury 'made them stand in the street outside the gate, making the said wife kneel a long time before him, and compelling them to thank him for their long inhabiting of the house and for their lives'. Salesbury and his associates also broke into a house belonging to one Hugh Fastolf near the Tower in a street called Thamistrete, 'wasted six casks of ale and a pipe of wine' and stole a sword and other items.[13] John Buntyng, called 'one of the chiefs of the insurgents' and later beheaded for his crimes, was convicted of blackmailing a chancery clerk named John Cranewys to the tune of 40*s* by threatening to burn down his London house with him inside it if he did not pay.[14]

The rebels aimed particular hate and venom at Flemish and other foreign merchants working in London, and at least 150 of these unfortunate people were killed and their goods stolen. No fewer than thirty-five Flemish men were dragged out of the church of St Martin in Vintry where they had, in vain, sought sanctuary, and were beheaded one after the other on a single block of wood. A shibboleth was demanded: men thought to be foreign were made to say the words 'bread and cheese', and if they could not pronounce it correctly were murdered. Prisons were broken open and the prisoners set free.[15] The uprising also gave cover to those who wished to commit simple blackmail and looting, and a year later it was described in the chancery rolls as 'the late devilish insurrection'.[16]

Thursday 13 June was the feast of Corpus Christi. Walsingham says that as the day grew warmer, the rebels took to drinking wine looted from the wine cellars of the wealthy in expensive goblets. As they grew more and more drunk, or not so much drunk as mad, he says, they began to discuss their next move, which was aimed at the duke of Lancaster. Unable to lay hands on John of Gaunt in person – if he had been anywhere near London it is virtually certain that Gaunt's head would have ended up being paraded around on a spike – the rebels took out their rage on his magnificent London palace of the Savoy, located on the Strand next to the Thames. It had been built in the thirteenth century by Peter of Savoy, uncle of Henry III's queen Eleanor of Provence, and was named after him; a famous hotel named the Savoy now stands on the site.

The palace was left a smoking ruin. The rebels poured through it, smashing gold and silver vessels into pieces with their axes or throwing them into the river or the sewers, tearing or trampling Gaunt's luxurious clothes, and grinding precious stones and jewels into dust in mortars. One of Gaunt's tunics was set up as a dummy on a spear and used for target practice by archers, and when that amusement had palled it was cut to pieces. Finally, they set fire to the palace all round and deliberately destroyed the building.[17] The Kirkstall chronicle also writes that the Savoy was razed to the ground and that all the duke of Lancaster's possessions inside, including money, jewels, bed hangings and tapestries, were either consumed by fire or thrown into the waters of the Thames and lost, and the *Vita* says the rebels 'found an almost infinite variety of objects' within the palace and after looting it left hardly one stone on top of another. The *Anonimalle* adds the detail that as well as drinking

Gaunt's wine, the rebels gorged themselves on his food.[18] One of the men named as responsible for burning the Savoy was Stephen Hulle, a draper from London, who was held in captivity in the prison of the king's household and on 19 August 1381 was sent to the sheriff of Surrey.[19]

In 1383 John of Gaunt brought a case in the court of common pleas against the men he and his advisers believed had sacked his residence, and claimed that they had stolen and destroyed goods worth £10,000. The case was dropped, but a very long list of men's names – many dozens – was given, often including their professions; they were tailors, mercers, skinners, fullers, tanners, drapers, shipmen, taverners, cordwainers, brewers, carpenters, masons and many others.[20] Also destroyed or badly damaged and plundered on 13 and 14 June 1381 were the archbishop of Canterbury's palace at Lambeth; Clerkenwell Priory, where the rebels drank much of the wine they found and poured away the rest, and which burned for seven days; and Temple Bar, where statutes, books and muniments were burnt and other goods stolen.[21] Richard II, trapped in the Tower, could do little but look on in horror: the *Anonimalle* gives a vivid account of the fourteen-year-old king climbing various turrets and, 'pensive and sad', looking out over the fires spreading through his capital in every direction.[22]

Finally, 'Friday dawned, a day of anger, of distress and trouble, a day of calamity and sorrow.'[23] On this day, 14 June, Richard II agreed to ride out of Tower and meet the rebel leaders again, this time at Mile End. Ultimately there was little else he and his advisers could do at this point but try to disperse the rebels peacefully and to listen to their demands. Chronicler Henry Knighton says that the knights who should have accompanied him stayed in the Tower, and the *Anonimalle* that Richard's mother and half-brothers, and some magnates, went with him.[24] It was still a huge risk; although the rebels professed loyalty to their king, it would only have taken one rogue archer to kill Richard from a distance, or for a small group of men to set an ambush as the king and his supporters made their way through the narrow streets of London. One man did in fact grab the bridle of the former mayor Nicholas Brembre and halt him in his tracks as Richard and his party rode along Aldgate, which shows that it would have been equally easy for anyone to do the same to the king. Probably at this point, Richard's mother Joan of Kent and others turned back to the Tower.[25]

In the end, the rebels' attitude towards Richard was respectful, and he responded as diplomatically as he could to the demands, stated again, for the heads of Sudbury, Hales, Gaunt and others, and for a standard rent of 4*d* per acre of land. The *Vita* says that the young king, who after all was still only in his early teens and who had been carefully protected all his young life, 'appeared like a lamb among wolves; he even greatly feared for his life, and addressed those surrounding him in an ingratiating manner'.[26] It must have been a terrifying experience. Richard, astonishingly, granted all the rebels' requests, 'provided that you follow my banners and go back to your own places in the way I told you'. This was an incredibly important moment in the history of the uprising and of England itself.[27] It has often been assumed that Richard was being insincere and cynical or was even outright lying, and had no intention of granting the rebels' radical requests, and only pretended to be willing to do so in order to extricate himself from a very dangerous situation. Indeed the *Vita* says that the leaders of the Mile End crowd would not let the king leave until he had granted what they demanded, even though it was 'to the very great prejudice of the crown and realm of England'. Yet historian Juliet Barker provides evidence that Richard was sincere and acting in good faith, and seems genuinely to have sympathised with the rebels' grievances and to have desired the abolition of villeinage or serfdom. Later, however, the young king was prevented from doing what he wished and intended to do. He had acted alone and spontaneously at Mile End, and his councillors, once the immediate danger was over and things had returned more or less to normal, had to backtrack.[28]

The king and his companions leaving the Tower was the cue for an invasion of the fortress: apparently the guards simply opened the gates and let the mob in. Sudbury and Hales, the rebels' main targets, were discovered hiding in the chapel of St John in the White Tower, the oldest part of the Tower of London. The two men were beaten, dragged out of the fortress, and beheaded on Tower Hill. Walsingham says that it took eight strokes of the axe to remove the unfortunate Sudbury's head (and also that the rebels now controlled that part of the city and had even seized goods belonging to Richard II being taken into the Tower). The same chronicler says that Sudbury faced death with calm equanimity, saying to those who had come to drag him out of the Tower, 'It is good that you have come, my sons. Here I am, the archbishop you are looking for, though no traitor or plunderer.' Once on Tower Hill, he asked, 'My dearest sons, what is it that you are proposing to do? What sin have I committed against you that you wish to kill me?'[29]

Sudbury's head was finally removed from his shoulders on the eighth attempt, not before he had (surely instinctively) put up a hand to try to defend himself and lost some fingers as well, and it was set on a spike with a red hat nailed to it to indicate that he was a bishop. It was carried through the city to shouts of 'Here is the predator's head', then displayed on London Bridge.[30] Astonishingly, Simon Sudbury's mummified skull still exists in the church in his hometown of Sudbury in Suffolk, and in 2011 his face was revealed by a forensic artist. A chaplain of Bridgewater in Somerset called Nicholas Frampton was pardoned in February 1382 'for all treasons and felonies committed by him in the late insurrection between 1 May and All Saints, provided that he did not kill Simon, late archbishop, Robert Hales, or John Cavendish', and the actual killers of Sudbury, Hales and others are not known for certain, though one of them may have been a man called John Starling.[31] Walsingham upgraded those responsible for the murder of the archbishop from mere wastrels and bare-legged rascals to 'demoniacal wastrels'. Always a man able to turn a phrase, he added that their yelling in triumph on discovering Archbishop Sudbury and Robert Hales inside the Tower was beyond any human imagining and like the ghastly shrieks of the inhabitants of hell, or 'the devilish cries of peacocks'. He also describes their 'limbs of Satan' as they laid hands on Sudbury.[32]

Also left behind in the Tower when Richard rode off to Mile End was his cousin Henry of Lancaster. The boy, who like Richard was fourteen, much later (after he became king of England) pardoned a man of Southwark named John Ferrour who had taken part in a rebellion against him, because in June 1381 Ferrour saved his life in a 'wonderful and kind manner'.[33] The whole thing must have been a terrifying experience for the teenager: to see rebels swarming into the Tower which he and the others must have thought entirely safe and impregnable, to see men he knew well being dragged out to their deaths, and to know that he was personally in great danger because he was his father John of Gaunt's son and heir, and his father was detested. We do not know how John Ferrour saved Henry's life, perhaps by concealing him somewhere or by fighting off rebels who tried to seize hold of him, but the fourteen-year-old would never forget it. It is entirely probable that without Ferrour's act, Henry of Lancaster would also have been dragged out and executed; his youth is not likely to have spared him given that fourteen-year-olds were held liable for paying the poll tax, and given the almost universal loathing of his absent father.

As Henry and his son and grandson were all to reign as kings of England, John Ferrour thus inadvertently had a major impact on English history. Even hundreds of miles away in Yorkshire, the constable of John of Gaunt's castle at Pontefract was too afraid to allow his wife the duchess of Lancaster, Henry's stepmother Constanza of Castile, to enter, and she and her household were forced to travel on to Knaresborough Castle to seek refuge. Constanza waited there 'until better news could reach her'.[34] The rebellion had in fact spread to Yorkshire: in and around Scarborough, 50 miles from Knaresborough, houses were robbed and burned down, and other crimes committed, by a group of rebels who wore a kind of uniform of white hoods in order to identify each other. 'Certain evildoers' were also said to have 'risen in insurrection' in the town of Beverley, 50 miles from Knaresborough.[35]

Richard had not returned to the Tower after its sacking, instead staying at a royal house in Blackfriars. From here he rode out to meet the rebels again on Saturday 15 June, this time at Smithfield. The young king took a large bodyguard and fortified himself beforehand by praying at the shrine of St Edward the Confessor in Westminster Abbey.[36] On this occasion he met the famous Wat Tyler, who apparently had not been at Mile End (or at least, only one chronicle puts him there; it is unclear who spoke to the king at Mile End). William Walworth, the mayor of London and one of the king's attendants, killed Wat Tyler in some way during this encounter. The Kirkstall chronicle says that Tyler refused to make reverence to Richard II, 'either by gesture or word', and was arrested and immediately beheaded, and the *Vita* that Tyler approached the king with his head covered and spoke to him with threatening and insulting words. Walworth then wounded Tyler with his sword and someone else nearby quickly cut off Tyler's head, the *Vita* goes on to say. Tyler's head was placed on London Bridge in place of Archbishop Simon Sudbury's.[37] The *Anonimalle* also comments on Tyler's rudeness to Richard, and says that he demanded a jug of water because it was so hot and then a flagon of ale as well. There was then a scuffle between Tyler and Walworth which ended with Walworth stabbing the other man in the shoulder; Tyler managed to stagger away, bleeding profusely, and then collapsed and died. The account of Wat Tyler's death at the hands of William Walworth is widely supported, though not in the finer details, by Thomas Walsingham,

Jean Froissart and Henry Knighton, and Walsingham and Froissart add that Tyler was carrying a dagger and whipped it out.

Whatever the details, it is beyond doubt that William Walworth killed Wat Tyler and that many of the assembled masses saw their leader die. The situation became even more dangerous and threatening, and according to Walsingham (though no one else) Richard II stood in great personal danger as the rebels prepared their bows to loose arrows at their king. Whether Richard himself was in danger or not, those attending him probably were, and it was a very tense moment. Just when all seemed lost, fourteen-year-old Richard gathered himself and cried out, 'My men, what is this? What are you doing? Surely you don't want to shoot your king? Don't be upset or sad at the death of a traitor and a rascal. I will be your king, your captain and your leader. Follow me to the open ground where you shall be granted all the requests which it shall please you to make.' The *Vita* gives a similar story and has Richard riding his horse among the people and shouting, 'I am your leader. Follow me.'[38] Even Walsingham, who rarely praised Richard II in any way, had to admit at this point that the teenager was 'inspired by an ability unexpected in one so young and fired with courage'.[39] The king's strategy was, of course, designed to lead the crowds away from the city, and it worked: 'The rest were dispersed, an almost countless number who fled in all directions like wandering sheep.'[40] Suddenly deprived of their leader, the rest were lost and confused, and within weeks order had been restored all over the country.

The immediate crisis had, thanks to the fourteen-year-old king's quick thinking and courage, been averted. Now he, or rather his councillors, had to deal with the aftermath. There was some uncertainty as to the exact nature of the crimes committed by the rebels: Edward III's Statute of Treasons in 1352 had defined treason in narrow terms which did not include popular insurrection, and local commissioners trying the rebels often defined their offences as felony and let them off lightly.[41] A few were, however, imprisoned or executed. On 2 July 1381, Richard's council ordered all the king's subjects, especially in the counties of Northumberland, Yorkshire, Lincolnshire, Nottinghamshire, Leicestershire, Northamptonshire, Huntingdonshire and Hertfordshire, to give safe conduct to John of Gaunt, who 'is by the king's command coming to him in haste with an armed power'.[42] The following day, Richard declared that Gaunt was innocent of the treason imputed to him by the rebels, and on the 5th the duke was given permission to have a retinue of armed men to protect himself. Gaunt had sought refuge in Scotland and only returned to England after 3 July.[43] Also on 5 July, it was proclaimed that no one was to leave the country without Richard's express permission.[44] Wat Tyler was already dead, and the famous preacher John Ball was put on trial in St Albans in July 1381 before the harsh justice Robert Tresilian (who would himself be executed not many years later) and was hanged and then beheaded. On 3 August 1381 the bailiffs of St Albans were told to hang 'certain traitors and felons' in chains and to leave them to 'hang there as long as they should endure', as 'diverse evildoers' had cut down the bodies, presumably to bury them.[45]

Thomas Walsingham puts a famous speech in Richard II's mouth: 'Serfs you are and serfs you are still; you will remain in bondage, not as before but incomparably harsher. For as long as we live and by God's grace, we will strive with mind, strength and goods to suppress you so that the rigour of your servitude will be an example to posterity.'[46] It is highly doubtful that Richard ever said this or anything like it, and Walsingham is such an anti-Richard source it is not always possible to take everything he says about him as true or even vaguely true. Letters were sent to all the counties of England on 2 July 1381 revoking 'letters of manumission and pardon, lately issued in haste' to the rebels.[47] As Juliet Barker points out, this was eighteen days after the meeting at Mile End and seventeen after the king had drafted two letters to the men of Somerset and Hertfordshire which stated that 'we have freed and quitted each of them from bondage'. The letters also stated that Richard would 'withdraw sentences of outlawry against them ... And we hereby grant our complete peace to them and each of them.' The delay between granting these astonishing concessions and revoking them suggests that Richard was reluctant to do so. In the parliament held in November 1381, Richard stated via the new chancellor that he would willingly free the serfs if parliament authorised him to do so.[48] He was still only fourteen and not acting under his own agency, and it would be another eight years before he declared his majority and began to rule alone.

Richard II was not old enough to push through his own probable wishes regarding the affairs of his realm and his subjects, though it is likely that events of 1381 and the part he played in them remained with him for the rest of his life. And soon came another important milestone in the young king's life: his marriage.

7

'She Came Adorned Hither like Sweet May': The King Marries the Emperor's Daughter, 1382–1383

An official contract of marriage between Richard II and Anne of Bohemia was made on 2 May 1381, shortly before the uprising, and Richard lent Anne's half-brother King Václav 20,000 florins or about £3,500, a fact which made the marriage unpopular in England. Richard also agreed to lend Václav another 80,000 florins a few days later, of which half would not need to be paid back if Anne of Bohemia arrived at Calais before Michaelmas or 29 September 1381, which in the end she did not.[1] Marriage to Caterina Visconti would have brought the English treasury a considerable sum of money, but Richard's marriage to Anne of Bohemia not only brought him no dowry but in fact cost him a considerable amount, and his subjects grumbled about it. It is also interesting to note that although negotiations for the marriage were progressing well at the beginning of the 1380s, Richard and his council were still hedging their bets. In or around February 1381, Richard sent a letter to King Pedro IV of Aragon touching on the possibility of his marrying the Infanta Isabel, and gave a silver cup to Pedro's ambassador Guillem Marques.[2] This must mean Pedro's daughter of this name with his fourth wife Sibilla of Fortia; Isabel was only a small child in early 1381. Richard further declared himself willing around this time to enter into peace negotiations with King Juan I of Castile, who had succeeded his father Enrique of Trastámara, usurper and killer of his half-brother King Pedro, in May 1379. Peace would ultimately be negotiated via marriage, when Juan I's son and heir married Richard's cousin Catalina of Lancaster.

Richard II's new queen Anne of Bohemia was eight months older than he, born in Prague (now the capital of the Czech Republic) on 11 May 1366, when her father was already fifty. He was one of the most powerful men in fourteenth-century Europe: Karl or Charles IV, Holy Roman Emperor and king of Germany, Italy and Bohemia. Anne of Bohemia's mother Elżbieta or Elizabeth of Pomerania, daughter of Duke Bogislaw of Pomerania – a region which nowadays is divided between Poland and Germany – and granddaughter of the king of Poland, was thirty years younger than Anne's father and his fourth wife. The couple married in Krakow, southern Poland on 21 May 1363 when Karl was forty-seven and Elżbieta about sixteen, and Elżbieta was crowned as queen of Bohemia in Prague that June and as Holy Roman Empress by Pope Urban V in Rome on 1 November 1368 (only a pope could crown an emperor or empress). Karl IV himself had been crowned emperor in Rome by Innocent VI on 5 April 1355, and Richard II's father Edward of Woodstock gave the very generous sum of £13 to the three imperial messengers who brought him news of the coronation.[3]

The imperial couple spent the period from 2 April 1368 until 20 August 1369 in Rome, accompanied by Karl's daughter Katharina from his first marriage, though it is unclear whether the infant Anne also accompanied them or remained behind in Prague or Nuremberg. She was the eldest of the couple's four children, followed by Zikmund or Sigismund, Holy Roman Emperor and king of Hungary, Croatia, Germany, Italy and Bohemia, born in Nuremberg, Germany on 14 February 1368 a few weeks before his parents set off for Rome for Elżbieta's coronation; Johann von Görlitz (a town east of Dresden now on the German-Polish border), margrave of Moravia and Brandenburg, born in Prague in June 1370; and Markéta, who married the Hohenzollern burgrave of Nuremberg and who was born in September 1373 as the youngest of Karl IV's many children, almost forty years younger than his eldest child. (The word 'burgrave' is the Anglicisation of the German word *Burggraf*, literally 'castle count'; 'margrave' is *Markgraf* or 'March count', equivalent to a marquis.) On 1 February 1349 six months after the death of Karl IV's first wife Blanche de Valois, Edward III had appointed Wilhelm, duke of Jülich 'to treat for a marriage' between Karl and Edward's eldest daughter Isabella of Woodstock, Richard II's aunt, but nothing came of this, and a little over a month later Karl married Anna of the Palatinate (also sometimes called Anna of Bavaria) instead.[4]

Elżbieta of Pomerania's maternal grandfather was *Kazimierz III Wielki* or Casimir III the Great, king of Poland, who lived until October 1370 when Anne of Bohemia was four and a half, so she may have been just old enough to have some memories of her great-grandfather. Kazimierz was the son of King Władysław, who bore the excellent nickname 'the Elbow-High' in reference to his shortness, and was a highly effective ruler of Poland for almost forty years and is still often remembered as such today, increasing his kingdom's land area by a third. A Polish proverb says that Kazimierz 'found Poland dressed in timber and left her dressed in brick'. He was a friend to the Jewish population of his kingdom and extended their rights and privileges; the Kazimierz district of Krakow, which until the Second World War was the Jewish quarter of the city, is named after him.

Unfortunately, not all of Anne of Bohemia's family were as friendly to their Jewish populations as Kazimierz. Her half-brother King Václav may have encouraged a notorious pogrom in Prague at Easter 1389 which killed hundreds of Jewish residents, and he certainly had the survivors arrested and their goods confiscated, though he publicly pretended to be dismayed by the murders.[5] As he left only daughters from his four marriages, one of which was bigamous, Kazimierz the Great was the last of the Piast dynasty which had ruled Poland since the 900s, and was succeeded as king by his nephew Ludwik I of Hungary. Anne of Bohemia's great-grandmother Aldona, the first of Kazimierz's four wives, was Lithuanian, the daughter of Gediminas, grand duke of Lithuania. Queen Aldona was buried in Krakow in 1339. On her father's side, one of Anne's great-great-grandmothers, Kunigunda or Koungouta Rostislavna, queen of Bohemia, came from Kievan Rus' in modern-day Ukraine, and Kunigunda's father was prince of Novgorod in Russia, ruled lands in Ukraine, Hungary and Croatia and proclaimed himself emperor of Bulgaria. Anne's ancestry stretched far across Europe, as did Richard's; his grandmother Queen Philippa's great-great-grandmother Erzsébet the Cuman also came originally from the area of Ukraine, Russia and Kazakhstan before her nomadic people settled in Hungary.

Anne's father the emperor Karl IV and great-grandfather Kazimierz III of Poland were not only great political and military leaders, but also pioneers in education: Karl founded the Charles University (*Univerzita Karlova* in Czech) in Prague in 1348, which still exists and is the oldest university in central Europe, and Kazimierz founded the Jagiellonian University in Krakow in 1364, the second-oldest. Anne's brother-in-law Duke Rudolf IV of Austria, first husband of her much older half-sister Katharina, founded the third-oldest university in central Europe in Vienna in 1365, and her father Karl was also responsible for founding the University of Pavia in Lombardy, northern Italy in 1361. Karl IV transformed the small and insignificant backwater of Prague into a thriving metropolis and made it the third-largest city in Europe at the time after Rome and Constantinople; it became the cosmopolitan and dynamic crossroads of Europe and a great cultural centre. The main square in Prague, one of the biggest city squares in the world, is still named *Karlovo Náměstí* or Charles Square after him, as is the famous *Karlův Most* or Charles Bridge.

The emperor Karl died at the Hradčany Palace in Prague on 29 November 1378 when Anne was twelve, having made an unsuccessful attempt to arrange her marriage to Richard earlier that year. When Anne was a child in 1370 Karl had already attempted to arrange her future marriage with Duke Albrecht II of Bavaria, whose sister Katharina had been proposed as Richard's bride in 1380, but this had not worked out (though Anne's half-brother Václav married Albrecht's sister Johanna as his first wife). Other potential suitors for her hand before her engagement to Richard were the future Charles VI of France, who was a little her junior and her close relative, and the German prince Friedrich, margrave of Meissen and elector of Saxony, also some years her junior. Karl IV's desire to conclude a marriage alliance with England is perhaps surprising: a few months before his death, he and his son Václav went on a visit to the emperor's long-term ally France, and the two men rode into Paris with the emperor's nephews King Charles V of France and the dukes of Berry and Burgundy on 4 January 1378.[6]

Anne's father's sister Jutta of Bohemia, who was renamed Bonne after her wedding, married the future King John II of France in 1332 but died a few months before he acceded to the throne in 1350, and was the mother of King Charles V and his siblings, who were Anne's much older first cousins. Another of her first cousins was Erik, king of Sweden, Denmark and Norway. Her half-brother Václav, born in Nuremberg in 1361 and five years Anne's senior, succeeded their father as king of Germany and Bohemia and was unkindly though accurately nicknamed *der Faule* or 'the Idle', and 'the Drunkard'. He was the son of Karl IV's third wife Anna Świdnica (also sometimes called Anna von Schweidnitz, the German form of her name), who like Anne of Bohemia's mother Elżbieta was Polish and who died in childbirth in July 1362, ten months before Karl married Elżbieta. Anne may have been named in honour of her father's late wife, or perhaps after her great-grandmother Aldona of Lithuania, queen of Poland, who took the name Ona or Anna when she was baptised into Christianity.

Anne's step-grandmother Beatrice de Bourbon, King John the Blind's much younger second wife who lived until 1383 and whom Anne probably knew well, was a member of the French royal family. Beatrice's brother Pierre, duke of Bourbon and father-in-law of Charles V of France, was killed fighting against Richard's father at the battle of Poitiers in 1356. Anne and Richard thus came from families which had long been enemies, and although the marriage brought England no financial benefit nor, as it turned out in the long run, much if any diplomatic or military benefit either, its detaching of the powerful house of Bohemia-Luxembourg from its long alliance with France was reckoned a triumph in the early 1380s. The last English royal to take a German bride had been Richard II's namesake Richard of Cornwall, second son of King John and brother of Henry III. Richard was elected king of Germany in 1257, and in 1269, when he was already sixty, married Beatrix von Valkenburg, who was the daughter of the count of Valkenburg and only fifteen or sixteen years old. Although Henry I of England's daughter Maud, the mother of Henry II by her second marriage, wed the king of Germany and Holy Roman Emperor Heinrich V in 1114, and Henry II's eldest daughter Matilda married Henry 'the Lion', duke of Saxony and Bavaria, in 1168, no medieval king of England had married a German woman before.[7]

Anne of Bohemia, like most of her family, was a polyglot. Her two native languages were German and Czech, and she was also fluent in French and Latin and could read all four languages. She presumably knew at least some Polish given that she had a Polish mother (her brother the emperor Zikmund was sent to Krakow as a boy to learn good Polish, and some members of Anne's retinue in England came from Poland), and learnt English well enough after her marriage in

1382 to have a copy of the four Gospels in that language. She also brought to England with her a New Testament written in Czech, German and Latin and separate editions of the Gospels written in Czech and German.[8] French was the lingua franca of European royalty and nobility in the fourteenth century, and this was probably the language in which Anne and Richard communicated when she first arrived in England, or perhaps in a mixture of French and Latin, before she learnt English; in fact they may well have continued to speak mostly in French throughout their married life, depending on the level of fluency Anne managed to achieve in English. Zikmund spoke Czech, German, Latin, French, Italian, Polish and Hungarian, and their father the emperor Karl spoke Czech, German, French, Italian and Latin, and was fluent enough in Latin to be able to write his autobiography and a biography of Saint Václav, patron saint of Bohemia and (nowadays) the Czech Republic and his ancestor, in Latin.[9] The emperor had originally been called Václav like Anne's half-brother and after their illustrious ancestor, and changed his name in honour of his uncle and godfather King Charles IV of France, at whose court he grew up; in May 1323, when he was only seven, he married his first wife, Blanche de Valois, in Paris, and lived at the French court for a few years. Anne of Bohemia herself probably grew up partly at the Hradčany Palace in Prague and at the *Kaiserburg* or imperial castle in Nuremberg.

Anne left Germany for the last time in September 1381, and spent a month in Brussels with her aunt Johanna, duchess of Brabant, and Johanna's husband, Anne's uncle Václav, duke of Luxembourg. Duke Václav had last seen his half-brother the emperor in January 1378, during Karl IV's visit to Paris: the duke rode behind his nephew Charles V of France, and Anne's half-brother the king of Bohemia and Germany, also Václav, rode behind their father, precedence and etiquette being of prime importance during such ceremonial occasions, as it no doubt also was during Anne's visit to her aunt and uncle's court.[10] On her way to England Anne also visited Louis, count of Flanders, in Bruges, and was conducted through that county by a force led by Sir Colard van den Clite, which included eleven crossbowmen and archers and twenty-two lances. The account of expenses relating to this trip refers to Anne as *la royne Dengleterre*, 'the queen of England', though she had not yet married Richard. She was entertained during the journey through Flanders by minstrels thoughtfully provided by Count Louis.[11]

Anne was met at the port of Gravelines between Calais and Dunkirk by Richard's half-brother John Holland, the earls of Salisbury (Joan of Kent's former husband William Montacute) and Devon (Richard II's kinsman Edward Courtenay), and Richard's chamberlain Simon Burley and steward John Montacute, who escorted her to England. Holland, Burley and John Montacute were tasked with this duty in the room of Westminster Palace called the *Redechaumbre* on 30 November 1381.[12] On 13 December, five days before the young woman even arrived in England, Richard ordered several sheriffs to proclaim a general pardon, supposedly at the request of 'the most serene lady, Lady Anne, by the will of God our future consort'.[13] Anne landed at Dover on 18 December 1381, stayed there for three days, then travelled the 40 miles to Leeds Castle also in Kent where she spent Christmas. She had a lucky escape: most of the fleet in which she and her retinue had travelled, including her own ship, was destroyed in a storm after she arrived.[14] The captains of the three Dunkirk ships that carried Anne and her retinue from Dunkirk were paid £13 10s to Dover; Anne's half-brother King Václav had paid for her journeys on the continent, and Richard took over from Calais.[15]

The author of the *Brut* chronicle says that Anne was met at Blackheath by the Londoners, who staged a grand entry for her into the city and put on a series of pageants for her entertainment, though unfortunately little is known about this event.[16] Anne was accompanied to England by a noblewoman named in English records as the *lantegravissa de Lucembergh* or 'landgravine of Luxembourg', who is difficult to identify as this title seems not actually to have existed; whoever she was, the lady left Anne behind in her new country and returned to Dunkirk in a ship called the *Fligut*.[17] Given that this lady returned to the Continent shortly after Anne's wedding, she cannot be identified as Anne's well-known lady-in-waiting Agnes Launcecrona, who was still in England in the late 1380s, as has sometimes been surmised. Przemylaus, duke of Cieszyn, who had been one of the queen's deputies for contracting her marriage with Richard and who also travelled with her, remained in England with his retinue until August 1382.[18] He was given an annual allowance of 500 marks by Richard on 1 May 1381. Konrad Kreyger and Peter Wartenberg, who had come to England from King Václav to negotiate Richard and Anne's marriage – they were respectively the master of Václav's household and of his chamber – received 250 marks each annually. Other Bohemians were granted smaller annual allowances from the English Exchequer as well.[19] Duke Przemylaus's daughter Margrethe remained in England with Anne and married Richard's standard bearer Sir Simon Felbrigg, who lived until 1443 and remained devoted to Richard's memory long after the king's deposition and death: his and his wife's brass effigies at the church of St Margaret in Felbrigg, Norfolk are rich with symbolic references to Richard and his kingship.[20]

Anne's arrival in England attracted surprisingly little comment, especially given that she was the daughter of a powerful ruler over much of Europe, though the Westminster chronicler rather rudely called her a 'tiny scrap of humanity' (also sometimes translated as 'a tiny bit of flesh' or 'a tiny portion of meat') who came to England as a purchase that had cost too much rather than as a gift.[21] In addition to lamenting the proposed match to Caterina Visconti, which would have brought England a large sum of money, the *Eulogium Historiarii* complains that Richard should have married the daughter of the count of Flanders, which would have brought the entire county of Flanders under his control, and that Richard married Anne without the consent of the realm.[22] The 'daughter of the count of Flanders' was Marguerite, who was born in 1350 and was thus seventeen years Richard's senior, making it incredibly unlikely that she would ever have been considered as his bride.[23] Walsingham wrote a typically snide and sarcastic account of the arrival and wedding of 'the imperial girl', as he called Anne: 'Each and every one strove with all his strength to honour these great nuptials with gifts and favour over and above what was demanded. A delegation was sent to meet this magnificent maiden and conduct her with all worldly glory to the port of Dover...Tournaments were also held for some days in order to enhance such celebrations, and in them the English publicly demonstrated their virtue.'[24]

It is, unfortunately, difficult to say very much about Queen Anne, her personality, her likes and dislikes, or even about her household or her day-to-day life in England. None of the records relating to her and her household that surely once existed still survive, and it may be that a grieving Richard had them destroyed after her death, when he ordered the royal palace where they had spent much time together to be torn down.[25] One of the damsels of Anne's chamber bore the excellent name of Perrin or Perrine Wytteneye and was married to Richard's squire Thomas Clanevowe; another was the aforementioned Agnes Launcecrona, who would be abducted around 1386/87 by

Richard II's great friend Robert de Vere; and another was Eliska, the wife of Sir Here Mistilburgh, presumably also Bohemian or German.[26] Anne's chaplain in England, or one of them, came from Warsaw and was called Henryk Reybutz.[27] The queen and her retinue must have appeared weirdly foreign to the English, wearing fashions which looked outlandish to English eyes and speaking Czech and Polish, languages barely if at all known or heard of in England (German, their other main language, was fairly close to English and would not have been so alien and exotic).

If the effigy of Anne which Richard had made after her death and which still exists today in Westminster Abbey is any guide, she was round-faced, tending somewhat to plumpness and perhaps somewhat plain, at least in comparison to her extravagant and fabulously dressed husband, who was described as 'beautiful' by several contemporaries. On the other hand, it is possible that Richard found Anne, coming from a sparkling cosmopolitan court and wearing splendid costly clothes and crowns, glamorous and appealing; he placed a great emphasis on regal appearance. Given their close and affectionate partnership, he seemingly also found her sexually attractive, and after her death Richard declared his queen to have been 'beautiful in body, fair and mild of face'. According to Walsingham, Richard said that he had chosen Anne as his bride 'above all others' and would rarely permit her to leave his side.[28] Anne's brother Zikmund, twenty-one months her junior, was called 'the ginger fox' by contemporaries in reference to his hair colour, which perhaps she shared. Her mother Empress Elżbieta was known for her unusual physical strength, and during festivities organised by her husband would bend and snap metal objects such as swords, large knives and even horseshoes for the amusement of their guests.[29] There is no indication that Anne of Bohemia inherited her mother's enormous strength, though she must have witnessed Elżbieta's impressive performances as she was growing up, assuming the story is true and not legend; Elżbieta had a reputation as a woman willing to fight fiercely for her children's rights, as her husband tended to put his children with his third wife Anna Świdnica before hers.

Anne of Bohemia's heraldic symbol was an ostrich, and in an extant treasure roll of Richard's possessions two collars are recorded, one 'set with rubies in an ostrich' with seventeen great pearls and thirty-five smaller pearls, and the other of gold, 'with an ostrich enamelled white and a diamond'. Anne also brought to England with her many items of silverware for her table and her chamber, marked with the arms of her father the emperor.[30] A magnificent and extremely ornate crown now held in the *Schatzkammer* (treasury) of the Munich Residenz may have belonged to Anne and later passed to Henry IV's daughter Blanche, who in 1402 married the count palatine of the Rhine. Formed in the shape of a *fleur-de-lis* or lily, made of gold and measuring 18 centimetres high and around, it is studded with diamonds, pearls, rubies, sapphires and emeralds.[31] Anne also had at least five gold and jewelled chaplets and a dozen gold belts.[32]

Anne of Bohemia seemingly had a rather retiring personality, and although contemporaries recognised her own attractive personal qualities, they moaned about her expensive and scandal-prone Bohemian retinue and Richard's habit of marrying off Bohemian women to English noblemen. It would, however, be a mistake to dismiss Anne as a mere cipher or to assume that her quiet personality necessarily made her boring and unimportant, or that she herself was unpopular in England. Complaining about the size of a queen consort's retinue was a common medieval habit – the same thing happened to Richard's second queen Isabelle de Valois a few years later – and should not automatically be taken as a comment on Anne herself. For the dozen years of their marriage until her premature death at the age of twenty-eight, Anne supported Richard loyally and staunchly in all matters.

Their marriage was a resounding success; only fifteen when they married, they were to develop a close relationship. In one respect, however, it can be deemed unsuccessful: the royal couple had no children together, and there is no real evidence of any pregnancy in a dozen years except for a rather vague implication around 1385 that Anne may have had a miscarriage (this is only one possible reading of a letter of hers to her brother Václav, however).[33] It is pushing the evidence too far to suggest they had a chaste marriage and no sex life, as one modern historian has suggested. Richard admired Edward the Confessor, the king of England who died in 1066 and who was canonised as a saint in 1161, and who quite probably did have a chaste marriage with his wife Edith Godwinson. It has been suggested that Richard emulated his predecessor in this regard.[34] But Richard knew that he needed heirs, and more recent research has shown that he and Anne had a perfectly normal intimate relationship which for reasons beyond their control did not result in any children.

It is highly likely that one of them was infertile.[35] Contemporary chroniclers noted their childlessness with some sadness when Queen Anne died in June 1394. Shortly before her sudden death at the age of twenty-eight, twelve and a half years after her wedding, Anne evidently had still been hoping to become pregnant.[36] In November 1382, ten months after the royal wedding, Richard II granted a concession to Robert Bealknap, chief justice of the Common Bench, that 'his corn, hay, animals, poultry or other goods, carriage or men shall not be taken by any purveyor or buyer for the use of the king or queen or their children (when God gives them) nor his houses for their entertainment, against his will'. Five months after this in April 1383, Richard gave permission to three men in Warwick to found a guild in honour of St George the Martyr, as long as they promised to 'celebrate divine service daily for the good estate of the king, the queen and their children'.[37] These two entries in the chancery rolls strongly imply that the teenage couple had a perfectly normal and functional intimate relationship which the king assumed would eventually result in children (and the Warwick grant took place fifteen months after their wedding and when both king and queen were still only sixteen). Ultimately and unfortunately, Richard's lack of offspring was to contrast sharply with the fertility of his cousin and rival and later his deadly enemy Henry of Lancaster: by 1390 when he was still only twenty-three, Henry already had four sons with Mary de Bohun, and they later had two daughters as well.

The nature of Richard II's sexuality is unclear; that he deeply loved Robert de Vere, earl of Oxford and later also duke of Ireland, is beyond doubt, but how he loved him is impossible to know for sure. The St Albans chronicler Thomas Walsingham said that Richard and de Vere had an 'obscene familiarity', and that Richard 'loved him so much'.[38] Jean Froissart wrote that de Vere's hold over the king was such that if the earl said that black was white, Richard would not contradict him.[39] Oxford himself evidently was a lover of women who, according to three chroniclers, had his marriage to Richard's royal cousin Philippa Coucy annulled because he had fallen in lust with an attendant of Queen Anne and wished to marry her, though of course this does not preclude the possibility that he was capable of loving men as well. It is perhaps revealing that Richard II did not father any illegitimate children as his father Edward of Woodstock and grandfather Edward III, and even his great-grandfather Edward II – certainly a lover of men but also the father of an illegitimate son called Adam – had, and he is not known to have had any extramarital female lovers. It is impossible after so many centuries to determine the true nature of people's private relationships, even when one of the people was the king of England; they did not write personal letters or keep diaries, and we can only speculate as to their true feelings. Whatever Richard felt for the earl of Oxford, whether their relationship was romantic and sexual or a close friendship or both, it is beyond doubt that he loved Anne of Bohemia deeply as well, and his terrible grief when she died in 1394 stands as testimony to this. In letters to the dowager empress Elżbieta, he addressed her as *mater nostra carissima* (or *precarissima*), 'mother of our beloved'.[40]

Anne entered London on Saturday 18 January 1382, and married Richard two days later at Westminster Abbey. The king had turned fifteen two weeks before his wedding; Anne was also fifteen, and would turn sixteen in May 1382. She was crowned queen of England on 22 January 1382, in a ceremony which contemporary chroniclers unfortunately mostly ignored, with the result that we know few details about it, though as with Richard's coronation of July 1377 people travelled from far and wide to see it.[41] On 30 July 1381, William Courtenay, formerly bishop of Hereford then of London, had been elected archbishop of Canterbury as the successor of the murdered Simon Sudbury. He was a great-grandson of King Edward I and thus Richard's second cousin, though was decades the king's senior, and performed the wedding ceremony of Richard and Anne, and Anne's coronation as queen. Richard's cousin Henry of Lancaster was among those who attended the royal wedding, and who took part in the jousts held at Smithfield in late January to celebrate it. Some weeks before, Henry had received New Year gifts from Richard and his mother Joan of Kent.[42]

Not everyone in London was happy about the marriage of Richard of Bordeaux and Anne of Bohemia: an inquest was held before the mayor John Northampton and the city sheriffs John Rote and John Hend on 28 January to discover which 'evildoers' were responsible for tearing down 'certain shields, on which were painted the arms of the king and the emperor [Karl IV] together, and another shield bearing the arms of the king alone, which shields had been erected round the Conduit in honour of the king and Anne the queen-consort'. On Monday 21 January, the day between Richard and Anne's wedding and the new queen's coronation, three shields 'were violently and maliciously pulled down to the grave dishonour and scandal of the king and queen and to the manifest danger and damage of the city'. A twist in the tale was that one of the people found to be responsible for the vandalism was a German man called Godescalkus or Godschalk of Westphalia, a resident of London for ten years and the servant of a goldsmith named John Porter, who was, despite his very English-sounding name, French and a subject of the king of France. Godschalk was pardoned 'for having abraded and broken the arms of the king and queen, depicted on the Conduit in London' on 18 May 1382, at Anne's request.[43]

Some months later, Richard paid 100 marks for jewels for his new queen: a fillet for her hair with a large ruby and two sapphires, and three rings with a large diamond and four pearls in each.[44] He pardoned a Hugh Garwell of Lincoln at Anne's request on 20 May 1382 for any felonies he had committed during the uprising the previous year, 'provided that he did not kill Simon, archbishop of Canterbury, Robert Hales or John Cavendish'.[45] Probably during her first visit to London, Queen Anne was presented with a request by the mayor, aldermen and citizens of London that she would intercede with the king to support and confirm the privileges and liberties of the city. Written in Latin and in a style which went far beyond elaborately formal, part of the text reads

> ... whereas you are their supreme and natural liege lady, and whereas it pertains to your most benign piety, as well by right of your imperial majesty, of which you are possessed by birth, as of your royal dignity, by the emblems of which your position is made more resplendent, to assume, with bowels of compassion, the office of a mediatrix with that most excellent prince and puissant lord, our lord the king, your lord and ours, and in the exercise of your magnificence to recommend your subjects to our very noble lord aforesaid, as did other our queens, who preceded your most excellent highness in your realm of England – may it please your most clement and pre-eminent nobility thus to mediate by gracious words and deeds with our lord the king...[46]

Anne fulfilled the traditional role of a queen by acting as an intercessor with her husband, and accompanied Richard on almost all his travels; the royal couple rarely separated. Richard also kept in touch with Anne's family. On 7 March 1384, a royal minstrel called John Wylton was pardoned for the murder of a man in Brabant at the request of Anne's mother Elżbieta and the empress's stepson King Václav.[47]

In the meantime, another parliament had taken place at Westminster in November and December 1381, and again from 24 January (two days after Queen Anne's coronation) to 25 February 1382. Understandably, proceedings were dominated by the aftermath of the uprising and its aftershocks, though chroniclers focused more on an enormous quarrel between the royal uncle John of Gaunt and Henry Percy, earl of Northumberland. The Westminster chronicler dramatically exclaimed that this row threatened to destroy the whole of England, and Thomas Walsingham and the author of the *Anonimalle* also devoted considerable space to it.[48] Gaunt seemingly accused Percy of refusing to offer him hospitality in the north of England when he escaped there during the uprising, and the quarrel became so heated that both men arrived at parliament with large numbers of armed men, seriously threatening the stability not only of the parliament itself but of the city of London; a violent confrontation seemed highly likely.[49] Eventually, an armed altercation was avoided, and Percy was forced to make a humiliating public apology to Gaunt on his knees in the middle of parliament. Also rather humiliatingly, Percy had to be pardoned by Richard II three years later for 'twice letting Berwick Castle fall into the hands of the Scots since the king's coronation'.[50]

A sad death took place on 15 February 1382: William Ufford, the popular earl of Suffolk, who had carried the sceptre at Richard's coronation and been part of his royal council, died suddenly in Westminster Hall during parliament, only a few weeks after the death of Edmund Mortimer, earl of March. Feeling perfectly well, Suffolk entered the hall and was ascending the stairs to the chamber where the lords were meeting when he suddenly collapsed and died. Another parliament took place at Westminster in May 1382, and may have been brought to a premature end when an earthquake struck the south of England on 21 May. And a dreadful event happened on 6 August 1382 at Windsor: young William Montacute, the only son and heir of William Montacute, earl of Salisbury from Salisbury's second marriage to Elizabeth Mohun, was killed while jousting. This was not an uncommon occurrence in the fourteenth century, jousting being a remarkably dangerous sport, but what made the young nobleman's death particularly tragic was that he was accidentally killed by his own father. The bereaved earl of Salisbury, first or second husband of Richard's mother Joan of Kent, was now forced to accept his younger brother John and John's son the younger John as his heirs, though he despised them. John Montacute the younger, who ended up succeeding his uncle as earl fifteen years later, was a poet who wrote in French and was apparently the leading knightly patron of the Lollards or followers of John Wycliffe, and was, unlike his uncle, a descendant of Edward I. John Mowbray, the young earl of Nottingham and another descendant of Edward I, also died on 8 February 1383, still only in his teens, leaving his younger brother Thomas as his heir and as heir to their grandmother Margaret, countess of Norfolk.

Richard II and his council were endeavouring to extract some value from the alliance with the king's brother-in-law King Václav of Germany and Bohemia, and on 16 August 1382 sent three men to negotiate an alliance between England and Václav 'against Charles [VI], present occupant of the kingdom of France (*contra Karolum modernum occupatorem regni Franciae*)', his brother Louis, count of Valois and future duke of Orléans – who in 1382 was only ten years old – and his uncles the dukes of Anjou, Berry and Burgundy. Nothing came of it, however; despite his willingness to make an alliance with Richard and England and his ignoring Charles V's pleas in 1380 not to do so, Václav had no wish to break off all relations with the powerful kingdom of France and his close kinsman the young Charles VI.[51] Richard ordered numerous ships on 27 November 1382 to bring his uncle Edmund of Langley, earl of Cambridge, and other nobles home from the unsuccessful expedition to Portugal, and granted them a safe conduct.[52]

According to Jean Froissart, when Edmund returned to England he discussed the whole situation in the Iberian peninsula with his brother John of Gaunt, and the latter realised how difficult it would be for him to conquer Castile for himself and his wife Constanza and that the whole enterprise seemed doubtful. Froissart also says that at this time Robert de Vere, earl of Oxford (who was now twenty, five years Richard II's senior), 'had the sole management of the king' and was hostile to the royal uncles, and was trying to create a breach between them and Richard. De Vere counselled Richard that the war in Spain would cost the entire annual revenue of England and would ultimately be fruitless, and that it would be more prudent for the king to keep men and money at home in England where he needed them. Froissart goes on to claim that 'the young king was well inclined to follow the advice of the earl, for he loved him with his whole heart, they having been brought up together'.[53] This is an early indication of the sway Robert de Vere held over Richard's heart, and that he also held considerable influence over him politically. On 16 January 1383, ten days after Richard's sixteenth birthday, a safe conduct was issued for King Carlos II of Navarre, coming to England, and orders were also given to the cities of Bayonne and Bordeaux (under English control) to provide a fleet for him.[54]

As for Portugal, the kingdom was plunged into crisis on 22 October 1383 when King Fernando died in Lisbon, still only in his late thirties. His only child was ten-year-old Beatriz, who the year before had been betrothed or married to Richard's first cousin Edward of York, Edmund of Langley's son. In the end, this marriage was annulled and Beatriz instead married King Juan I of Castile, son of Enrique of Trastámara, a few months before her father's death. Juan of Castile invaded Portugal in late 1383 to press his and his wife's claim to Fernando's throne, but on 14 August 1385 the Portuguese won a great victory over Castile at the battle of Aljubarrota, and the late king Fernando's half-brother João I succeeded as king of Portugal in place of his twelve-year-old niece Beatriz. Beatriz of Portugal continued to reign as queen-consort of Castile until her death around 1420, but had no children; Juan I of Castile's heir was his elder son Enrique III from his first marriage to the ubiquitous Pedro IV of Aragon's daughter Leonor.

During the parliament held at Westminster between 23 February and 10 March 1383, Michael de la Pole was made chancellor of England. Then probably in his early fifties, Pole was the son of a wool merchant from Hull, William de la Pole, who had become Edward III's chief financier a few decades before. Michael de la Pole had once served Edward of Woodstock, and was Richard II's unconventional choice to fill the important role. Henry Despenser, the nobly born bishop of Norwich (he was a grandson of Edward II's notorious favourite Hugh Despenser the Younger, the brother of Lord Despenser, who died in 1375, and a descendant of Edward I) had at the previous parliament declared his intention of leading a military campaign in Flanders, under attack by the French, and this request was finally, albeit reluctantly, accepted near the end of the parliamentary session. The royal uncle John of Gaunt, who like many other nobles favoured an expedition to the Iberian peninsula rather than to Flanders, walked out of parliament in disgust at the decision. The bishop's army left England two months later and his campaign proved an utter fiasco, and Despenser was impeached in the next parliament, held between 26 October and 26 November 1383. The chancellor Michael de la Pole prosecuted Bishop Despenser with some zeal, though Richard II comforted his distant kinsman as best as he could by assuring him that he himself 'remained well disposed towards him'.[55] The king's great friend and favourite Robert de Vere, who had come of age (twenty-one) a few months earlier, was summoned to this parliament as earl of Oxford for the first time, and was made a Knight of the Garter probably in 1384.

In 1382 and 1383 King Richard took Queen Anne on two major itineraries through his realm, both to show England and his subjects to his wife and for the people to see her too. Richard and Anne had become inseparable, and Richard was immensely proud of his queen, her royalty and her status as the daughter of an emperor. They always travelled together – Richard was loath to allow Anne to leave his side unless absolutely necessary – and on the rare occasions they were apart, sent each other letters. In April 1383, as noted above, sixteen-year-old Richard gave permission for several men in Warwick to found a guild, as long as they promised to 'celebrate divine service daily for the good estate of the king, the queen and their children'.[56] In May and June that year Richard and Queen Anne went on pilgrimage to the shrine of Our Lady of Walsingham in Norfolk, which was particularly associated with fertility.[57] It seems that at this time the royal couple were both interested in praying to Our Lady to help them produce offspring. Perhaps they were concerned that after nearly eighteen months of marriage Anne had not yet become pregnant, and it is highly unlikely, as has sometimes been suggested, that they had a chaste marriage if they were expecting to produce children. And yet the lack of such cannot have loomed too large in the couple's minds quite yet: in June 1383 Richard was still only sixteen and Anne recently turned seventeen. They must surely have thought that they had plenty of time. Even Richard's cousin Henry of Lancaster, who was to have half a dozen children with Mary de Bohun, did not become a father until September 1386 when he was nineteen.

At an uncertain date, most probably sometime in the mid-1380s, Anne of Bohemia sent a letter in Latin to her half-brother Václav, king of Germany and Bohemia, which is the only extant letter from Anne to her family and is thus of much interest. Anne, addressing Václav as *magne celsitudinis* or 'great highness' and referring to herself as 'by the grace of God queen of England and France, your sister', began by congratulating him on his successes in Hungary and Poland. This seems almost certain to be a reference to Václav's campaigns on behalf of Anne's younger full brother Zikmund, who was trying to secure control of those countries by right of his wife Maria of Hungary. Although he never took control of Poland, Zikmund succeeded in Hungary in 1387 and was crowned king at Székesfehérvár, a town south-west of Budapest and then the capital of the kingdom, on 31 March that year with the holy crown of Saint István.

After congratulating Václav and reporting that England was at peace, Anne went on to tell him that two of her lady attendants had died but that she hoped Václav would send her three more, called by their initials L, I and F, to console her, and informed him that a 'Lord Nicholas' had found favour with Richard II. The penultimate sentence expresses her sorrow that she had not yet borne a child, but hoped to do so soon. The letter provides some useful insights: that Anne was politically active and astute, informed about the activities of her brothers on the other side of Europe and in contact with them, and that she and Richard evidently had an active sex life which she was hoping would produce children. She told Václav that she had everything in her life that she needed and was mostly happy, but that 'we write grieving that still we are not rejoicing in our *puerperio*,' i.e. childbirth. She added a pious hope that she was healthy enough in the near future for this to change, if God permitted. It is also not impossible – the Latin of the letter and especially this part is complicated and not easy to unpick – that the queen was telling her brother that she had suffered a miscarriage.[58] Richard II's own feelings on his and Anne's continuing childlessness are not recorded, but Anne herself stated that she was 'grieving' and that everything in her life brought her happiness except this. If the letter to Václav does date to around 1384 or 1385, Richard and Anne were heading towards their late teens and had been married for about three years, and perhaps were growing more than a little concerned that their close, contented marriage had not yet proved fertile and were worried – correctly as it turned out – that it might never do so.

During the royal visit to the shrine of Walsingham in Norfolk in the early summer of 1383 an accident befell Sir James Berners, a knight of Richard II's chamber and a friend of the king. As the royal party was passing through the town of Ely, a sudden and violent thunderstorm forced them to take shelter. Berners was actually struck by lightning during the storm, which supposedly left him blind and half crazed. Richard II, distressed, ordered all the clergy with him to proceed to the shrine of St Etheldreda the Virgin in Ely Cathedral and pray for the afflicted man. When Berners appeared before the shrine in person he saw Etheldreda and St John the Baptist in a vision, and was, so it was told, miraculously cured of his blindness and insanity.[59] On 3 August 1383, Richard II confirmed a grant to Ely Cathedral made by his grandfather Edward III. The sixteen-year-old king spoke at length about what he had seen: 'Now the king, out of devotion to St Etheldreda, whose holy body was translated in the church of Ely, where, while he was there present, the king saw many wonders wrought by the divine power on the intercession of that glorious virgin, among others in the bestowal of sight upon a knight of the king, who was blinded by lightning in the night-time, which miracle took place in the king's presence in the company of many persons...'[60] Nor was this the only time when Richard II expressed his belief in miracles. He was once informed by Thomas Arundel, bishop and archbishop, of a miracle which had taken place at the Canterbury shrine of St Thomas Becket, the archbishop of Canterbury killed in 1170, and replied, 'We are strictly bound to thank the High Sovereign Worker of Miracles and to offer gratitude and thanks, which we desire to do unfeignedly and with all our power.' He also told Arundel that the faith of anyone who criticised the Church would be strengthened by this miracle.[61] Although many in the twenty-first century might deem Richard credulous for expressing his faith in miracles and the supernatural, there is little doubt of the king's sincerity regarding this matter, which provides an interesting insight into his and his era's religious beliefs.

8

'By Envy's Hand and Murder's Bloody Axe': An Invasion of Scotland and Murder, 1384–1385

English attitudes towards France in the late 1370s and 1380s can be most confusing to follow: England sometimes sought a peace settlement and sometimes preferred to make more aggressive and hostile overtures, although generally this amounted to little more than posturing. Suspicion fell on a man called James Bynd on 14 February 1385. Bynd was arrested and imprisoned in Newgate prison, London, because he 'used to make lonely journeys to diverse parts of France and so had fallen under suspicion of being a spy who carried news of the king's counsels to those parts'.[1] In September 1383, the French invaded the county of Flanders next to France's northern border. According to Thomas Walsingham, when Richard II heard the news he kicked a table in rage and rode to London from Daventry in haste, waking the abbot of St Albans in the middle of the night in order for the latter to provide him with a fresh horse, 'as if he planned to slay the king of France that very night'.[2] Nothing came of this, however, and Richard seemingly lost interest in the whole matter. (Riding through the night in great urgency and then failing to do anything at all reveals quite a lot about the king's character.)

On 8 September 1383, John of Gaunt, duke of Lancaster, was appointed as an envoy to Charles VI with a novel proposal for the two kings to settle their disputes. Either Richard, aged sixteen, would engage in single combat with Charles, aged fourteen going on fifteen, or there would be a combat between the kings and their uncles, or there would be a general battle.[3] Not entirely to anyone's surprise, this combat did not occur. The parliament held in the bishop's palace in Salisbury between late April and late May 1384 failed to ratify an Anglo-French treaty which had been drafted, and Richard's uncles John of Gaunt and Thomas of Woodstock spent much of the summer of 1384 on the Continent trying to work out a formula of peace acceptable to both sides. In the end, they only managed to secure a seven-month extension of the ongoing truce, taking it up to 1 May 1385.[4]

Richard spent the feast day of St Nicholas, 6 December 1383, at Westminster, where he gave a pound to the 'boy-bishop' who officiated in his chapel.[5] Although they were not allowed to celebrate the Eucharist, 'boy-bishops' were choristers who blessed people, were expected to give at least one sermon, and gave out alms to the poor from the feast of St Nicholas until the feast of the Holy Innocents, 28 December. The following day, Anne of Bohemia's half-uncle Václav, duke of Luxembourg, died. He left his widow Johanna of Brabant, who was duchess of Brabant in her own right; she was fifteen years Václav's senior, and they had married when Václav was only fourteen and Johanna at the end of her twenties. Perhaps unsurprisingly, the couple had no children. Duchess Johanna survived her much younger husband by many years and lived until 1406. Duke Václav's mother, Anne of Bohemia's French step-grandmother and the dowager queen of Bohemia Beatrice de Bourbon, outlived her son by sixteen days and died on 23 December 1383. Louis, count of Flanders, died some weeks later as well, and the county passed to his daughter Marguerite and her husband Duke Philip of Burgundy, Charles VI's uncle. Luxembourg, meanwhile, passed to Duke Václav's nephew and namesake the king of Germany and Bohemia, Richard II's brother-in-law, and King Václav arrived there in August 1384 to take the homage of his nobility.[6]

Anne of Bohemia was made a Lady of the Garter in April 1384, with several other highborn ladies: Richard's aunt by marriage Eleanor de Bohun, countess of Buckingham (Eleanor's sister Mary, married to Henry of Lancaster, was raised to the honour in 1388); Richard's kinswoman Anne Hastings, *née* Manny, dowager countess of Pembroke, younger daughter of Margaret, countess of Norfolk (Anne did not have long to enjoy the honour as she died that month); the royal cousin Catalina of Lancaster, aged about eleven, only child of John of Gaunt and Constanza of Castile; Elizabeth Montacute, *née* Mohun, countess of Salisbury, second wife of Joan of Kent's former husband William Montacute; and Elizabeth's mother Joan, Lady Mohun. Richard II's half-sister Joan Holland, duchess of Brittany, died in 1384. She left no children, and her widower Duke John IV (previously married to Edward III's daughter Margaret) married his third wife Juana of Navarre, teenage daughter of Carlos II 'the Bad', in 1386. According to the Westminster chronicle, Richard and Queen Anne were present at Arundel Castle for the wedding of his kinsman Thomas Mowbray to the earl of Arundel's daughter Elizabeth in July 1384, and Richard's itinerary does indeed place him at the earl's castle of Arundel in Sussex on 6 and 7 July that year. The chronicler says the wedding festivities lasted for an entire week.[7] Despite their youth – they were still teenagers, almost exactly the same age as the king himself – both Thomas Mowbray and his new wife had been married before: Elizabeth to the earl of Salisbury's son William Montacute, accidentally killed by his father during a joust in August 1382, and Mowbray to the daughter and heir of Lord Lestrange of Blackmere, who died within months of their wedding.

Parliament took place in the Wiltshire town of Salisbury between 29 April and 27 May 1384. During this parliament Richard II lost his temper with the earl of Arundel, who gave a harshly critical speech about the king and his government, claiming that England was on the brink of destruction and collapse because it 'lacks prudent government'. The Westminster chronicle says that Richard II went 'white with passion' on hearing this speech and was completely engulfed by fury, and shouted at the earl, 'If it is supposed to be my fault that there is misgovernment in the kingdom, you lie in your teeth. You can go to the devil!' A complete hush followed because no one dared to speak, eventually broken by the king's uncle the duke of Lancaster, who hastened to interpret the earl's speech in a tactful and wise way and thus managed to calm Richard II down.[8] Evidently the king had recovered himself enough to enjoy Arundel's hospitality at his daughter Elizabeth's wedding a few weeks later. Richard Fitzalan, earl of Arundel, was born in about 1346 as the eldest son of Richard Fitzalan the elder and Eleanor of Lancaster, one of the six sisters of Duke Henry of Lancaster. His father, who died in early 1376, was probably the richest man in England in the entire fourteenth century, or at least the second-richest behind his brother-in-law Duke Henry, and the younger Richard inherited this enormous wealth.[9] The earl of Arundel had a harsh personality, and Richard came to hate him, especially in and after 1387.

Richard II was prone to outbursts of temper and rage: the Westminster chronicle says that he was so infuriated with his kinsman the archbishop of Canterbury's criticisms of his reliance on his councillors in late 1384 that when he encountered Archbishop Courtenay in his barge on the Thames, the king drew his sword and would have run Courtenay through had he not been physically restrained by two household knights, John Devereux and Thomas Trivet. Richard then turned his anger onto these two men, who, afraid for their lives, jumped from Richard's barge into the archbishop's.[10] Nor was this the only time when Richard came close to attacking Archbishop Courtenay. At Lent 1385, says the *Historia Vitae et Regni Ricardi Secundi*, the king reacted furiously when Courtenay reprimanded him for his arrogance and the bad governance of the kingdom: his uncle Thomas of Woodstock had to physically prevent him striking Courtenay. Richard was forced to content himself with shouting 'many foul words' at the archbishop, who, grossly offended, took himself off away from the king.[11] Richard's supposed over-reliance on favourites and courtiers was a common complaint of chroniclers, as it had been of his great-grandfather Edward II as well. The *Vitae et Regni* says that he was 'too apt to prefer and to follow the recommendations of the young' rather than older and wiser nobles, and similar comments can be found in the works of other writers, even ones generally favourable towards Richard.[12]

Richard tended to overreact and to make hasty judgements on the spur of the moment, without thinking matters through. The Westminster chronicle also says that when the king heard of a supposed plot against him involving his uncle the duke of Lancaster, he immediately ordered Lancaster's execution in a fit of passionate rage. Fortunately, however, he soon came to his senses.[13] The king also physically assaulted the earl of Arundel at Queen Anne's funeral in 1394 and spilt his blood, and proceedings had to be temporarily postponed while the shocked monks re-consecrated the abbey. In fairness, Richard's bad temper was hardly unique among the medieval kings of England. His great-grandfather Edward II in the 1320s had also flown into a yelling, furious rage against the archbishop of Canterbury, who was forced to make excuses in order to escape from the king's wrathful presence, and Edward I had to pay compensation to a servant for assaulting him at his daughter Margaret's wedding in 1290. Edward I also ripped his daughter Elizabeth's coronet from her head during an argument with her in 1297 and threw it on the fire, and had to pay for a replacement.

And although Richard II insulted Archbishop Courtenay and came close to striking him physically on one occasion, his cousin and successor Henry IV went much further in 1405 when he actually had an archbishop, Richard Scrope of York, beheaded for treason.

The Salisbury parliament of 1384 is also famous for the affair of a Carmelite friar called John Latimer, which was the occasion of Richard ordering John of Gaunt's execution in a temper.[14] One day Latimer celebrated mass in the king's presence, then in the chamber of Robert de Vere, earl of Oxford, suddenly began ranting that John of Gaunt was planning to have Richard killed and would then attempt to seize the throne for himself. On hearing this, without stopping to think, an enraged Richard ordered that his uncle must be put to death (at least, according to the Westminster chronicler). Thomas Walsingham says that John of Gaunt's brother Thomas of Woodstock rushed into the king's chamber and furiously declared that he would attack and kill anyone – even Richard himself – who suggested that Gaunt was a traitor.[15] Some people in attendance on the king rather bravely pointed out that Richard was acting rashly and that it was unjust for anyone, let alone the king's own uncle, to be put to death without being heard, and fortunately Richard calmed down somewhat and conceded the point.

News of Latimer's claims came to the ears of Gaunt himself, who entirely understandably demanded an audience with Richard so that he could set matters straight. The friar John Latimer was led away to be imprisoned and interrogated, but had the misfortune to fall into the hands of the king's half-brother Sir John Holland, a violent and aggressive young man. Holland and his men tortured Latimer in the most horrible ways, and he died of his injuries, having said nothing of use on the matter of exactly who, if anyone, had persuaded him to accuse Gaunt of plotting Richard II's death. He named the courtier William la Zouche of Harringworth as someone who would have knowledge of the affair, but Zouche strenuously denied all knowledge of it, and the matter remains unclear. It is not impossible that Robert de Vere, earl of Oxford, in whose chamber John Latimer made the allegation against John of Gaunt, was the chief mover in the whole business, his aim to create conflict between the king and his eldest uncle. De Vere found little favour with contemporary and near-contemporary chroniclers, who mostly criticised him harshly for his hold over the king and his apparent attempts to sow conflict, though Jean Froissart did comment that de Vere had 'sensitivity, honour, fair speech and generosity'.[16] He also wrote that there was much discontent in England owing to the excessive influence wielded by Robert de Vere over Richard II.

A few months later in August 1384, the draper and former mayor of London John of Northampton was put on trial at a meeting of the royal council in Reading.[17] He was accused of inciting disorder in London after losing an election the previous autumn. When Richard II proposed that the council should move to judgement on Northampton, the latter stood and declared that he hoped Richard would not proceed to judgement against him in the absence of his uncle the duke of Lancaster. The king, overreacting once again, angrily pointed out that he had not only the ability to sit in judgement on John of Northampton, but on the duke of Lancaster as well if he wished. Anne of Bohemia quickly intervened with her husband and spared Northampton's life.[18] On 26 September, John of Northampton and his allies John More and Richard Norbury, who 'lately made insurrection against the king's peace', were spared the terrible death of hanging, drawing and quartering 'by the king's grace', and it was decreed that 'they shall be sent to prisons in different counties 100 leagues distant from the city for ten years, and not then be released until they have found security that no evil or prejudice shall befall the city or any of the king's lieges thereby'.

On 3 June 1386 it was declared that 'although since their removal from the city tranquillity and good government prevailed, where as long as they remained they drew together so great a multitude of fools for their evil purpose that constant dissension arose between the king's lieges, yet that the king's uncle John, duke of Lancaster, has so urgently besought the king to be gracious to them that he [Richard] is unwilling to refuse some remission of their punishment'. Richard thus released the men from prison on condition that they did not come within eighty leagues of London, on pain of death. The matter was finally resolved on 28 July 1390 when Richard was staying with John of Gaunt at Leicester, and at his uncle's request permitted John of Northampton to receive back his forfeited goods and 'liberty to go where he will throughout the realm, notwithstanding his exile, but he is not to come to the city [London] except as a stranger, or stay or hold any office therein'.[19] The Westminster chronicle says that John of Gaunt skilfully played his nephew by saying, 'God forbid that your power be so cramped that you could not extend grace to your subjects when circumstances demanded it.' Richard grumbled that friends of his were also living in exile, but did allow the duke of Lancaster to sway him on the matter.[20]

The second parliament of 1384 was held at Westminster and officially began on 12 November. Richard arrived 'secretly' at Westminster on 13 November 1384 from his palace of Eltham, and paid £2 5s 'to dine and to inspect his jewels, and upon other of his private affairs'.[21] He may have been aware that 13 November was the date of his grandfather Edward III's birth in 1312, the feast day of the obscure saint Brice and two days after the far more famous saint, Martin. The palace of Eltham in Kent had been given to Richard's great-grandfather the future King Edward II in 1305. Edward III spent over £2,000 remodelling it in the 1350s, and it must have been a delightful place for Richard to stay.[22] Eltham lay in a great park, was surrounded by a large moat and had a garden with a vineyard and a turf garden built by Richard 'for the pleasure of the king and queen'. It had a king's chamber and a queen's chamber with a *pentice* or covered way connecting them, and Richard added a dancing chamber, a new bath-house and a 'painted wall'. He also had accommodation built for his friends and courtiers, both chambers and apartments, probably free-standing buildings. John of Gaunt, Robert de Vere and Thomas Mowbray were among those who had their own apartments.

Richard also spent time, though not very often, at the palace of Langley in Hertfordshire, which had been his great-grandfather Edward II's favourite residence; the king had founded a priory of Dominican friars there in 1308, and had his beloved Piers Gaveston buried there after his 1312 murder. Richard's uncle Edmund was born at Langley in 1341 and would die there in 1402, and Richard himself would be buried at Langley for a few years until his body was moved to Westminster Abbey. Robert de Vere and Thomas Mowbray also had their own chambers here, and Richard rebuilt the bath-house, which had ten glazed windows and a great oven underneath. Finally, Richard and Queen Anne's favourite residence was the palace of Sheen on the River Thames west of London, which was built around two courts and consisted of free-standing timber buildings. The king had yet another luxurious bath-house built here, with 2,000 painted tiles and a bath with large bronze taps for hot and cold water, and added small fireplaces to the chambers. Richard also built three Great Houses for his courtiers, all of which had chambers with private latrines and fireplaces, and had a garden pavilion built on an island in the Thames called La Neyt or La Nayght as a private retreat for himself and Queen Anne.[23]

On 31 December 1384, the great religious reformer John Wycliffe, who had translated part of the New Testament into English, died. In July 1382 the chancellor, proctors and theologians of Oxford University had been ordered to hold an inquisition into the works of Wycliffe and three others, including a professor of theology called Master Nicholas of Hereford, who were condemned as 'heretics'.[24] Some months after this Wycliffe was summoned to appear before a synod in Oxford, but he was not excommunicated. Three years after Wycliffe's death, in March 1388, all his and Nicholas of Hereford's 'compiled and published books, booklets, schedules and quires containing heresies and manifest errors injurious to the Catholic faith' were to be confiscated and brought to the royal council. It was prohibited to buy or sell such books on pain of imprisonment and forfeiture, or even to 'maintain or teach these doctrines'.[25] The year 1388 saw a renewed onslaught on Wycliffe and his followers: on 16 April four men including the sheriff of Yorkshire were ordered to confiscate all books they found 'containing diverse heresies and errors injurious to the Catholic faith ... weakening the orthodox faith and to the evident subversion of many persons', and to proclaim that no one was allowed to sell, buy or make such books or to 'maintain or teach any such heretical opinions' on pain of arrest. This commission was also given to Henry Despenser, bishop of Norwich, on 29 May.[26]

On 2 May 1388, a knight called Thomas Latimer was ordered to come to London and appear before the king's council to explain his possession of books and pamphlets 'concerning the error and perverse doctrine of the Catholic faith, as is said'.[27] John Wycliffe's supporter Master Nicholas of Hereford was invited on 12 December 1391 to appear before the royal justices 'on account of his zeal in preaching privately to false teachers subverting the Catholic faith and infecting not only the laity but also the clergy and the learned with their heresies and errors'; Nicholas was being 'sued maliciously by his enemies ... with a view to his imprisonment and to prevent him further resisting their depraving doctrine'.[28] As late as 18 July 1395, Richard II, talking of 'his zeal for the Catholic faith, whereof he is and by God's help shall be the defender', told the chancellor of the University of Oxford 'under pain of forfeiture' to examine Wycliffe's book the *Triolagus*. All the heresies and errors it was found to contain should be made known to the royal council so that Richard could take further steps to support the true faith; for he had heard of the 'great number of nefarious opinions and detestable allegations ... and unsound doctrine' within it which 'may infect the Christian people'.[29] In 1415, during the reign of Henry V, John Wycliffe was declared a heretic, and his remains were dug up, burned and thrown into a river. Richard II's cousin and successor Henry IV passed a notorious law in 1401 called *De heretico comburendo*, which translates as 'concerning the burning of heretics', which was aimed at Wycliffe's followers, known as the Lollards.

Richard II himself did not persecute heretics. Although he supported and most probably held orthodox Christian views, especially in and after the mid to late 1380s, and was concerned about 'unsound doctrine', he refused requests to have people burned alive for the crime of heresy. The king's mother Joan of Kent named three prominent Lollard knights as the executors of her will in 1385, and Richard retained their and other Lollards' services. This perhaps reveals that privately he had some sympathy with Lollard and Wycliffite beliefs, while presenting an entirely orthodox public face.[30] The king's position on heresy, however, hardened somewhat in the 1390s.[31] In or shortly before December 1389, Richard was present when a Jewish man called Richard de Cicilia converted to Christianity and was baptised at the royal manor of Langley by Robert Braybrooke, bishop of London.[32] Presumably Richard de Cicilia had had another name when he was Jewish, and took the king's name when he was baptised; Richard II was his sponsor. Richard de Cicilia was to receive £10 a year from the Exchequer for life. On 2 May 1392, a convert to Christianity called William Piers was granted 2*d* a day from the Exchequer for life, 'to induce the unbelieving to accept the catholic faith'.[33]

Richard, rather interestingly, showed considerable devotion to some fairly obscure saints of Anglo-Saxon England in Edmund, Erkenwald, Winifred and Etheldreda, along with his especial devotion to the much more famous Edward the Confessor, the penultimate king of Anglo-Saxon England who died in January 1066.[34] St Edmund, a king of East Anglia murdered by Danish invaders in the ninth century, and Edward the Confessor were two of the three saints on the Wilton Diptych, which Richard had made in the 1390s, and the Confessor's feast day of 13 October was an important day in Richard's calendar. Richard's ancestor Henry III was also a devotee of Edward the Confessor and St Edmund: his two sons King Edward I and Edmund of Lancaster were named after the saints, and Henry thus brought two archaic Old English names back into fashion. As for John the Baptist, the third saint on the Wilton Diptych, Richard II was delighted in April 1398 to acquire one of the saint's teeth, and gave the man who had presented it to him, one John Glasier or Glazier, a gift of 4*d* a day from the Exchequer 'for life or until further order'. Twelve years before, Richard had also received the 'dish wherein the head of St John the Baptist lay after it was cut off' from John de Lunde, parson of the church of All Saints upon the Pavement in York, and thereafter kept it in his chapel.[35] Richard's confessor early in his reign was one Brother John de Woderoue or Woodrow, apparently a Dominican; by 1383 Woodrow had been replaced by Thomas Russhok, and by 1390 by Alexander Bache, bishop of St Asaph. Late in the king's reign, his confessor was John Burghill, bishop of Llandaff.[36]

On 8 May 1385, Richard granted an annual income of 10 marks for life to Edith Willesford, his late father's mistress, to be taken out of the £100 a year given to his half-brother Sir Roger Clarendon, Edith's son.[37] Edward III had granted Roger this income on 26 January 1372, which Richard confirmed on 12 June 1388 as the original document had been accidentally lost.[38] Clarendon was a knight of the king's chamber in the early 1390s and probably before and after as well, and in October 1391 was given permission to leave England from any port he wished and gifted £100 for the expenses of his journey.[39]

Richard II's first cousin Richard of Conisbrough, third child of Edmund of Langley and Isabel of Castile, may have been born in 1385, and if so he was considerably younger than his siblings Edward and Constance of York (though it is not impossible that he was born much earlier, around 1375). A question mark hangs over Richard of Conisbrough's paternity, and it has been postulated that he was the son of Richard II's half-brother John Holland, earl of Huntingdon, who supposedly had an affair with Isabel of Castile, rather than of Edmund of Langley. Edmund did not even mention Richard of Conisbrough in his will of November 1400 and left him no lands or money, though did mention 'my most dear son of Rutland', i.e. his elder son and heir Edward of York, earl of Rutland, and Isabel, 'late my wife, whom God pardon'. This latter formulation, however, is a conventional expression of piety common in this era, and not too much needs to be read into it.[40] Duchess Isabel's own will of January 1392, made a few months before she died, asked King Richard to grant her younger son Richard of Conisbrough, who was his godson, an income of 500 marks a year.[41] The king did so, and treated his young cousin with conspicuous favour.

In the summer of 1385, Richard II decided to go on a military campaign to Scotland. Possibly he was intending to thwart a possible two-pronged attack by Scotland and France, always a fear for the kings of England: a famous French knight called Jean de Vienne gathered a great fleet in 1385 and sailed to Scotland with the assent and blessing of the young king of France Charles VI. Now eighteen, Richard had never previously been north of Nottingham, so it was at least a chance to see some of the northern parts of his kingdom at long last.[42] He marched out of Newcastle on 30 July 1385 with the greatest army seen in England since the Crécy campaign of 1346, burning Melrose Abbey and the city of Edinburgh, where he was on 12 August. The king was back in Newcastle on the 20th, presumably because he had heard of the death of his mother the dowager princess of Wales.[43]

As so often with medieval armies, disease spread and feeding the large numbers of men and horses became a significant and pressing problem. Richard II also quarrelled with his uncle John of Gaunt, abusing him to his face and accusing him of treason when Gaunt suggested pressing on past the Firth of Forth rather than retreating. It was all very well, Richard declared, for great lords such as Gaunt, who had brought large quantities of food for themselves, while the rest of the army went hungry. 'I shall return home with my men,' the king stated. 'But I am one of your men,' Gaunt pointed out. 'I see no evidence of that,' Richard sniffed.[44] Chronicler Jean Froissart wrote that in the summer of 1385, Michael de la Pole (sometime chancellor of England and earl of Suffolk) told Richard that John of Gaunt 'wishes for nothing more earnestly than your death, that he may be king'. Whether Richard ever truly believed at any point that his uncle wanted him dead or not is unclear, and his complex relationship with his uncle ebbed and flowed throughout his reign.[45]

In York in July 1385, during the English's army journey north to Scotland, a brawl took place during which two squires of Richard's half-brother Sir John Holland were killed by an archer in the retinue of Ralph Stafford, eldest son of Hugh, earl of Stafford. Such brawls and unnecessary deaths were hardly uncommon in fourteenth-century England, when all young men went about armed, but this one was to have tragic consequences. John Holland, in a rage, went to investigate what had happened, and came upon Ralph Stafford. Either failing to recognise Stafford, or so blinded by his fury at the death of his men that he did not care, John Holland killed the young nobleman.

Once he realised what he had done, he fled to Beverly Minster to seek sanctuary. Ralph Stafford was almost exactly the same age as the king, and his close friend and loyal ally. Heir to the earldom of Stafford, he was also a descendant of Edward I via his grandmother Margaret Audley, a great heiress who inherited a third of the old earldom of Gloucester and who was such a marital prize that she was abducted and forcibly married in 1336 by Ralph Stafford, namesake grandfather of the younger Ralph. Ralph the elder, first earl of Stafford, had been a long-term close friend of Edward III and one of the men who helped the king arrest his mother's favourite Roger Mortimer in 1330. The young Ralph seemingly was highly thought of by contemporaries despite his youth, but now, at only eighteen or so, he was dead. The king had him buried at Langley Priory, where he would have his brother Edward of Angoulême re-interred some years later.

Richard II was furious and deeply upset at the shocking killing of his friend and kinsman, and refused to forgive his half-brother, despite their mother Joan of Kent's pleading with him to do so. The *Historia Vitae et Regni Ricardi Secundi* says that the king even sent letters to Joan, ordering her not to receive or comfort her son John.[46] Holland was a violent and dangerous young man: he had already had the friar John Latimer tortured and murdered after Latimer accused John of Gaunt of conspiring to kill the king. Joan of Kent was dying in July 1385, and the author of the *Vitae et Regni* thought, whether correctly or not, that the refusal of one of her sons to forgive one of the others caused her such grief that it hastened her death (though the knowledge that her son John Holland was a thuggish killer and torturer must surely also have caused Joan considerable grief, and it hardly seems reasonable to hold Richard II partly responsible for her death).

On 7 August 1385, Joan made her will at her castle of Wallingford near Oxford, which began, 'I, Joan, princess of Wales, duchess of Cornwall, countess of Chester and Lady Wake.' She left to 'my dear son the king' her new bed of red velvet, 'embroidered with ostrich feathers of silver, and heads of leopards gold with boughs and leaves coming out of their mouths'. She also left beds to her other two sons Thomas and John Holland (beds were valuable and thus were frequently bequeathed to close family members, and Richard had also inherited three from his father). Joan asked to be buried with her first (or second) husband Sir Thomas Holland at the Greyfriars church in Stamford, Lincolnshire, rather than in Canterbury Cathedral next to her royal husband Edward of Woodstock, father of her son the king.[47] To have been lain to rest next to her royal husband would have been a far more prestigious location, and Joan's choice to lie for eternity at the far more obscure Stamford next to Thomas probably reveals her strong feelings for her Holland husband even a quarter of a century after his death. A few weeks before Joan died, on 12 June 1385, Richard exempted thirteen men of her retinue from the general array (to Scotland) on the grounds that they should 'assist continually about the person of the king's mother for her comfort and security … rendering other services befitting the estate of so great a lady'.[48]

A week after making her will, on 14 August 1385, Joan of Kent, granddaughter, niece and mother of kings, who would have been queen consort of England herself if Edward of Woodstock had lived longer, died in her late fifties, probably while still in residence at Wallingford Castle. (She died on the same day as the great Portuguese victory over the kingdom of Castile at the battle of Aljubarrota.) Illness is a far more likely explanation for her death than Richard II's fury over his half-brother's murder of his kinsman; Joan had grown so hugely overweight by this time that she could barely stand.[49] Her funeral was delayed for some months until January 1386, partly because Richard was absent in Scotland but also because there was usually a long delay between a royal death and funeral in the fourteenth century, Edward III's being one exception. Richard attended his mother's funeral, but not, apparently, her interment; he did not go anywhere near Stamford in January 1386, but instead remained at Westminster, Eltham and Sheen.[50] Neither did Richard spend much money on Joan's funeral or on the commemoration of her death, with the notable exception of the tenth anniversary, 7 August 1395, when he spent over £20 remembering his mother. On 29 June 1386 he ordered glaziers to repair the chapel at Stamford where his mother lay, but otherwise seemingly took little interest in her resting place.[51]

Compared to Richard's grief at the loss of Queen Anne and close members of his circle, and his respect for the brother he could surely barely remember, paying a considerable amount of money to have Edward of Angoulême's body brought to England in the early 1390s and buried, his neglect of his mother's remains seems striking. Historian Michael Bennett has speculated that Richard was rather embarrassed about his mother and her lively marital affairs, and also comments that although Richard paid for his father's tomb in Canterbury and observed the anniversary of his death every year, he otherwise made little effort to honour Edward of Woodstock's memory either.[52] For all Edward's immense popularity and larger-than-life reputation, Richard II was so different from his father that he may have experienced Edward's legacy as a burden rather than a source of pride. The king did honour his mother's dying wish to lie beside Thomas Holland rather than next to his father, but that did not necessarily mean that he was happy about it. Richard surely loved Joan of Kent as a son, but from his perspective as a king she was perhaps something of a liability, with her chequered marital past and relationship with a humble knight, the incorrectly formulated dispensation for her marriage to Edward of Woodstock and his grandfather Edward III's alleged displeasure at the marriage, not to mention Joan's old habit of dressing in the style of a freebooter's mistress, which can hardly have increased respect for her. Joan was sarcastically known to one chronicler as the Virgin of Kent, and even the rebels in 1381 demanding kisses from her, though it may indicate that they liked her and found her considerably more approachable than other members of the royal family and the nobility, does not imply deference for a royal person and the king's mother. It is difficult to imagine anyone demanding a kiss from Joan's predecessors Philippa of Hainault or Isabella of France, or from Henry of Lancaster's mother Duchess Blanche.

Rumours were rife throughout Richard's lifetime that he was not really the son of Edward of Woodstock, and although there is no real reason to suppose that Richard or anyone important believed this to be true, it does demonstrate how Richard's mother caused him problems in some ways. Not a whiff of scandal attached itself to Duchess Blanche, whose background was as royal as Joan of Kent's was. Henry of Lancaster's maternal grandfather Duke Henry of Lancaster was one of the great figures of the English fourteenth century, but by contrast, Richard's maternal grandfather Edmund of Kent had died on the scaffold as a convicted traitor (although he was posthumously pardoned only months later by his nephew Edward III). With a father whose warlike legacy surely weighed heavy on him, a scandalous mother and an executed traitor as grandfather, and a great-grandfather who was so disastrous a king that his own wife led a rebellion against him and forced him to abdicate his throne – not to mention a maternal half-brother who murdered one of his closest friends – Richard's family could hardly have been a source of much pride and contentment to him.

9

'Thy Glory like a Shooting Star Fall to the Base Earth': The King of Armenia Visits, 1385–1386

Belatedly, the king did pardon John Holland for the death of Ralph Stafford on 18 February 1386 as part of an agreement with Stafford's father Hugh, the earl of Stafford, and at John of Gaunt's request, according to the Lancastrian chronicler Henry Knighton. Holland agreed to pay for three chaplains to say prayers for Ralph's soul, two at the place of the murder and one at Langley Priory, Ralph Stafford's burial site. The number of chaplains praying for Ralph's soul at Langley was increased to three in November 1387.[1] Hugh, earl of Stafford, died in October 1386 on the island of Rhodes on his way back from pilgrimage to the church of the Holy Sepulchre in Jerusalem, where he had presumably travelled on pilgrimage to pray for his late son's soul. His heir was now his second son, who also died young, and the earldom passed to the third son and ultimately to the fourth son Edmund, who was the ancestor of the later earls of Stafford and dukes of Buckingham. In 1388, Richard made John Holland earl of Huntingdon, a sign that he had forgiven him by then both for the murder of Ralph Stafford and for the torture of the friar John Latimer (or at least that he was willing to act in public as though he had forgiven Holland).

While in Scotland in the summer of 1385, Richard II upgraded the titles of his uncles Edmund of Langley and Thomas of Woodstock, and made them both dukes: Edmund became duke of York, and Thomas duke of Gloucester. The promotion of these two sons of a king to the same title as their elder brothers was entirely normal and expected, and attracted no criticism. According to a chronicler called Henry Knighton, Richard's chamberlain Simon Burley was made earl of Huntingdon at this time, though this appointment is not recorded in the Charter Rolls as the others are. Neither did Richard refer to Burley as earl of Huntingdon at any point.[2] On 6 August 1385, a few days before his mother's death, Richard made his chancellor Michael de la Pole earl of Suffolk, a title which had fallen vacant on the death of the childless William Ufford in February 1382. This was an astonishing promotion for a man who was born as the son of a wool merchant, and is evidence of Richard's trust in and affection for Pole. Walsingham, as cutting as ever, declares that Pole 'had grown old in peace among money-changers, not in war with soldiers'.[3] Although the family was of humble origins, Pole's descendants were destined to play important roles in fifteenth-century English history: his grandson William de la Pole was raised to a dukedom under Henry VI and was Lord High Admiral of England, and his great-grandson John married one of the sisters of Edward IV and Richard III. The family also intermarried with the descendants of Geoffrey Chaucer when Michael de la Pole's grandson William married Chaucer's granddaughter Alice Chaucer.

Another astonishing promotion later in 1385 was that of Robert de Vere, already earl of Oxford by hereditary right, the king's dearest friend and perhaps his lover, now made marquis of Dublin – an unprecedented title. This immediately gave de Vere precedence over all the earls of England, and at the next parliament de Vere pushed past the earls in order to take a higher seat in the hall, at least according to Walsingham.[4] Richard II pontificated proudly on the 'absolute integrity and outstanding wisdom of his dearest kinsman' de Vere and declared that he 'desir[ed] that the excellence of his name should be the consequence of the earl's magnificent deeds', though de Vere's integrity, wisdom, excellence and magnificence were not immediately apparent to anyone but the king.[5] Finally, the king's friend and kinsman Thomas Mowbray had already succeeded his late elder brother John (who died in 1383) as earl of Nottingham, and on 30 June 1385 became Earl Marshal of England for life, a title once held by his great-grandfather Thomas of Brotherton, son of Edward I and elder brother of Richard II's grandfather Edmund of Woodstock. Mowbray replaced the king's half-brother Thomas Holland in the position.[6] He had married the earl of Arundel's daughter Elizabeth in July 1384, and their first son Thomas was born on 17 September 1385 when Mowbray was eighteen or nineteen. In September 1392, Richard II gave £200 to Mowbray for a future marriage between a son of Mowbray and his wife Elizabeth, *née* Fitzalan, and a daughter of Richard's half-brother John Holland and his wife Elizabeth of Lancaster. Thomas Mowbray the younger was thus betrothed to the king's half-niece Constance Holland (who presumably was named after the duchess of Lancaster Constanza of Castile and may have been her goddaughter).[7]

Beginning in the mid-1380s and continuing for a few years, Richard actively promoted the canonisation of his great-grandfather Edward II, who was also his great-uncle on his mother's side. The king later travelled to Gloucester to discuss the evidence of miracles performed at Edward's tomb there and to oversee the production of a book of miracles to send to the pope to support the canonisation, and perhaps also to discuss and arrange a translation of Edward's body to Westminster Abbey, though in fact this never happened. Richard was in fairly frequent contact with the pope about the sainthood of 'the glorious king Edward, our beloved [great-]grandfather', though it never happened either.[8] On 30 November, Richard paid £2 to Arnold Brocas, clerk of the king's works at Westminster and the Tower of London, 'for making a tabernacle over the head of an image, made in the likeness of the king, placed at the end of the great hall' in Westminster palace.[9] Richard enjoyed his own image, and fortunately we still have two magnificent examples of it: the portrait in Westminster Abbey, and the gorgeous Wilton Diptych. He probably adopted his mother's image of a white hind as his own famous white hart, and he adopted the broomcod as his personal symbol.[10] Richard may have chosen the white hart and found it particularly appealing because of the play on his name *Richart*, i.e. 'rich' and 'hart'.[11] In the ninth year of his reign, 1385/6, Richard wore a long red velvet gown embroidered with harts of pearl and crowns. For Easter 1386, Richard and Queen Anne had long blue velvet gowns and hoods embroidered with white harts lying under trees of gold.[12]

At the parliament of 20 October to 6 December 1385 which had made de Vere marquis of Dublin, the English lords issued thirteen recommendations to improve the conduct of government.[13] A document was presented to Richard II called 'The Advice of the

Lords Touching the Good Government of the King and of the Realm'. It emphasised the need for Richard to be guided and advised by the members of his council rather than 'informers' and for suitable persons to be appointed as his chief ministers. Richard was not amused, and declared that he would change his ministers when it pleased him. He also stated 'the king will do as he pleases' in response to the idea that his household and the exchequer should be subject to annual external review. Part of the 'advice' was, 'May it please the king to attach to himself persons of estate, probity and honour, and to associate with them and eschew the company of others; if he does this great good and honour will come to him, and he will win the hearts and love of his people. But if he does the opposite, then the contrary will happen, to the great danger of himself and his realm, which God forbid.'[14]

In late 1385 and January 1386, the titular king of Armenia – or more accurately, the king of Armenian Cilicia, the southern coastal region of Anatolia or Asia Minor, modern-day Turkey – visited England. He was Levon V, born in 1342 as Leo de Lusignan, son of John de Lusignan, constable of Armenia and nephew of King Gosdantin II of Armenia. Levon's mother may have been the daughter of the king of Georgia and she may not have been married to his father, and Levon was the successor and distant cousin of Gosdantin IV or Richard, who perhaps acted as Richard II's godfather in January 1367 and who was assassinated in 1373. Levon surrendered his kingdom to the Mamluk forces who had invaded Armenian Cilicia in 1375, and spent the rest of his life as an exile outside his kingdom, much of it in Spain and then in Paris, where he was to die in November 1393. Other members of his family were taken to Cairo as prisoners (the Mamluks were a Muslim warrior dynasty of former slaves who ruled Egypt and Syria from the middle of the thirteenth century until 1517, when they were overthrown by the Ottomans).[15] In late 1393 Levon was to be buried at St Denis in Paris, where most of the kings of France are also buried, and his tomb can still be seen there.

Richard granted Levon and his household a safe conduct to travel to England on 24 October 1385, and gave the master of his household, John Rusp, permission to bring a large amount of wine to England for Levon's use.[16] Levon arrived at Dover in late 1385 and was met by Edmund of Langley and Thomas of Woodstock, and was taken to the palace of Eltham in Kent, where he met the eighteen-year-old king and spent Christmas with him and Queen Anne. Levon had little Latin or

French and of course no English, so communication must have proved somewhat tricky and required interpreters. During Levon's visit, Richard showed him round Westminster Abbey at night in candlelight, dressed in his 'most impressive finery', to show the other king the royal insignia used at his coronation, which was the second time in a few months that Richard had apparently spontaneously decided to visit the abbey at night. Two or three years later, Richard – always interested in royal history – commissioned a monk of Westminster Abbey to learn whether his regalia dated from the time of King Alfred in the late ninth century and had been used by him.[17] A few days before Christmas 1385, Richard had paid £2 to the painter Walter Walton to make two images 'in likeness of the king' and someone called 'Houell' or Howell, unidentified, to be placed at the end of the king's great hall at Westminster; perhaps he showed these to Levon as well.[18]

At some point during his sojourn in England Levon gave a gift of a 'tablet of jasper' to Richard's aunt by marriage Isabel of Castile, which on her death in 1392 Isabel left to her brother-in-law John of Gaunt, and stayed with Richard's uncle Thomas of Woodstock at Pleshey in Essex.[19] Walsingham says sourly that Levon came to England on a pretext of making peace between Richard and Charles VI of France, but that 'he alone saw the profits of his arrival' and that Levon 'wheedled many gifts from Christian kings, to such an extent that he was more fortunate as a fugitive in foreign lands than as ruler of his realm with his own people'. The Westminster chronicler also wrote that Levon was 'very cunning'.[20] Certainly, Richard settled £1,000 on Levon when he left England on 3 February 1386, which was intended to be an annual settlement given in two instalments at Easter and Michaelmas until 'by God's assistance' Levon recovered his kingdom from which he had been expelled, according to Richard, 'by the enemies of God [i.e. the Mamluks] and his own deluded subjects'. Richard added fiercely, 'The curse of God, St Edward [the Confessor] and the king on any who contravene this grant!' (He had used the same formulation a few months earlier when granting his beloved Robert de Vere the royal castle of Queenborough in March 1385.)[21] Levon responded by making Richard an executor of his will.[22]

Richard evidently was most impressed with Levon and perhaps shared his vision of the kings of England and France uniting in the future against a common enemy, the Turks, and appears to have found Levon congenial company. The English magnates, however, regarded

Levon as a sponger and a spy, and therefore prevented his return to England later in the year and again some years later, despite Richard granting Levon a safe conduct to visit him on 18 March 1386 and another one on 11 December 1392.[23] The two men did keep in touch, though: Levon wrote to Richard from Bruges in the county of Flanders on 2 November 1386, and Richard replied in French probably not long afterwards, addressing Levon as 'Lyoun by the grace of God king of Armenia, our very dear and beloved cousin' (although they were only very distantly related, this was a polite and conventional way of writing to a fellow king).[24] The letter discusses a possible treaty between England and France and Levon being received in Paris on 4 October. Richard referred to Charles VI as 'our adversary of France' and added 'king of France' to his own list of titles, as he almost always did.

The festivities of the feast of Saint George were held somewhat later than usual in April 1386 after Richard sent messengers to various Knights of the Garter in the west of England to delay the feast, without explaining why, on 3 April.[25] This April, the new Ladies of the Garter included Robert de Vere's mother Maud, *née* Ufford, dowager countess of Oxford; Thomas Mowbray's wife and the earl of Arundel's daughter Elizabeth, *née* Fitzalan, countess of Nottingham; and Richard II's first cousin Constance of York, only daughter of Edmund of Langley and Isabel of Castile. Constance was about ten or eleven, but had already been married for some years to Thomas Despenser, son and heir of Lord Despenser and nephew of the bishop of Norwich, a descendant of Edward I but still perhaps rather a poor match for a girl who was the granddaughter of two kings. The earl of Arundel, Richard Fitzalan, was one of only two new Knights of the Garter in 1386, the other being Richard's standard-bearer Sir Nicholas Samesfield, who had been one of the executors of Edward of Woodstock's will. The following year, 1387, Constance's brother Edward of York became a Knight of the Garter, and the new Ladies of the Garter included Katherine Swynford, rather remarkably as she was at that time merely the former governess of John of Gaunt's two eldest daughters, the child of a herald and the widow of an unremarkable knight. She was also, of course, Gaunt's long-term mistress and father of four of his children, though she did not accompany him during his long sojourn in Spain which began in 1386. In May 1386, Arnold Brocas received £5 for painting and maintaining images in the great hall at Westminster, including the recently painted images of the king himself, and for repairing a bridge there.[26] Some years later, Richard II employed a man named John Lettreford full time on wages of 6*d* a day for the sole purpose of repairing the borders and dorsers of his tapestries.[27]

On 28 April 1386, Richard and Juan I of Castile made a treaty of alliance and mutual assistance, and at this time Richard also made a treaty of perpetual alliance with King João I of Portugal.[28] This was a confirmation of his grandfather Edward III's treaty with João's father King Fernando in 1373, and in the twenty-first century is still in force. John of Gaunt decided to try to make good his and his wife Constanza's claim to the throne of Castile, and departed from England with an army in the summer of 1386.[29] Gaunt would not return to England for well over three years, not until November 1389, and Richard would miss his calming influence. The duke began planning his journey in early 1386, and took with him his daughters Philippa, Elizabeth and Catalina. John of Gaunt was soon to become, whether he was happy about it or not, the father-in-law of Richard's unpleasantly violent half-brother Sir John Holland.

On or around 24 June 1386 at Plymouth, shortly before departure, Holland married Gaunt's second daughter Elizabeth of Lancaster, the younger of his two daughters from his first marriage to Blanche of Lancaster. Elizabeth had previously been married to the young earl of Pembroke, grandson of the countess of Norfolk, who was almost a decade her junior and still only thirteen years old in the summer of 1386. Elizabeth was apparently already pregnant by Holland at the time of their wedding, and her marriage to Hastings therefore had to be hastily annulled. Ultimately she and Holland had six children, of whom four survived childhood, and their eldest son was named Richard after his uncle the king. Holland sailed to Spain with his wife and father-in-law; for all his brutal behaviour he was not much of a soldier, as it turned out, and failed to make much impression as constable of John of Gaunt's army or even to maintain discipline in their ranks.[30] He returned to England in April 1388, and a few weeks later was made earl of Huntingdon by his half-brother the king with an income of about 2,000 marks a year. John of Gaunt's other two daughters Philippa and Catalina were still unmarried in 1386, and Gaunt hoped to use their marriages, if necessary and if his campaign proved unsuccessful, to bargain away his claims to Castile.[31] Philippa and Catalina of Lancaster as the granddaughters of a king were, one assumes, resigned to this fate.

On 5 July 1386, Richard II paid over £25 for a hunting knife 'to be used in the woods', and for a hunting horn ornamented with gold which weighed sixteen ounces and also had tassels of green silk.[32] The king may not have been a fan of jousting, or rather of taking part in a joust himself, but in other ways his tastes were more conventional for a man of his station in the late fourteenth century, and an enjoyment of hunting was certainly conventional. His cousin Edward, son and heir of Edmund of Langley and later duke of York, wrote a book about hunting called *The Master of Game* in the early 1400s; it is the oldest treatise on hunting in the English language (although is mostly a translation from an earlier French work). William Twiti, chief huntsman of Richard and Edward of York's great-grandfather Edward II, wrote the first book on hunting in England in the 1320s, though it was in French. A year later, Richard spent 20 marks, or £13 6s 8d, on a sword for himself, which was ornamented with silver and gilt.[33] When, or if, he ever had a reason to use a sword is unclear; presumably it was merely intended for ceremonial occasions.

In or around 1386/87, the royal favourite Robert de Vere fell in love (or more probably in lust) with Agnes Lanchecron or Launcecrona or Landkrona, one of Queen Anne's close personal attendants and herself apparently of quite high birth. Two of de Vere's attendants, John Banastre of Lancashire and William Stanley of Cheshire, were imprisoned in chains at Winchester Castle sometime before 5 March 1389, having been arrested for abducting Agnes, called 'late damsel of the queen's chamber', at de Vere's command. Both men had escaped from Winchester Castle shortly before this date and were pardoned for 'breaking prison'.[34] Agnes has sometimes been identified as a landgravine – Jean Froissart calls her one – though this identification is not certain, and may represent a confusion with the rather mysterious and unidentified 'landgravine of Luxembourg' who accompanied Anne on her journey to England in late 1381 (and in fact returned to the Continent shortly afterwards).

According to Thomas Walsingham, Jean Froissart and the Westminster chronicler, de Vere had his marriage to Richard II's first cousin Philippa Coucy annulled in order to marry Agnes Launcecrona instead in 1387. Supposedly the 'divorce' of de Vere and Philippa Coucy was declared invalid by Pope Urban VI on 17 October 1389, at least according to the Westminster chronicle. It is unclear what became of Agnes Launcecrona, whether she truly married de Vere or not, and if she did, if she accompanied him abroad when he was exiled or remained in England. Nothing at all is known about her except what is said by three gossipy chroniclers, and one entry on the Patent Roll which states that she was abducted on de Vere's orders by two of his men sometime before early 1389 and presumably before he fled from England in late 1387. Thomas Walsingham says venomously but certainly incorrectly that Launcecrona was a saddler's daughter, *sellarii filiam*, and that she was 'low class and foul' or 'ugly'.[35] If she was an attendant of the queen, as the Westminster chronicle, Froissart and the entry relating to her on the Patent Roll state, being 'low class and foul' seems very unlikely.

Froissart says that de Vere was hated as a wanton who wilfully degraded his wife with 'promiscuous adulteries', and that he 'greatly trespassed against the lord of Coucy's daughter, who was his wife lawfully spoused, and forsook her without any title of reason, but by false and evil temptation and deceit took another wife, a damsel of the queen of England's'. The Westminster chronicle says that de Vere's mother Maud, *née* Ufford, had such a great love for Philippa, even more than if she had been her own daughter, that she did not hesitate to curse her own son for bringing about the divorce. It claims that de Vere sent a clerk named John Ripon to the pope in order to obtain a divorce, and that Ripon did so by obtaining false witnesses gathered for that purpose. This story cannot be verified.[36] Walsingham also says that Richard II and Anne of Bohemia themselves asked the pope to annul the marriage of Robert de Vere and Philippa Coucy, and that Philippa's uncle Thomas of Woodstock was at the forefront of the barons furious at de Vere's, and the king's, treatment of a royal lady. The poet John Lydgate (*c.* 1370–1450) also refers to the annulment in his short work *Of the Sodein Fal of Princes in Oure Dayes*, written in the 1430s:

> This Duc of Yrland, of England Chaumburleyn.
> Which in plesaunce so he ledde his lyf,
> Tyl fortune of his welth hade disdeyn,
> That causeles he parted was frome his wyf,
> Which grounde was of gret debate and stryf,
> And his destruccion, if I shal not lye,
> For banned he was, and did in meschef dye. (Lines 43–49)

The supposed annulment of Robert de Vere's marriage to his royal wife and subsequent remarriage to an attendant of Queen Anne, presumably a Bohemian lady, would therefore seem to be a historical fact, though it is curious that there is little if any confirmation of the story in other, more reliable sources. There are no extant petitions to the pope either from de Vere or from the king or queen of England asking for the annulment to be granted, no petitions from Philippa Coucy protesting it, no real confirmation that de Vere married Agnes Launcecrona, no record of why Richard II – for all his undoubted love of de Vere – would have permitted such an insult to a woman who was the granddaughter of a king and his own cousin, not even a copy of or any reference to the alleged annulment at all. The entry on the Patent Roll which states that two of de Vere's men had been imprisoned in chains for abducting Launcecrona hardly indicates that she went to de Vere willingly or that there was anything romantic or loving about this situation at all; entirely the opposite, in fact.

Immediately after discussing this matter, Walsingham goes on to claim that Robert de Vere maintained a hold over the king by forcing Richard II to do his bidding by magical spells, so his testimony on this point hardly seems trustworthy. It is entirely plausible that de Vere would have embarked on a brazen extramarital affair with Agnes Launcecrona or even that, as the king's favourite and a highborn nobleman, would have felt entitled to her and so had her brought to him by his men whether or not she was willing. It is also plausible that de Vere and his wife Philippa did not get on well and lived apart; their marriage produced no children, and of course not all arranged marriages among the medieval nobility proved successful on a personal level.

It is not at all clear, however, why de Vere would have felt the need to end his marriage to the king's cousin in order to wed his mistress. Medieval noblemen often took mistresses, sometimes perfectly openly; no one batted an eyelid. It is true that in 1396 John of Gaunt married his long-term mistress Katherine Swynford, mother of four of his children, which was scandalous enough, but this was only after his second wife Constanza of Castile had died after more than two decades of marriage. It surely did not enter Gaunt's mind to annul his marriage to Constanza in order to marry Katherine, a woman of much lower rank than himself and his two previous wives Constanza and Blanche of Lancaster. Philippa Coucy, who had no brothers, was the joint heir with her elder sister Marie to their father the lord of Coucy, and Robert de Vere therefore stood to benefit financially from his marriage to her, as well as the immense prestige which came from marrying a king's granddaughter. (In 1401 Philippa and Marie Coucy agreed, after much legal process, that Philippa would receive their parents' English lands and Marie their father's French ones.)[37] Marriage to an obscure Bohemian or German woman could not begin to match these advantages.

Throughout the 1390s and into the 1400s, Philippa Coucy was always referred to in the chancery rolls as 'Philippa, duchess of Ireland' (de Vere was made duke of Ireland in 1386) or 'the king's kinswoman the duchess of Ireland' or 'Madam of Ireland' or 'Philippa late the wife of Robert de Vere', which strongly implies that she, not Launcecrona, was de Vere's widow.[38] After de Vere's death overseas in 1392, Philippa was assigned dower as his widow.[39] There is not a single mention of Agnes Launcecrona as de Vere's wife in the chancery rolls, or any official confirmation that de Vere ever married her. On 18 October 1389, an entry on the Patent Roll refers to 'the king's kinswoman Philippa, duchess of Ireland' and a grant made to her by 'her husband Robert de Veer, late duke of Ireland', and another on 16 November 1389 also makes it clear that de Vere was then Philippa Coucy's husband.[40] An inventory of de Vere's goods made after his flight from England reveals that among his possessions in Chester were two new saddles *pour damoiselles de Boeme*, 'for young ladies of Bohemia', and an old saddle in Bohemian style, though this only implies that Agnes was at some point in de Vere's company (which we know anyway from the Patent Roll entry relating to her abduction), not necessarily that he married her.[41]

Divorce as we know it was impossible; only death could end a marriage. It was possible in some rare situations for the pope to grant an annulment, which meant that the marriage had never been valid in the first place and required some kind of pre-existing impediment: that the couple were too closely related and no dispensation for consanguinity had been awarded, for example, or that there was a spiritual connection, if the close relative of one partner was the godparent of the other partner and no dispensation for this had been received. Robert de Vere could not simply say to the pope that he had grown tired of his wife and wished to marry his mistress instead so please could he have a divorce. There is no entry in the Calendar of Papal Letters to indicate when or why Pope Urban VI annulled Oxford and Philippa's marriage, if he ever did and if the whole story is more than mere gossip.[42]

One of the very few references to Anne of Bohemia in the Calendar of Papal Letters is undated, and has nothing to do with her supposed encouragement of de Vere's divorce: she was given permission by Pope Boniface IX, on an unstated date sometime between his election on 2 November 1389 and Anne's death four and a half years later, to 'enter as often as she please, with a suite of fifty honest persons of either sex, any monastery of enclosed religious women and to eat and drink therein, but not to pass the night'.[43] Her seventeen-year-old brother Johann von Görlitz, margrave of Moravia and Brandenburg, married in Prague on 10 February 1388. His bride was Richardis of Sweden and Mecklenburg, sometimes also called Katherine, daughter of the king of Sweden and duke of Mecklenburg. As Anne was apparently kept well informed of her brothers' activities, she and Richard II were surely aware of Johann's wedding. At an uncertain date after 31 March 1387, Richard sent a letter in Latin to his mother-in-law the dowager empress Elżbieta congratulating her on the coronation of her elder son Zikmund as king of Hungary, the ceremony having taken place in Székesfehérvár on that date. As always, Richard addressed Elżbieta as 'the most excellent and serene princess, mother of our beloved' and 'your most excellent imperial highness'.[44] It is likely that Elżbieta kept herself informed about the state of her elder daughter and son-in-law's marriage and about events in faraway England, and that she too felt sorrow over their ongoing childlessness.

10

'Our Sea-Walled Garden Is Full of Weeds': A Threatened Invasion of England, 1386–1387

In the spring and summer of 1386, the French planned an invasion of England which was to be led by the seventeen-year-old Charles VI in person. They and their Castilian allies raised a great army at Sluys in Flanders, the largest force seen on either side thus far in a war that had begun half a century earlier. 'Never, since God created the world, had so many ships and great vessels been seen together as there were that year in the port of Sluys and off the coast,' gasped Jean Froissart; there were 1387 of them. Froissart also wrote that 'right through the summer until September there was a continual milling of flour and baking of biscuits' all along the coast of northern France and Flanders as the king fed his army, and that supplies of salt, eggs, onions, flour, beans, wine, hay, tallow and other provisions and clothes were pouring into Flanders all the time. He added that the French had taken possession of all the big ships from Seville in southern Spain to Prussia in northern Germany.[1]

For several months from April until October 1386, invasion was expected in England at any moment, and it caused great anxiety. The ever-spiteful Thomas Walsingham described the panic among the citizens of London: 'They grew very fearful, and like frightened rabbits and anxious mice they sought secluded spots ... they rushed like drunkards to the walls, pulled down, demolished and destroyed the adjacent houses ... Not a single Frenchman set foot on ship, no enemy set sail, but the Londoners, as though all the land around had been vanquished and conquered, were as fearful and agitated as though they could see the enemy before their gates.'[2] The mayor of London Nicholas Brembre took measures to ensure the capital was prepared for a possible invasion, and on 5 September ordered that all Londoners who had left the city return within two weeks 'in view of an expected attack by the enemy.'[3]

Earlier in 1386, in anticipation of 'imminent invasion of the coasts of England by the king's enemies of France, Spain [i.e. Castile], Flanders and Brittany', Richard II and his council ordered all the inhabitants of the Isle of Thanet in Kent to take themselves and their goods to Dover Castle or to the towns of Rye or Sandwich, 'there to remain safely'. The inhabitants of Sandwich were told to remain in the town to defend it and to resist the invasion. Simon Burley, as the warden of the Cinque Ports, was empowered to imprison anyone who refused.[4] Richard's former brother-in-law the duke of Brittany was one of the men urging Charles VI to invade, and according to Froissart so was another of his brothers-in-law, the count of St Pol. These men and the royal uncle the duke of Burgundy supposedly said to the French king, 'Why shouldn't we go over to England for once and have a look at the country and people? We'll get to know our way about there, just as the English did in their time in France.' The Canterbury chronicler William Thorne reported that the French wished to invade England 'to wipe out all its people and to destroy its language', a common theme, and blamed Richard's chamberlain and close ally Sir Simon Burley (whom he called 'the crafty turncoat') for creating discord in the realm which caused the French to plan their invasion.[5]

On 12 and 22 September Charles VI was 'reported to be about to invade England', and as late as the middle of October 1386, the French invasion was still feared: there are references to Welsh archers and knights ordered to assemble at various English ports 'to resist the malice of the king's enemies'.[6] No one was quite sure where the invasion force might land – though on 26 September the location was thought to be Orwell in Suffolk – and castles along the coast in places as far apart as Cornwall and Norfolk were ordered to be repaired and strengthened from April 1386 onwards.[7] There were those who sought to benefit from the panic and chaos: on 25 September knights in four counties were ordered to investigate certain 'armourers or vendors of arms, armour or horses' who were raising their prices to take advantage of the men joining the king's army. It was to be proclaimed that such equipment had to be sold at the same rates as previously.[8]

Jean Froissart says that the English plan was to light torches and build big fires on hillsides as a warning if they saw the French fleet approaching, and to let Charles VI and his army land and march around unopposed for three or four days. The English would then attack the French ships, steal their supplies and also lay the countryside to waste, so that Charles and his army would go hungry and would be unable to retreat to France as their ships had been captured. In the end, despite the massive expenditure on ships, soldiers and supplies for which the unfortunate French people had been taxed to the hilt, the planned invasion of England in 1386 did not take place thanks to various delays, illness, mishaps and arguments among the commanders, and indeed never would take place. William Thorne declared that 'the good Lord, through the merits of those saints who defend Kentishmen, considered our king's innocence and the traitor's [Simon Burley's] plans, and by a persistent contrary wind, He prevented the royal fleet from leaving port'.[9]

A parliament opened at Westminster on 1 October 1386 which sat until 28 November and became known as the Wonderful Parliament. On 13 October, the nineteen-year-old king gave his dearest friend Robert de Vere, earl of Oxford, the unprecedented title of duke of Ireland. Before this, the only dukes in English history had been members of the royal family: Richard's then seven-year-old father Edward of Woodstock, duke of Cornwall, was the first in 1337, the wealthy royal cousin Henry of Lancaster was the second in 1351 and Edward III's second son Lionel of Antwerp the third, followed by Duke Henry's son-in-law John of Gaunt as the second duke of Lancaster and then Edward III's fourth and fifth sons Edmund and Thomas. Richard II's controversial decision demonstrates the depth of his feeling for de Vere, and proved remarkably unpopular. De Vere was a nobleman of ancient and impeccable lineage and married to a granddaughter of Edward III, but was not of royal birth, and Richard's decision to elevate him to the same title as his uncles John, Edmund and Thomas caused a scandal. The date of de Vere's elevation was also significant: it was the feast day of St Edward the Confessor, one of the king's favourite saints.

Also during this parliament, Richard II made the very ill-advised comment that he would seek help from his cousin Charles VI against those who infringed his liberty. Almost certainly this was simply a spontaneous riposte to hostility or perceived hostility by a man who often did overreact, but it was a foolish thing to say, especially given the very recent, and indeed still ongoing, threat of a French invasion of

Richard's kingdom. The duke of Gloucester and his ally the bishop of Ely, who was the earl of Arundel's younger brother Thomas Arundel, were provoked into reminding Richard of the fate in 1327 of his great-grandfather Edward II (who was also Gloucester's grandfather). In effect the two men threatened him with deposition by reminding him that 'if a king by his folly and injustice alienated himself from his people' then he could be deposed and replaced with another member of the royal dynasty, as had happened in the not too distant past.[10] It is possible that they would have chosen to attack Richard on the grounds of illegitimacy, given his mother's previous marriages to two men at the same time and the irregularity of his parents' union.[11]

On the other hand, Edward II's baronial enemies had also threatened him with deposition several times during his reign, and there were certainly no grounds for attacking Edward's legitimacy or his right to be king; there was no doubt whatsoever that he was the eldest surviving son of Edward I, and legitimate. What had provoked Gloucester and Arundel's threat was Richard II taking himself off to his manor of Eltham in a fury, where he remained for most of the parliament, after the lords and commons demanded the impeachment of his chancellor Michael de la Pole. Richard declared that he would not 'dismiss the meanest scullion from his kitchen at their behest'. The duke of Gloucester and Bishop Arundel were the men sent from parliament to Eltham to inform Richard that they could make no progress until he returned, to which he replied that he would go back within three days, and apparently did so. Michael de la Pole was subsequently removed from the office of chancellor. Sometime before 19 November 1386, Richard was also forced to consent to the formation of a committee of reform called the Commission of Government, which was to comprise fourteen lords (of whom few were friends of the king) who would control the royal administration and rule the kingdom for one year. This was a deep humiliation for Richard II, who was now nineteen yet still not even close to being the real ruler of his realm. Richard and his friends retaliated a few months later by posing ten questions to judges on the legality of the proceedings; Richard's critics responded by formally accusing the king's five leading supporters of treason.[12]

The working period for the commissioners was one year from the date of the committee's formation, i.e. from November 1386 until November 1387. Richard tried to thwart them by spending most of this year travelling around his kingdom; with the exception of a few days in early

February 1387, he did not set foot in London or Westminster between mid-October 1386 and 10 November 1387. Instead he undertook what became known as his 'gyration' as he progressed around his kingdom for nine months between February and November 1387, and visited Chester for the first time that July.[13] The king appointed Robert de Vere as justice of Chester on 8 September, and Cheshire was the part of the country where his support was at its strongest and from where his future bodyguards the notorious Cheshire archers would come.

At Banbury on 17 June 1387, Richard made a payment of five hundred pounds to Wilhelm, duke of Jülich and Guelders, as his annual fee for paying homage and fealty to Richard.[14] While at Westminster in early February 1387, Richard dealt with the situation of a whale which had been beached in Lincolnshire and which by right belonged to Queen Anne, but which had been stolen by 'certain evildoers'. On his return to Westminster nine months later, the king ordered a skinner of London 'to take as many pelterers [dealers in animal skins] and artificers as may be necessary for the peltry [pelts or fur] of Queen Anne'.[15] In April 1383, as noted above, Richard had given permission to men in Warwick to found a guild in honour of St George the Martyr as long as they promised to 'celebrate divine service daily for the good estate of the king, the queen and their children'. On 25 November 1387, Richard again gave permission to a group of men to found a guild in Lichfield in honour of the Virgin Mary and John the Baptist, but on this occasion asked only for daily prayers for 'the good estate of the king and queen and for their souls after death and the souls of their progenitors'.[16] Any possible children of the royal couple were not mentioned, and perhaps, almost six years after their wedding, Richard had given up hoping that he and Anne might produce any.

Meanwhile on the first day of 1387, Richard's kinsman and possibly one of his godfathers King Carlos II 'the Bad' of Navarre died a horrible death: he was burned alive in his own palace in Pamplona, apparently when the alcohol-soaked sheets he had wrapped himself in to cure his leprosy or another disease caught fire. This hideous demise became the talk of Europe. Just five days later, on 6 January 1387, in Barcelona, another Spanish king died: Pedro IV of Aragon, who had reigned for over fifty years, been married four times, and who had imprisoned his nephew, Richard's godfather Jaime IV of Majorca. Pedro of Aragon was succeeded by his eldest son Juan I, child of Pedro's third wife

Leonor of Sicily, while Carlos II of Navarre was succeeded by his eldest son Carlos III, a first cousin of Charles VI of France.

England was still heavily involved in the affairs of the Iberian peninsula, and John of Gaunt, duke of Lancaster, had left England to travel there again in the summer of 1386. In February 1387, Gaunt's eldest child Philippa became queen-consort of Portugal when she married King João I, usually known to history as João of Aviz. Born on 31 March 1360, Philippa was almost twenty-seven at the time of her wedding, an advanced age by the standards of the time when most royal women (her aunt Isabella of Woodstock being a notable exception) married in their early or mid-teens. King João was three years Philippa's senior, and already had three illegitimate children, including a daughter, Beatriz, who later married two English noblemen. João himself was also illegitimate, the son of King Pedro I (who died in January 1367) and a woman named Teresa, and had formerly taken monastic orders: he was the grand master of the chivalric Order of Aviz, a military monastic order in Portugal in the style of the defunct Knights Templar.

Between 1388 and 1402 Philippa of Lancaster and João I of Portugal had nine children, of whom six survived infancy and are known to Portuguese historians as the Illustrious Generation (Ínclita Geração). They included a saint of the Catholic Church, the early explorer Henrique or Henry the Navigator, Isabel, duchess of Burgundy, and Duarte, the eldest, João's successor as king and named after his English forebears (Duarte being the Portuguese equivalent of the English name Edward). Philippa's younger half-sister Catalina of Lancaster married her cousin Enrique of Trastámara, heir to the throne of Castile, sometime before September 1388 in the cathedral of Palencia north of Madrid; she was fifteen or sixteen and he not yet nine. John of Gaunt had finally accepted that he and his wife Constanza would never rule Castile, and officially surrendered their claims to the throne: he made a peace treaty with Castile on 12 June 1387.[17] The marriage of their daughter Catalina to Enrique, grandson of the usurper Enrique of Trastámara, provided an elegant solution which united the rival branches of the Castilian royal family. Catalina and the younger Enrique succeeded as king and queen of Castile on the death of Enrique's father Juan I in 1390, and were the parents of Juan II (b. 1405), himself the father of the famous Isabel the Catholic, queen of Castile in her own right, and grandfather of Henry VIII of England's first queen Katherine of Aragon.

11

'Sorrow's Eye, Glazed with Blinding Tears': The Merciless Lords Appellant, 1387–1388

Five noblemen formed a group at the parliament of late 1386 and somewhat later called themselves the Lords Appellant because of their intention to appeal some of the king's chief supporters for treason, bring them to trial and reduce their influence over the king. The five men were Richard's uncle Thomas of Woodstock, duke of Gloucester; the earl of Arundel, Richard Fitzalan; Thomas Beauchamp, earl of Warwick; and, surprisingly, Richard's cousin Henry of Lancaster, earl of Derby, and Thomas Mowbray, earl of Nottingham, usually an ally and friend of the king. Mowbray was the earl of Arundel's son-in-law, which perhaps swayed his decision to join the other men, and it seems that there was also fierce rivalry between Mowbray and Robert de Vere and a long struggle between them over access to the king and his favour. By mid-1387 Mowbray had admitted defeat and left court.

Henry of Lancaster, in the absence of his father John of Gaunt in Spain, may also have resented the influence of de Vere, who was much closer to the king than he himself was.[1] This, however, can only be speculation as there is little evidence to explain precisely how Henry of Lancaster and Thomas Mowbray joined the three senior Appellants. There was something of a disconnect between the three older men, who were all much the king's senior (they were born around 1338, 1346 and 1355 respectively) and were decidedly 'old school', and the fashionable young courtiers who surrounded Richard.

Thomas of Woodstock, duke of Gloucester, was, however, a rather more rounded and interesting personality than one might assume from his frequent aggression and his hostility to his nephew. He was literate and left numerous books on his death in 1397, and enjoyed music; he kept a blind harper in his household (this may have been William Dodmore, who received an income of £10 from Richard II in January 1392 and who was then described as a blind harper in the king's service). For his house in London, Thomas purchased tapestries featuring angels playing musical instruments.[2]

Earlier in 1387, the earl of Arundel, accompanied by his son-in-law Thomas Mowbray, had led a highly successful naval expedition to France, and captured sixty-eight ships. More than 8,000 barrels of wine were also seized, which were sold in England at less than half the usual price. According to Thomas Walsingham, Arundel did not keep even one barrel for himself but allowed 'the commons of England' to enjoy all of it, which, as it was no doubt intended to do, made him extremely popular. Walsingham goes on to declare that Richard II's friend Robert de Vere belittled the earl of Arundel's deeds to the king on the grounds that he had done nothing out of the ordinary except attack merchants, and at this juncture makes his famous criticism that the men who surrounded Richard II were knights of the goddess of love Venus rather than of the god of war Mars. Apparently de Vere's whispering campaign against Arundel and his expedition was so successful that when Thomas Mowbray came to Richard, the king was dismissive and did not even smile at him.[3] The king's behaviour on this occasion may have been one of the factors which pushed Mowbray into joining the Appellants.

King Richard finally returned to his capital after his travels on or around 10 November 1387. On the 14th, the duke of Gloucester and the earls of Arundel and Warwick marched to Waltham Cross in Hertfordshire and formally accused, or appealed, five of Richard's main supporters of treason. These five supporters were Robert de Vere, duke of Ireland; Michael de la Pole, earl of Suffolk and formerly chancellor of England; Alexander Neville, archbishop of York, a nobleman by birth and closely related to the earls of Stafford, whose inclusion in the list of the Appellants' chief targets is rather puzzling; Nicholas Brembre (or Bramber), former mayor of London and a wealthy merchant of the city, a member of Richard's council when the king asked the judges about the legality of the reform commission in 1387, and who had subsequently tried to rally support for Richard in the capital; and Robert Tresilian, chief justice of the court of King's Bench, who had probably drafted the questions to the judges and who was said to have given aid and counsel to de Vere, Pole and Neville. He was also the infamously harsh judge who had condemned many rebels to death after the 1381 uprising. In the summer of 1387 Richard's advisers had counselled him to take revenge on those men who had humiliated him in the last parliament.[4] Mediators arranged a meeting with Richard II at Westminster on 17 November, where the three older Lords Appellant reiterated their intention to proceed against the five men. With little other choice, Richard agreed that their appeal should be heard in the parliament to be held in February 1388.

The three older Lords Appellant met at Huntingdon in arms on 12 December 1387 and were joined there by Henry of Lancaster and Thomas Mowbray, and set off for Waltham Cross. Supposedly Richard set ambushes for Gloucester, Arundel and Warwick, but they evaded them and gathered in the wood of Haringey near London with a large following. Richard went to Westminster hoping to attack the men with the help of the city. The archbishop of Canterbury intervened and begged Richard to allow the three men into his presence and not to harm them, and conducted the men to Richard's presence in the great hall of Westminster.

Richard was furious. 'How dare you rebel and take up arms against the peace of our kingdom?'

His uncle the duke of Gloucester answered. 'We are not rebels, nor do we arm ourselves against the peace of your kingdom but to protect your life against the enemies of ourselves and of the realm, for which cause any man might bear arms.' Gloucester went on to ask Richard to hold a parliament on 2 February 1388 and to have his 'sycophants' appear there as well.

This speech did nothing to dissolve Richard's anger. He snapped, 'You shall have a parliament, but I shall not harm them, and I shall treat you as less than the lowest of your kitchen-boys.'

'You should treat me as no less than a king's son,' Gloucester retorted. Hastily remembering to whom he was talking, he dropped to one knee before his nephew and reminded him that he was indeed a king's son.[5] Richard's reaction to this statement is not recorded, and it might not have been favourable, reminding him as it did of the rather awkward fact that although he was a king he was not the son of a king, whereas his hated uncle was. Richard originally agreed to meet all three lords the following day and to permit reform to take place, but then changed his mind and took himself off to the Tower.

Meanwhile, Michael de la Pole, earl of Suffolk, and Alexander Neville, archbishop of York, fled to the north of England. Robert de

Vere travelled to the royalist stronghold of Cheshire to raise an army, then returned towards London 'with the king's banner unfurled' in an open declaration of war.[6] It fell to twenty-year-old Henry of Lancaster to cut off de Vere and prevent him reaching London. Henry secured the bridges across the Thames, which de Vere would have to cross, having moved swiftly to reach them first. The royal favourite fell into Henry's trap at Radcot Bridge between Cirencester and Oxford on 20 December 1387. The bridge had been deliberately broken in three places and Henry of Lancaster and his men, in thick fog, were waiting for de Vere. The latter, seeing that he was trapped, jumped onto his fastest horse and galloped as hard as he could west along the river, his escape aided by the winter fog. No one was able to catch up with him, and he managed to strip off his armour and swim across the Thames, reach his Kent castle of Queenborough safely, and from there flee abroad.[7]

Walsingham says that Richard's letters to de Vere were found among the possessions de Vere was forced to leave behind by the Thames, and that they urged de Vere to come to London with great power. If he did so, *rex cor apponeret ad vivendum et moriendum cum eo*; that is, Richard was promising to bestow his heart on de Vere and to live and die with him.[8] De Vere, although his family was relatively poor by the standards of the fourteenth-century English nobility, acquired great riches thanks to his close relationship with the king. The inventory of his goods taken after his flight from England included, as well as the three Bohemian saddles mentioned above, silver plate with a value of almost £100 and other items worth almost £300. He also owned a set of bed hangings embroidered with butterflies.[9]

Also on 20 December 1387, Michael de la Pole, earl of Suffolk, was ordered to be arrested, though he had probably already fled.[10] The Lancastrian chronicler Henry Knighton tells a story that Pole escaped to Calais and disguised himself as a Flemish poulterer carrying a basket of capons.[11] Pole never saw England or Richard II again: he died still in exile in Paris in September 1389, in his late fifties. His son Michael the younger, almost exactly the same age as the king, was lucky enough to be married to the earl of Warwick's niece Katherine Stafford and survived events of 1387, and was restored to his father's earldom a few years later. A distraught Richard II spent Christmas 1387 at Windsor, with 'Queen Anna and her Bohemians', according to Thomas Walsingham.[12] He then moved the few miles to the Tower of London, a much safer and more defensible location, and the five Lords Appellant also arrived there on or about 27 December.

Some of the king's allies who had accompanied him, including his uncle the duke of York and the bishops of Ely, Hereford and Winchester, went out to negotiate with the Appellants, and on 30 December 1387 the five Appellants entered the Tower with at least 500 armed followers, locking the gate behind them. Richard greeted them with as much courtesy as he could muster and led them into his private chapel to talk to them.[13] It seems that at least two of them, the duke of Gloucester and the earl of Arundel, temporarily withdrew their homage to the king, and it is likely that Richard was formally deposed for two or three days. It also appears likely that Thomas of Woodstock, duke of Gloucester, wished to take the crown for himself, or at least this was widely believed at the time, and Thomas was forced to deny it when parliament opened again in February 1388. Henry of Lancaster, earl of Derby, strongly opposed such an act, understandably: Thomas was only Edward III's fifth son (in fact the seventh, but the fifth to survive childhood), and his father John of Gaunt and he had a far superior claim to the throne.[14] According to a version of a chronicle called the *Polychronicon* by a monk of Chester named Ranulph Higden, the Appellants deposed Richard for three days, but then argued over who should be king in his place:

> [T]he majority wanted to promote Thomas of Woodstock to be king, but Henry, duke of Hereford [*sic*; Henry of Lancaster had not yet received this title] took a contrary position, protesting that he was the son of the elder brother, and claiming for this reason that he ought to be king.

Supposedly the others viewed this discord between uncle and nephew with some alarm, and, 'fearing that they would be perceived as traitors, they joined in the deliberations and reinstated Richard as king again'.[15] The Westminster chronicler says that the lords rebuked Richard for his duplicity and misgovernance, and warned him that he must correct his errors and rule more wisely in the future. The king was also told that he had an heir of full age, and that the heir was fully prepared to take on the governance of the realm with the advice of the Appellants.[16] Presumably this was a reference to the duke of Gloucester; the king's heir general Roger Mortimer, heir to the earldom of March, was still only thirteen so not yet of full age, and John of Gaunt was away from England and would hardly offer to govern the kingdom with the Appellants' advice.

On 4 January 1388, the mayor and sheriffs of London were told to seize all Robert de Vere's goods in the city and deliver them to Chancery.[17] Nicholas Brembre, the former mayor of London and currently a prisoner at Gloucester Castle, was to be brought back to the city on 28 January 'upon certain articles of treason' laid on him by the five Lords Appellant, named in order of rank as the duke of Gloucester followed by the earls of Derby (Henry of Lancaster), Arundel, Warwick and Nottingham. Also arrested were the knights Thomas Trivet, John Beauchamp and Nicholas Dagworth.[18] The Lords Appellant demanded the removal of several women from court. They were Blanche, Lady Poynings, who in fact was Thomas Mowbray's aunt; Lady Mohun, whose daughter Elizabeth was married to the earl of Salisbury, former husband of Joan of Kent; and Lady Moleyns.[19] Richard II turned twenty-one on 6 January 1388; it can hardly have been a happy birthday. The king was still keen to look after Robert de Vere's interests as much as he could, and sent letters to Charles VI of France asking him to protect de Vere and other Englishmen who had fled abroad after Radcot Bridge. Taking the advice of his uncles, the French king received them honourably, showered them with gifts and entertained them lavishly, and even held a jousting tournament in their honour. A grateful Richard II praised Charles for his gracious behaviour and sent envoys to the French court to thank him.[20]

A long parliament opened at Westminster on 3 February 1388 which became known as the Merciless Parliament, and remained in session until 20 March and again from 13 April to 4 June. Its aim was basically to clear away the royal courtiers whom the Lords Appellant found most noxious, and their supporters as well, even the humble ones. The accusations against Robert de Vere, Alexander Neville, Simon Burley, Michael de la Pole, Robert Tresilian, Nicholas Brembre and others – some present, some such as de la Pole who had already fled abroad – somewhat predictably stated that they encroached on royal power and came between the king and his natural advisers, i.e. the Lords Appellant. The five Appellants declared that their three chief targets, Robert de Vere, Archbishop Neville and Michael de la Pole, were 'false traitors to and enemies of the king and kingdom, perceiving the tender age of our said lord the king and the innocence of his royal person, so caused him to believe many falsities devised and plotted by them against loyalty and good faith, that they caused him to devote his affection, firm faith, and credence entirely to them, and to hate his loyal lords and lieges, by whom he ought rather to have been governed'.[21]

Another chief Appellant target, Robert Tresilian, formerly of King's Bench, sought sanctuary in Westminster Abbey. Tresilian's hiding place was betrayed by an abbey odd-job man named John Paule, who would himself be executed in May 1392. Tresilian had concealed himself 'above the gutter of a house abutting the palace wall at Westminster' where he could watch the comings and goings, but was discovered by a group of squires, having disguised himself in hermit's clothes of an old tunic made of russet and poor-quality red boots, and was heavily bearded (a false beard, says chronicler Henry Knighton). The unfortunate Tresilian was led before parliament to the words, 'We havet hym, we havet hym!' He refused to confess and remained completely silent, which availed him nothing: the next day he was dragged by horses to his execution at Tyburn. He refused to mount the scaffold and had to be manhandled there by force, and was hanged naked and had his throat cut for good measure. When his clothes were removed before his death, they were found to be full of protective charms which had entirely failed to protect him.[22]

Alexander Neville was captured off the northern coast of England in mid-June 1388 trying to sail across the North Sea in a small boat, and although he was not executed he was deprived of his archbishopric and translated to St Andrews in Scotland. This was a purely nominal appointment. He later went to the continent and in 1389 met his fellow exiles Robert de Vere and Michael de la Pole in Paris, and died in Louvain in 1392.[23] Two London politicians, Thomas Usk and John Blake, were executed on 4 March 1388: they were dragged to Tyburn and 'there among the gallows they quickly fell asleep'.[24] Usk was called 'a false and wicked person of their persuasion', i.e. of de Vere, de la Pole and Neville. He and Blake were said to have received 'great bribes' from the three men to take part in 'false quarrels and purposes to the destruction of the king and his kingdom'. The former mayor Nicholas Brembre, called 'false knight of London' in the records of the parliament, was sentenced to death on the grounds that 'he was aware rather than ignorant' of the charges against him, one of which was that he had unlawfully taken twenty-two criminals out of Newgate prison at night and had them beheaded at a place called the 'Foul Oak' in Kent. He was hanged at Tyburn.[25] Robert de Vere and Michael de la Pole were also sentenced to death in absentia.

There was an adjournment of parliament beginning on 21 March; Richard II spent the next few weeks mostly at his manors of Kennington and Eltham, probably with the queen. Three knights of the king's chamber, John Beauchamp, James Berners (who had been struck by lightning in Ely some years before and supposedly cured miraculously) and John Salisbury, were executed in May 1388, having been accused of treason on the grounds that they took advantage of Richard's delicate years to turn him against his natural advisers and obstructed the work of the royal council. The royal chamberlain Sir Simon Burley was charged with the same offences, and also of helping Michael de la Pole, earl of Suffolk, to flee abroad, encouraging the king to keep the company of Robert de Vere, filling the royal household with Bohemians, and illicitly using the great seal.[26]

The duke of Gloucester and earls of Arundel and Warwick were in favour of Simon Burley's execution, though the two younger Appellants Henry of Lancaster and Thomas Mowbray were strongly opposed to it, and these two men were joined by the duke of Gloucester's brother Edmund of Langley, duke of York. Edmund quarrelled fiercely with his brother about the matter and protested that Burley had always been loyal to the king, though to no avail: Gloucester retorted that Burley had been false to his allegiance. Edmund angrily called his brother a liar, Gloucester shouted the same back at him, and the king himself, of all people, had to intervene between them.[27] Queen Anne went down on her knees to pray for Simon Burley's life to be spared, supposedly for three hours, and Richard added his own pleas, but Gloucester and the other senior Appellants ignored them.[28] Burley had been one of the ambassadors who came to Anne's brother's court to undertake the negotiations for her marriage to Richard, and therefore had been the first English person she had probably ever met. Richard II would never forgive or forget this insult to his queen, the daughter of an emperor and the woman he loved dearly. According to the confession of the duke of Gloucester in 1397, the duke told Richard in May 1388 that he would have to choose between saving Burley and keeping his crown, though as this statement was made under duress after Gloucester was arrested and imprisoned it should perhaps not be given too much weight.[29]

On 5 May 1388, Sir Simon Burley, then probably in his mid to late fifties, was condemned to death, and on the same day was taken through the city of London with his hands tied behind his back. He was beheaded 'on level ground beside the Tower of London'.[30] The sentence had originally condemned him to the full agonies of the traitor's death by hanging, drawing and quartering, though this was respited to mere beheading on account of his high status. Some years later, after Queen Anne herself had died as well, Richard II asked the abbey of 'St Mary Graces by the Tower of London' to pray for the souls of Anne, Simon Burley, James Berners and John Salisbury on the anniversaries of their deaths.[31] The chronicle of Kirkstall Abbey commented of Simon Burley that 'no one of his rank could be compared to him in all the fine trappings of his horses, and he excelled the other lords in all worldly pomp'.[32] A bed which belonged to Burley, of green 'cloth of Tarteryn' and embroidered with ships and birds, came into the possession of the bishop of Salisbury, and Richard bought it from him at a cost of over £13.[33] Burley had owned twenty-two books, of which only one was in English: *Item, j. liure de Englys del Forster et del Sengler*, 'a book in English of the forester and the wild boar'. There were also two books of the Ten Commandments, one of them new and both with red covers; one 'little book which begins *Miserere Mei, Deus*' (i.e. the fifty-first Psalm); a book about 'William Bastard', who appears to have been Henry II's illegitimate son William Longespée, earl of Salisbury (*c.* 1176–1226) rather than William the Conqueror as might be expected from the name; the prophecies of Merlin; and, rather intriguingly, a book 'with diverse words of diverse languages', perhaps a kind of rudimentary dictionary.[34] The book about the life and deeds of William Longespée perhaps indicates that Burley shared and had inspired Richard II's interest in English history.

The Westminster chronicle says that Richard spent the entire autumn of 1388 hunting and arranging jousting tournaments at Eltham to try to relax and escape from the stress caused by the Lords Appellant and their attacks on him. He also celebrated Christmas at Eltham.[35] It is very difficult to say much about Richard II personally in 1388; he is curiously absent from chroniclers' accounts and from the official documents of the Merciless Parliament. We may fairly assume that he was distraught at the executions and exile of his friends, especially his old tutor Simon Burley, angry, and surely deeply humiliated at his inability to protect them.[36] The cruel, vindictive brutality of the Appellants took its toll on the king and was to reap bitter rewards later in the reign. Richard kept his rage inside himself and waited until he could gain revenge on his enemies; it would take him almost a decade.

12

'I See Some Sparks of Better Hope': The King Comes of Age, 1389–1390

There was still considerable discontent in the south-east of England later in 1388, and a petition in Kent was recorded by the chronicler Henry Knighton. It complained to Richard II that 'peace and right justice in your land, which you are bound to maintain, is not administered equally between rich and poor, as God and right demand ... your poor people cannot survive, nor bear the burden of aiding you and your realm as they should do'. The petition also declared that 'to remedy these faults ... there is need first to change the governance of yourself and your land, that you, our liege and natural lord, shall ... be honoured and feared and perfectly loved by the people for the good and just governance, that is, most honoured lord, in doing right justice to all persons as well to the poor as to the rich equally'.[1]

Meanwhile, the battle of Otterburn took place either on 5 or 19 August 1388, when the Scottish nobleman James Douglas, earl of Douglas, led a raid into north-east England and defeated an army led by Sir Henry 'Hotspur' Percy, son and heir of the earl of Northumberland and married to the earl of March's sister Elizabeth Mortimer. Hotspur was taken prisoner, and Richard II agreed to pay £3,000 towards his ransom. An instalment of £500 was made on 15 July 1389, and another £1,000 in late 1390.[2] It seemed in 1388 as though everything that could go wrong in England went wrong. Thomas Mowbray, earl of Nottingham and Earl Marshal, replaced Hotspur as warden of the English–Scottish marches. A Scottish chronicler was most unimpressed: 'Immediately on getting the post he [Mowbray] spoke very scornfully and arrogantly to the English borderers, criticising them for allowing the Scots – who were subhuman, he said – to gain a victory over them at Otterburn.' Mowbray also declared that if he could get the supplies he needed to fight the Scots he would do so, even if they outnumbered his forces two to one. Robert, earl of Fife, thereupon gathered an army and invaded England as far south at Tynemouth in the east and Appleby in the west, devastating the countryside. Nobles of the north of England marched into Scotland and returned the favour.[3]

Neither did events improve much as 1389 came around, and a most unpleasant event took place in Oxford in April that year. A man called John Kirkeby, a chaplain called Thomas Speek and 'other evildoers' formed a gang, armed themselves, and went into the town of Oxford on Thursday and Good Friday to seek out as many Welsh people as they could find. They either killed or badly wounded all those whom they found in a particularly horrible manner, by smashing their heads into walls. As the gang roamed the streets, they shouted out, 'War, war, war, sle [slay], sle, sle the Walshe dogges and her helpes, and hoso [whoso] loketh out of his hous, he shal be dede [dead].' The men also broke into numerous houses and university halls, stealing and looting such diverse items as linen cloth, books of grammar, doors and windows, swords and axes, cloaks, tables, and bows and arrows. Six years later the men were all pardoned for these revolting acts 'out of regard for Good Friday'.[4] Violent crime in fourteenth-century England could be stomach-churningly awful. To give just one example of many, a pregnant woman named Juliana Gylle was pardoned in 1391 at the request of Queen Anne after she broke into a house in Buckinghamshire with other thieves, stole the owners' goods, and not only beat up the woman of the household but tore out her eyes and tongue.[5] This was a long way from being a unique instance of its kind, and the rate of violent crime and homicide in England in the fourteenth century far exceeded that of the modern era.

On 3 May 1389, Richard II finally declared himself of age and able to rule his kingdom himself. Charles VI of France, almost two years younger than Richard, had done the same thing the year before.[6] Richard, as he was generally prone to do, made a drama out of the whole situation. He swept into his council room and demanded that his councillors tell him how old he was. They replied that he was twenty years old, an error either on their part or more likely by the St Albans chronicler Thomas Walsingham, who recorded the tale; Richard, born on 6 January 1367, was now twenty-two. 'Then,' said Richard, 'I am of full age to govern my house and household and also my kingdom. It seems to me unjust that my state should be worse than that of the least person in the kingdom. Surely any heir of my kingdom when he has reached the age of twenty [*sic*] years and his parent is dead, is permitted to conduct his affairs freely. Why therefore should this be denied to me, when it is conceded by law to anyone else of lower rank?' The barons replied that of course nothing should be denied to Richard, and that he should have the rule of his kingdom, as was his right. The king exclaimed, 'Well! Know that I have for long been ruled by tutors, and it was not possible for me to act at all, or almost at all, without them. Now henceforth I will remove those from my council, and, as heir of lawful age, I will appoint whom I will to my council, and conduct my own affairs. And I order that in the first place the chancellor should resign to me his seal.' Thomas Arundel, now archbishop of York and brother of the earl of Arundel (both men the king disliked intensely), did so, and Richard collected the seal in a fold of his clothing and went out of the room briefly. After a short while he returned and gave it to William Wykeham, bishop of Winchester, who reluctantly accepted it. Richard removed his uncle the duke of Gloucester and the earl of Warwick Thomas Beauchamp from the council, and a few others. He did not, yet, attempt to take any revenge against the Lords Appellant.

Not long afterwards, twelve years into Richard II's reign and mere weeks after he began to rule personally, it is apparent that not all his subjects were happy with him. On 14 July 1389, two royal sergeants-at-arms were sent to the Forest of Dean in Gloucestershire to arrest certain people for 'blaspheming the king's person'.[7] And also in July 1389, Richard ordered the arrest of a Londoner who had said, rudely if rather amusingly, that he was 'unfit to govern and should stay in his latrine'.[8] A William Mildenhale appeared before Chancery in London on 9 December 1391 and admitted that his father Peter Mildenhale, now dead, had uttered these words and expressed a wish that Richard II might stay in his latrine forever without doing any more governing. Peter had apparently also stated that he could seize hold of the king with only twelve men whenever he wished, and that this would be especially easy as Richard often rode from his manor of

Sheen to London with only a small escort and would not be able to resist; 'and he spoke many other disrespectful words disparaging the king's person'. Because his son William had not denounced his father's 'iniquity' to the king as he should have done owing to his allegiance, he was imprisoned, but was soon released thanks to Richard's 'kindness' and because he admitted his fault. William Mildenhale promised that thereafter he would endeavour to speak as respectfully of the king as possible, and 'if he heard unlawful words or abuse of the king spoken by any person of the realm, he would declare it as speedily as he could'.[9]

A three-year truce between England and France was concluded on 18 June 1389, which in 1392 and again in 1393 was extended.[10] Richard II gave gifts to a French notary and two esquires of Charles VI, travelling to Scotland with news of the ratification of the treaty, on 23 August 1389: three silver cups with gilt covers bought from a goldsmith of London called John Fraunceys (whose name means 'Frenchman'), two silk cloths 'called baudekyns' and a whole cloth of violet.[11] Richard had realised by now, as did Charles VI, that it would make more sense for the two of them to unite as Christian leaders against the Turkish threat rather than fight each other: in the 1380s Turkish forces were overrunning parts of south-eastern Europe and were threatening the city of Constantinople itself, and Richard was aware that it would be wise for the Christian rulers of Europe to unite against a common enemy.[12]

For all the criticism of him by some or many of his subjects, Richard did at least try to rule moderately and wisely, and when his uncle John of Gaunt, duke of Lancaster, returned to England in late 1389 – the king had written to him on 30 October requesting him to come home at last after more than three years away – Richard greeted him amicably with the kiss of peace at Reading, having ridden 2 miles to meet him.[13] In March 1390, Richard even bestowed the duchy of Aquitaine on his uncle for life, and in July 1390 the king and queen were guests of the duke at a splendid hunting party at Leicester.[14] Their earlier conflict was now forgotten, and Richard made an effort to get on better with Gaunt and to heed his advice.

And yet even now that he was into his twenties, Richard II was still unable to control his temper or prevent himself from lashing out. Walsingham says that around this time rumours reached the king's ears that his uncle Thomas of Woodstock was raising armies against him. Predictably, without even waiting to think about it or to try to confirm the rumours, Richard furiously summoned his uncle to him, and on learning that the rumours were false, 'blushed in his confusion' (yet more evidence of Richard's rapid changes of colour and that his emotions could clearly be seen in his face). Walsingham also says that some of those who had spread the rumours in the first place were present at the reconciliation of uncle and nephew, and that Gloucester wished to denounce those who had lied to Richard about him but dared not, and that Richard protested his love for him and asked him not to take the matter further. As soon as Thomas of Woodstock was gone, says Walsingham, the rumour-mongers again began to whisper to the king.[15] There is no other confirmation of this story, but it does seem entirely typical of the character of Richard II himself and of the general character of his reign: endless plots and counter-plots, schemes by courtiers to bring down others, and the king's inability to discern bad and self-interested advice from wise counsel or to stop himself overreacting. After the duke of Gloucester's actions as an Appellant in 1387/88 and his executions of some of the king's dearest friends, Richard understandably found it impossible to trust him again.

On 15 October 1389, the Roman pope Urban VI, born Bartolomeo Prignano, died, and was succeeded on 2 November by Piero Tomacelli, who took the name Boniface IX. Meanwhile, the Avignon pope Clement VII or Robert of Geneva continued as the other pontiff, and died on 16 September 1394. His death did not heal the great papal schism, as he was succeeded twelve days later by the second Avignon pope, Benedict XIII, a nobleman of Aragon whose real and startlingly long name was Pedro Martínez de Luna y Pérez de Gotor. The official position now of the Catholic Church is that Benedict XIII was an anti-pope, as all of the Avignon popes.

Richard and Queen Anne spent Christmas 1389 at the royal palace of Woodstock near Oxford, birthplace of Richard's father the prince of Wales almost sixty years earlier. Tragedy struck on 30 December when one of the festive jousts went horribly wrong, and seventeen-year-old John Hastings, heir to the earldom of Pembroke, was killed. The man who killed him, a knight called Sir John St John, was pardoned in July 1391 on the grounds that the accident had happened by misadventure, not malice. St John was also pardoned for his subsequent outlawry, which implies that he had fled, terrified of the consequences of killing such a highly-born nobleman and kinsman of the king.[16] John Hastings, last of the Hastings line – he was an only child and his father and grandfather had also been only children – left his fourteen-year-old widow Philippa, younger sister of Roger Mortimer, earl of March, and granddaughter of Richard II's uncle Lionel of Antwerp. Hastings' childless death also left his cousin Thomas Mowbray, earl of Nottingham, as sole heir to their grandmother Margaret, countess of Norfolk.

Philippa Hastings, *née* Mortimer, married the widowed Richard Fitzalan, earl of Arundel, a man thirty years her senior, in mid-August 1390 when she was still only fourteen years old. Probably predictably given the Appellant Arundel's long hostility to the king, the couple did not seek permission from Richard to marry as they should have done, and paid a fine of 400 marks in exchange for a royal pardon in November 1391. Given their vast combined wealth, this was a paltry sum which they can barely even have noticed. The couple also married without a properly formulated papal dispensation for consanguinity, which they required as they were related both by birth and marriage; Boniface IX declared their marriage legal on 16 September 1391.[17] Despite the huge age difference, Philippa and Arundel's marriage proved a happy (though childless) one, and the earl renamed his castle of Shrawardine in Shropshire 'Castle Philippa' in her honour: his will, dated 4 March 1392, was written at 'Castle Philipp', though in it the earl asked for his body to be buried at Lewes Priory in Sussex next to his first wife Elizabeth de Bohun.[18] The marriage of Philippa and Arundel may have been a love-match, and in his will Arundel frequently referred to his 'dear wife' and left her many valuable items, though no doubt he also appreciated the political benefits of the marriage: it made him the brother-in-law of Richard II's first cousin once removed and heir general Roger Mortimer, who might one day inherit the throne. The succession was an ongoing and vital issue as Richard and Queen Anne failed to produce any children, and the Westminster chronicler claimed in 1387 that if the king were to die without heirs of his body, the succession to the throne would fall to the Mortimer family.[19] It is notable, however, that Richard rarely showed much favour to his kinsman Roger Mortimer, earl of March, and only one rather unreliable chronicle mentions that he named him as his heir to the throne; no other evidence supports this. After eight years of marriage, the king must have realised that he and Queen Anne were now most unlikely to produce any offspring, and it may well have suited Richard to keep the question of the succession to his throne open.

At the festivities held to mark St George's day on 23 April 1390, Richard knighted several men, though did not create them Knights of the Garter. One was Roger Mortimer, who had turned sixteen a few days before. Although still some years underage, Roger Mortimer was generally already addressed as the earl of March. Another new knight was Thomas, heir to the earldom of Stafford since the murder of his brother Ralph in 1385; he was about seventeen or eighteen. Sometime in 1390, Thomas Stafford married Richard's first cousin Anne of Gloucester, second child and eldest daughter of his uncle Thomas of Woodstock and only a child at this time.[20] A third man knighted by Richard II in April 1390 was Alfonso, son of the count of Denia in Aragon, who spent many years as a hostage in England (albeit a hostage treated with much honour and respect) and whose ongoing captivity had caused such problems for his captors Robert Hawley and John Shakell a few years before. Possibly Richard was attempting to woo a valuable future player in the endless game played between England, France and the Iberian kingdoms.[21] The only two men made Knights of the Garter in 1390 were Wilhelm, duke of Guelders and Jülich, and another Wilhelm, this one from Hainault, the count of Ostrevant and heir to his father the duke of Bavaria, a kinsman of Richard.

Wilhelm of Guelders and Jülich – territory which nowadays lies partly in the Netherlands and partly in Germany – arrived in England on 8 May 1390.[22] 'The king honoured [him] magnificently' and installed him as one of the Knights of the Garter at Windsor. In May 1390, a series of duels took place between English and Scottish knights in London, the most famous of them being a match between Lord Welles and Sir David Lindsay which took place on London Bridge. One Scottish chronicler says that Richard II and Anne of Bohemia watched the duel from a 'summer palace', apparently a temporary pavilion, on London Bridge.[23] In the summer of 1390, Richard visited Gloucester where his great-grandfather Edward II had been buried in December 1327 at St Peter's Abbey, now Gloucester Cathedral. He discussed the possibility of Edward's canonisation, a matter in which he took a great interest, and spent time preparing a dossier to promote Edward's canonisation, to be presented to Boniface IX. Richard presumably glossed over Edward's many faults and his relationships with men, and emissaries were sent to the pope on 24 April 1395 with the final dossier.[24] Queen Anne, as ever, was close to Richard physically and emotionally, and he often granted the petitions she presented to him on behalf of others. On 24 August 1390 at Anne's request, for example, the king pardoned two men for stealing a horse with saddle, cloths, a beaver hat and a 'silk purse with five silver-gilt rings'; they had, perhaps rather harshly, been sentenced to death. Richard himself was capable of acts of rather extraordinary kindness and generosity: in 1388 he paid the debts of all the prisoners in the London gaol of Newgate.[25]

The royal couple had spent part of July 1390 as guests of John of Gaunt at Leicester, where they took part in a magnificent hunting party which drew the attention of the Westminster chronicler. Gaunt hosted lavish banquets for his nephew and the queen, and several days were spent in festivities.[26] Richard by now openly showed favour to his uncle by publicly wearing the Lancastrian collar of Ss. He was forced to defend this action in parliament some years later in early 1394, and declared that 'soon after the arrival of his said uncle of Guyenne [i.e. Gaunt], when last he came from Spain to England, our same lord the king took the collar from the neck of his same uncle and put it on his own neck, and said that he would wear it as a sign of the great and whole-hearted love between them, as he had done with the liveries of his other uncles'.[27]

In October 1390 Richard held a spectacular jousting event at Smithfield, inviting Wilhelm of Hainault, count of Ostrevant, whom he wished to court as an ally. Wilhelm of Hainault was so impressed by the magnificence of the occasion and the warmth of his reception that although he did not officially enter into an alliance with Richard and England – his wife Marguerite of Burgundy was the daughter of Charles VI's uncle the duke of Burgundy and one of his sisters was married to Burgundy's son and heir, and thus he was closely tied to the French court – he thereafter consistently upheld the English cause. Wilhelm, duke of Guelders and Jülich, Wilhelm of Hainault's brother-in-law, was another nobleman drawn into the English field of influence in such a manner.[28]

Wilhelm of Ostrevant was the son and heir of Duke Albrecht of Bavaria and a grandson of Ludwig of Bavaria, predecessor of Richard's father-in-law Karl IV as Holy Roman Emperor. Richard II had in 1380 had sent men to discuss his possible betrothal to Wilhelm's sister Katharina of Bavaria, and in the early 1380s John of Gaunt had entered into negotiations for Wilhelm to marry his eldest child

Philippa, who later became queen of Portugal.[29] Jean Froissart says that Wilhelm visited his father Duke Albrecht in Le Quesnoy, Hainault before he travelled to England. Albrecht tried to dissuade his son from attending the tournament, saying, in a rather magnificent example of fourteenth-century 'As you know, Bob' dialogue: 'My good son, you have nothing to do in England: you are now connected by marriage with the blood royal of France, and your sister is the wife of the eldest son of our cousin the duke of Burgundy: you have no occasion, therefore, to seek other connections.' Wilhelm answered that he had no intention of forming new alliances in England but merely wished to see his cousins, whom he had never met, then applied emotional blackmail by claiming 'should I not go thither, after the particular invitation I have had, for a purpose messenger brought it me, my refusal will be considered as the effect of pride and presumption. I feel myself bound therefore in honour to go.' Albrecht rather petulantly agreed that his son was his own master, but that peace would be better served if he did not go to England.

Also present at Smithfield in October 1390 were Richard II's half-sister Maud, *née* Holland, and her second husband Waleran, count of St Pol. Wilhelm of Ostrevant travelled to Dover with them, and they were met by Maud's brother John Holland, earl of Huntingdon, and half-brother the king in London. They had stopped in Canterbury on the way and prayed at the shrine of St Thomas Becket, and presumably saw the tomb of Richard's father Edward of Woodstock while they were there. Richard had sent heralds to proclaim the Smithfield event throughout western Europe. According to Jean Froissart, the coronation of Charles VI's wife Isabeau of Bavaria as queen of France in August 1389, a splendid occasion when the queen led a procession through Paris, prompted Richard to hold an equally magnificent event, and therefore he organised the jousting tournament at Smithfield. During the tournament, the feast of Edward the Confessor was held with the usual solemnity on 13 October 1390. Richard sat beside Queen Anne at Mass and at table, both of them dressed in their full coronation regalia, with his half-sister Maud and her husband the count of St Pol.[30] Richard was either at Westminster or, less probably, Kennington for the feast of Edward the Confessor, and according to the Westminster chronicler, who is likely to be a reliable source on this issue, the king was in the abbey for prime (six a.m.), vespers (sunset), compline (bedtime) and matins (midnight) with Queen Anne and all his chaplains. He and Anne also heard High Mass while sitting, crowned, in the choir.[31]

Historian Alison McHardy has described the Smithfield tournament as 'the social highlight of the reign'.[32] Froissart, a huge fan of pageantry and impressive royal display – as Richard II himself also was – gives a vivid account of the Smithfield tournament. Around three o'clock in the afternoon of Sunday 10 October, sixty squires each riding a war-horse ornamented for the occasion paraded out from the Tower of London, followed by sixty richly dressed ladies each riding a palfrey and each leading an armed knight by a silver chain. This parade, accompanied by minstrels and trumpeters, went through the streets of London towards Smithfield, where the king and queen, attended by Anne's ladies and damsels, were already waiting 'in chambers handsomely decorated'.

The tournament began with an advance by the count of St Pol and his companions, and such was the enthusiasm for the event that only the falling dark persuaded the combatants, reluctantly, to break off for the night. Queen Anne stayed in the bishop of London's palace near St Paul's, where a great banquet was held that evening. Wilhelm of Ostrevant arrived in the evening and was warmly received by Richard and Anne, and dancing also took place after the banquet in the presence of the king and queen, the three royal uncles John of Gaunt, Edmund of Langley and Thomas of Woodstock, and other members of the nobility. Richard's half-brother John Holland, earl of Huntingdon, distinguished himself on the first day and won the prize for the best 'defender' at the tournament, while the count of St Pol won the prize for best 'challenger'. The jousting continued with blunted lances on the Monday with both Richard and Anne in attendance, Richard surrounded by dukes, lords and knights and the queen by her ladies and damsels. Sir Hugh Despenser, kinsman of the bishop of Norwich and a distant relative of the king, won this day's prize as the best defender, a very rich golden clasp, and the count of Ostrevant was adjudged the best challenger and won a golden crown. The event continued for several more days, and it must have been quite a party; after a day of jousting between squires on Tuesday, the dancing went on until daybreak on Wednesday, when the exhausted revellers finally took themselves off to bed. Richard II hosted a banquet on Thursday evening for all the foreign lords, knights and squires, while Queen Anne entertained their ladies and damsels. On the Friday, it was the turn of

John of Gaunt, duke of Lancaster, to host yet another magnificent banquet. Even after the end of the jousting on the Saturday, almost a week after it had begun, the festivities continued, and Richard invited the counts of St Pol and Ostrevant to Windsor and held yet more lavish feasts for them.[33]

The Westminster chronicle says that Richard took part personally in the Smithfield tournament, which is certainly not impossible. This statement, however, may represent the monk of Westminster's confusion that one of the king's representatives, his half-brother John Holland or his kinsman Sir Hugh Despenser, had won prizes, though indeed Froissart also comments that Richard came fully armed on the second day of the Smithfield tournament, and the king had ordered armour for a previous tournament in 1386.[34] At this juncture Richard invited Wilhelm of Ostrevant to become a Knight of the Garter, and Wilhelm accepted. This, as his father Albrecht of Bavaria had foreseen, caused some problems regarding his relations with France. Jean Froissart recorded the muttering of Wilhelm's French attendants in England, who conveniently reiterated the nobleman's relationship to the French royal family for Froissart's readers who had already forgotten it: 'This count of Ostrevant plainly shows that his heart is more inclined to England than France when he thus accepts the order of the Garter, which is the device of the kings of England. He is purchasing the ill will of the court of France and of my lord of Burgundy, whose daughter he has married, and a time may come for him to repent of it.'[35]

Richard's cousin Henry of Lancaster, earl of Derby, missed the Smithfield tournament: in the summer of 1390, he had set off on a crusade to Lithuania.[36] The grand duke of Lithuania, Vytautas, had become Christian as recently as 1387, and the country was undergoing a process of Christianisation, the last country in Europe to do so. Anne of Bohemia's great-great-grandfather the Lithuanian grand duke Gediminas had been a pagan, though his daughter Aldona, queen of Poland, Anne's great-grandmother, was baptised into Christianity on 28 June 1325 and became a devout Christian. After she did so, she took the name Anna or Ona instead of her original pagan name Aldona. Anna/Aldona's nephews including Vytautas converted Lithuania to Christianity. Henry of Lancaster subsequently travelled from Lithuania to Jerusalem to go on pilgrimage. He passed through Prague, where Queen Anne's half-brother King Václav greeted him with honour at his palace of Bettlern and took him hunting, and later also met Anne's full brother Zikmund, king of Hungary and Croatia, and Wilhelm of Ostrevant's father Duke Albrecht of Bavaria, at his residence on the other side of the Danube in Vienna.[37] The crusading spirit was not dead in the royal family: Richard's uncle Thomas of Woodstock was given permission to go to Prussia in September 1391 also on crusade.[38] It is unlikely that King Richard was sorry to see his uncle Thomas leave, and he may not have been sorry to see his cousin Henry spend time away from England either; the two young men had an awkward relationship.

In the parliament held between 12 November and 3 December 1390, Duke John IV of Brittany was deprived of his English lands. Since the death in 1384 of his second wife, Richard's half-sister Joan Holland, the duke had been adopting a cooler tone towards England and favouring France, and had been involved in the French plans to invade England in 1386. This was quite a startling change of heart given that the duke had played an important role in Richard's coronation nine years before. On 2 October 1386 John IV had married his third wife, Carlos II 'the Bad' of Navarre's daughter Juana, who was about thirty years his junior and was the mother of all eight or nine of his children. Juana later became queen-consort of England when she married Henry IV in 1403.

Sometime in the early to mid-1390s, Richard II had the famous portrait of himself made which hangs to this day in Westminster Abbey. Although heavily restored in the more than 600 years since it was painted, it gives a good impression of what Richard really looked like, and is the earliest realistic portrait of any English king. Most probably some years after this, perhaps in the late 1390s, Richard also had the Wilton Diptych made, and it fortuitously survives as an outstanding example of medieval art at its finest. Richard is depicted as a young man wearing a crown, kneeling with his hands stretched out in prayer, and smiling as the infant Jesus, held in the arms of His mother Mary, blesses him. Behind Richard stand three saints, John the Baptist, Edmund the Martyr (the king of East Anglia killed by the Danes in the ninth century) and Edward the Confessor, who present him to the Virgin Mary and Christ Child in the opposite panel. The Virgin and Child are surrounded by eleven angels in blue, all of whom wear Richard's symbol of the white hart as brooches on their chests. It has been described as 'a strikingly narcissistic image of sacral kingship'.[39]

Around 1390, Richard's master cook produced a book called *The Forme of Cury*, the first cookbook in English. It called Richard 'the best and ryallest [most royal] vyander of alle cristen [Christian] kynges'. A *vyander* means a provider of viands, i.e. foodstuffs. *The Forme of Cury* consists of 196 recipes, including such delights as venison broth, deer livers, roast hares, porpoises, whales, herons and seals, pheasant spiced with cinnamon, cloves and ginger, and oysters in Greek wine. There are also 'potages', soups or stews, and 'subtleties' or desserts such as *moree* (mulberries cooked with honey) and *blank dessorre* (ground blanched almonds and white wine), which were coloured, carefully shaped and intended to be pleasing to the eye. Spices such as ginger, cinnamon, nutmeg, saffron, mace and spikenard were used liberally. One sauce was called 'Sauce Madame', and one recipe was called *Douce ame* or 'Sweet soul', which began 'Take gode Cowe mylke'.[40] The *Forme of Cury* gives an excellent impression of the kind of food Richard and his court would have eaten.

13

'To Meet at London London's King in Woe': Conflict in London, 1391–1393

On 27 April 1391, Richard had the body of his elder brother Edward of Angoulême transferred to England and buried at Langley Priory in Hertfordshire. Edward's marble tomb cost 100 marks, or £66 13s 4d, and Richard later also paid over £8 for a missal book and a silver cup for the priory church.[1] This burial at a priory founded by his great-grandfather Edward II may have prompted Richard to continue to promote the latter's canonisation. Richard II always had a strong sense of history, and he was very aware of his great-grandfather's fate and how much he resembled him in many ways. In July 1391 he gave 40 marks to a Master William Storteford to go to the papal court to plead for Edward II to be canonised, and another 52 marks to 'certain proctors, notaries, scribes and messengers' engaged on the same business.[2] Rather confusingly, the record speaks of 'the canonisation of King Edward, great-grandfather of the said now lord the king, whose body was buried at Westminster'. Edward II was buried at St Peter's Abbey in Gloucester, now Gloucester Cathedral, not at Westminster. His father Edward I, who was both Richard II's great-great-grandfather on his father's side and his great-grandfather on his mother's, was indeed buried at Westminster; yet it seems unlikely that Richard was trying to promote the canonisation of Edward I as well as of Edward II, and this is probably a clerical error.

The king bought himself some new horses – six coursers and eight others – on 9 May 1391, appointing a man named William Gilden to buy them 'in whosesoever hands found, at prices to be agreed on between him and the owners'.[3] A few months later he sent men to Ireland to buy three goshawks and eight tercels for his use.[4] In July that year, Richard gave £1 6s 8d to two minstrels sent to him by the king of Aragon, Juan I, eldest son of the late Pedro IV, for their performance.[5] And on 23 October 1391, Richard II granted an income of 10 marks each at the exchequer to three minstrels in his household: William Launde, a lute player, Richard Kyrton, who played the guitar, and John Hilton, a harper. He also gave permission to the canon of St Stephen inside his palace of Westminster to take up permanent residence in the 'place which is called *la Salcerie* at the right hand within the second gate of the palace, with the chambers built over it'.[6]

Earlier in the year, a French initiative had seen Sir Thomas Percy and Sir Lewis Clifford invited to Paris in order to negotiate a personal meeting between Richard II and Charles VI at Midsummer 1391, and although this ultimately was not to take place, Percy and Clifford returned to England with their arms full of expensive gifts from Charles.[7] Richard and the queen spent Christmas 1391 and New Year 1392 at Langley near St Albans, Hertfordshire, where he had had his brother buried a few months before. A few days before Christmas 1391, Richard's kinswoman Margaret Courtenay, *née* de Bohun, dowager countess of Devon, died at the age of eighty; via her mother Elizabeth, who died in 1316, Margaret was a granddaughter of Edward I and a first cousin of Richard's mother Joan of Kent. Her death left Margaret, countess of Norfolk as the sole surviving grandchild of Edward I.

On Christmas Day 1391, a dolphin appeared and played in the River Thames in London, which prompted chronicler Thomas Walsingham to write a charming account of dolphins' behaviour and their supposed abilities, including the rather hilarious 'fact' that 'they hear men's voices more quickly when the wind is in the north, but when the south wind blows, their hearing is blocked'.[8]

At Westminster on 9 February 1392, Richard granted Walter Vesecok, the master of his barge, an income of 2d a day on account of his age and infirmity and for his long service to the king and his father Edward of Woodstock, and on the grounds that Vesecok had never previously had any income for his work.[9] A few months later, Richard appointed his servant John Winterbourne as the keeper of his camel, who may have resided at the royal manor of Langley, where a camel had been kept for a century or so. Richard also owned an ostrich, whose keeper was one Henry Wyscheley succeeded by John Sparowe at 3*d* a day 'for his wages and for the sustenance of the ostrich'. Two ostriches were given to Richard by 'the good men of Ghent' in modern-day Belgium in or shortly before July 1384, and by September 1385 one of them had died.[10] The ostrich was the heraldic symbol of Richard's queen Anne of Bohemia, presumably the rationale behind the gift, and she and Richard owned a double cup of ostrich egg mounted in silver-gilt with ostriches in opaque white enamel inside. At Christmas 1385, Richard had a ceremonial sword carried before him with a sheath and belt covered in black velvet and embroidered with gold thread and ostrich feathers.[11] As had been the case with all the kings of England since Henry III (who reigned from 1216 to 1272), Richard kept lions in the Tower of London. One hopes the animals were not harmed – or that they managed to escape and cause mayhem – when the rebels invaded the Tower during the uprising.[12] Richard also appointed a man on several occasions to 'keep the king's swans in the [River] Thames and elsewhere in the realm'.[13] Near the end of his reign, Richard II granted to the dean of his chapel in Windsor 'all unmarked swans flying in the River Thames' and gave him and his men permission to 'search for the said swans throughout the said river and all streams flowing to and from it between Gravesend and Oxford bridge'.[14]

The young Charles VI of France suffered his first mental breakdown on 5 August 1392, which news reached England within weeks, when it was reported that 'the king of France has lost his reason'.[15] Richard II addressed a letter in French to 'the very high and mighty prince C., by the grace of God our very dear cousin of France' seventeen days later on 22 August, in which he declared that he would be joyous and greatly comforted to hear of Charles's good health. This may simply be a conventional and not necessarily very meaningful wish – such phrases were common in fourteenth-century letters – or it may indicate that Richard had heard of the French king's recent affliction.[16]

Problems continued in London in the early 1390s; civil unrest and antagonism towards government in the capital was a permanent and often pressing issue throughout the Middle Ages, and the second half of Richard II's reign proved no exception. Richard, short of money, asked London to make him a large loan apparently of either £5,000 or 5,000 marks, offering a jewel as security. The Londoners refused, and Richard was furious, claiming that they were willing to lend money to foreigners but not to their king. The chief citizens of the city were summoned to Nottingham and informed of certain charges of 'many derelictions of duty' against them, and the mayor John Hend was committed to prison at Windsor Castle and the two sheriffs John Shaddeworth and Henry Vanner at Odiham and Wallingford, two other royal castles. Sir Edward Dalingrigge was made keeper of the city, and on the advice of the chancellor and treasurer, the king moved all his courts from London to York.[17]

The mayor, sheriffs and twenty-one aldermen were pardoned on 29 September 1392 in exchange for acknowledging a massive debt of £10,000 to the king, and the formal procedures which marked the king's reconciliation with his capital were among the greatest ceremonial occasions of the entire reign.[18] A letter still exists by an anonymous writer to an unspecified English lord describing this reconciliation, one of the main sources for what happened in the city at this time. Amusingly, the letter begins with the statement that the unknown author was 'a little out of sorts in my head' when he arrived in London on Sunday 18 August 1392. Despite this, Richard ordered the writer to ride with him and Queen Anne through the city. As soon as Richard was a little beyond Wandsworth, the warden and aldermen of London approached him on foot and presented him with the keys of the city. Nearby, the city guilds all dressed in their respective uniforms lined both sides of the road on horseback, and the king rode through past them. As Richard approached the city he was met by all the religious men of London, monks, friars, priests and clerks, singing the hymns *Te Deum Laudamus* and *Summe Trinitati*. At London Bridge, the warden and aldermen gave Richard a magnificent gift of two large coursers (horses) wearing trappings of cloth of gold mixed with red and white and silver-gilt saddles, and also presented Queen Anne with a palfrey wearing trappings of the same colours and a golden saddle. On arrival at Cheapside, 'between the two crosses, there came two angels out of a cloud,' carrying two crowns, one for Richard and the other for Anne. Richard halted the procession for some time while he went into St Paul's to pray and make an offering.

He rode on to Ludgate, where he and the queen each received a 'beautiful tablet of pure gold for an altar' which had a value of 100 marks, and at Westminster went inside his palace and changed his clothes: he put on a long robe because he had ridden all day in a short one. In his chamber at Westminster, Richard sat on a high seat which had been made in front of his great throne and was covered with cloth of gold, with Queen Anne and Archbishop Courtenay standing on one side of him and Robert Braybrooke, bishop of London, on the other. Queen Anne knelt before Richard to ask him to show mercy and clemency to the disobedient inhabitants of London; Richard's grandmother Queen Philippa had done the same to Edward III to pray for the lives of the burghers of Calais many years before.[19] Anne apparently had no wish to exercise political power, being content to be Richard's supportive partner behind the scenes, and to intercede with him as the role of English queen-consort demanded. This gave Richard an opportunity to back down without losing face, and to pardon the men, which he did: he 'took them all into his grace and granted them all their privileges as freely as they had ever had them'. He ate spices and drank wine and then rode away to Kennington to dine. The next day, Richard and Anne ate with the city warden again; he received yet another gift, a tablet of silver and enamel large enough to be used as decoration behind his altar, and the queen was presented with a crystal goblet and a ewer inlaid with gold.

When the king and queen left London for Westminster, they were accompanied along the river by a large crowd of guildsmen dancing and making loud music in finely decorated boats. Richard invited them into his palace and gave them all drinks, and afterwards they departed 'with very great joy and comfort'. Another present given to Richard and Anne was a silver-gilt table 9 feet in length with a value of 500 marks, and some months later at Epiphany 1393, Richard's twenty-sixth birthday, representatives of the city came to visit him and Anne at Eltham bearing yet more gifts. These were 'a dromedary [camel] with a boy sitting on it', presumably not a real animal but a depiction or figure of one, and for the queen 'a great and wonderful bird with a very wide throat'.[20] In a poem written to celebrate Richard's reconciliation with London, Richard of Maidstone exclaimed over the king's captivating beauty: he wrote that Richard was as handsome as Troilus or Absalom, and says that if Nature had more generously bestowed beauty on him, envious Venus might have shut him away in her chambers.[21]

On 13 October 1392, Richard spent over £2 sending his clerk Stephen Percy from London to Queenborough Castle in Kent (built by his grandfather Edward III and named after his grandmother Philippa of Hainault) to collect his great crown and bring it to Westminster to celebrate the feast of St Edward the Confessor. Several archers accompanied Percy to ensure that the crown was not stolen on the way.[22]

The king received sad news in the late summer or autumn of 1392: sometime before 5 August, his beloved Robert de Vere (to whom he had granted Queenborough in 1385) had died while still in exile, probably in Louvain, at the age of only thirty. One chronicler says that de Vere was killed by a wild boar while hunting, though there is no other confirmation of this story.[23] Richard had not seen him for almost five years, and surely missed him greatly. As he had had no children with his wife Philippa Coucy – nor any with his supposed second wife, or more probably his abducted mistress, Agnes Launcecrona – de Vere was succeeded as earl of Oxford by his father's younger brother Aubrey in January 1393 after Aubrey successfully petitioned for the restoration of his inheritance. His title of duke of Ireland was never used again, though Philippa Coucy continued to be addressed as the duchess of Ireland or 'Madam of Ireland' for the rest of her life.[24] De Vere's mother Maud, *née* Ufford, outlived her son by more than twenty years and died in 1413. Richard II had pardoned her for travelling overseas without licence to Brabant 'to confer with her son Robert de Veer, earl of Oxford, and for relieving him with certain gifts' on 10 May 1391.[25] Two of Maud's damsels and seven male members of her household were also pardoned for travelling with her. The king's ally Alexander Neville, former archbishop of York, had also died in exile earlier in 1392.

Just before Christmas 1392, on 23 December, came yet another death: Richard's aunt by marriage Isabel of Castile, duchess of York, only in her late thirties. In accordance with her will, Richard granted her younger son Richard of Conisbrough 400 marks on 16 March 1393, and had Isabel buried at Langley Priory in Hertfordshire where he had buried his brother Edward of Angoulême the year before (and where Isabel's husband Edmund would also be interred in 1402).[26] Thomas Walsingham says that Duchess Isabel 'was a pampered and voluptuous lady, but men said that she was very sorrowful and repentant at the end'.[27] Isabel also left her two older children, Edward of York, earl of Rutland and future duke of Albemarle, and Constance, Lady Despenser, and bequeathed to them her crown and a 'fret of pearls' respectively. It is notable that Isabel left her husband

Edmund no bequests in her will, though she left items to Richard II, her brother-in-law John of Gaunt (a jasper tablet given to her some years before by Levon of Armenia) and her sister-in-law Eleanor de Bohun, duchess of Gloucester.[28] The marriage of the Yorks had apparently not been a particularly happy or close one, and the two were mismatched. Among the duchess's possessions were sleeves sewn with pearls, several objects decorated with the Yorkist symbol of a falcon, and two small brooches with fetterlocks, Isabel's personal badge.[29] Richard II's half-sister Maud, *née* Holland, countess of St Pol and Ligny, was yet another person who died in 1392. There is little to suggest that the king was or ever had been particularly close to either of his two Holland half-sisters, both of whom were now dead.

Richard sent letters to his first cousin Catalina of Lancaster, her husband Enrique III of Castile (still barely into his teens), and Enrique's council on 12 and 18 February 1393. Rather embarrassingly, though fortunately, as it turned out, not too disastrously for international relations, Richard's clerk got Enrique's name wrong and addressed the Spanish king in both letters as *Johanni* rather than *Henrico*, actually the name of his late father Juan I.[30] Richard also sent a letter on 1 April 1393 to Margrete Valdemarsdatter, queen regnant of Denmark and also queen of Sweden and Norway by marriage, addressing her as 'our beloved sister' (*sorori nostra carissime*) rather than as his cousin, even though they were only very distantly related. Margrete was more closely related to Queen Anne, and was succeeded on her death in 1412 by Anne's first cousin Erik of Pomerania, Margrete's great-nephew.[31] An envoy and commissioner of Queen Margrete, who bore the excellent name Sweyn Stalefote, was in London in 1393, and was given permission to hire 'three large vessels of war'.[32] Just over a year later, Richard gave Margrete a gift: she had bought a gold cup from a London goldsmith for £40, and Richard paid for it for her.[33]

In February and March 1393, Richard ordered the mayor and sheriffs of London and the bailiffs of Westminster to clean the city on the grounds that the banks of the River Thames and the river itself between Westminster and London were being polluted with 'unclean entrails, issues and intestines of beasts, dung, dunghills, ordure, rubbish and filth'. Anyone who continued to pollute the river banks or to dispose of dead animals anywhere except in the deepest part of the Thames 'when the tide begins to ebb' faced a heavy fine.[34] The king made a progress to Canterbury in May 1393: he left the palace of Sheen on the 20th and crossed over London Bridge with a large company of lords and bishops, passing under a portal set with images of himself and the queen and shields bearing his, Anne's and St Edward the Confessor's arms, which he had recently had made.[35] He spent the period from 23 May to 11 June 1393 at St Augustine's Abbey in Canterbury, and spent Trinity Sunday at the conventual church of Holy Trinity. It was the seventeenth anniversary of his father's death, and the king spent £14 on 100 torches of wax to burn around Edward of Woodstock's tomb in Canterbury Cathedral.[36]

On or around 15 April 1393, Richard's mother-in-law the dowager Holy Roman Empress Elżbieta of Pomerania, widow of Karl IV, died at Hradec Králové or 'Queen's Castle', now a city in the Czech Republic. She was about forty-six or forty-seven. Richard had kept in contact with her, and so had her daughter: Queen Anne sent the empress two worsted cloths and one cloth of Rennes on 2 July 1389, and Richard sent a letter to his customs collectors in London, Dover and Sandwich telling the men to let the gift pass through the ports without paying the usual customs.[37] Richard and Queen Anne presumably heard about the shocking act of Anne's half-brother King Václav, Elżbieta's stepson, on 20 March 1393 just weeks before Elżbieta died: he had a man called John of Nepomuk or Jan Nepomucky tortured and drowned in the Vltava River in Prague supposedly for failing to reveal the private confession of Václav's young second queen Sophia of Bavaria. Nepomuk later became the patron saint of Bohemia. Richard ordered a Requiem Mass to be celebrated in St Paul's Cathedral for Elżbieta's soul on 12 June 1393, after his return to his capital from Canterbury.[38] Elżbieta was buried next to her husband the emperor at St Vitus's Cathedral in Prague, which he had built, and where his three previous wives Blanche de Valois, Anna of the Palatinate and Anna Świdnica were also buried. Richard II ordered the construction of a 'very unusual imperial shrine, the like of which had never been seen before' in St Paul's around the time of Elżbieta's Requiem Mass.[39]

Right: Edward III, grandfather of Richard II. (Courtesy of the British Library)

Below: Miniature featuring Edward of Woodstock, father of Richard II. (Courtesy of the British Library)

The famous contemporary portrait of Richard II in Westminster Abbey. (© Dean and Chapter of Westminster. Used with kind permission)

The effigies of Richard and his first queen Anne of Bohemia. (© Dean and Chapter of Westminster. Used with kind permission)

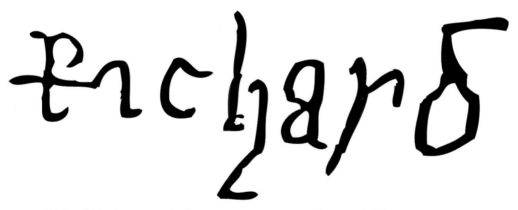

Richard II's signature, the first surviving signature of an English king.

Canterbury Cathedral, where Richard's father Edward of Woodstock was buried in 1376. (Courtesy of Matthew Black under Creative Commons)

Stamford, Lincolnshire, where Richard's mother Joan of Kent was buried in 1385.

Bordeaux, Richard's place of birth. (Courtesy of Luca Sartoni under Creative Commons)

St André Cathedral, Bordeaux, where Richard was baptised three days after birth. (Courtesy of Einalem under Creative Commons)

Painting of the royal castle in Prague in 1607, birthplace of Richard's first queen Anne of Bohemia in 1366.

Charles Bridge, Prague, named after Richard's father-in-law the emperor Karl or Charles IV. (Courtesy of Charles Sharp under Creative Commons)

St Vitus's Cathedral, Prague, built by Karl IV; he and his four wives, including Richard's mother-in-law Elżbieta, are buried here. (Courtesy of Jay8085 under Creative Commons)

A 1493 illustration from the Nuremberg Chronicle of the Kaiserburg or Imperial Castle in Nuremberg, Germany, where Anne of Bohemia partly grew up.

The Alcazar in Seville, built by King Pedro the Cruel of Castile, probably Richard's godfather; Pedro's two daughters married Richard's uncles John and Edmund in 1371 and 1372.

The town of Angoulême, now in the Charente department in southern France, birthplace of Richard's brother Edward of Angoulême in 1365.

Hradec Králové, a city now in the Czech Republic, where Richard's mother-in-law Empress Elżbieta died in April 1393.

Ely Cathedral near Cambridge, where Richard believed he had seen a miracle in 1383.

Above and below: The Louvre in Paris, birthplace of Richard's second queen Isabelle de Valois in 1389 when it was a royal palace. (Above courtesy of Zoetnet under Creative Commons)

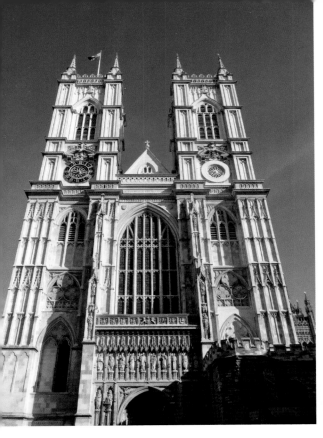

Left: Outside Westminster Abbey, where Richard was crowned on 11 July 1377 and where he was buried in 1415, at the start of Henry V's reign.

Below: The Tower of London, from where Richard watched the uprising in June 1381, and where he was imprisoned in September 1399. (Courtesy of Dave Addey under Creative Commons)

Wallingford Castle near Oxford, where Richard's mother Joan of Kent died in 1385. (Courtesy of Bill Tyne under Creative Commons)

Smithfield Market, London. Richard held great jousting tournaments at Smithfield throughout his reign, most famously in 1390. He met Wat Tyler here on 15 June 1381. (Courtesy of Steve Cadman)

Blackheath, London, where Richard first encountered the mass of rebels on 13 June 1381.

The ruins of Pleshey Castle, Essex, where Richard arrested his uncle the duke of Gloucester in July 1397. (Courtesy of tz1_1zt under Creative Commons)

Anne of Bohemia's funeral in 1394. (Courtesy of the British Library)

Right: A contemporary example of Richard II's badge of the hart. (Courtesy of the Metropolitan Museum of Art)

Below: Berkeley Castle, Gloucestershire, where Henry of Lancaster met his and Richard's uncle Edmund of Langley in July 1399.

Conwy Castle, North Wales, where Richard stayed shortly before his surrender to Henry. (Courtesy of Patana Rattananavathong)

Flint Castle, North Wales, where Richard surrendered to his cousin Henry of Lancaster in August 1399. (Courtesy of ARG_Flickr under Creative Commons)

Pontefract Castle, Yorkshire, now a ruin, where Richard probably died by starvation in February 1400. (Ruin courtesy of Tim Green; coin courtesy of the Metropolitan Museum of Art; model courtesy of Rept0n1x)

Above: Windsor Castle, where Richard's grandfather and predecessor Edward III was born and where both kings held annual celebrations for the Knights of the Garter on 23 April.

Left: Henry IV, depicted as king in a manuscript from 1451–1480. (Courtesy of the British Library)

14

'Let's Talk of Graves, of Worms, and Epitaphs': A Tragic Death, 1393–1394

A parliament was held at Westminster beginning on 27 January 1394. Richard Fitzalan, earl of Arundel, declared that he had 'certain matters close to his heart' which he could not 'conceal from his conscience' and angrily criticised the king's closeness to his uncle John of Gaunt: the duke of Lancaster walked arm in arm with Richard, and Richard and his household wore Gaunt's livery. This was hardly a fair or reasonable criticism on Arundel's part. Richard and Gaunt were, after all, uncle and nephew, and an alliance between the king and the wealthy, influential duke of Lancaster could only bring stability to the kingdom. Arundel petulantly complained that Gaunt was being presumptuous and 'often spoke such harsh and overbearing words in council and parliaments that the said earl and others often dared not to declare their full intent', and that it did the king no favours to show him such honour. For once Richard did not lose his temper, but skilfully argued against Arundel's points and defended his and his uncle's behaviour: 'Sir, inasmuch as it seems to the king and to the other lords, and each of them, that you are much grieved and displeased by my words, it beseems me to beseech you, of your good lordship, to stay your anger towards me.' The earl was forced to apologise to them both and retract his allegations.[1] Richard II could act wisely and prudently when he chose to, and it is a shame that he did not do it more often, rather than losing control of himself and shouting.

A most curious wedding had taken place on or around 4 November 1393: Richard's uncle Edmund of Langley, duke of York, aged fifty-two and the widower of King Pedro the Cruel's younger daughter Isabel of Castile, married Joan Holland, aged about thirteen and said to be a 'beautiful young lady'.[2] Joan was one of the daughters of Thomas Holland, earl of Kent, the elder of Richard II's two half-brothers, and thus the king's half-niece became his aunt. The new duchess of York was younger than at least two of her new husband's three children with Isabel of Castile, Edward and Constance of York, and the young woman, only just into her teens, became the third lady in England on her marriage behind Queen Anne and Constanza of Castile, duchess of Lancaster. Duchess Constanza, however, did not have long to live. She died on 24 March 1394, probably aged only forty or a little less, and left as her sole heir her daughter Catalina, then twenty-one and far away in Spain. Constanza and John of Gaunt never managed to take back her father Pedro's kingdom, and it remained in the hands of the Trastámara dynasty, but at least Catalina of Lancaster became the queen consort of Castile in 1390 when her husband and cousin Enrique III of the house of Trastámara succeeded his father on the throne.

Another royal lady died in the summer of 1394: Mary de Bohun, countess of Derby, younger daughter and co-heir of the late earl of Hereford, and wife of Richard's cousin Henry of Lancaster. Mary, who was no more than twenty-five at her death, left her widower and her six children, four sons and two daughters. Her heir to the half of the earldoms of Hereford and Northampton she had inherited from her father was her eldest son Henry of Monmouth, the future King Henry V, though Mary's widower Henry of Lancaster was entitled by English law to hold her entire inheritance as long as he lived.[3] Some years later, Henry of Lancaster was made the first duke of Hereford. He did not marry again until 1403, some years after he became king, though in 1401 fathered an illegitimate son, Edmund Lebourde.[4]

As though fate had not yet struck hard enough at the women of the royal family in 1394, far worse was to come for the king. On 7 June, the feast of Pentecost, at the royal palace of Sheen where the royal couple spent much time together, Anne of Bohemia died suddenly, a month past her twenty-eighth birthday. The cause of the queen's death is unclear: it has often been suggested as plague, but seemingly there was no outbreak of plague in England that year. Historian Kristen Geaman has examined Anne's extant apothecary accounts from June 1393 to June 1394 and found that the queen was not preoccupied with a long-term serious illness, but seems rather to have been a woman in the prime of her life concerned with maintaining her general good health.[5] Whatever killed Anne, perhaps an infection or influenza, must have affected her fairly quickly and lethally. She had recently purchased large quantities of medicines associated in the fourteenth century with fertility and conception such as water of plantain, trisandali, spikenard and trifera magna, so had evidently still not given up hope of conceiving a child.[6] Richard II was utterly devastated at the sudden and shocking loss of his beloved companion of the last twelve and a half years, the woman who had supported him loyally through thick and thin and whom he adored.

He paid £7 6s 8d to send messengers asking all the archbishops, bishops, abbots, priors and deans of cathedral churches in England to say prayers for Anne's soul on 10 July, and bought £1,500 worth of wax in Suffolk and had it transported to London where a *chaundeler* or candle maker called Roger Elys would fashion them into candles to burn on Anne's hearse. Richard wrote to Anne's half-brother Václav of Germany and Bohemia to inform him of the sad news, and presumably to Anne's younger brother Zikmund of Hungary and Croatia as well (the king's half-brother John Holland had been sent on an embassy to Zikmund earlier in 1394, so the brothers-in-law certainly remained in contact).[7] Four days even before the queen's death, Richard paid 3s for the transport of 'the statue made in likeness of Anne, late queen of England' from London to Sheen.[8] This, presumably, is a reference to the effigy which would lie on top of her tomb, and it is curious that it was made some days before Anne died and that she was already called 'late queen' when she was still alive; this must surely mean that she was believed to be close to death already. Anne was survived by her younger siblings Zikmund, king of Hungary and Croatia, Johann, margrave of Moravia and Brandenburg, and Markéta, burgravine of Nuremberg, and her older half-siblings Václav, king of Germany and Bohemia, and Katharina, duchess of Bavaria and Austria.

Shortly after Anne's death, Richard sent a letter to Wilhelm, duke of Guelders and Jülich, postponing a reception of the duke because he was suffering from the 'heaviest sadness and bitterness of heart, and therefore could not show as much courtesy for your friendship as we would like'.[9] The *Vitae et Regni* says that 'although she died childless, this queen was held to be glorious and beneficial to the realm of England, insofar as she could be, so that both nobles and commoners greatly mourned her death'.[10] On 10 June, three days after her death, the king ordered members of the English nobility and the English bishops to accompany Queen Anne's body from Sheen to Westminster.[11] Four hearses were built 'upon the days of celebrating the solemnity of the exequies of the said queen', and these hearses were taken bearing Anne's body, surrounded by the candles made by Roger Elys, to Wandsworth, the priory of St Mary Overie (later Southwark Cathedral), St Paul's Cathedral and Westminster Abbey at various times between June and August 1394.[12] Some months later, Richard gave 100 marks to be shared out among the monks of Westminster as a reward for their efforts in performing Anne's funeral.[13] Her effigy can still be seen in the abbey, next to Richard's with the couple holding hands, though bizarrely, few of her remains still survive in the coffin: over the centuries, most of the queen's bones were removed through a hole in the side of the tomb by curious visitors.

On 9 August 1394, the king agreed to give Westminster Abbey £200 a year in two instalments in return for their prayers for his good health and the well-being of his realm, and for Anne's soul on the anniversary of her death every year. Richard also asked them to pray for his own soul after he died on the anniversary of his death, and gave very precise instructions to be followed on his anniversary: the abbot, prior and convent should chant *placebo* and *dirige* with nine lessons and with 'the solemn tolling of bells', and place a hundred wax candles around his tomb, each one weighing 12 lbs. The abbot should say a solemn Mass before the high altar, every monk should say a private Mass, and the lay brothers should say the Lord's Prayer, the creed and the Hail Mary. Every poor person who visited the abbey on the anniversary should receive 1*d* in alms and be fed in the precincts of the abbey, in return for saying 'clearly and devoutly' the Lord's Prayer, the creed and the Hail Mary for the souls of the king and queen. Richard's very long and detailed instructions went on and on in similar vein.[14] His preoccupation, even obsession, with every minor detail of the ceremonies he intended to take place on the anniversary of his own death – he was, after all, a young man, still only twenty-seven – provides a valuable insight into his grieving and morbid state of mind two months after losing his beloved Anne. The king returned to this topic some years later in 1398, on the feast of St George or 23 April, and granted the abbey several lands, tenements and rents intended to make up the promised £200. He added 'and lest the foregoing be forgotten, in each year on the aforesaid anniversary [of his death] the whole of the foregoing charter shall be read in the chapter before the whole convent'.[15]

Queen Anne's funeral and burial took place at Westminster Abbey on Monday 3 August 1394. Richard's grief and temper broke out against Richard Fitzalan, earl of Arundel, when the earl arrived late for the queen's funeral and, to add insult to injury, requested that he might also leave early. Unable or unwilling to control himself, furious at this insult to his consort and hardly a friend of Arundel anyway, the king seized a cane or a staff and laid about the earl with it, causing him injuries and forcing the funeral to be interrupted and delayed until well into the night as the monks had to re-consecrate the abbey, desecrated as it was with Arundel's blood. It may even be, as Thomas Walsingham claims, that Richard would have killed the earl if he had not been physically restrained. It would certainly fit with what we know of Richard II, who tended to overreact at the best of times, and this was the worst of times and the worst insult Arundel could have offered him. A no doubt shaken Arundel was temporarily imprisoned in the Tower of London and only released when he was bound over for the staggeringly large amount of £40,000, a sum which even he, enormously wealthy as he was, would never have been able to pay.[16]

Within months, Richard was planning his own tomb and effigy, next to Anne. On 1 April 1395 he commissioned Henry Yevele and Stephen Lote, stonemasons of London who also worked on Westminster Hall, to construct a 'tomb of pure marble … for the said lord the king and Anne, late queen of England'. This would cost Richard £650.[17] The king also paid £20 to a sacristan of the abbey for 'painting the covering of the tomb of Anne, late queen of England' and for 'the removal of a tomb near the tomb of the said queen; also for painting the said tomb so removed, and for painting an image to correspond with another of the king placed opposite in the choir'.[18] Another £2 13s 4d went to 'diverse masons, carpenters and other labourers' working on Richard's renovations at Westminster Hall and to 'certain artificers for forming two images of copper in likeness of the king and queen'. *Chaundeler* Roger Elys received over £40 for his expenses relating to the queen's burial.[19] In April 1399, only some months before his downfall, Richard would pay £100 to two coppersmiths of London 'for gilding two images, resemblances of the king and queen, made with copper and latten, and crowned, with their right hands joined, and the left hand of the said statues holding a sceptre, with a rod and cross between the statues'.[20]

Richard II also decided on the epitaph he wished to appear on his and Anne's joint tomb, probably in April 1395. It was written in Latin in rhyming couplets, and gives a useful insight into his grandiose opinion of himself:

> Prudent and pure, Richard by right the second, vanquished by fate, lies here depicted under marble. Truthful in speech he was, and full of reason. Tall of body, prudent in mind, like Homer. A friend of the church, he subdued the mighty; he cut down anyone who violated royal rights. He struck down heretics and scattered their friends. Oh merciful Christ, to whom he was devoted, oh [John the] Baptist, keep safe him who put you first in his prayers. Beside him under stone, Anne now lies entombed. While she lived in the world she was married to Richard the second. Devoted to Christ she was well known for her deeds; she favoured the poor, always receiving thanks for her gifts. She settled disputes and relieved the oppressed. She was beautiful in body, fair and mild of face. She proved a comfort to widows, and a tonic to the sick. In the year 1394, in June, the seventh of the month, she departed this life.[21]

Famously, Richard ordered the palace of Sheen – all of the sprawling complex, not only the private area of La Neyt where he and Anne had lived and where she had died – to be razed to the ground. This order was not given until 9 April 1395, ten months after Anne's death, and therefore Richard was not acting in the first wave of terrible grief, but much later when he had had more time to think about it.[22] This tends to emphasise the idea that he ordered the palace's destruction because of the painful memories of the happy times he had spent there with Anne, whom he had lost, and that he genuinely could not face the prospect of visiting and staying at Sheen without her. For a year Richard also refused to enter any chamber in which Anne had been, excepting churches.[23] The order to level Sheen was given to the clerk of the king's works, John Gedney, and included 'as well the houses and building in the courtyard within the moat and within the courtyard outside the moat, as the houses and buildings of La Neyt beside the manor'. It cost the king a considerable amount of money for masons, bricklayers and other labourers to reduce Sheen completely.[24] It is also possible that around this time Richard destroyed Anne's household accounts, correspondence and other records, as almost nothing has come down to us.[25] Richard of Bordeaux's beloved Anne of Bohemia therefore remains, sadly, something of an enigma to us, for all Richard's undoubted adoration of her.

15

'So Sweet a Guest as My Sweet Richard': A Second Royal Marriage, 1394–1396

The issue of the succession to the English throne was becoming ever more acute. Richard was now a widower in his late twenties with no immediate prospect of fathering a child, and his cousin Roger Mortimer, the earl of March, came of age in April 1395. The king, however, showed few signs of favour either to March or to another potential heir, his first cousin Henry of Lancaster. The earl of March was the king's heir general, while his heir male was his uncle John of Gaunt followed by Gaunt's son Henry. Gaunt remained loyal to Richard throughout the 1390s, which cannot always have been easy given their occasionally tense relationship and Richard's often prickly and difficult personality, and was perhaps a quid pro quo if Gaunt expected that he or his son might be named as heir to the throne. Richard, however, showed much more affection and favour towards his cousins Edward of York and Richard of Conisbrough – the latter his godson and namesake – than he did towards Henry of Lancaster.

Only one chronicle is known to have written a commentary on the succession to the throne during Richard's reign. The chronicler commented probably in 1387 that Edward III's second son Lionel married the heiress of the earldom of Ulster, Elizabeth de Burgh, and had one daughter with her, i.e. Philippa of Clarence. It was to Philippa's two sons Roger Mortimer, earl of March, and Edmund Mortimer, said the chronicler, that 'the kingdom of England would descend if – which God forbid – the king were to die without children'.[1] There is, however, no known document of Richard II's reign in which he acknowledged March as his heir to his throne, though one chronicler claims that at one of his parliaments he had it publicly proclaimed that if he died childless March should be his heir.[2] There is no evidence for this statement in the extant records of parliament.

In late August 1394, ambassadors from Scotland were given safe conducts to visit England and met the bishop of Durham and the earl of Northumberland to discuss the possibility of a marriage between the royal families of England and Scotland.[3] Presumably the grieving Richard was not yet thinking of taking another wife – though perhaps he was, given the urgency of the succession question – and if he was not the intended groom it is not entirely clear who the potential marriage partners were intended to be. In 1394 the king of Scotland, since the death of his father Robert II in April 1390, was Robert III, second of the house of Stewart. Robert III's wife Annabella Drummond was either pregnant at this time with her youngest child, the future King James I, or he had recently been born; James would eventually marry Joan Beaufort, daughter of Richard II's first cousin John Beaufort, with whom he fell in love while a prisoner in England. Another meeting was arranged 'between English and Scottish princes' for 3 July 1395, though Richard wrote to King Robert and Queen Annabella postponing it to 1 October.[4]

On 3 December 1394, Richard paid 100 marks to two London goldsmiths for 'two collars, and one stud of gold ornamented with pearls and precious stones' for himself to wear.[5] Some weeks before, he had spent just under £250 on gifts for the viscount of Melun, a French envoy from Charles VI: these included a 'great gold cup', two gold rings (one with a ruby and one with a diamond), a velvet cloak 'worked with gold of Cyprus', two pieces of blue cloth-of-gold (material shot through with gold thread) and six pieces of black cloth-of-gold.[6] Also in December 1394 he sent a messenger to Pope Boniface IX 'upon the secret affairs of the lord king', with a gold ring set with a ruby to be given to Boniface as a gift.[7] This may have been connected to Richard's ongoing efforts to have his great-grandfather Edward II canonised: on 24 April 1395 he made a belated payment of £6 19s to two men, Peter Merk and James Monald, for travelling from London to Florence some years before to see Urban VI (who had died in October 1389) with a gift of a gold cup and a gold ring with a ruby, and most importantly, one *Book of the Miracles of Edward, late King of England, whose body was buried at the town of Gloucester.*[8]

Richard adored jewels and was somewhat preoccupied with his appearance. Clothes at his court, in the latter years of his reign if not also before, were lavish and extravagant, at least for men, whose short and skin-tight clothing was far more sexualised than women's. Men often wore a hood on their heads, and long arms and legs, broad shoulders and a slender waist were prized and emphasised.[9] Courtiers wore shoes with long points called *cracowes*, after the Polish city of Krakow (where Richard's parents-in-law Karl and Elżbieta had married in 1363), the points of which had to be tied to men's legs so that they could walk. The disapproving author of the *Vitae et Regni* commented that 'from Bohemia there came with the queen into England that execrable abuse, namely shoe-soles with long points, called in English "cracows" or "pyks", half a yard long, so that it was necessary to bind them to the shin with silver chains, before one could walk in them'.[10] The same author claims that Richard had made for himself a 'tunic of pearls and precious stones and gold, and worth thirty thousand marks' or £20,000, which must be a gross exaggeration – Richard certainly spent a lot of money on garments, but it is impossible for an item of clothing to have cost this much – and comments that he was 'extravagantly splendid' and 'too much devoted to luxury'.[11]

Then again, royalty and nobility were expected to look the part and to appear opulent, wealthy and powerful in order to set themselves apart from the common people, to display open-handed generosity and lavishness of living, and generally did spend enormous sums on clothes and jewellery; Richard II was far from alone in this. His mother Joan of Kent and paternal grandparents Edward III and Philippa of Hainault spent notoriously large amounts of money on their clothes, and so did his uncle John of Gaunt and cousin Henry of Lancaster. In 1393/94, Richard II spent over £24 on 'two very curious garments' to wear at a masque, one a dancing doublet and the other a *hanselin* or loose jacket. The *hanselin* was embroidered with leeches, water and rocks, and embellished with fifteen whelks and fifteen mussels made of silver-gilt, and fifteen cockles of white silver. The doublet, meanwhile, was embroidered with gold orange trees and adorned with 100 oranges of silver-gilt.[12] The seventeen-year-old Richard, concerned as ever with cutting a fine royal figure, spent £20 on buttons in June 1384, bought from a London jeweller named Pincheron, and also owned an 'eagle of pearls with a silk belt' which he perhaps wore with his staggeringly expensive eagle-shaped pearl buttons, previously mentioned.[13] Among the items belonging to Richard inventoried at Haverford Castle in 1399 were a wall-hanging of red worsted embroidered with stags, a blue cloth embroidered with golden elephants' heads, and a white and blue cloth embroidered with dogs.[14] He and Queen Anne owned an elaborate standing mirror supported on a foot shaped like a tree, enamelled with roses and set with pearls, and wore matching belts decorated with their initials R and A. The king and queen owned numerous other belts, some of which had bells hanging from them, which were perhaps intended for dancing.[15]

Richard was ill sometime before March 1395: his physician, Master John Middleton, paid over £15 that month to two apothecaries of London for 'spices and electuary for the king's body ... for the use of the lord king'.[16] Other payments were made in 1395/96 to Richard's secondary physician Geoffrey Melton and his surgeon William Bradewardyn as well as to another apothecary, and it may be, as one modern historian has postulated, that Richard was suffering from calculus, i.e. accretions of salts forming in the internal organs.[17] He was also treated for a stone in the urinary tract at an uncertain date.[18] Among the medical staff employed by the king were several surgeons or 'leeches' who included one called, appropriately enough, John Leche, as well as John of Salisbury and Dan (Master) Robert Tidman or Tideman of Winchcombe, made bishop of Llandaff in 1393 and in 1395 translated to the bishopric of Worcester (Richard II attended his installation as bishop there in early 1396). The *Vita* accuses Tidman, probably unfairly, of spending nights in drunken revelry with the king and Thomas Merk, later bishop of Carlisle and a strong supporter of Richard II.[19] John Leche was forced to give up his job in May 1383 owing to weak eyesight, but continued to receive an income of 7½d a day from Richard until this was replaced in September 1386 by the grant of a manor in Cheshire for life without rent.[20]

Despite his illness, the king began making plans for a visit to Ireland, of which the kings of England had been lords (at least nominally) since 1171. Richard would be the first English king to visit the country since John, his great-great-great-great-grandfather, in 1210, and would also be the last king of England to set foot there for another 300 years,

William III being the next royal visitor in the 1690s. Richard paid £2 for two large wooden chests bound with iron to transport 16 lbs of gold and silver to Ireland with him, and at the beginning of October set off himself, landing in Waterford on 2 October 1394.[21] The main aim of the visit was to bring down Art MacMurrough, who had styled himself king of Leinster, and Richard had been planning the visit since at least 2 July 1394, less than a month after the queen's death (perhaps he thought that visiting a country neither he nor Anne had ever visited would help distract him from his grief and loss).[22] Accompanying him was an army of 7,000–8,000 men and many of the English nobility, including the king's half-brother John Holland and his nephew Thomas Holland; the earl of Nottingham, Thomas Mowbray; Thomas, Lord Despenser; and Sir Thomas Percy, the earl of Northumberland's brother.

Richard left his uncle Edmund of Langley, duke of York, as *custos regni* or 'keeper of the realm' in his absence, though Edmund's son Edward of York was one of the men who travelled to Ireland with Richard.[23] The king was in Dublin from 6 November 1394 until 18 January 1395, and sailed again from Waterford on 1 May 1395. At Drogheda during the visit, Richard presented his cousin Edward of York with a fine gift, a silver cup decorated with a golden beech tree.[24] English chroniclers knew little about Ireland and hence barely mentioned Richard's visit, and Jean Froissart, citing an English squire called Henry Crystede 'who spoke French quite well' as his source, called it a 'strange wild place consisting of tall forests, great stretches of water, bogs and uninhabitable regions'. Froissart also said that four Irish kings – O'Neill of Meath, O'Brien of Thomond, MacMurrough of Leinster and O'Conor of Connaught – were personally knighted by Richard in the cathedral church of Dublin on Lady Day (25 March) 1395, and sat at his table with him that day.[25] O'Brien of Thomond sent a letter to Richard II which began 'to the excellent lord the king, with all humility, reverence and honour' and went on to declare that he would have submitted to him 'heartily and humbly and with all subjection' if he had known earlier of the king's arrival in Ireland. Richard elsewhere was addressed in letters as 'your highness' and 'your majesty' and 'most serene prince and lord' by men who called themselves his 'humble liegeman' and so on.[26] The expedition was in fact a great triumph for Richard, and when he returned to England in early May 1395 he had good reason to feel pride and joy in his achievements.[27]

The date 21 June 1395 marked the eighteenth anniversary of the death of Edward III and Richard's accession to the throne, and he ordered one of his sergeants-at-arms, John Elyngeham, to bring his second crown to Leeds Castle in Kent, where he was staying. A group of archers was to attend Elyngeham to ensure that the crown was not stolen.[28] In July that year, the Hainaulter chronicler Froissart, who had been in Bordeaux when Richard was born there at the beginning of 1367, visited England. Froissart landed at Dover and on 13 July travelled to Canterbury where made a special point of visiting the tomb of Richard's father Edward of Woodstock, and saw the king himself there 'with a noble company of lords, ladies and damsels'. Froissart followed the royal court to nearby Leeds Castle, where Richard was staying from 7 to 18 July 1395.[29] Froissart was presented to Richard – it was the first time he had seen him as an adult – and gave him letters from the duke of Bavaria (presumably Richard's kinsman Albrecht I, son of the Holy Roman Emperor Ludwig of Bavaria and father of Wilhelm of Ostrevant), but had no time to give the king the gift he had brought him as Richard was 'sore busied in council'.

The court moved on to the royal palace of Eltham in Kent, where Froissart met his old friend Sir Richard Sturry and walked with him in the gallery and garden in front of the king's chamber, 'where it was very pleasant and shady'. Attending Richard at this time were the earls of Derby, Arundel, Northumberland, Kent and Rutland, the archbishops of Canterbury and York, and the bishops of London and Winchester. Froissart had brought an illuminated book for Richard when he finally met him, which he laid on the king's bed; it was covered with crimson velvet, with ten silver and gilt buttons and roses of gold, and with two large clasps of silver and gilt. Richard asked what the book was about, and was delighted to hear that it 'treated matters of love'; he opened it in Froissart's presence and read some of it from different pages, at which juncture the chronicler commented on the king of England's excellent ability to read and speak French. A knight of the royal household took the book into Richard's private chamber.[30] John of Gaunt, duke of Lancaster, was in Aquitaine at this time so there was no chance for Froissart to meet him, but the chronicler had time for a chat with Gaunt's brother Edmund of Langley, duke of York, who remembered Froissart's loyalty to his mother Queen Philippa. In Froissart's account of meeting Richard II, the man who was usually gossipy and a great storyteller comes across as curiously unengaged, and the account is rather abrupt and with few details or descriptions of Richard personally (though there are many details of the English court and courtiers more generally).

Some years later, Froissart claimed that in the late 1390s rumours were rife in London that Richard II was not really the son of Edward of Woodstock.[31] Presumably he heard gossip during this trip to England in the summer of 1395, though it is doubtful if he believed it. Froissart had been in Bordeaux at the time of Richard's birth, after all, and mentioned no vicious rumours or gossip at this time that Richard was not truly his father's son. The irregular marriage of Richard's parents continued to haunt the king, though these rumours are also evidence of his subjects' discontent with him, and probably if he had not alienated a substantial proportion of his kingdom by the time of his downfall in 1399, few people would have cared so much about the 1361 marriage of Edward of Woodstock and Joan of Kent and whether or not they had a correctly formulated dispensation, or whether Joan had been married before. In the summer of 1395, Richard had been widowed from Anne of Bohemia for a year: 7 June marked this sad anniversary.

On 22 November 1395, the body of Robert de Vere, earl of Oxford and duke of Ireland, was brought back from Louvain to England for burial, having been exhumed from its original resting place.[32] Richard II attended the funeral at Earls Colne Priory in Essex, where most of the de Veres were buried. Rather morbidly, at least according to the sometimes unreliable Thomas Walsingham, the king had the cypress wood coffin opened to see de Vere's face one last time and looked at it for a long time, and touched de Vere's corpse: he placed gold rings on de Vere's fingers as a sign of his respect and affection. De Vere's mother Maud, *née* Ufford, attended, as did the archbishop of Canterbury and various other bishops and abbots, but the entire English nobility stayed away because they 'had not yet swallowed the hate they had conceived against Robert'.[33] Robert's widow Philippa Coucy apparently did not attend either.

Richard II did not take another favourite after Robert de Vere; although in the late 1390s he showed much favour to his cousin Edward of York, earl of Rutland and by then duke of Albemarle, he does not seem to have been anything like as infatuated as he had been with Robert, and chroniclers did not comment on it. It was hardly surprising, after all, that the king should show favour to his own royally born cousin, who was the grandson of two kings (Edward III and Pedro of Castile). Richard spent Christmas 1395 and New Year 1396, the second festive season he had spent without Queen Anne, at the royal manor of Langley and at his father's former favourite residence of Kennington.

Richard's uncle John of Gaunt, duke of Lancaster, caused a great scandal at the English court on or shortly after 14 January 1396: he married his long-term mistress Katherine Swynford, mother of his four illegitimate children John, Henry, Thomas and Joan Beaufort, born in the 1370s. Katherine was now duchess of Lancaster, and the highest-ranking lady in England until Richard married again. It was an astonishing marriage. Gaunt's first wife had been a great heiress, of the highest noble birth, and partly royal; his second was a king's daughter and the rightful queen of Castile in her own right. Now he had married a woman whose father was a mere herald and who was the sister-in-law of the poet Geoffrey Chaucer, and who had been Gaunt's mistress for many years. Froissart says that John of Gaunt's sister-in-law Eleanor de Bohun, the duchess of Gloucester, and Philippa Mortimer, countess of Pembroke and Arundel, sister of the earl of March and Gaunt's great-niece, led the list of ladies who refused to enter any place where Swynford was present and who declared that the duke 'has sadly disgraced himself by marrying his concubine'.[34] Froissart adds that Gaunt's brother Thomas of Woodstock was also outraged and called the duke a doting fool, and stated that he would never honour Swynford by calling her his sister.

By contrast, Richard II showed considerable affection and support to the new duchess, and later supported his uncle's request to Pope Boniface IX to legitimise his Beaufort cousins. This was done on 4 February 1397, a year after Gaunt and Swynford's wedding, and was announced in the parliament then being held at Westminster: 'John, knight, Henry, clerk, Thomas, *donsel*, and Joan, damsel ... since we thought in our inner contemplation how ceaselessly and with what honours we have been blessed by the paternal and sincere affection of our uncle ... you may hold, enjoy and exercise as fully, freely and lawfully as if you were born in lawful wedlock any statutes or customs of our realm of England ... by virtue of the plenitude of our royal power, and by assent of our parliament, we legitimate you, and any children you may have'. Later the proviso 'the royal dignity being excepted' was added by the Beauforts' half-brother Henry IV, indicating they had no claim to the throne.[35]

Now legitimate and able to marry members of the high nobility, the four Beaufort children and their descendants rose high. John, the eldest, was made earl of Somerset on 10 February 1397, six days after he was legitimised, and was the father of Joan Beaufort, queen consort of Scotland, and, via his granddaughter Margaret Beaufort, the great-grandfather of Henry VII. The second Beaufort son, Henry, became a cardinal and bishop of Winchester, Thomas became duke of Exeter and Joan became countess of Westmorland and was the grandmother of Edward IV and Richard III via her youngest child, Cecily Neville.[36] Between the death of the queen, Anne of Bohemia, in June 1394 and the wedding of John of Gaunt and Katherine Swynford nineteen months later, the first lady in England had been, rather astonishingly, Joan Holland, duchess of York. She was Richard II's half-niece and the second wife of his uncle Edmund of Langley, and was still only in her mid-teens; her husband was forty years her senior. The English nobility of the late fourteenth century was fiendishly interrelated. Joan Holland was also the niece of the earls of Arundel and Huntingdon, sister-in-law of the earl of March, and a first cousin of Eleanor de Bohun, duchess of Gloucester and also the king's aunt by marriage. Joan Holland and Eleanor de Bohun's uncle Thomas Arundel, brother of the earl of Arundel, was translated from the archbishopric of York to the archbishopric of Canterbury in 1396, to the great displeasure of the king, who loathed him (a feeling heartily reciprocated).

Richard did not have long to grieve for Anne of Bohemia. It was imperative that the king marry again and father a child, an heir of his body; it was still unclear whether the next heir to the English throne was Roger Mortimer, John of Gaunt or Henry of Lancaster. Richard made it plain that he would accept no one but the daughter of a king as his new queen.[37] Already in the second half of 1394, Richard's council began to search for a new royal bride, and by February 1395 had settled on Yolande of Aragon, even though she was already betrothed to Louis of Naples.[38] Yolande was the daughter of King Juan I of Aragon and granddaughter of Pedro IV, and was a great-granddaughter, via her mother Yolande of Bar, of John II of France. Born in the early 1380s, she was almost a decade and a half Richard's junior, and she and her older half-sister Joana, countess of

Foix, were King Juan I's only children to survive childhood. Joana of Foix renounced her claim to the throne of Aragon on her marriage, and therefore, in the absence of any brothers, Yolande had a very good claim to the throne. In the end, however, her father was succeeded as king of Aragon on his death in May 1396 by his younger brother Martin I.

The putative England–Aragon alliance caused some alarm in France, and Charles VI, or rather his advisers, stepped in to prevent Yolande marrying Richard by offering Charles's own daughter Isabelle instead. Yolande of Aragon ultimately married Louis, king of Naples, who was already her fiancé in 1394/95. She became the mother-in-law of Charles VI's fifth son and successor Charles VII, and was the grandmother of Marguerite of Anjou, who married Henry VI of England in 1445. Richard responded favourably to the putative marriage alliance with France; the king's instinct to make peace with that kingdom rather than pursue his father and grandfather's claim to the French throne grew stronger in the 1390s. Richard's envoys regarding his marriage included his cousin Edward of York, earl of Rutland, his more distant cousin Thomas Mowbray, earl of Nottingham, William Scrope, his chamberlain, and the archbishop of Dublin. The kingdoms of France and England had been on the verge of signing a final peace treaty in the early summer of 1393. On 16 June that year, eighteen drafted articles were agreed between the dukes of Lancaster and Gloucester on the English side and the dukes of Berry and Burgundy on the French, who had been negotiating hard in a town between Boulogne and Calais. The treaty foundered, however, when the English were asked to renounce sovereignty over the duchy of Aquitaine in south-west France.[39] Now the possibility of arranging a real peace, sealed by a royal marriage, had come at last.

The marriage was approved and agreed in Paris on 9 March 1396, and a dispensation for consanguinity, necessary because both Richard and Isabelle were descended from Philip IV of France's brother Charles de Valois, was issued by Pope Boniface IX on 27 July.[40] Richard also wrote to Charles VI in July 1395 and again in June 1396, proposing two further marriages: that of his cousin Edward of York to Charles's second daughter Jeanne (b. 1391), and that of his cousin Henry of Lancaster's eldest son Henry of Monmouth (b. 1386, future King Henry V) to Charles's then youngest daughter Michelle

(b. 1395, so only a baby at this time).[41] In the end, nothing came of these suggestions, though Henry V did marry Charles VI's daughter Katherine (b. 1401) in 1420.

Edward of York instead made a rather peculiar marriage at an uncertain date in the late 1390s: his bride was Philippa Mohun, who was many (probably at least twenty) years his senior and who had been widowed twice, her previous husbands being the rather obscure knights Sir Walter Fitzwalter and Sir John Golafre. Both of her previous marriages were childless, and she and Edward produced no family either; she may already have been past childbearing age when they wed. As Edward was the grandson of two kings, heir to the dukedom of York and one of the greatest noblemen in Europe, he might have expected to make a far more impressive union, which suggests that – despite the huge age difference and his wife's probable inability to give him heirs – his marriage to Philippa was a genuine love match.[42]

In a letter of May 1396 Richard addressed Charles VI as 'the very high and mighty prince C., by the grace of God our very dear and beloved father of France', a rather elegant way of writing a letter to Charles with the courtesy he deserved without acknowledging him as king of France. This was a title Richard used himself, albeit, tactfully, not in this particular letter, where Richard called himself 'R. by the same grace king of England etc.'. In correspondence four years previously, Richard had begun letters to Charles with 'by the grace of God our very dear and beloved cousin of France', and in September 1395 with 'our very dear and beloved brother and cousin of France'; despite his wish for an alliance with Charles, he refused to acknowledge him as king.[43] The king of England told his ambassadors Edward of York, Thomas Mowbray and the archbishop of Dublin to tell the French that 'if it happens by God's grace that from the marriage of our lord king with Isabelle, daughter of his cousin of France, there should be a son, then that son should be duke of Normandy and count of Anjou and Maine'.[44] As the kings of England had lost Normandy, Anjou and Maine to the French in 1204, almost 200 years before, this was a rather startling declaration. Richard also stated that if he and Isabelle might have any younger sons, 'if by chance it can be found that the realm of Scotland should be in any manner confiscated, or otherwise that it ought to come to the kingdom of England', that Charles VI should send soldiers to help him conquer Scotland for Richard's son and Charles' grandson.

Needless to say, Richard's grandiose plans to take control of a sovereign nation and parts of France which his ancestors had lost two centuries previously came to nothing. Charles VI's daughter Isabelle of France, also often known as Isabelle de Valois, was born into the Valois dynasty which had ruled France since her great-great-grandfather Philip VI had succeeded his Capetian cousin Charles IV in 1328. Isabelle was many years Richard's junior; born in late 1389, she was, in fact, only five years old when her marriage to the English king was proposed. Why did Richard think it was a good idea to marry a young child, who would not be able to produce a child and heir to the English throne for a decade? There would, of course, be no question of consummating the marriage until Isabelle was considerably older. Richard would turn thirty at the beginning of 1397, and now had no prospect of fathering a child until he was close to forty. He may not have seen any problem with fathering children so late: his father Edward of Woodstock had been thirty-six when he was born, and his mother thirty-nine or forty. Richard was surely also aware that Edward I had been almost forty-five when his successor and Richard's great-grandfather Edward II was born in 1284, and sixty-two in 1301 at the birth of his youngest son, Richard's grandfather Edmund, earl of Kent. Equally, it may have been an indirect declaration that as he had had no children with his beloved Anne of Bohemia, he had no wish to father them with another woman either, or perhaps he thought that peace with France was worth the cost.

Isabelle's dowry may have made it worthwhile: 800,000 francs, of which 300,000 would be paid at the time of the wedding and the rest in yearly instalments.[45] The French author Philippe de Mézières wrote his celebrated *Letter to King Richard* (*Epistre au Roy Richart*) in the summer of 1395 recommending the then five-year-old Isabelle to the English king, on the not entirely female-friendly grounds that it was easier to train elephants and camels while very young, and that an immature princess would be easier to mould to Richard's wishes.[46] Richard's subjects may have hoped that he would marry a woman who could begin to bear him children more or less immediately. It was not to be, and it is even possible that Richard himself never expected children to result from his union with Isabelle.[47] A clause was added to the marriage contract that in the event of Richard's death, Isabelle would be free to return to France with her jewellery; this, as it turned out in 1399/1401, would be a relevant and important point for the young girl. Charles VI sent the most important envoys he could to the English king, his brother the duke of Orléans and his uncles the dukes of Berry, Burgundy and Bourbon. A truce of twenty-eight years was negotiated, to begin at sunrise at Michaelmas (29 September) 1398 and to last until Michaelmas 1426.[48]

Richard's soon-to-be father-in-law Charles VI, who was born on 3 December 1368 and thus was almost two years younger than he, had married his queen, Isabella or Isabeau of Bavaria, in the summer of 1385 when he was sixteen and she about fifteen. Isabeau was half-German and half-Italian: her father Stephan was the duke of Bavaria and a grandson of the Holy Roman Emperor Ludwig of Bavaria, and her mother Taddea Visconti (whose younger sister Caterina had once been put forward as Richard's bride) the eldest of the seventeen legitimate children of Bernabo, lord of Milan. In French she is known as Isabeau de Bavière, in German as Elisabeth von Bayern-Ingolstadt or Elisabeth von Wittelsbach, the name of her dynasty. Somewhat humiliatingly, the French had demanded before the 1385 marriage that Isabeau be brought from Germany and paraded before Charles VI for his inspection and agreement, to the displeasure of her father Stephan. Finally the duke begrudgingly agreed, but only on the condition that neither Isabeau nor anyone else was informed of the true reason for her visit to the French court in case the young king rejected her and returned her to Bavaria. As it happened, Charles VI fell in love when he saw her, and the teenage couple married in Amiens on 17 July 1385 only days after their first meeting.[49]

Isabeau's coronation as queen of France took place belatedly on 22 August 1389, five days after the wedding of her brother-in-law Louis, later duke of Orléans, to her cousin Valentina Visconti. Valentina was the daughter of Gian Galeazzo, lord and later the first duke of Milan, and his first wife Isabelle of France, daughter of King John II and Bonne of Bohemia. Valentina was thus her husband Louis's first cousin, and she and Isabeau had a rather awkward relationship as Valentina's father had murdered his uncle Bernabo, Isabeau's grandfather. The 1389 coronation of the queen consort of France was a splendid event which, Froissart says, inspired Richard's tournament at Smithfield a few months later after the English king and his uncles heard detailed accounts from knights who had been present. Isabeau made a formal entry into Paris followed by the royal and noble ladies of France in strict order of precedence, watching a number of pageants enacting scenes from history and from the Bible as she went, including a magnificent depiction of the great general Saladin jousting with Christians. This latter detail may have particularly interested Richard when he heard about it, as he had inherited a tapestry featuring Saladin from his father, and may have been named in honour of Saladin's great adversary Richard Lionheart, the first King Richard of England.[50]

Queen Isabeau was six and a half months pregnant with Richard II's future queen at the time of her coronation. Isabelle de Valois, born in the Louvre in Paris on 9 November 1389, was the third of Charles and Isabeau's twelve children and the first to survive infancy. (The Louvre, now a world-famous museum, was originally a strong fortress on the edge of the city built in the late 1100s, and was converted by Isabelle's grandfather Charles V into a more comfortable royal residence.) Isabelle's brother Charles was born and died in 1386, the year after their parents' wedding, and her sister Jeanne was born in June 1388 and died in 1390. Her nearest sibling was another Jeanne, born in January 1391 and only fourteen months her junior, who later married John V, duke of Brittany, a grandson of King Carlos II 'the Bad' of Navarre via his mother Juana. Throughout Isabelle's early years and until she was eighteen, her mother Queen Isabeau regularly gave birth to Isabelle's siblings, though half of them died in childhood or early adulthood, including all but one of the royal couple's six sons; King Charles VII, the fifth son and the third to be given the name Charles after their father, born in 1403, was the only one to survive past the age of eighteen.

The royal daughters fared better, and five of the six lived into adulthood: two queen consorts of England, a prioress, and the duchesses of Brittany and Burgundy. At the time of Isabelle's marriage to Richard II in late 1396, she had four younger siblings – Jeanne, a second Charles who died as a child, Marie and Michelle – and the queen of France was pregnant again with her third son, Louis, who was born in January 1397. The tenth of Charles VI and Isabeau's children, born in 1401 and twelve years Isabelle's junior, was also a queen of England: Katherine, wife of Henry V, mother of Henry VI, grandmother via her son Edmund Tudor of Henry VII, and thus the ancestor of the Tudor dynasty. Supposedly Isabelle's parents were disappointed when she was born in 1389, having hoped for a son; the birth of another daughter fourteen months later must have compounded the disappointment. A previous marriage had been considered for Isabelle, with Jean of Alençon, later duke of Alençon, whose grandfather Charles was the younger brother of Philip VI.[51]

Isabelle was not yet three years old in August 1392 when her father Charles VI – still only twenty-three – suffered the first bout of the mental illness he would endure for the remaining thirty years of his life. Charles sometimes suffered from the delusion that he was made of glass and would shatter if anyone touched him. He also tried to kill his younger brother Louis of Orléans, demanded to be addressed as George, and often failed to recognise his wife and children, though he did also have periods of lucidity such as in the winter of 1395/96 when he corresponded with Richard about the marriage with his eldest daughter and a few months later when they met in person. Richard II was dismayed at the news of Charles's affliction; whatever his personal feelings about the French king may have been, Charles was as royal as he himself was. The rumours that Charles was the victim of poison or sorcery can only have increased Richard's own worries about his safety, and the news that Charles was so afflicted that he sometimes begged his courtiers to put him out of his misery can only have distressed him.[52]

Nor was Charles VI the only person suffering at the French court. His sister-in-law Valentina Visconti, duchess of Orléans, was, according to Froissart, looking after her own son and the three-year-old son of Charles VI and Queen Isabeau in 1395 when someone slipped a poisoned apple through the open window of the chamber in an attempt to kill the king's son. Valentina's own four-year-old son ate it instead, and died. As well as the horror of losing her child, Duchess Valentina was wrongfully accused of trying to poison her nephew, and was reviled as a traitor and enemy of France. Her father Gian Galeazzo, now duke of Milan, became involved, demanding that his beloved daughter be restored to her honour. The French court was far from a happy place in the 1390s, and the mutual bitterness and hostility with the court of Milan did not help matters. Richard II, when he met Charles VI in late 1396, promised to aid him militarily against Gian Galeazzo, though nothing came of it.

Richard II travelled to Calais between 7 and 22 August 1396 to meet Charles VI's uncle Philip, duke of Burgundy, to discuss how the two kings would meet and how and where the royal wedding would take place. During the visit, Burgundy gave Richard a gift of a liturgical book entirely covered with pearls, perhaps a Book of Hours.[53] A week before Richard departed, his kinsman William Courtenay, archbishop of Canterbury, died after almost exactly fifteen years in office, and was succeeded a few weeks later by Thomas Arundel, translated from the archdiocese of York. The king of England and the French royal duke arranged that Richard would return to Calais later in the year, and servants on both sides worked furiously to arrange the large amounts of food, drink, and sleeping accommodation that would be required. Richard appointed his uncle Edmund of Langley, duke of York, as regent of England in his absence as he had done when he visited Ireland, sailed from Dover, and arrived again in Calais on 21 October 1396. The letters patent appointing Duke Edmund as keeper of the realm gave the official reason for Richard's visit to France as 'a personal inspection of the castle and town of Calais and other castles and fortresses in Picardy'.[54]

Richard was accompanied by a large retinue, including his uncle John of Gaunt, duke of Lancaster, Gaunt's new wife Katherine Swynford, and Richard's cousins Elizabeth and Henry of Lancaster, two of Gaunt's three children with his first wife Blanche; the youngest royal uncle Thomas of Woodstock, duke of Gloucester, Duchess Eleanor, *née* de Bohun, and their daughter Anne, countess of Stafford; Edmund of Langley's son Edward of York, earl of Rutland; Thomas Mowbray, earl of Nottingham and Earl Marshal of England; and Henry Percy, earl of Northumberland.[55] Richard had his six noble male attendants, John of Gaunt, Thomas of Woodstock, Henry of Lancaster, Edward of York, Thomas Mowbray and Henry Percy, dressed in red velvet suits with a white heraldic bend of the livery of his late queen Anne of Bohemia.[56] This rather pointed reminder of his beloved first wife on the occasion of his second wedding perhaps emphasises that Richard saw his new marriage as purely political. Charles VI for his part was accompanied by his brother Louis, duke of Orléans, his paternal uncles the dukes of Berry and Burgundy, and his maternal uncle Louis, duke of Bourbon. Queen Isabeau did not attend, perhaps because she was about six months pregnant (she gave birth to a son, Louis, on 22 January 1397) and therefore found travelling difficult and uncomfortable.

On 26 October 1396 Richard rode from Calais towards his castle of Guisnes, accompanied by John, duke of Berry, and they were met by the duke of Orléans and 500 men. Richard dined with the two royal French dukes that night, and gave them rich gifts: to Berry a collar worth 500 marks, and to Orléans a gold goblet and ewer worth 200 marks.[57] It was arranged that the two kings would meet in the middle of the afternoon on Friday 27 October at a great encampment set up at Ardres, 10 miles from Calais, in a field which, not coincidentally, would also be used as the location for the Field of the Cloth of Gold 124 years later in 1520 when Henry VIII of England met Francis I of France. Tents and pavilions were erected for both the English and French sides, and 400 noblemen were assigned to assist events.

On 27 October 1396, the two kings met for the first time as arranged, at a central point in a pavilion, having advanced exactly the same distance towards each other. Richard looked magnificent in a long gown of red velvet bearing his symbol the white hart, and on his head wore a chaplet full of precious stones which Charles had sent him; Charles was dressed in a knee-length gown also of red velvet trimmed with a band of black and white, black leggings and spurs, and red and white shoes. On his head he wore a chaplet of black cloth covered with jewels, and wore both his own livery and Richard's, the white hart. Shortly before the meeting, Charles had entered the area and arrived at his own tent to the sound of loud music, and entered the pavilion with a retinue of 100 men. Both men took off their hoods, shook hands and kissed, while all their attendants – who had been forbidden to carry a sword, dagger or staff in their presence – knelt.

According to an English eyewitness, Charles VI looked as though he might faint at one point, and Richard took him by the arm, helped and comforted him.[58] Presents were exchanged: Charles gave Richard a gift which had been given to him as a New Year gift that year by his uncle the duke of Berry. It was a gold *nef*, a decorative ship used to collect alms at a feast, and the splendid and costly item stood on a bear and had tigers, the badge of Charles VI, at the prow and stern. The tigers wore jewelled collars and were looking at themselves in mirrors.[59] Richard gave the French king a large gold goblet and matching ewer which had been made for his grandfather Edward III about thirty years before.[60] After wine and sweetmeats had been consumed, Charles took Richard to his own marquee and visited

Richard in his, the two kings walking hand in hand, then they said their farewells at the central meeting point, shook hands and retired to their own quarters.

Saturday 28 October 1396 also saw some festivities, though these were interrupted by heavy rain, and some of the French delegation were forced to seek shelter in the English pavilions as many of their own had been washed away.[61] Richard on this day was wearing a calf-length gown of red and white velvet, while Charles wore the same clothes as the day before. They exchanged more gifts: Charles gave Richard two 'large golden pouches stuffed with precious stones', a panel with the image of the Trinity – probably a nod to his father, who had been devoted to the Trinity – in gold and encrusted with precious stones, and three equally luxurious and costly panels of Jesus Christ and Saints George and Michael. At dinner the two kings were served by the dukes of Berry, Burgundy and Bourbon, the latter – apparently something of a born entertainer – amusing them with his jokes.[62] The language of discourse was of course French, Richard and probably most of his accompanying nobility being fluent in the language. The French, on the other hand, had no reason or incentive to learn English. On Sunday Richard dined at Guisnes with the duke of Berry, and later with the duke of Orléans.[63] At some point during the visit, Marguerite, duchess of Burgundy, countess of Flanders and a descendant of Philip V of France, entertained Katherine Swynford, duchess of Lancaster, among other English nobility; evidently she was more forgiving of the duchess's humble origins than some of the English ladies.[64] Richard II gave Duchess Marguerite a particularly valuable badge of a white hart, his personal emblem, on this occasion or somewhat later.[65]

On Monday 30 October 1396, Richard II met his young bride-to-be Isabelle de Valois at the central spot in the pavilion where he had met her father some days before: the two kings waited together and watched as Isabelle was ceremoniously brought in. Richard gave Charles a gold hanap and ewer as they were waiting. Charles announced, 'Dearest son, I commend you to this creature, the dearest to me over all creatures in the world, except the Dauphin [his son] and our wife.' Richard, wearing a full-length gown of cloth of gold and blue, took Isabelle by the hand and thanked Charles for the precious gift. Isabelle wore a 'narrow gown of old-fashioned style' in blue velvet embroidered with the French fleur-de-lis and a hugely expensive crown, and had arrived at the pavilion on a richly caparisoned palfrey horse. Coached well in how to behave, Isabelle curtseyed twice to Richard, who raised her and gave her a formal kiss of peace.[66] Later in the day Richard hosted a dinner, and during this day gave Charles a courser, a fast and expensive horse ridden by knights, with a silver-gilt saddle. Charles gave him a brooch and a spice-plate decorated with the arms of France and unicorns, the latest items in the frantic and competitive mutual gift-giving between the English and French royals which marked the occasion.

At Richard's final banquet with Charles, having evidently learned that the French king was something of a carnivore, boiled and baked meats were served in line with Charles's preferred eating habits.[67] Isabelle subsequently travelled the few miles to Calais in the company of Richard's aunts by marriage the duchesses of Lancaster (Katherine Swynford) and Gloucester (Eleanor de Bohun), and the countesses of Huntingdon (his first cousin and sister-in-law Elizabeth of Lancaster) and Stafford (Anne of Gloucester, another of his first cousins and Eleanor de Bohun's daughter, who was only thirteen).[68]

The king of England and the king of France's daughter married in the church of St Nicholas in Calais on 4 November, the ceremony conducted by Thomas Arundel, the new (since 25 September) archbishop of Canterbury. The new archbishop of York, Robert Waldby, notified the king the day before his wedding that Boniface IX's dispensation for his marriage to Isabelle had arrived.[69] Richard's uncle Thomas of Woodstock, for all his hostility to the king and his opposition to the French marriage, had too much courtesy to show his displeasure to a little girl, and gave Isabelle some precious gifts on the eve of her wedding. They included a golden eagle adorned with precious stones from himself, and a great covered gold cup from Duchess Eleanor and six other cups from their children. On the day of the royal wedding, Thomas also gave Isabelle a golden crown, and his nephew Henry of Lancaster at some point gave her a gold greyhound.[70] The royal pair had a good and safe journey across the Channel to England which took only three hours, though others were not so fortunate: a storm suddenly blew up and took several of Richard's ships to the bottom of the sea, losing many of the precious props used at Ardres in the process.[71]

The new queen of England turned seven just five days after her wedding, on 9 November 1396. Despite her extreme youth she travelled to England and did not remain with her parents, and though leaving her family and her home at such a young age would normally have been difficult, even traumatic, for such a young child, Isabelle may well have found moving to England preferable to her life in France. Because of her father's madness, a power struggle arose between his brother Louis, duke of Orléans, and his uncle Philip the Bold, duke of Burgundy and later Philip's son and heir John the Fearless (*Jean sans Peur* in French). Over the years and decades, this struggle became extraordinarily vicious and resulted in the assassinations of Isabelle's uncle and her father's cousin. This can hardly have been a happy environment for the royal French children to grow up in.

On the other hand, Isabelle and her siblings were close to their mother Queen Isabeau, who was once thought by chroniclers and historians to have been an appallingly neglectful mother, a cruel wife to her unfortunate husband, and an adulteress with her brother-in-law Louis of Orléans, but these allegations have been disproved by more recent historians. Isabeau was in fact an involved and affectionate mother who found it painful and difficult to see her children leave her when they married, who took a keen interest in their education, and who bought them books, toys, clothes, birthday presents and pets, including parrots and turtledoves. She bought a Book of Hours for her daughter Jeanne in 1398 and an alphabet psalter for her daughter Michelle in 1403. The queen came from an affectionate and close-knit family in Bavaria, and, far from allegations that she left her children to go hungry, dirty, cold and dressed in rags while she slept with her brother-in-law and cruelly taunted her husband, did her best to recreate the warmth of her natal family ties with her own offspring.[72]

Sweetly, Isabelle de Valois took her dolls with her to England, all 'trimmed and provisioned with silver utensils', and her mother bought her a 'golden mill fitted out with pearls and little brooms for the amusement of my lady Ysabel'.[73] Isabeau also bought a small casket with a gold key for her daughter, and others sent her little mirrors, rings and rosaries.[74] As she was not only a little girl who loved playing with dolls and toys but the daughter of a king and now the wife of a king, however, Isabelle also took two ornate crowns with her – one with sapphires, rubies and clusters of pearls set around small diamonds – plus chaplets and other headdresses, brooches, numerous jewels and a belt entirely of gold and gems.[75]

Although to modern sensibilities the marriage of a man of almost thirty to a child of just turned seven might seem revolting and abusive, in fairness to Richard, he treated his young wife as though she were his sister and showed the little girl much kindness and affection, which she eagerly reciprocated. According to a chronicle called the *Traison et Mort*, Richard referred to Isabelle as 'my dearest sister and lady, my dearest and beloved companion Isabel of France'.[76] Owing to Isabelle's youth, she did not live with the king and they of course did not consummate their marriage – indeed, with Richard's deposition and death when Isabelle was barely ten, they never would. Under different circumstances, she might have expected to become Richard's wife in more than name only at the age of about fifteen (assuming that Richard ever had it in mind to consummate the marriage). Richard's fluency in French must have made communication between them very easy. The young queen lived sometimes at Windsor Castle and sometimes at Wallingford with her governess Marguerite, Lady Courcy, a French noblewoman who is not to be confused with Richard's first cousins the Coucy sisters Philippa, duchess of Ireland and countess of Oxford, and Marie, countess of Soissons and Bar. Lady Courcy was accused of profligate spending and lack of discretion, and was sent back to France in some disgrace in June 1399 with other members of the young queen's household only a few weeks after she was made a Lady of the Garter.

The Saint-Denys chronicler claimed that Queen Isabelle was treated in an appalling manner in England, and that all her household except one confessor and one lady-in-waiting were returned to France and that the little girl lived a solitary existence at Wallingford, forbidden to receive any French visitors in private or even converse with them in public. Charles VI, Queen Isabeau and the rest of the French royal family were furious at this, and the chronicler thundered, 'May it serve as an example to strike fear into the hearts of any French noblewoman intending to marry an Englishman! These perfidious foreigners have always distrusted the French.'[77] This statement about the bad treatment of the young queen is not borne out by any other source and seems to be merely a nationalistic rant (the English were also said to be 'naturally fickle' and to have mistreated the little queen 'out of hatred for the French') written after Richard's downfall. Jean Creton, a French chronicler who spent time with Richard II in 1399, continued the nationalistic theme, commenting that 'evil and unreasonable people as they are, the English mortally hate the French', but that Richard himself was ultimately deposed because 'he loyally loved his father-in-law the king of France with a love as true and sincere as any man alive'.[78]

Isabelle continued her lessons after she moved to England, and kept in touch with her mother Isabeau – though perhaps not with her afflicted father – via a messenger called Pierre Salmon.[79] There is evidence that Richard was deeply concerned about the mental state of his father-in-law the king of France and attributed it to malign forces around Charles VI at the French court. It may also have increased his own paranoia, to which he was increasingly to fall prey in 1397.[80] The *Historia Vitae et Regni Ricardi Secundi* says that Isabelle de Valois entered London on 23 November 1396 and was led through Southwark towards Kennington. Many of the citizens crowded onto London Bridge to see her, but because of the mass of people, some were crushed and trampled to death.[81]

16

'My Sorrow's Dismal Heir': A Coronation and the Succession, 1396–1397

Richard II spent Christmas 1396 at Coventry, and New Year and his thirtieth birthday, Saturday 6 January 1397, at the palace of Eltham in Kent. He paid more than £116 for jewels to give to Queen Isabelle 'at the feast of the Nativity of our Lord', and also gave lavish gifts to other family members at the end of 1396. John of Gaunt, duke of Lancaster, received a 'worked tablet' with four sapphires and four rubies, which cost £26; Thomas Mowbray, earl of Nottingham and Earl Marshal, also received a 'worked tablet' of gold with two sapphires, two rubies and pearls, which cost £25; Richard's first cousin Edward of York, earl of Rutland, received a 'tablet of gold worked with the image of Saint Katherine with rubies, sapphires and pearls' at £28; and John of Gaunt's new wife Katherine Swynford, duchess of Lancaster, was given a 'gold stud set with three sapphires and three rubies', which cost the king over £15. Even the cousin Richard often ignored, Henry of Lancaster, earl of Derby, received a gift, a diamond ring which cost £6, though perhaps the shine was rather taken off this sign of royal favour for Henry when the exact same thing was given to Joan, Lady Beauchamp, who was the earl of Warwick's sister-in-law and one of the daughters of the earl of Arundel. Finally, two sapphire rings were given to 'the companion of the queen's confessor and Herteman Hauberk', unidentified, and a diamond ring worth £5 to Blanche, Lady Poynings.[1]

Blanche Poynings, *née* Mowbray, was the widow of Thomas, Lord Poynings and the aunt of Thomas Mowbray, earl of Nottingham, and

a particular favourite of the king: in 1398 Richard gave her a gift of
£40. In 1388 she had been expelled from court by the Lords Appellant,
evidence of how close she was to Richard II, and in November 1396
was one of the noble ladies who accompanied Queen Isabelle to her
wedding. Blanche had been made a Lady of the Garter in 1386, the
same year as Richard's cousin Constance of York, Elizabeth Mowbray,
née Fitzalan, and Robert de Vere's mother Maud.[2] Isabelle de Valois
herself also sent out presents to Richard, the duke and duchess of
Lancaster, the royal cousins Edward of York and Henry of Lancaster,
and several others. These included a gold cup worth £72 to Richard.[3]

The day after her husband's thirtieth birthday, on Sunday 7 January
1397, Isabelle de Valois was crowned queen of England at Westminster
Abbey.[4] She had been brought to London a few days before and stayed
at the Tower of London, and on the day of her coronation was taken
from there along Cheapside to Westminster.[5] Richard showered her
with presents this year, and indulged and cosseted her.[6] One of the
gifts he gave her was a whistle inlaid with precious stones, previously
given to him by the bishop of Durham, and he also spent the massive
sum of £400 on a carriage for her. Other gifts the king bestowed on
the young queen between 1397 and 1399 were a golden candlestick
with a snuffer, a Venetian goblet, a jewelled hart and a crown, three
circlets and a chaplet.[7] As had also been the case with Anne of
Bohemia, people – predictably – complained about the excessive size
of the little queen's retinue.[8] Despite her youth, Isabelle was granted
her own dower lands on 8 December 1396, including the castle and
lordship of Pembroke in South Wales, and in 1397 she was made a
Lady of the Garter, the only one created that year.[9] The king restored
all rights, liberties and privileges to the mayor, sheriffs, aldermen and
citizens of London on 12 June 1397, supposedly 'at the supplication
of Queen Isabel'.[10]

A parliament was held at Westminster between 22 January and
12 February 1397, during which Richard tried unsuccessfully to raise
money for a military campaign against Gian Galeazzo Visconti, duke of
Milan, in aid of his new ally and father-in-law Charles VI of France.[11]
Richard did his best to convince those attending, and himself argued
in favour of the expedition. Considering how 'in the past there had
been very great trouble and unbearable destruction between the two
realms of England and France', he thought that the greatest good he
could do was to aid Charles VI, his kinsman, 'in his trouble and need'

so that 'great benefit and promise' might bring about the salvation of the kingdom. Richard went on to argue that he and Charles VI 'are considered two of the most worthy and valiant Christian princes', and therefore were bound to 'destroy such a tyrant and destroyer' of good Christian people, as Visconti supposedly was, and to restore those who had been oppressed. The king finished by saying that 'he wished to be at large and at liberty to command his people, and to send them to aid his friends, and to dispose of his own goods at his will, where and whensoever he chose'. This articulate pleading failed to move the commons, who announced that they were opposed to any such expedition and did not wish to be charged or burdened as a result of it. If the king wished to send a force of armed Englishmen to Milan to support the king of France, he would have to pay for it himself.

Richard's hostility towards Gian Galeazzo might also be interpreted as hostility towards his cousin Henry of Lancaster, a friend of the duke. This was also the parliament where Henry's half-siblings the Beauforts were legitimised and where the king declared himself 'entire emperor in our realm of England'. It is perhaps best known for a petition presented to it by a royal clerk called Thomas Haxey, which was disclosed to parliament on Friday 2 February 1397 (the feast of the Purification, or Candlemas) after Richard II had eaten dinner. Haxey made four specific complaints, the last and most interesting of which was that there were 'too many bishops and ladies' plus their hangers-on at Richard II's court, and that the costs of the king's household were much too high and should be curtailed, most particularly by reducing the number of bishops and ladies present.[12] As noted elsewhere, Richard very much seems to have enjoyed the company of women, and he responded to Thomas Haxey's points in person. Haxey was at first condemned to death for treason on 7 February 1397, though was already in the custody of the new archbishop of Canterbury Thomas Arundel, who sought mercy for him in the company of all the other prelates. Haxey was officially pardoned by Richard II 'of his royal pity and of his special grace' on 27 May 1397 for his request for a 'remedy for the grievous expense of the king's household by the stay of the bishops and multitude of ladies therein etc'.[13]

In or shortly before February 1397, Richard took a remarkable step: he adopted his first cousin Edward of York, earl of Rutland, as his brother. Edward first appears on record as 'the king's brother' on 27 February 1397, when he, Thomas Mowbray and William

Scrope were given 'instructions concerning the negotiations at Calais', i.e. related to Richard's marriage to Isabelle de Valois, and to propose a marriage between Henry of Lancaster, earl of Derby, and 'the daughter of the king of Navarre'. A year previously, when commissioned to deal with the English–French royal marriage, Edward of York had not been called 'the king's brother'.[14] Edward of York has often had a bad press, mostly owing to his occasionally indifferent loyalty to both Richard II and his other first cousin Henry of Lancaster, yet he was a highly intelligent and capable man whom one chronicler, later in Edward's life, called 'a second Solomon'.[15] Rosemary Horrox believes that Edward was called Richard II's brother solely on the strength of his possible future marriage to Queen Isabelle's sister Jeanne, proposed in 1395/96, yet Richard's desire to make Edward his heir to the throne and the conspicuous favour he showed to Edward and his father Edmund of Langley in the late 1390s suggests that something deeper was going on.[16]

It is highly likely that Richard II at this stage of his life was a deeply lonely man. He had lost the companionship of his beloved Anne of Bohemia when he was only twenty-seven, he had lost his father when he was nine and his mother when he was eighteen, and he had no children and no surviving siblings except for his illegitimate half-brother Roger Clarendon and his much older Holland half-brothers, with whom he seems not to have been particularly close on a personal level. He had not seen his dearest friend, or lover, Robert de Vere since late 1387 when he was only twenty, and de Vere had been dead since 1392. It seems probable therefore that Richard yearned for affection and close relations or family ties, and thus elevated a cousin of whom he had always been fond to an even higher position. Given that any brother of Richard would automatically have been next in succession to the childless king's throne (excluding of course the illegitimate Roger Clarendon and the Hollands, who were related to the king on his mother's side), and given also that Richard had made York's father Edmund of Langley keeper of the realm in 1394 and 1396, it seems likely, though not certain, that the king was publicly declaring that Edmund and Edward were his desired heirs to the throne. Richard's friend Sir William Bagot claimed later that the king told him sometime in 1398 that 'he had no desire to live longer than it took to see the crown of England held in such high respect, and obeyed with such lowly humility as by all his lieges, as it had been in the times of other kings ... so that it would forever be chronicled that with skill and wisdom he had recovered his royal dignity and his honourable estate; following which, he would renounce his crown the next day. And he said moreover that if he were to renounce it, the most able, wise and powerful man to whom to renounce it would be the duke of Aumale', that is Edward of York (who was shortly to become duke of Albemarle).[17]

Richard was therefore pushing Roger Mortimer, John of Gaunt and Henry of Lancaster to one side, though it is not entirely clear how he expected Edward of York to take the throne or why he thought anyone would accept him as king when he was only the son of Edward III's fourth son. William Bagot, rather unwisely, told Richard this, and the king responded that if Henry of Lancaster became king he would be 'as wild a tyrant to holy church as ever there was'.[18] Henry of Lancaster's biographer Ian Mortimer has pointed out how rarely Henry was given grants or favours by his cousin the king, and that he was sent on no important diplomatic missions; Henry would have been the ideal person to send to France to negotiate Richard's marriage to Isabelle, for example, but Edward of York and Thomas Mowbray were sent instead. Given Henry's royal birth, the esteem in which he was held by the English barons and by royalty across Europe and the fact that on John of Gaunt's death he would come into an enormous inheritance, it is difficult to avoid the impression that Richard was deliberately ignoring him, and thus insulting him. There is no evidence of an open breach between the two men or any real conflict, but it is almost impossible to avoid the conclusion that Richard favoured other men far above his cousin. A handful of pardons were issued to various people throughout Richard's reign 'at the supplication of the king's cousin the earl of Derby', and he witnessed some of the king's charters, but otherwise there are remarkably few references to Henry in the chancery rolls or other documents.[19]

On the subject of Henry's proposed marriage to a daughter of the king of Navarre in early 1397, Henry did eventually marry Juana, daughter of King Carlos II 'the Bad' of Navarre, but only after he became king of England, and she cannot have the woman intended as his bride in February 1397 as her first husband, Duke John IV of Brittany, lived until November 1399. Henry's potential Navarre bride in 1397 was presumably one of Juana's nieces, the daughters of her brother Carlos III. There were also plans in the late 1390s to marry

Henry to Lucia Visconti, one of the many children of the late Bernabo, lord of Milan, but she ultimately married Richard II's half-nephew Edmund Holland, earl of Kent. Lucia met Henry in person when he stayed with her cousin and brother-in-law Gian Galeazzo in Milan in 1393, and evidently was quite smitten: she declared that she would wait forever to marry Henry, even if she were to die three days after their wedding.[20]

Edmund Holland's father, Richard II's half-brother Thomas, earl of Kent, died on 25 April 1397 at the age of about forty-six. His will, written three days before his death – in the Middle Ages people generally only made their wills when they thought they were dying – is one of the earliest surviving wills made in English.[21] His widow Alice, sister of Richard, earl of Arundel, Joan, dowager countess of Hereford, and Archbishop Thomas Arundel, lived until 1416, and was mentioned in the will: 'Praying my wyf for al the love and trust that hath ben bywtyn us.' Holland's eldest son, also Thomas, succeeded him as earl, though was to die childless with the result that his younger brother Edmund became the next earl of Kent. Richard II and his other half-brother John Holland were now the only two surviving children of Joan of Kent.

The elderly William Montacute, earl of Salisbury, also died on 3 June 1397 at the age of nearly seventy. Half a century earlier, he had been the first or perhaps the second husband of Joan of Kent, and had outlived her, her other two husbands and all but two of her six children. His lands were taken into the king's hands on the day of his death. Salisbury was succeeded as earl by his nephew John Montacute, himself already in his late forties, who was a poet and supposedly a Lollard (supporter of the late John Wycliffe) but who became a close ally of Richard II. John Montacute swore homage and fealty to Richard and was granted his full inheritance on 6 February 1398.[22] The famous French poet Christine de Pisan met John Montacute in Paris in 1398, and praised his fine poetry.[23]

Richard spent 25 marks to celebrate the festivities of the Order of the Garter at Windsor on 23 April 1397, two days before Thomas Holland's death; it was exactly twenty years since he had been invested himself as a ten-year-old.[24] The Knights of the Garter in 1397 were John Montacute, soon to become earl of Salisbury; Richard's standard-bearer Sir Simon Felbrigg, married to the late Queen Anne's attendant Margarethe of Cieszyn; Albrecht, duke of Bavaria; and Ruprecht, count palatine of the Rhine. In the summer of 1397, Ruprecht performed a ceremony of homage to Richard II in Heidelberg, witnessed by Richard's envoys Sir Nicholas Rybenuzo and John Parant, and was given an income of 1,000 marks a year as he 'had become homage vassal and liege of the king'. His son Ruprecht the younger did the same and was granted 100 marks a year from Richard until the death of his father, when he too would receive 1,000 (this was duly granted on 25 April 1398).[25] Ruprecht the elder met three of Richard's envoys at Bacharach on 16 June 1397: Edward of York, Thomas Mowbray and Thomas Merk, the new bishop of Carlisle and a doctor of theology.[26] Friedrich von Saarwerden, archbishop of Cologne and duke of Westphalia, was another important German man who swore homage to Richard and received an annual allowance of £1,000, as well as badges of Richard's white hart given to him and fourteen of his retinue. The archbishop's nephew Friedrich, count of Moers, and Wynand von Holizheim, were two more men who swore homage to Richard in 1397, with an allowance of 50 marks a year each, and a third was Hugh Hernorst, provost of Saintes and archdeacon of Cologne, at £100 a year.[27]

The king of England almost certainly harboured ambitions to follow in his father-in-law Karl IV's footsteps and become Holy Roman Emperor, an elected position and one which would have made him ruler and overlord of huge territories over much of Europe. Walsingham states that 'knowing the rashness and ambition of the king', messengers from Germany including the dean of Cologne visited England around 24 June 1397 to intimate to Richard that he either had been or was about to be elected emperor.[28] It is even possible that Richard was intending to renounce his English crown if elected as emperor, and to allow his throne to pass to one of his cousins, presumably his adopted brother Edward of York, as William Bagot was to claim.[29] When the Beauforts were legitimised in early 1397, Richard called himself 'complete emperor of his realm of England' before parliament, which gives some idea of the way his mind was working in the last years of his reign. The king, who was always interested in prophecies and who tended to have a very high opinion of himself, felt encouraged to be told by self-proclaimed prophets that he would be raised to the imperial dignity and deserved to be counted among the greatest princes of the world.[30]

17

'Show Fair Duty to His Majesty': The King's Strange Behaviour, 1397

Richard II's uncle Thomas, duke of Gloucester, meanwhile, was expressing his complete dissatisfaction with his nephew to his retainer Sir John Lakenheath, in a long and revealing speech, or rather rant, recorded by Jean Froissart. The speech is too long to be quoted in full but included the following:

> If only we had a real king in England, someone who would fight the French for the heritage which they have tricked out of him, that man would find 100,000 archers and 6,000 men-at-arms behind him ready to put their lives and substance at his service across the Channel. But no, we don't have a king like that in England ... if only I were able to make my voice heard I would be the first: the first to go back to war, the first to right all the wrongs which in our silliness and softness we have let them do to us. Our lord the king has actually allied himself by marriage with his enemy. That's no way for a true warrior to behave. No, not on your life it isn't. The man's arse is too heavy to be shifted. All he ever wants to do is eat, drink and sleep, dance and caper about and laugh the hours away with women. What sort of life is that for a man of action? ... I tell you that before long we will see a great uprising in this country. People are starting to complain. They are not going to put up with all this business much longer.[1]

There could hardly be a more stark account of the differences between Richard II and his father Edward of Woodstock and grandfather Edward III. It is also interesting to note that Thomas of Woodstock believed that his nephew enjoyed the company of women, which is borne out by other evidence such as the Haxey petition earlier in 1397. It is not necessarily the case that Richard took women as lovers, but that he enjoyed socialising with them. Beginning in 1397, Richard's character and kingship noticeably changed; he became more paranoid, stood much more on his royal dignity, and was accused by chronicler Thomas Walsingham of tyrannising his people.[2] This change has always fascinated historians of the reign and led them to making some rather extreme and astonishing judgements on the king. Anthony Steel in 1941 speculated that Richard had always been neurotic and that in and after 1397 he became insane in 'the last stage of his illness', and was a 'pitiful neurotic' with a 'schizoid mind', and even a 'mumbling neurotic, sinking rapidly into a state of acute melancholia'.[3] Eleven years later, A. R. Myers agreed, declaring that Richard 'was always mentally unbalanced, and finally mad', and in 1959 May McKisack stated that he was 'perhaps dangerously mad ... The malice and cunning with which he carried through his acts of revenge, his mounting recklessness, his dark suspicions ... all suggest a sudden loss of control, the onset of a mental disease.'

As late as 1993, it was declared that Richard 'suffered from a moderate, even possibly an acute, depression which bordered at times on manic-depressive insanity'.[4] Richard's biographer Nigel Saul in 1997 argued that the king had always been neurotic and narcissistic, and certainly became more aloof in 1397, drawing attention to Richard's tendency to intense anger when criticised, his burning desire for revenge on those who did criticise him, his sense of his own uniqueness, and his tendency to self-worship.[5] Alison McHardy in 2000 made the rather more measured suggestion that Richard had always lacked confidence, made use of dramatic gestures and also used non-verbal means of communication, and reacted aggressively to any suggestion of criticism because of his lack of confidence.[6] If Richard were truly a narcissist, he would have been incapable of loving anyone beside himself, and judging by his wild grief after her death, it seems beyond doubt that he genuinely loved Anne of Bohemia. His troubling nightmares, insomnia and visions of a ghostly earl of Arundel after the latter's execution on his command in September 1397 argue that Richard had a conscience and empathy and was able to feel guilt and remorse over his actions, which would also argue against his being a genuine narcissist (who do not feel these emotions). It is possible that Richard had tendencies towards narcissism without being a full-blown narcissist, but it is impossible after more than 600 years to correctly diagnose Richard as neurotic or narcissistic or 'dangerously mad', or to know what was really going on inside his mind. We should be wary of trying to analyse a person so many centuries dead, a person who lived in a world very different from our own and who had been raised from the earliest childhood to see himself as set apart from other mortals.

It should be pointed out that Richard II's alleged madness is the invention of twentieth-century authors and not based on any primary source, with one possible exception: one of the charges against him at his deposition in 1399 was that he was guilty of *vecordia*. This Latin word has sometimes been translated as 'insanity' but really means foolishness or folly, even cowardice.[7] Whatever was really going on with Richard, it does seem clear that in and after 1397 he was increasingly prone to retreating into his own private fantasy world, unaware of his immense unpopularity among his subjects, preferring to surround himself with yes-men and sycophants rather than real advisers who could have given him sensible and impartial counsel. After June 1394 Richard is not known to have had any intimate partner or lover or perhaps even a close, real friend: Queen Anne and Robert de Vere were both dead, and Isabelle de Valois, for all Richard's undoubted fondness of and kindness towards her, was only a child and could not be his true companion for many years to come.

Perhaps Richard lived the last few years of his life in celibacy. There are no hints that after Anne's death he took a lover, and as previously noted, he fathered no illegitimate children. The three prominent courtiers in the last years of the reign, John Bushy, William Bagot and Henry Green, were sycophants out for what they could get from the king rather than genuine caring friends. Edward of York was the king's cousin and his adopted brother, yet ultimately showed little real loyalty to Richard when it mattered, going over to the side of his other cousin Henry of Lancaster in 1399 when it became expedient. Even loyal allies such as Thomas Despenser and John Montacute were practised courtiers who, though Richard surely enjoyed their company, were probably not friends in a real sense. For the last few years of his life, Richard II appears to have been intensely lonely and isolated. In the autumn of 1395 he formally impaled the arms of St Edward the Confessor with his own in a 'heraldic marriage' with the royal saint, which gives credence to the notion that he now sought to emulate the Confessor and live in permanent celibacy.[8]

One oft-repeated story about Richard II's behaviour in 1397/98 is found in *An English Chronicle*, a continuation of the *Eulogium Historiarum*: it says that on solemn days 'the kyng ... [would] make in his chambir a trone, wherynne he was wont to sitte fro aftir mete unto evensong tyme, spekynge to no man, but overlokyng alle menn, and yf he loked on eny mann, what astat [estate] or degre that evir he were of, he moste knele'.[9] According to the *Anonimalle* chronicle, Richard's father Edward of Woodstock had behaved in very similar ways while he was prince of Aquitaine in the 1360s: he made important lords wait four or five days before he deigned to admit them to his presence, would only allow them to approach him kneeling, and would make them kneel to him for long periods.[10] Richard's behaviour therefore was not unprecedented and he may have taken his own father's actions as an example, and it is perhaps revealing that only one chronicle mentions that he did this.[11] The elaborate forms of address Richard came to prefer (for which see below) were also not entirely unprecedented, though had previously been reserved for written language rather than speech; this had been the style adopted by his great-grandfather Edward II when writing to his father-in-law Philip IV of France, and the French kings had been addressed as 'your majesty' for over a century.

Richard had always had a strong sense of his own royalty and sacral kingship and of his separateness from his subjects, which he expressed most obviously in art and also, according to this one chronicle, in his behaviour in and after 1397. Although Richard was not old enough to have more than vague, if any, memories of his father's court in Aquitaine – he was only just four years old when they left for good and travelled to England in early 1371 – he must have heard frequent tales of Edward of Woodstock's pomp and ceremony. As well as keeping important people waiting for days to speak to him and only allowing them into his presence on bended knee, the prince of Wales and Aquitaine travelled around his duchy accompanied by large retinues of earls and barons, and Froissart (who knew Edward well) comments that his court was one of the most magnificent in Europe, so splendid and rich that no other lord's could even begin to match it.[12] It would hardly be surprising if Richard sought to emulate it, especially if he had begun to harbour ambitions of being elected emperor.

Walsingham says that in 1397 Richard II began to cultivate more elaborate forms of address. The Speaker of the Commons in Richard's 1397 Revenge Parliament, Sir John Bushy, 'imputed to the king in his statements not human, but divine, honours, finding strange and flattering words hardly suitable for mere mortals; so that whenever he addressed the king, who was seated on his throne, he would extend his arms and supplicate with his hands, as if praying to him, entreating his high, excellent and most praiseworthy majesty that he might deign to concede these or those things. And the young king, courting honours and seeking praise, did not stop these words, as he should, but rather delighted in them.'[13] Richard always had a tendency to theatricality and drama, and often dramatised himself. This behaviour, if it is recorded accurately, tends to reinforce the idea that in the last years of his reign the king began living in some kind of isolated fantasy world where he was surrounded by sycophants who did not dare speak the truth to him. Froissart said that 'in those days there was none so great in England that dare speak against anything that the king did or would do'. One of the Articles of the Deposition in 1399 stated that when people were 'giving their advice according to their discretion [they] were suddenly and sharply rebuked and censured by him [Richard] so that they did not dare to speak the truth about the state of the king and the kingdom'.[14]

Richard grew more introspective and retreated more into himself. He had always been prone to overreacting and to nervous irritability, and as he grew older these tendencies only became worse, not better. The king also had a tendency to think of and portray himself in a Christ-like manner; his self-image became ever more grandiose. On the other hand, and emphasising the contradictions to which the king was prone, Richard showed considerable affection for his personal retainers, his Cheshire archers, whom he allowed to call him by the pet name Dickon and who referred to themselves as his *nurres* or foster children. They were tasked with guarding the king day and night, and to contemporaries took on the appearance of a private army.[15] The archers, as northerners, attracted the opprobrium and prejudice of Walsingham in St Albans, who called them 'by nature bestial' and 'evildoers' who were guilty of 'shamelessness' and 'pride, disdain and cruel insolence'.[16] The criticisms of the king's Cheshire archers were perhaps based more on prejudice than reality, but to contemporaries they took on the alarming appearance of a royal army. They ate and even slept alongside Richard. The leaders of the Cheshire archers supposedly told the king *Dycun slep sicury quile we wake, and dreed nouzt quile we lyve*, 'Dickon, sleep securely while we wake, and dread nothing while we live.'[17] (Richard must have spoken English with these men, who were of too low birth and status to know French.) For archers to address the king himself in such familiar terms is rather startling, and sits oddly with Richard's high and mighty behaviour on other occasions.

It is easy to gain the impression that Richard II in the late 1390s was a frightened man who could only sleep when he knew he was surrounded by his archers, who were of much lower status than he and whom he therefore believed (correctly) he had no reason to fear. There is more evidence of Richard's tyrannical behaviour in the last years of his reign. The Dieulacres chronicle says that in 1399 he had 'blank charters' drawn up and made people swear faithfully to acquiesce to whatever might be written on them in future, and thus 'evil rumours began to spread through the whole community, because of the harsh bondage to which they were subjecting themselves'.[18] According to the *Vitae et Regni*, Richard was given to 'grievously extorting taxations from his people every year of his reign ... which were wasted on his extravagancies as soon as they reached his treasury'.[19] Whether he knew it or not, whether he cared or not, Richard was becoming grossly unpopular and hated among many of his subjects, and if the chroniclers are correct, they had good reason.

Sometime after June 1397, perhaps in 1399, Richard II – said by Walsingham to be an 'inquisitive searcher for antiquities relating to his royal ancestors' – was himself rooting around in the Tower of London when he came across several chests which were locked and which he was unable to open.[20] When a servant broke one of the chests open, the king found a container of oil and some writings of Thomas Becket, archbishop of Canterbury, murdered in 1170 and canonised soon afterwards. This oil was brought to England in 1308 by Edward II's brother-in-law Duke John II of Brabant when the duke attended Edward's coronation, but was not used to anoint the king. In 1317 Edward changed his mind and asked Pope John XXII for permission to be re-anointed with the holy oil, but this did not happen. It was then presumably locked away in the Tower and forgotten for eighty years, though it may have been returned to Brabant at some point, and Walsingham claims that Duke Henry of Lancaster (d. 1361) discovered it in a church in France and gave it to Edward of Woodstock to be used at his coronation as king of England.[21] The holy oil was found in the late 1390s in a flask or ampoule contained within a golden eagle. Richard kept the eagle and oil and took them to Ireland with him in 1399, and they were taken from him at Chester Castle (or possibly at Flint Castle) that year by his enemies. The oil was used to consecrate Richard's cousin and usurper Henry IV in 1399.[22]

Before this happened, however, Richard finally managed to gain revenge on the three men who had forced him to hold the Merciless Parliament in 1388 and who had executed and exiled his dearest friends. The days of the three senior Lords Appellant were numbered.

18

'The Last Leave of Thee Takes My Weeping Eye': The King's Revenge, 1397

Almost a decade after their successes, on Tuesday 10 and Wednesday 11 July 1397, Richard II suddenly and dramatically ordered the arrest of the three senior Lords Appellant: his uncle Thomas of Woodstock, duke of Gloucester; Richard Fitzalan, earl of Arundel; and Thomas Beauchamp, earl of Warwick. Two months later the three were put on trial at parliament, when the record of the Merciless Parliament of 1388 was overturned. Richard dined at the London home of his half-brother John Holland, Coldharbour (later called Poultney's Inn), behind the church of All Hallows on the banks of the Thames, on 10 July 1397. According to Thomas Walsingham, the king invited the duke of Gloucester and the earls of Arundel and Warwick to this banquet. Only Warwick turned up; Gloucester claimed that he was too ill to travel, and Arundel, also fearing the king's intentions, remained at his Sussex castle of Reigate. Richard therefore personally arrested his uncle Gloucester at Gloucester's main seat of Pleshey in Essex, having set off from London under cover of darkness with John Holland, Thomas Mowbray, a large force of Londoners and household knights.

They arrived so early at Pleshey (35 miles from the capital) that it was still dark when they arrived, and the duke, accompanied by his wife Eleanor and their children and attended only by a skeleton household, was still asleep. Gloucester came downstairs and dropped to his knees before the king. Richard at first greeted his uncle with courtesy as *bel oncle* or 'fair uncle' and even bowed to him, then suddenly had him arrested and told him that he would show him as much mercy as Gloucester had shown to Simon Burley nine years before.[1] The *Vitae et Regni* says that the duke was ill at this time, and that Richard II disregarded the 'grief, tears and prayers' of Duchess Eleanor and their household. On the other hand, the Dieulacres chronicle says that 'for a servant or a subject to rebel against his lord is ridiculous. In order therefore that no crime should remain unpunished, God directed the king's heart towards finding a way to punish these rebels, whereupon the rightful king came secretly with his followers at dawn' to arrest the duke of Gloucester.[2] Gloucester was taken by Richard's nephew the earl of Kent and Sir Thomas Percy to the town of Calais in northern France, which at this time belonged to England. Thomas Mowbray was captain of the town and Thomas of Woodstock was handed over into his custody.

The earls of Warwick and Arundel were also arrested, surely much to their surprise. Warwick and his wife Margaret Ferrers had recently received a visit from the young queen Isabelle de Valois, so it seems probable that he was not expecting his sudden arrest.[3] Walsingham says that Archbishop Arundel persuaded his brother the earl of Arundel to give himself up, and according to the French author of the *Chronique de la Traison et Mort de Richart Deux Roy Dengleterre* or the 'Chronicle of the Betrayal and Death of Richard II, king of England' (who probably came to England with Queen Isabelle), the earls of Rutland and Kent with a large company of armed men and archers arrested him.[4] The mayor and sheriffs of London and eleven counties were also ordered to arrest all the members of the three men's retinues whom they found armed or making assemblies in their jurisdictions and who were 'sowing evil words and inciting the people against the king'.[5]

Richard wrote to all the sheriffs of England on 15 July, ordering them to issue a proclamation that the three Appellants had been arrested with the assent of his cousin and adopted brother Edward of York, earl of Rutland; his half-brother John Holland, earl of Huntingdon; Holland's nephew Thomas Holland, earl of Kent; Thomas Mowbray, Earl Marshal and earl of Nottingham; the king's cousin John Beaufort, earl of Somerset; John Montacute; earl of Salisbury; Thomas, Lord Despenser, brother-in-law of Edward of York; and Richard's chamberlain William Scrope. Richard stated that he had ordered the three men's arrest because of a 'great number of extortions, oppressions, grievances etc. committed against the king and people'.[6] This list of men may represent the king's allies who had foreknowledge of the arrests of the duke of Gloucester and earls of Arundel and Warwick. Richard also said that he was acting with the assent of his other two uncles, John of Gaunt and Edmund of Langley, the dukes of Lancaster and York, and Gaunt's son Henry, earl of Derby. Not everyone was happy about the downfall of the three men: on 28 July Richard was forced to order the keepers of the peace in Sussex, Kent, Surrey and Essex to arrest and imprison anyone found to be 'stirring against the imprisonment' of the Appellants and who 'are purposing to go from town to town and place to place in [the four counties] disseminating abuse of the king's person and act, so that they might stir up the people against the king and his act, and resist the king'.[7]

The three older Lords Appellant had been sidelined by 1397; even the duke of Gloucester, although Richard's uncle, played little role in the king's council, and the earls of Arundel and Warwick seemingly played no role in politics at all by this time.[8] Walsingham's account of July 1397 makes it seem that Richard had planned a coup against the three lords for some time, whereas French chronicles more sympathetic to the king state that Richard had recently uncovered evidence of a new Appellant plot against him, and thus acted pre-emptively in his own defence.[9] The *Traison et Mort*, among others, says that the three Appellants' plan was for Richard and his two older uncles John and Edmund to be seized and perpetually imprisoned, and for other members of his council to be drawn and hanged.[10] It is difficult to know what was really happening, though it is perhaps significant that on 6 July 1397, just days before the arrests, Richard made his uncle John of Gaunt duke of Aquitaine for life (an appointment first made in March 1390), his previous rancour against the duke and his belief that Gaunt was plotting against his life apparently now forgotten. Aquitaine would not pass to Gaunt's son Henry of Lancaster but would revert to the Crown on Gaunt's death.

It seems unlikely that the three Appellants genuinely were plotting afresh against the king in the summer of 1397, and perhaps this idea was fabricated by Richard's sympathisers to explain his sudden actions against them. It may indeed be that the king did fear an attack by the three men, though this does not necessarily mean that they were planning one; the king was increasingly prone to paranoia and fear. Revenge for the Merciless Parliament and the cruel executions of the king's friends, which had been stewing in Richard's mind for nine years until at last he found his opportunity and knew he could enjoy the support of a large group of loyal noblemen, perhaps seems more plausible. In his proclamation of 15 July, Richard was at pains to point out that the three men had not been arrested because they had 'made assemblies and ridings within the realm', a reference to events of 1387/88, but for 'other offences against the king's majesty which shall be declared in the next parliament'.[11] Various entries in the chancery rolls in 1398, however, recite Richard's 1397 charges against Gloucester, Arundel and Warwick, and indicate that they were indeed 'convicted of high treason against the king's majesty' because of their actions in 1387/88: the men 'rose against the king and their allegiance, whom at that time the king might not resist without too great peril of his person and of his lieges, and by compulsion caused the king to summon a parliament at Westminster on the morrow of the Purification 11 Richard II [3 February 1388] ... therein rendering a number of judgements for manslaughter ... and publishing diverse statutes and ordinances'.[12]

Shocking news reached England shortly after the opening of parliament on 17 September 1397. Thomas of Woodstock, duke of Gloucester, son and uncle of kings, was dead at the age of forty-two. It is virtually certain that Gloucester was murdered in Calais on the orders of Thomas Mowbray, and Mowbray can only have been acting on the command of the king; he would never have dared to kill a king's son without Richard's consent and order. Richard II, therefore, had his own uncle killed. There is no justification for such a terrible act, though the king no doubt believed that Gloucester's viciousness and vindictiveness during the Merciless Parliament, and in particular his insistence on Simon Burley's execution, meant that his uncle deserved his death.

Parliament was told that Gloucester died on 25 or 26 August 1397, and rumours had been circulating in England by about mid-August that he was already dead, but his confession was dated 8 September, which may have been the date of his death.[13] Gloucester's supposed confession (in English) of 8 September 1397 was presented to Richard and was read out in parliament on 24 September, but was tampered with and altered. The duke supposedly confessed that he had done evil and acted wickedly and slandered his liege lord and acted against

Richard's regality and high estate. It included the highly unlikely line that, realising what he had done wrong, Gloucester 'submitted myself to my lord and cried to him for mercy and grace, and still do, as lowly and meekly as a man may'.[14] On the same day, 24 September, Gloucester was declared guilty of treason and his lands and goods therefore forfeit to the Crown. Richard had sent a man called William Rikhill to Calais on 17 August to have a conference with the duke of Gloucester, and on 21 September ordered Thomas Mowbray to have Gloucester brought before parliament to answer the charges against him, but Gloucester was – as Richard surely knew very well – already dead by then.[15]

Sir William Bagot would present a bill to parliament in October 1399, at the start of Henry IV's reign, stating that in October 1397 he had been riding past the Savoy towards Westminster behind Thomas Mowbray, earl of Nottingham and by then also duke of Norfolk. Mowbray had seen Bagot and asked him if he knew anything about the duke of Gloucester's fate. Bagot had answered, 'No, by my troth, but the people say that you murdered him.' Mowbray swore great oaths to the contrary, and claimed that he had saved Gloucester's life contrary to the wishes of the king and certain other lords, for more than three weeks. He also said that he had never been as afraid for his life as the time when he returned to England from Calais and met Richard again, because the duke of Gloucester was then still alive. Richard appointed one of his own men to accompany Mowbray to Calais to ensure that the murder was carried out, and Mowbray also claimed that Edward of York, shortly to be made duke of Albemarle, was the man who first encouraged the king in the matter of the arrest of the three lords and everything that came after.[16] It also came out at the start of Henry IV's reign that one of Thomas Mowbray's valets, John Hall, was the man responsible for killing the duke. Hall confessed that Thomas Mowbray told him Richard II had ordered him to kill Gloucester, and so the duke was taken to a house in Calais, told to lie down on a bed, and then was suffocated with a feather mattress.

Richard probably felt he had no way to rid himself of Gloucester other than by murder. Putting a king's son on trial was a difficult proposition, especially as Gloucester's brother John of Gaunt was high steward of England and would preside over the trial, and would probably, for all his loyalty to his nephew Richard, balk at pronouncing the death sentence on his own brother.[17] Observing the niceties due to a man he loathed but who was nonetheless the son of a king and the son of his grandfather, Richard had prayers said for Gloucester's soul on 6 and 9 October 1397, and on the 14th ordered Thomas Mowbray to deliver the duke's body to the royal clerk Richard Maudelyn (a man who resembled the king so closely that in later years he was used as Richard of Bordeaux's impersonator after the king's downfall). Maudelyn was then to deliver the body to Gloucester's widow Eleanor de Bohun or to her attorney. Richard went so far as to tell Duchess Eleanor on 31 October that she must bury her husband at Bermondsey Priory, though he had previously given her permission to bury him in the church of Westminster Abbey.[18] Eleanor, as the wife of one Appellant and niece of another (Arundel), was hardly high in the king's favour in 1397, though Richard did allow her possession of some of her late husband's goods on 28 December.[19]

Parliament began at Westminster on 17 September 1397. As Richard was having Westminster Hall rebuilt at this time – the magnificent hammer-beam roof he had constructed is still there – proceedings were held in a kind of marquee in the palace yard, with Richard seated on an elevated throne from which he could observe proceedings.[20] Hundreds or perhaps even thousands of Cheshire archers, the king's personal bodyguard, had gathered in London. Chronicler Adam Usk even says that the archers surrounded the parliament building, and at one point, wrongly believing that there was some dangerous dissension afoot, prepared to loose arrows at the attendees until Richard calmed them down. Richard also asked his uncles John of Gaunt and Edmund of Langley, and his cousin Henry of Lancaster, to bring men-at-arms to Westminster for his protection.[21] The Westminster parliament of September 1397 is sometimes known as Richard II's Revenge Parliament.

Thomas Beauchamp, the earl of Warwick, less noxious to the king than the other two Lords Appellant, faced parliament on Friday 28 September 1397. Adam Usk paints a rather pathetic portrait of the unfortunate and frightened man 'sobbing and whining like a wretched old woman' as he broke down and 'foolishly, wretchedly, pusillanimously confessed to everything in the appeal'.[22] The *Traison et Mort* has Warwick admitting to parliament that he deserved a terrible death because of his treason, but begging the king for mercy anyway. Although he was sentenced to death, Richard II commuted this punishment on the grounds that 'almost everybody there felt moved by his [Warwick's] tears', and therefore the earl was sent into lifelong exile on the Isle of Man 'to pine away in perpetual prison'. Richard said to him, 'By St John the Baptist, this confession of yours, Thomas of Warwick, is worth more to me than the value of all the lands of the duke of Gloucester and the earl of Arundel.'[23] Warwick was almost sixty years old, so perhaps Richard felt that he had little to fear from him and that the earl would die soon anyway.

On 1 March 1398, Richard gave his half-nephew Thomas Holland the 'pieces of cloth of arras' depicting the legend of Guy of Warwick which had formerly belonged to Thomas Beauchamp.[24] The earl of Warwick was luckier than many other noblemen of the era: he survived Richard II's reign and outlived Richard himself, and died in April 1401. His son and heir Richard, born in 1381 and named in honour of his then fourteen-year-old godfather Richard II, became the governor and tutor of the child-king Henry VI in the 1420s. Warwick's wife Margaret Ferrers was granted an income of 250 marks a year from the Exchequer to maintain herself on 2 May 1398, backdated to 27 September 1397, and was acknowledged as the king's kinswoman at this time (she was descended from Edward I via his second daughter Joan of Acre).[25] Then again, one chronicle claims that in October 1398 Richard lost his temper with Countess Margaret when she came to plead with him on her husband's behalf, and even threatened to put her to death. Supposedly he said that he would do so immediately were she not a woman.[26] That Richard II would lose his temper is an entirely plausible story; that he would threaten a woman with execution perhaps less so.

A week earlier, on 21 September 1397, Richard Fitzalan, earl of Arundel, wearing a robe with a scarlet hood, had been brought to trial before parliament, where he faced the king and his allies, who were all dressed alike in red silk robes with white silk bands and powdered with gold lettering.[27] Arundel defended himself with spirit, wit and passion, telling John of Gaunt (as steward of England) that 'I see it clearly now: all those who accuse me of treason, you are all liars. Never was I a traitor.' The speaker of the commons, Sir John Bushy, informed him that his pardon for his actions as Lord Appellant had been revoked 'by the king, the lords, and us, the faithful commons'. Arundel retorted, 'Where are those faithful commons? I know all about you and your crew, and how you have got here – not to act faithfully, but to shed my blood.' Richard II's cousin Henry of Lancaster stood and accused him of plotting to seize the king in 1387. Arundel cried out, 'You, Henry earl of Derby, you lie in your teeth. I never said anything to you or to anyone else about my lord king, except what was to his honour and welfare.'

Walsingham says that the eight lords who were the king's allies tried to provoke the earl of Arundel with obscene gestures and prancing around, chief among them the earl of Kent, who was in fact Arundel's own nephew as well as the king's.[28] Arundel was convicted of treason despite his spirited and articulate defence, and was sentenced to be hanged, drawn, beheaded and quartered. Richard II commuted the sentence to mere beheading because of Arundel's high rank. The king had shown his true feelings by saying to Arundel, 'Did you not say to me at the time of your parliament [in 1388], in the bath-house behind the White Hall, that Sir Simon Burley was for various reasons worthy of death? And I replied that I neither knew nor could discover any reason why he should die. And even though my wife, the queen, and I interceded tirelessly on his behalf, yet you and your accomplices, ignoring our pleas, traitorously put him to death?'[29]

There being no such thing as death row in fourteenth-century England, Arundel was immediately taken away to his execution at Tower Hill on foot with his hands tied behind him, with 'no more shrinking or changing colour than if he were going to a banquet', says Walsingham. He was followed all the way along Cheapside to the place of execution by a great throng of people who, according to the *Vita*, 'mourned him as much as they dared'. Arundel may have hoped that he would be rescued by the crowd, but it was not to be; even if they had wanted to, few would have dared to defy the king so publicly in such a manner.[30] Arundel was the second member of his family to be executed within a few decades: his grandfather Edmund, earl of Arundel, had been beheaded without trial in November 1326 on the orders of Richard II's great-grandmother Queen Isabella and her favourite Roger Mortimer, lord of Wigmore and later the first earl of March, because of his loyalty to Edward II.

Arundel was about fifty-one at the time of his death. His son-in-law Thomas Mowbray and his nephew Thomas Holland were among the lords who accompanied him to his execution. Supposedly Arundel warned Mowbray and Kent that the time would come when men marvelled at their misfortune as they were doing now at his. This is a nice story but sounds very much like something written with hindsight, given that both young men were dead within little more than two years, one of plague while exiled from England and the other beheaded by a mob. Jean Froissart says that Thomas Mowbray tied the blindfold over his father-in-law's eyes, and that the earl's head was cleanly struck off with an axe.[31]

Arundel had written his will in 1392, asking to be buried at Lewes Priory in Sussex with his first wife Elizabeth de Bohun, a request the king ignored; he was buried instead at the church of the Augustinian friars in Bread Street, London. According to both Adam Usk and Thomas Walsingham, Richard II had vivid nightmares in the immediate aftermath of Arundel's execution. Walsingham says that the king was so tormented by dreams of the ghostly earl flitting about that he hardly dared sleep, and also that he heard rumours that miracles were being performed at Arundel's grave and that his headless body had remained upright after he was beheaded for as long as it took to recite the Lord's Prayer. The king therefore had the earl's body exhumed in a peculiar ceremony in the dead of night, in the presence of John of Gaunt, Edward of York, Thomas Holland, Thomas Mowbray and Henry Percy, earl of Northumberland. The monks who had buried the body had indeed sewn the head back on, and the two parts were once more separated and reburied in an unmarked grave with paving stones on top to discourage pilgrims from visiting it.[32]

Arundel's long will of 1392 had left bequests to numerous members of the English nobility, including Margaret, countess of Norfolk, whom Arundel called 'my mother of Norfolk' in the will: she was his daughter Elizabeth's grandmother-in-law. As was conventional, he referred to his three sons-in-law as his 'very dear sons', to his daughter Elizabeth, wife of Thomas Mowbray, Earl Marshal of England, as 'my daughter Marshal', and to his sisters Joan and Alice, dowager countesses of Hereford and Kent, as 'my dear sisters of Hereford and Kent' (he left them a 'cup with trefoils' and a 'cup with hearts' respectively). Eleanor de Bohun, duchess of Gloucester, was called 'my honoured lady and niece of Gloucester', being the daughter of his sister Joan, and he left a 'cup enamelled with a stag on top' to his 'dear and honoured brother' Archbishop Thomas Arundel. To his heirs in perpetuity, the earl of Arundel left his coronet, a Bible in two volumes, a large gold chain and other jewels and holy relics 'contained in a small box fastened with silver and massive lions gilt' and other items he had inherited from his enormously wealthy father.

Among the items Arundel left to his young second wife Philippa, *née* Mortimer, sister of the earl of March and great-granddaughter of Edward III, were 'a blue bed' embroidered with his own arms and those of his first wife Elizabeth de Bohun, a blue tapestry with red roses, 'two candlesticks of silver for supper in winter', and 'the apparel for the heads of ladies' with pearls and other attire which he had given her in life.[33] Philippa, who after all was a close relative of the king, was granted her enormous dower on 5 December 1397.[34] A hanap (drinking vessel) belonging to Arundel found its way into the king's possession and was later inventoried. Rather ironically, it was engraved with the Middle English words *Gode grant hym gude yend*, 'God grant him a good end'. A magnificent crucifix set with diamonds, rubies and pearls, which had belonged to the duke of Gloucester and was valued at £600, was another of the items which passed from the three Appellants to the king in December 1397, when their goods were taken under armed guard to Windsor and Richard selected the items he wanted. He also chose a hanging pyx of gold decorated with enamelled flowers and a canopy of red satin, a reliquary cross and a jewelled cross.[35] On 29 and 30 September, Richard II sent a group of men to travel through England and Wales and 'to seize into the king's hands all horses lately belonging to Thomas, duke of Gloucester, Richard, earl of Arundel, and Thomas, earl of Warwick', and 'to keep the same for the king's use'.[36]

Arundel's heir was his eldest surviving son Thomas, born in 1381, who became a ward of the king, and his younger sons Richard and John were given into the custody of the king's half-brother John Holland and Arundel's son-in-law Thomas Mowbray on 12 October 1397.[37] Supposedly John Holland humiliated his ward Richard by entrusting him to the care of a knight called John Schevele, who treated Richard like a menial servant and forced him to wait upon him.[38] This is only found in Walsingham, however, hardly a reliable and unbiased source. The earl of Arundel's brother Thomas Arundel, archbishop of Canterbury, was exiled from England on 25 September 1397, four days after the earl's execution, and was given no chance to defend himself; the king talked angrily of his 'untrustworthy and vengeful character'.[39] The archbishop went to the pope in Rome to plead against this injustice, and sometime later met up with Richard's exiled cousin Henry of Lancaster in Paris, despite the king's forbidding them to do so.

Possibly deliberately, Arundel's execution had taken place on the seventieth anniversary of the supposed murder of Richard II's great-grandfather Edward II on 21 September 1327. Given Richard's deep awareness of English history and his fascination with this particular ancestor, it is difficult to imagine that the king was unaware of the significance of the date. In late June 1397 Richard had made renewed efforts to have Edward II made a saint: he sent Richard Scrope, bishop of Coventry and Lichfield and shortly afterwards archbishop of York, as a special ambassador to the papal court in Rome, 'respecting the canonisation of Edward II, late king of England.' Scrope – who would be executed in 1405 by Richard's cousin and successor Henry IV after taking part in an uprising against the king – received 200 marks for his expenses from Richard.[40] While he was in Rome in early 1398, he was translated to the see of York, succeeding Robert Waldby as archbishop.

Eight days after the earl of Arundel's execution, on 29 September 1397, Richard upgraded the title of his elderly kinswoman Margaret, already countess of Norfolk, and made her duchess of Norfolk. She was the first Englishwoman in history to be made a duchess in her own right. Margaret, the last surviving grandchild of Edward I since the death in December 1391 of Margaret Courtenay, *née* de Bohun, dowager countess of Devon, must then have been in her mid-seventies or so: her parents Thomas of Brotherton and Alice Hales married around 1321, and she herself had borne her first child Elizabeth Segrave (Thomas Mowbray's mother) in 1338 and thus cannot have been born later than 1322 or 1323. Margaret's only brother, Edward of Norfolk, died as a child in the early 1330s, and her sister Alice died in the early 1350s after being brutally assaulted by her husband Edward Montacute, uncle of Joan of Kent's sometime husband William, earl of Salisbury. In the late 1390s, Margaret of Norfolk was a link to the distant past, born in the reign of her half-uncle Edward II, whom she may have just been old enough to remember. Her father Thomas joined his brother Edmund, earl of Kent, Richard II's grandfather, when the invasion force of their sister-in-law Queen Isabella arrived in England in September 1326. Duchess Margaret had outlived all her children and some of her grandchildren, and had several great-grandchildren. Her ultimate heir was her great-grandson John Mowbray, born in 1392 and five years old at this time.

On the same day as Margaret of Norfolk's elevation to duchess, various earls were also upgraded to the higher title of duke.

John Holland, earl of Huntingdon, was made duke of Exeter; his nephew Thomas Holland, earl of Kent, became duke of Surrey; Margaret of Norfolk's grandson Thomas Mowbray was made duke of Norfolk; Henry of Lancaster, earl of Derby, became duke of Hereford; and Edward of York, earl of Rutland, became duke of Albemarle, or 'Aumerle' as his ducal title was and is frequently referred to. The title of duke had been rare in England up to this point, and contemporaries derisively referred to the men as *duketti* or 'little dukes'. In addition, the newly legitimised John Beaufort, yet another royal first cousin, was made marquis of Somerset in September 1397, the title of marquis having been previously held only by Robert de Vere, and Richard bestowed the title of earl of Gloucester on his friend and first cousin by marriage Thomas Despenser. The great northern lord Ralph Neville was made earl of Westmorland, the royal chamberlain William Scrope earl of Wiltshire, and the earl of Northumberland's younger brother Thomas Percy, steward of the king's household, earl of Worcester.[41] The new marquis of Dorset John Beaufort married one of Richard II's many Holland half-nieces, Margaret, sister of the duchess of York, the duke of Surrey and the countess of March, before 28 September 1397.[42]

Also on 29 September 1397, the last day of the Westminster parliament, Richard granted the other two Lords Appellant, Henry of Lancaster and Thomas Mowbray, a pardon for everything they had done in this capacity in 1387/88, supposedly on the grounds that they had tried to restrain the malice and murderousness of the others and had eventually returned to the king's side. The two men, however, cannot have trusted the king an inch, as would soon become apparent. Richard revoked the 1321 judgements on the two Hugh Despensers, father and son 'favourites' of his great-grandfather Edward II: they had been charged with treason and perpetually exiled from England, though in fact returned within half a year, and Edward II reversed the judgement at the York parliament of 1322. In 1327, at the start of Edward III's reign, however, they were once more convicted of treason, having both been executed some months before in the presence of Richard's great-grandmother Queen Isabella and Roger Mortimer.

Hugh Despenser the Younger's great-grandson and heir Thomas Despenser was a descendant of Edward I and thus a distant cousin of Richard, and was the nephew of the bishop of Norwich, Henry Despenser. In 1397 Richard II gave Thomas Despenser the earldom which had belonged to his great-grandmother Eleanor's brother Gilbert de Clare, who was the eldest grandchild of Edward I and who was killed at the battle of Bannockburn in 1314. Gilbert's brother-in-law Hugh Despenser the Younger had coveted the earldom of Gloucester, and now, finally, it had passed to his great-grandson. Thomas of Woodstock, duke of Gloucester, being dead, Richard saw a good opportunity to ennoble a friend and ally. A lighter note was struck amid the doom and gloom of the downfall of the three Appellants when another of Richard's first cousins, Elizabeth of Lancaster, also his sister-in-law by her marriage to John Holland, won the prize for best dancer at the feast held to mark the end of parliament.[43]

In the autumn of 1397, Richard II was at the height of his powers. He had rid himself of his three most hated and most influential enemies, and had bent a compliant parliament to his will in the matter. His coffers were as full as those of any king of England since the downfall of Edward II, who had been aided by his despotic and highly efficient favourite Hugh Despenser the Younger. As well as the incomes of the three Appellants, which now filled Richard's coffers as the men had been convicted of treason and their lands and goods were thus forfeit to the Crown, on 7 November 1397 Richard acknowledged receipt of 100,000 francs from the French court as part of Queen Isabelle's dowry.[44] He had been able to create a faction of noblemen loyal to him and bestowed higher titles on them, he had made an excellent marriage into the powerful kingdom of France (following his first excellent marriage to an emperor's daughter) and made peace with that country, and he had established a close alliance with his most powerful subject, his uncle John of Gaunt. Thomas Walsingham also makes the point that in the summer of 1397, 'England seemed to be basking in peace and the future looked entirely favourable: the country had an impressive-looking king' who had not only secured great riches via his marriage into France but a thirty-year truce.[45] Had Richard II died at this time, at the age of thirty, historians would view his reign in a very different light.[46] But 'through the rashness, cunning and pride of the king', it was soon all to go terribly wrong for Richard.[47]

19

'And Sigh'd My English Breath in Foreign Clouds': Duel and Exile, 1398

Richard II probably travelled to Westminster to celebrate the feast of St Edward the Confessor on 13 October 1397 with the new *duketti*, and at this time sent a letter both grandiose and rather self-pitying to Duke Albrecht of Bavaria. It said that God had protected 'our royal throne and person since the very cradle from the hands of all enemies, and especially those of household and intimacy, whose contrivances are notoriously more destructive than any plague'. A conflict now arose between two of the greatest noblemen in the country and would be made famous by William Shakespeare 200 years later in the opening scenes of his play *Richard II*.

Sometime in December 1397, Henry of Lancaster, now duke of Hereford, was riding with his retinue between Brentford and London when he encountered his second cousin Thomas Mowbray, duke of Norfolk. The two men talked for a while, apparently in French, or at least the conversation was recorded in that language in the rolls of parliament. Mowbray opened the conversation with a warning: 'We are about to be undone' (*Nous sumes en point d'estre diffaitz*). Lancaster asked why, and Mowbray replied that it was because of what the two of them had done at Radcot Bridge ten years before. Lancaster demanded to know how this could be, 'since he [Richard II] has given us grace, and declared for us in the [recent] parliament, saying that we had been true and loyal to him'. Mowbray replied that, this behaviour notwithstanding, the king would do with them what he had already done to the other three Appellants, for he wished to wipe out the record of his shame at Radcot Bridge and what came afterwards. In short, Mowbray believed that Richard's pardons, protestations of friendship and elevation of himself and Henry of Lancaster to dukedoms could not be trusted. Lancaster said that it would be a great wonder if the king were later to annul that which he had said before the people.

Mowbray replied that this was a wondrous world and false, 'for I know well that if there had not been others there, my lord your father of Lancaster and you would have been taken or slain when you came to Windsor after the parliament', i.e. in early October 1397. Mowbray went on to explain that he, Richard's half-brother John Holland, the royal cousin Edward of York and the earl of Worcester Thomas Percy (younger brother of the earl of Northumberland) had sworn 'that they would never assent to destroy a lord without a just and reasonable cause', but that 'the malice of that deed was with' Richard's half-nephew Thomas Holland, the new earl of Wiltshire William Scrope and John Montacute, earl of Salisbury, who had also brought Thomas Despenser, the new earl of Gloucester, over to their cause. 'And these four had supposedly sworn to defeat the other six lords, namely, the dukes of Lancaster, Hereford, Albemarle, and Exeter, the marquis [of Dorset, John Beaufort], and himself.'

Why Thomas Holland was seeking the destruction of his uncle John Holland, the duke of Exeter, and why Edward of York was one of the intended victims, was not explained. Mowbray was describing what appears to have been a plot aimed at six members of the royal court by four others, something perhaps not entirely unexpected in the fevered atmosphere of Richard II's court in the late 1390s: the king's ally Sir William Bagot admitted to plotting to kill John of Gaunt and disinherit his children, and promised to pay the king £1,000 if it were proved that he had tried to disinherit them. Bagot's recognition in early March 1398 that he would be put to death without further legal process if he was ever proven to have slain the duke, his wife and children was recorded in the chancery rolls as though it were normal, unexceptional business.[1] When Bagot *was* put on trial for this early in Henry IV's reign, he admitted (according to Thomas Walsingham) that he had indeed plotted to kill John of Gaunt but had been pardoned for this by Gaunt himself and Richard II.[2] According to the chronicler Adam Usk, in the winter of 1397/98, months before the premature death of Roger Mortimer, earl of March, Richard II been intending to destroy March and had 'laid snares' for him.[3] Such was the atmosphere at Richard II's court in the last years of his reign.

Thomas Mowbray also explained to Henry of Lancaster that the king's allies Thomas Holland, William Scrope, John Montacute and Thomas Despenser planned to reverse the judgement made on Thomas, earl of Lancaster, which would 'be to the disinheritance of us, and many others'. This was a reference to a judgement made by parliament in early 1327, at the beginning of Edward III's reign, which annulled Edward II's charge of treason and forfeiture against his cousin Thomas, earl of Lancaster, in March 1322. The reversal of Edward's judgement gave Thomas's brother and heir Henry the entire Lancastrian inheritance in 1327. It passed on Henry's death in 1345 to his son Duke Henry, to the duke's daughter Blanche and her husband John of Gaunt in the early 1360s, and ultimately would pass to their son Henry of Lancaster on Gaunt's death. If Richard II reversed the 1327 reversal, it would mean that the Lancastrian inheritance rightfully belonged to the king and should have remained in his grandfather Edward III's hands in and after 1327. (On 20 February 1398, some months after this meeting between Henry of Lancaster and Thomas Mowbray, Richard 'with the full assent of the [royal] council after mature deliberation' released and discharged all his potential rights and claims to any of the Lancastrian lands arising from Thomas of Lancaster's 'treasons, seditions, insurrections, forfeiture etc in the time of Edward II'. In short, he promised his uncle Gaunt and cousin Henry that he would not try to claim any of their lands on the basis of the 1322 judgement against Thomas of Lancaster.[4] Gaunt and his son had apparently sought confirmation from Richard that he would not attempt to seize their lands, and given the timing it is highly likely that Thomas Mowbray's allegations lay at the root of this.)

'God forbid!' Henry of Lancaster exclaimed. 'It would be a great wonder if the king were to assent to that', as he, Richard, had given Henry such a warm welcome, so it seemed to him. It is hardly surprising that Henry of Lancaster was horrified: if the judgement of treason on his great-grandfather's brother was allowed to stand, he would be disinherited of his rich patrimony in an instant. Lancaster recovered himself enough to state to Mowbray that Richard had sworn by St Edward the Confessor to be a good lord to him and to all the others, perhaps trying to reassure himself that his cousin could not and would not disinherit his family.

Mowbray's reply was that Richard had done the same to him on many occasions, i.e. greeted him warmly and promised to be a good lord, and that he could no longer trust him because of this insincerity. He also told Lancaster that Richard was intent on convincing Roger Mortimer, earl of March, and other men with the assent and support of his four allies, to destroy the six others (though mere months later the king was allegedly 'laying snares' for March; it is extremely difficult to follow and make sense of all the plots and counter-plots of the late 1390s and to ascertain exactly who was in royal favour at any given time). The duke of Norfolk therefore implicated the king himself in this alleged plot against the six lords. Lancaster answered, 'If this were so, we could never trust in them.'

'Certainly not; since even if they may not accomplish their purpose at present, they would be intent on destroying us in our houses ten years hence,' Mowbray answered. He was himself confronting, and drawing his kinsman's attention to, the possibility that Richard II intended to strike against them whenever he could as punishment for their actions as Lords Appellant, even if he had to wait a decade; in short, that Thomas Mowbray and Henry of Lancaster could never feel safe from the king and that the axe might fall against them at any time. It was a nightmarish vision. Some months later, when Henry of Lancaster informed the king of this conversation, he widened his accusations against Mowbray, and according to one chronicler stated that Mowbray had misappropriated funds in his role as captain of Calais and ordered the murder of Thomas of Woodstock, duke of Gloucester. Getting carried away with himself, Henry also declared that Mowbray's machinations 'lay at the bottom of all the treasons committed in the kingdom these last eighteen years'. This would have been quite an achievement given that Mowbray was exactly the same age as Richard II and Henry himself and only thirty or thirty-one in late 1397/early 1398, so only twelve years old eighteen years before.[5]

Only some months before this conversation between Lancaster and Mowbray, Richard had seemingly made his cousin Edward of York his adopted brother, and now, according to Thomas Mowbray, the king was plotting against him, and even against his own half-brother John Holland (who was married to Henry of Lancaster's sister Elizabeth, perhaps a reason for Richard's supposed displeasure towards his half-brother), despite Holland's unceasing loyalty to him. The four lords accused of conspiring against the six others, Thomas Holland, William Scrope, John Montacute and Thomas Despenser, were all 'new men' at court, having been created earls or dukes that very same year, and were dependent on Richard II for favour and wealth, which is almost certainly the key to their actions. If they managed to bring down the house of Lancaster, they may have hoped that the vast Lancastrian inheritance would be shared out among themselves (Edward II's court favourites in the mid to late 1310s had probably done something similar to Thomas of Lancaster).

Of the six lords said to be the target of their plot, Henry of Lancaster was of course Lancastrian, as was his half-brother John Beaufort, the recently legitimised marquis of Dorset, and John Holland was his brother-in-law. Lancaster's father John of Gaunt was another target. Thomas Mowbray was partially Lancastrian via his paternal grandmother Joan, one of the sisters of John of Gaunt's long-dead father-in-law Duke Henry. Edward of York, the king's first cousin and adopted brother, heir of his uncle Edmund of Langley, is the odd one out, and according to other evidence Richard II hoped that Edward would succeed him on the throne. Perhaps he was targeted simply because he was John of Gaunt's nephew. There were plots and counter-plots and rumours of plots at Richard II's court near the end of his reign, alliances and counter-alliances and yet more alliances being made and broken, men who had long been friends becoming suspicious and wary of each other, no one sure whom he could trust or whether his continued political survival was assured; including, as it turned out, Richard II himself.

On Wednesday 30 January 1398, the second day of the second session of Richard's Revenge Parliament was taking place at Shrewsbury, and Henry of Lancaster came before the king holding a schedule or deed in his hand. Richard told him and the other attendees that he had heard ten days before how Thomas Mowbray, duke of Norfolk, 'had spoken many dishonourable words in slander of his person' to Lancaster. Richard ordered Lancaster to tell him what Mowbray had said to him, and Lancaster, who had written it down from memory, recited his recent conversation with Mowbray above.[6] On 4 February 1398, Richard ordered all the sheriffs of England 'to cause proclamation to be made that Thomas duke of Norfolk shall under pain of forfeiting life and limb etc appear in person before the king in person within fifteen days after such proclamation ... as in this parliament the said duke is by Henry duke of Hereford impeached of treasons, misprisions etc affecting the king's person and majesty'.[7]

Henry had already been pardoned on 25 January, five days before he spoke to parliament. He had been summoned to Richard's presence at Heywood in Shropshire, and told that the king knew about his conversation with Mowbray.[8] The constable of Windsor Castle was ordered on 26 February to 'receive and keep securely' both men, and on 23 April, the mayor and sheriffs of London were told to keep Mowbray 'securely within the king's wardrobe' (which was a department of Richard's household based in a building near Blackfriars, not a piece of furniture).[9] Two chronicles say that Mowbray admitted to laying an ambush or 'snares of death' for John of Gaunt, duke of Lancaster, but that Gaunt was forewarned and evaded it.[10] In the meantime, while Richard was staying in Bristol on 19 March, 'it was assented and agreed to ... that the process and determination of the matters abovesaid should follow the course of the law of chivalry', i.e. by battle.[11]

On 22 July 1398, Lancaster and Mowbray were ordered 'for particular causes nearly affecting the king' to appear before Richard with no more than twenty men each on the day after the feast of St Peter in Chains, i.e. 2 August, and the constable of Windsor Castle was told to give Mowbray permission to leave the castle, bearing a copy of the writ ordering him to come before Richard; this presumably means that Mowbray was being held securely in Windsor Castle at that point and was no longer in the king's wardrobe in London.[12] Richard sent out numerous messengers and couriers on 31 August 1398 to all the counties of England, bearing writs of privy seal ordering sundry bishops, the archbishop of Canterbury, lords, knights, squires and others to 'assemble themselves in person, with all haste' in Coventry on 16 September 1398 to an event which would determine the truth of the matter. A duel would be fought between the dukes of Hereford and Norfolk in Richard's presence.[13] The king, although he may not have taken part in jousts personally (or only on a handful of occasions), still enjoyed watching them and looking the part. In the late 1390s, his tailor Walter Rauf – who was married to the king's former nurse Mundina Danos – was ordered to make a number of doublets, cloaks and shoes for Richard to wear at 'tournaments and jousts'.[14]

The impending duel between two of the greatest noblemen of the realm aroused considerable interest throughout Europe. Henry of Lancaster sent to Milan, ruled by his friend Gian Galeazzo Visconti, for his armour, while Thomas Mowbray appears to have ordered his from Bohemia where Richard II's brother-in-law Václav ruled, and was attended by a Bohemian squire called Jacob Folin.[15] Henry also received items from, among other men, his brother-in-law João, king of Portugal (whose queen Philippa, Henry's eldest sister, had given birth to their sixth child some months before).[16] The Scottish duke of Albany's son Sir Walter Stewart travelled to England to watch the joust, as did Waleran, count of St Pol, widower of the king's half-sister Maud Holland, and Robert Waldby, archbishop of Canterbury.[17]

Richard II spent the night of 15 September before the joust at a house with a tower which belonged to Sir William Bagot in Baginton near Coventry, while Henry of Lancaster stayed at his father's great castle of Kenilworth, 8 miles away, and then moved to a town house in Coventry.[18] The tournament green was located at Gosford on the edge of Coventry, and Henry of Lancaster arrived at 9 a.m. accompanied by six attendants riding *beaulx coursiers* or 'fine coursers', having already called on the king at Baginton earlier that morning. He announced himself as 'Henry of Lancaster, duke of Hereford' and took an oath that he would do his duty against the 'false traitor' Thomas Mowbray, who, he said, was disloyal to God, King Richard, the realm and himself. Mowbray only arrived after Richard had already done so and taken his seat, accompanied by his usual retinue, his Cheshire archers and his brother-in-law Waleran of St Pol. The joust was conducted under the command of the dukes of Albemarle and Surrey, Edward of York and Thomas Holland, who were respectively constable and acting marshal of England (Surrey officially replaced Thomas Mowbray himself in the role of marshal of England the next day). The two dukes were dressed alike in short *houppelandes* or voluminous outer garments with full trailing sleeves made of plain red sendal (a kind of silk) with silver belts.[19] The two combatants having taken up their positions, Henry of Lancaster began to ride towards his opponent, Mowbray for the time being remaining motionless.

And then something entirely unexpected happened: Richard dramatically stopped the joust by standing up and crying out 'Ho ho!'[20] This was not unprecedented. John II of France some decades before had also stepped in at the last minute to stop the joust between

Duke Henry of Lancaster and Duke Otto of Brunswick. The onlookers, however, expecting to see an exciting battle and favouring Henry's cause, were disgruntled. Lancaster and Mowbray retired to their pavilions and waited, with everyone else, for two hours.[21] Finally, Sir John Bushy climbed onto the tribune and announced Richard's will on the matter. And it was truly shocking. Henry of Lancaster was exiled from England for ten years, although Richard may have reduced the sentence to six years before Henry departed.[22] For Thomas Mowbray came a far harsher penalty: he was sentenced to permanent exile from England, or as Shakespeare put it, 'The sly slow hours shall not determinate / The dateless limit of thy dear exile / The hopeless word of "never to return" / Breathe I against thee, upon pain of life.' The king claimed that as both men were so closely related to him, he wished to avoid any dishonour falling on the loser of the duel and that he needed to avoid the possibility that more quarrels and conflict would break out between them in future.

Both men were given several weeks to put their affairs in order. Thomas Holland, duke of Surrey and earl of Kent, was given Mowbray's title of marshal of England to hold during Mowbray's lifetime on 17 September, the day after the joust, and on 30 January 1399 was given the title permanently. During his office, Holland was permitted to carry 'a gold staff enamelled with black at either end, and ornamented at the upper [end] with the royal arms and at the lower with the duke's', both in Richard II's presence and when he was away from him, and notwithstanding that previous marshals of England were 'wont to bear a wooden staff'.[23] Thomas Mowbray was given a safe conduct on 3 October 1398 'to cross to foreign parts to stay in Almain [Germany], Bohemia and Hungary, and to traverse the great sea on pilgrimage' (suggesting he intended to go to Jerusalem), from any port on the eastern side of England between Scarborough in the north and Orwell, Suffolk in the south.[24]

Germany, Bohemia and Hungary were the lands ruled by Richard's brothers-in-law Václav and Zikmund. The *Traison et Mort* gives the same three permissible destinations, only stating a more specific part of Germany – Prussia – and also says that Mowbray's intention when crossing the great sea was to go to the land of the 'Saracen miscreants'.[25] Four knights and five clerks were appointed as Mowbray's council and to act on his behalf while he was abroad.[26] Also on 3 October, Mowbray was given permission to take forty people, £1,000 in cash, and jewels and plate abroad with him. A herald named Reginald was allowed to export cloths of russet and blanket for the use of Mowbray and his household on 13 October.[27]

Henry of Lancaster was given permission on 10 October to sail from Dover with up to 200 people accompanying him, £1,000 in cash, and as many horses, vessels, jewels and other property as he needed, and a week earlier had been given permission to stay in Calais for one month and in Sangatte for six weeks. Three of the king's sergeants-at-arms, one of whom bore the excellent name Thomas Totty, were ordered to requisition as many ships in Dover and Calais as were required for Henry to transport his retinue and his goods overseas.[28] He certainly was not being ordered overseas as a penniless exile with few or no companions, but as a man of royal birth with a large retinue and with as many rich possessions as he cared to take with him. Thomas of Lancaster, the second of his four sons, accompanied him overseas, though his two youngest sons John and Humphrey and his daughters Blanche and Philippa remained in England, and Henry the eldest with Richard.[29]

Richard II sent a squire called Hugh Curteys and a sergeant-at-arms called Robert Markeley to Calais on 7 December 1398, carrying a cash gift of 1,000 marks from Richard to Henry of Lancaster. Curteys and Markeley received £1 6s 8d for their expenses, and were told to hire horses during their journey if necessary to expedite their arrival with Henry.[30] Richard also promised Henry's eldest son Henry of Monmouth, who had recently turned twelve, a very generous annual income of £500 and paid him an instalment of £10 on 5 March 1399, which probably means that it was a weekly payment.[31] Henry of Lancaster was ordered to spend his exile in France or Spain and not to communicate with Thomas Mowbray or with Archbishop Thomas Arundel while abroad, though he did meet the latter.[32] All the people accompanying 'the king's cousin Henry de Lancastre, duke of Hereford' abroad were granted 'letters patent of general attorney for the time that he and they are absent, and that they be renewed from year to year during such term'.[33] On the same day, the following was issued: 'Grant to the king's cousin Henry of Lancaster, duke of Hereford, that if any succession or inheritances descend or otherwise fall to him in his absence, for which he ought to do homage, he may by his attorneys sue and have livery thereof, and that his homage and fealty may be respited for reasonable fine made, until it shall please the king that he return to do them in person.'[34]

Thomas Mowbray left England from Lowestoft on 19 October 1398 with his retinue and sailed to Dordrecht, and was to receive an income of £1,000 a year.[35] Richard II may well have been intending to recall him at some point – the sentence was extremely harsh and Mowbray was his kinsman and had been high in his favour for years – but events overtook them, and Mowbray died less than a year later on 22 September 1399 in Venice, Italy, apparently of plague. The day before he died, had Mowbray known it, the chronicler Adam Usk recorded the bitter speech of Richard II, now imprisoned at the Tower of London, at the mercy of his cousin Henry of Lancaster and soon to become the ex-king of England.

Henry of Lancaster himself, meanwhile, went to Paris in the autumn of 1398, where he was warmly received by the French court, despite its close ties to King Richard: Henry was royal and a great nobleman, and as such would find a welcome in any court. He had, according to Jean Froissart, been bid a sad farewell by large crowds of Londoners, lining the streets to see him off.[36] Apparently he had originally intended to go to the court of Wilhelm, count of Ostrevant, but on John of Gaunt's advice went to Paris instead.[37] Charles VI's uncles, especially the duke of Berry, were particularly hospitable, and according to Froissart Henry was given the Hotel de Clisson as his residence and it was widely believed in France that his cousin Richard was treating him unjustly. The chronicle of Saint-Denys claimed that Richard was annoyed about the respect shown to Henry at the French court, and wrote to Charles VI and his noblemen asking them not to show too much favour to his cousin (though if Richard did so, the letters have not survived).[38] Henry's exile did not mean that he was penniless, as he was allowed to draw from his revenues in England, and thus he cut a fine and wealthy figure.[39]

Henry was still in Paris when he heard of the death of his father some months later and officially succeeded him as duke of Lancaster, though he was not able to attend the funeral in London, which must have distressed him. In December 1398 Richard II sent his ally John Montacute, earl of Salisbury, to Paris, partly to claim the latest instalment of Queen Isabelle's dowry but also to put paid to the rumours of negotiations for a marriage between Henry of Lancaster and the duke of Berry's daughter Marie.[40]

Richard II must have thought in the autumn and early winter of 1398 that all his troubles were over: the two most troubling Lords Appellant, Gloucester and Arundel, were dead, while Warwick and now Mowbray and Lancaster were all exiled; yet well under a year later, he was imprisoned and no longer king, his victory turned to ashes in his mouth.[41] In late 1398, the king's half-brother Sir Roger Clarendon, illegitimate son of his father Edward of Woodstock, was in dire trouble: earlier in the year he had killed another knight called William Drayton in a brawl, was imprisoned at Wallingford Castle but escaped and fled, and on 9 October 1398 the king granted Clarendon's goods to his squire Richard Chelmeley.[42] This seems to have been the last contact between Richard II and his half-brother: Roger Clarendon remained on the run for several years, until after Richard's deposition and death. He was hanged by Richard's cousin and successor Henry IV in 1402, not because Henry saw him as a threat or as a potential claimant to the throne, but because he had become involved in a hare-brained scheme to overthrow the king.[43]

Richard II, for whatever reason, felt that he needed the company or support of his cousin by marriage Thomas Despenser, the new earl of Gloucester, and on 28 October 1398 a messenger was sent to Despenser with a writ of great seal requesting him not to cross the seas.[44] On 18 October Richard paid the messenger who brought news of a son born to his parents-in-law Charles VI and Isabeau of Bavaria, yet another brother of Queen Isabelle.[45] This was Jean, later dauphin of Viennois, born on 31 August 1398 and only nineteen months younger than his brother Louis. Louis and Jean would both die at the age of eighteen. Five days previously, on the feast of St Edward the Confessor, 13 October, Richard had granted the great poet Geoffrey Chaucer a cask of wine annually, and earlier in 1398 had taken Chaucer under his protection as he travelled around the kingdom on royal business, as Chaucer 'fears molestation from his enemies'.[46]

In the meantime, on 20 July 1398, Roger Mortimer, earl of March and Ulster, had died at the age of only twenty-four, killed in a skirmish in Ireland. March left as his heir his seven-year-old son Edmund, and his eight-year-old daughter Anne – the Mortimer men in the fourteenth century tended to marry and father children very young – who later married Edmund of Langley's younger son Richard of Conisbrough and was the grandmother of Edward IV and Richard III. Roger Mortimer's many lands in England, Wales and Ireland were taken into the king's hands on 5 and 12 August, as was customary, and Richard used some of them to benefit Queen Isabelle financially.[47]

March was succeeded as lieutenant of Ireland by Richard's half-nephew Thomas Holland, earl of Kent and duke of Surrey. The king had in fact removed March from his position as lieutenant and replaced him with Surrey on 26 July, before he had heard news of his kinsman's death, and it may be that the earl of March's premature demise saved him from political humiliation or worse on his return to England. Adam Usk claims that the duke of Surrey had been ordered to arrest March – his brother-in-law – and return him to England.[48] March had been out of favour with the king for some time, despite being Richard's heir general and close to the throne; he was not raised to a higher title in September 1397 as many of the king's other close relatives were, and Richard had ordered the arrest of his illegitimate half-uncle, adviser and friend Thomas Mortimer, formerly the earl of Arundel's steward and a supporter of the Appellants in 1387. At some uncertain date, and despite their rather strained relationship, March had sent Richard a superb gift: the base for a triptych featuring Richard's symbol of the white hart in enamel, with twelve pearls on the antlers.[49]

The death of Roger Mortimer, leaving a child behind as his heir, put an end to any possibility of a Mortimer succeeding as king of England. His widow Alianore Holland, the king's half-niece and sister of the duke of Surrey and the duchess of York, received her enormous dower some months later, and on 19 June 1399 was given permission 'to marry whom she pleases, without impeachment of the king or his ministers'.[50] Alianore married her second husband Edward, Lord Cherleton or Charlton of Powys, Wales before 10 May 1400 and had two daughters with him.[51]

The earl of March, despite his high status and proximity to the throne, had always been something of an outsider in English politics and there is little if any evidence that Richard II had ever been particularly fond of him, and on his death once again the vexed question of the succession to the throne arose. His son Edmund was only seven and the little queen of England barely older; she would not be able to give the king any children for many years. According to one chronicle, at some point in the 1390s John of Gaunt had tried to persuade Richard to make his cousin Henry of Lancaster his heir, but the earl of March protested and claimed to be the rightful heir.

Richard, apparently unwilling to deal with the situation, told both men to be quiet.[52]

Another chronicle says that Gaunt tried to resurrect an old legend that his first wife Blanche's great-grandfather Edmund, earl of Lancaster (d. 1296), had been the elder son of King Henry III, but had been set aside in favour of Henry's other son Edward I because he was a hunchback.[53] Gaunt's son Henry of Lancaster also resurrected this story when taking the throne in 1399. It is unlikely, however, that Gaunt used the story in such a way to Richard's face, as it would have denied Richard's right to his throne, and Gaunt's father Edward III's right to it as well, and made all the kings from Edward I to Richard II usurpers. Edmund of Lancaster, born in January 1245, was in fact five and a half years younger than his brother Edward I. Whether Richard believed that his successor was the earl of March, or John of Gaunt followed by Henry of Lancaster, or Edmund of Langley followed by Edward of York, he never publicly declared his heir, even at this stage of his reign. In late 1398 and early 1399, with the earl of March and the duke of Lancaster dead, Henry of Lancaster in exile and Edmund of Langley elderly, Edward of York perhaps believed that he was next in line to the throne, and Richard calling him his brother surely only strengthened this belief.

20

'The Dateless Limit of Thy Dear Exile': Perpetual Banishment, 1398–1399

Richard II spent Christmas 1398, his last as a free man, at Lichfield in Staffordshire, and it was a feast so magnificent it acquired almost a legendary status. Queen Isabelle de Valois was also present, and she and Richard received presents from the royal dukes of Berry and Burgundy, her father's uncles. Guests of honour at the Christmas court included the Genoese nobleman Hilario Doria, son-in-law and ambassador of the emperor of Byzantium, Manuel II Palaeologus (Doria was married to Manuel's illegitimate daughter Zampia). Richard II sent out invitations far and wide for the jousts and tournaments held every day around Christmas and New Year, and the biggest of all was held on 6 January 1399, the feast of Epiphany or the Three Kings and Richard's thirty-second birthday. On that day Richard knighted one of the Byzantine ambassadors to his court, probably Hilario Doria himself, and gave Doria a safe conduct to return to Constantinople on 20 January.[1]

Later in 1399, Richard II sent £2,000 to the emperor Manuel to help him 'resist the malice of the Saracens and others warring and fighting against the faith ... to the destruction of Christianity in those and the neighbouring parts'.[2] This was part of the long series of military campaigns against the Byzantine Empire by the Ottoman Empire which ultimately resulted in the fall of Constantinople, now Istanbul, in 1453. Manuel had begged for aid against the Turks besieging Constantinople from the Christian kings of Europe, including Richard, Charles VI of France and Richard's brother-in-law Václav, king of Germany and Bohemia. At the battle of Nicopolis on the River Danube on 25 September 1396, the Christian army – led by the late Queen Anne's brother Zikmund, king of Hungary and Croatia – was crushed by the Ottoman forces led by Sultan Bajazet or Bayezid. Zikmund himself fled the field and managed to escape, but all the noble leaders of the French contingent were captured and held for ransom.[3] Thomas Walsingham says that in 1399 the bishop of Chalcedon (a town which is now a district of Istanbul) came to England, carrying threatening letters from the pope asking or rather demanding that faithful Christians in the realm should send money to Manuel.[4] In October 1397 Richard had received a visit from Theodore Kantakouzenos, Manuel's uncle, who once again was seeking aid against the Turks.[5]

Earlier in 1398 Richard had sent a letter to the Emperor Manuel, which is worth quoting extensively as it gives an excellent insight into his thoughts and his opinion of himself:

> To the most illustrious prince the lord Manuel, by the grace of God the emperor of Constantinople, our very dear brother, Richard, king of England and France and lord of Ireland, greeting and the continuous abundance of successful wishes ... you know what I believe is notorious throughout all quarters of the world, how some of our subject magnates and nobles, while we were yet of tender age and afterwards also, have made many attempts on the prerogative and royal right of our regal state, and have wickedly directed their malevolence even against our person. Wherefore when we could no longer endure their rebellion and wantonness, we collected the might of our prowess, and stretched forth our arm against these our enemies; and by the aid of God's grace, we have by our own valour trodden on the necks of the proud and haughty, and with a strong hand have ground them down, not to the bark only, but even to the root and have restored to our subjects peace, which by God's blessing may endure forever.[6]

Whatever Richard may have thought about restoring peace to his kingdom, in truth he had become enormously unpopular, at least in the south-east of his kingdom. In 1398, even Richard was forced to admit to his counsellors that he could not safely ride through England because of the hatred of the people of London and the seventeen counties adjoining it.[7] In the spring of 1398, an uprising took place in the Thames Valley led by a man called Thomas Geldesowe of Witney in Oxfordshire, who used the *nom de guerre* 'Thomas, the young earl of Arundel', the son and heir of the executed earl of Arundel (Thomas, aged seventeen, had gone into exile). This rising was intended to seek out Richard II and destroy him, and took place, almost certainly not coincidentally, in the area around Radcot Bridge, where Robert de Vere had been defeated in December 1387. There was also considerable opposition in Warwickshire and Gloucestershire to Richard's friend Thomas Despenser and his nephew Thomas Holland.[8] The year 1399, probably because it was close to the turn of a century, caused a certain amount of fear and anxiety among some of the inhabitants of Europe. Thomas Walsingham commented that in this year 'the laurel trees throughout almost the whole of England suddenly withered', and the French chronicler of Saint-Denys exclaimed that God was deliberately 'humiliating France in the person of its king' and that almost every nation of Christendom was racked by war, rebellion and treason.[9]

On 3 February 1399, John of Gaunt, duke of Lancaster and former titular king of Castile, died at Leicester Castle. He was not quite fifty-nine years old, and left his slightly younger brother Edmund of Langley, duke of York, as the only surviving child of Edward III. In his will, made on the day he died, John of Gaunt asked to be buried next to his first wife Blanche of Lancaster at St Paul's Cathedral in London, and left to his third wife Katherine Swynford, who survived him, his two best brooches, 'excepting that which I have allowed to my lord and nephew the king'.[10] Gaunt also left Katherine (among many other items including £2,000 in cash) a large gold cup which Richard had given him before his visit to Gascony some years before as well as 'all the buckles, rings, diamonds, rubies, and other things, that will be found in a little box of cypress wood, of which I carry the key myself, and all the robes which I bought of my dear cousin [Margaret] the duchess of Norfolk,' and gave another gold cup to Richard which had been a gift to Gaunt from Duchess Katherine the previous New Year.

Gaunt also left valuable items to all his daughters – Philippa, queen of Portugal; Catalina, queen of Castile; Elizabeth, duchess of Exeter; and Joan, *née* Beaufort, countess of Westmorland – and to all his sons – his heir Henry of Lancaster and the Beaufort brothers John, Henry and Thomas – and grandsons Henry and John, the future King Henry V and the duke of Bedford, the first and third sons of Henry of Lancaster (though none of Gaunt's numerous other grandchildren are mentioned). He asked for a chantry to be founded at the 'New Church of Our Lady of Leicester' for the soul of his second wife, Constanza of Castile, who had been buried there in 1394, and for the anniversary of her death on 24 March to be kept there forever. Although Gaunt's will does not mention any of his in-laws or most of his grandchildren, overall it gives a most agreeable impression of a man who remembered, honoured and cared deeply about his loved ones, both dead and alive.

John of Gaunt may have been taken ill before Christmas 1398. According to a disgusting – and, one hopes, untrue – story written in the 1440s, he showed Richard the ulcerated flesh around his genitals as a warning against lechery.[11] It is likely that Richard did visit his uncle in the New Year, as Gaunt was at Leicester, not too far from where Richard held his glittering festive court at Lichfield. Historian Michael Bennett notes that on or just after 8 January 1399, and certainly before 20 January, messengers took letters to the English magnates and clergy inviting them to attend Gaunt's funeral at St Paul's on the Thursday before Passion Sunday. This was several weeks before the duke's actual death.[12] Perhaps Gaunt had been desperately ill and near to death early in the year, and invitations to his funeral were issued prematurely.

Also rather unpleasantly, Gaunt asked in his will for his body to remain above ground for forty days after death before being buried, and not to be embalmed. Michael Bennett wonders, given that his demise had been announced prematurely, if he feared being buried alive.[13] Richard was among those who attended John of Gaunt's funeral at St Paul's, with, among others, his first cousin Philippa Coucy, duchess of Ireland, Gaunt's widow Katherine Swynford, Gaunt's three Beaufort sons and his nephew Edward of York, and Richard's half-brother and half-nephew the dukes of Exeter (Gaunt's son-in-law) and Surrey. Not present was Gaunt's exiled son and heir Henry. For all his influence over the king, and for all Richard's undoubted affection for and trust in his uncle in the last decade or so of his reign, Gaunt had been unable to prevent Richard exiling his son and heir. In the last months of his life, Gaunt must have been devastated about this.

The duke's demise left Richard with a dilemma: his cousin Henry of Lancaster, recently exiled for six (or ten) years, was now the rightful duke of Lancaster and heir to Gaunt's inheritance. It is likely that Richard had not anticipated his uncle's death so soon, and that the king was forced into an important decision far sooner than he would have wished. Gaunt was in his late fifties and of course no longer young, but might have been expected to live some more years, given that his father Edward III had lived to be sixty-four and given that when the king had stayed with his uncle in September 1398, Gaunt was still in good health.

The Lancastrian patrimony was so vast it was almost another kingdom within England, and the Lancasters had been a thorn in the side of Richard's great-grandfather Edward II. Edward also had a first cousin who was earl of Lancaster (both of them were grandsons of Henry III): Thomas, who had done much to ruin Edward's reign. Thomas of Lancaster's brother Henry (d. 1345) and Henry's son Henry the younger (d. 1361), the first duke of Lancaster, were loyal to Edward III, both because Edward III was a much more effective ruler than either his father Edward II or grandson Richard II and because of the respective personalities of the Lancasters. The Lancastrian inheritance came back into the royal family with John of Gaunt's marriage to Duke Henry's daughter and heir Blanche in 1359. Gaunt had been completely loyal to his nephew, but a cousin was a different matter.

In the late 1390s, Henry of Lancaster, thanks to a custom called the 'courtesy of England', also held his late wife Mary de Bohun's considerable inheritance, half of the earldoms of Hereford and Northampton, for as long as he lived, when they would pass to his and Mary's eldest son Henry of Monmouth. This was on top of the enormous Lancastrian patrimony, which included the earldoms of Leicester, Derby and Lincoln. Now Richard faced the same prospect as his great-grandfather had eighty years earlier: a Lancastrian first cousin who had the potential to become an over-mighty subject, almost a second king, a cousin whom Richard had never much liked or trusted. He had two choices, neither of which was particularly appealing. He could allow Henry to take over his rightful inheritance and to control the enormous revenues and patronage of the duchy, and almost certainly become a threat to Richard's security on the throne even though he was abroad, and one day in the not too distant future allow him to return to his homeland; or he could disinherit him and exile him permanently.

Richard, perhaps in an attempt to take his mind off his troubles, went outside with his birds: on 11 February 1399, eight days after his uncle's death, he paid over £77 to his master falconer Sir Baldwin Bereford for two 'bold falcons', two lannerets and other birds Bereford had bought for him. Richard also purchased falcons for other men: three lannerets for King Carlos III of Navarre, son of Carlos 'the Bad', and two falcons for John Montacute, earl of Salisbury.[14]

On 18 March 1399, just two days after John of Gaunt's funeral, Richard made his decision, and took the astonishing step of banishing his cousin Henry, now the rightful duke of Lancaster, from England for life. He also confiscated all his lands. This was the act which would, within a short time, lose him his throne. Henry of Lancaster was not a man to sit quietly by and watch his inheritance be taken from him, and numerous other English noblemen, quietly appalled, agreed with him. If the king's own royal cousin could have his patrimony taken by the king, so could any of them. It flew in the face of law and custom.

On the other hand, on 8 October 1398, shortly before his departure from England, Richard had promised Henry that if his inheritance fell to him during his exile, he or his attorneys could have livery of it, and the homage which he was required to perform to the king would be postponed until he returned. It seems as though Richard was anticipating that Henry would return to claim his inheritance: various grants of lands and favours made to the king's allies between March and May 1399 after the death of John of Gaunt included the proviso that they could only hold the lands 'until Henry, duke of Hereford, or his heir, has sued for the castles, lands and tenements of his inheritance out of the king's hands by the law of the land or obtained another grant from the king in this respect'. This included a grant to Richard's uncle Edmund of Langley that he could hold the office of steward of England once held by his brother John of Gaunt only until Henry of Lancaster 'shall sue for the said office according to law or shall have some grant thereof from the king'.[15]

Beginning several days before John of Gaunt's death and continuing for months afterwards, numerous grants of lands and income made by Gaunt to his followers, witnessed and confirmed by Henry of Lancaster, were inspected and again confirmed.[16] It does not seem as though Richard had complete and permanent confiscation of his cousin's lands in mind. His ally Sir William Bagot told parliament in

September 1399 that he had heard Richard make a vow that Henry of Lancaster would never return to England while he, Richard, was alive, but that he would prefer to restore the sons of the three dead or exiled Lords Appellant, Gloucester, Arundel and Warwick, and others condemned 'for withstanding his power and malice', to their lands.

Bagot declared that he had personally sent a messenger to Henry of Lancaster in France informing him that the king his cousin was his sworn enemy, and that he must 'help himself by force'. The messenger, Roger Smart, acknowledged the truth of this in the presence of Henry's companion Peter Bukton. That Bagot sent a messenger to Henry of Lancaster is certainly possible, but he gave this confession at the parliament which deposed Richard II and was trying desperately to save his own skin after Richard's downfall, so his supposed overhearing of Richard's vow to exile Henry forever should perhaps be taken with a pinch of salt. Bagot went on to state that he had heard Edward of York, duke of Albemarle, say to Sir John Bushy and Sir Henry Green (who were both rather conveniently dead by this point), 'I would gladly give twenty thousand pounds to see this man dead.' 'Which man?' they replied. 'The duke of Hereford,' said Edward of York, 'not because I am afraid of him, but because of the misery and trouble which he is likely to cause in the kingdom.'[17] Bushy, Bagot and Green climbed to power in the late years of Richard II's reign and were grossly unpopular thanks to their influence over the king, and deemed sycophants of the worst order. Their notoriety down the centuries was assured when they appeared as characters in Shakespeare's play about Richard 200 years later.

On 24 March 1399, Edward III's first cousin Margaret, duchess of Norfolk and the last surviving grandchild of Edward I, died, probably in her late seventies. Her heir was her grandson the exiled Thomas Mowbray, who died in Venice six months later. Thomas's eldest son Thomas (who was also a grandson of the earl of Arundel executed in 1397) succeeded Margaret and his father as earl of Norfolk and Nottingham, but was executed by Henry IV in 1405, leaving his brother John as his heir.[18] Margaret of Norfolk had been unhappily married to her first husband John Segrave, Thomas Mowbray's maternal grandfather, but made a much happier second match to Walter, Lord Manny, a Hainaulter who had come to England as a page of Edward III's queen Philippa and rose high in the king's favour, and who was the grandfather of John Hastings, the earl of Pembroke killed jousting at Christmas 1389. Manny's will of December 1371 mentions his two illegitimate daughters, both nuns, the rather intriguingly named Mailosel and Malplesant.[19] The income from the lands of Margaret's exiled grandson Thomas Mowbray now belonged to the king, joined by the vast income of Henry of Lancaster. Richard II was now astonishingly wealthy. An inventory of his crowns, jewels and plates taken made in or shortly before 1399 runs to forty membranes, and the king also squirreled away enormous amounts of treasure at the remote Holt Castle in Cheshire, sending wagon after wagon loaded with expensive possessions there.[20]

Richard II wrote his will on 16 April 1399 at Westminster. He remembered his father's devotion to the Trinity, and the will began, 'In the name of the holy and undivided Trinity' and went on to name the Virgin Mary and the saints John the Baptist and Edward the Confessor, two of the three saints presenting him to Mary and the Christ Child in the Wilton Diptych. He referred to himself as 'we Richard, who by the grace of God have already for some time since our tender age submitted our neck by the mercy of the supreme king to the burden of the government of the English', a rather astonishing phrase which reveals much about his anxious and unhappy state of mind at this time. The king expressed his wish to be buried in Westminster Abbey next to Queen Anne 'of glorious memory', with his body dressed in white velvet or satin in befitting royal manner and wearing a crown, sceptre and ring with a precious stone.

The king bequeathed generous sums of money to several of his relatives and friends: 10,000 marks to his nephew Thomas Holland, duke of Surrey; 3,000 marks to his half-brother John Holland, duke of Exeter; and 2,000 marks each to William Scrope, earl of Wiltshire, and to Richard's first cousin Edward of York, duke of Albemarle, whom he named as his 'dear brother'. The little queen Isabelle was not forgotten, and Richard granted her all the jewels she had brought to the marriage with her if she outlived him, in accordance with the treaty he had made with her father Charles VI in 1396. The dukes of Surrey and Exeter and the earl of Wiltshire were also left one golden ring each. Richard's cousin Henry of Lancaster was, perhaps rather pointedly, not left any bequests, though the king did appoint as supervisors of the will his uncle Edmund of Langley and his kinsman Thomas Percy, earl of Worcester, steward of the royal household and brother of the earl of Northumberland.[21]

Ten days after making his will, Richard made a large payment to Adam Attewoode or Atwood, keeper of his beds. Adam received more than a £112 for himself and two servants for looking after the king and Queen Isabelle's beds in the Tower of London for half a year, an entry which reveals how expensive and important beds were in the fourteenth century.[22] The king made eight Ladies of the Garter in April 1399, his last appointments: they included his second cousin Katharina of Bavaria, duchess of Guelders and Jülich; his half-niece Joan, *née* Holland, duchess of York, who was also his aunt by marriage; his first cousin and Henry of Lancaster's half-sister the legitimised Joan Neville, *née* Beaufort, now countess of Westmorland; the duchess of York's sister Margaret, wife of Joan Beaufort's brother John the marquis of Dorset and yet another of the king's Holland nieces; and Queen Isabelle's attendant Marguerite Courcy, who mere weeks later was packed off back to her native France in disgrace.

In the spring of 1399 Richard began preparing for his second visit to Ireland, which he had been intending to visit since the summer of 1397; the arrest of the Lords Appellant hindered him on this occasion. He took with him the dukes of Albemarle, Exeter and Surrey, the earls of Gloucester, Salisbury and Worcester, the abbot of Westminster, numerous other lords, and two young men perhaps intended as hostages: his first cousin Humphrey of Gloucester, only son of the Thomas of Woodstock, duke of Gloucester, and then seventeen, and Henry of Lancaster's eldest son Henry of Monmouth, then twelve. He treated them well and kindly, however, and knighted Henry in Ireland.[23] Adam Usk thought that Richard intended to crown his nephew the duke of Surrey (who was his lieutenant in Ireland) as king of that country, which seems most unlikely.[24] The king paid £100 for the 'repairs of decayed ships and for necessary alterations', and for the construction of others, for his voyage to Ireland, and took a contingent of his Cheshire archers with him.[25] Less is known about Richard's second visit to Ireland than his first in 1395, though his aim may have been once more to compel Art MacMurrough, king of Leinster, to submit. The Irish expedition of 1399 proved notably less successful than Richard's previous one.[26]

Probably to mark the feast of St George on 23 April 1399 before he departed for Ireland, Richard held a jousting tournament at Windsor in honour of the young queen Isabelle, in which forty knights and their squires, all dressed in green, took part.[27] Isabelle was now nine and a half. She could not have known it, but this would be the last time she would see Richard, who treated her with enormous affection, swinging her up off the ground to bid her a last farewell and promising her that she would soon join him in Ireland. On the other hand, Richard arranged with William Scrope, earl of Wiltshire, that after he had departed for Ireland, Wiltshire would send Isabelle's governess Lady Courcy back to France, with twenty other of the little girl's domestic servants. This seems both calculating and rather unkind to the little girl, and her uncle Louis, duke of Orléans, was furious about it.[28]

Richard later entrusted Queen Isabelle, then living at Wallingford Castle, which had once belonged to his mother, to the official care of Wiltshire, John Bushy, Henry Green and William Bagot, the four courtiers he trusted implicitly. The French author of the *Traison et Mort* says that Isabelle 'was ill with grief from losing her lord', and so Richard sent her a long and affectionate letter to comfort her. The same writer gives an amusing account of the Irish people at the end of the fourteenth century: there 'are two races speaking two languages, the one speak bastard English, and ... have always been friendly to good King Richard; the other are a wild people, who speak a strange language, and are called Crichemons'.[29]

Richard II arrived in Waterford on 1 June and a month later had reached Dublin. The first day of his twenty-third and last regnal year was 22 June 1399, and on this day he appointed Thomas, bishop of Chrysopolis, to receive money to aid Manuel II Palaeologus, emperor of Byzantium, in his endless campaign against Sultan Bayezid and the Ottoman forces.[30] Eight days later, Richard made a payment of £8 13s 4d to a goldsmith of London for making him a *nef* of silver. He also asked the goldsmith to repair six silver shields engraved with 'diverse arms' which had formerly belonged to his uncle John of Gaunt and which the king was giving to the abbot of Westminster.[31] Richard sent his ally Thomas Despenser to treat with Art MacMurrough, and Despenser met the king of Leinster in a glen in Wicklow, but failed to compel him to submit to Richard.[32]

Meanwhile in Paris, Richard's exiled cousin Henry of Lancaster was gathering allies. Charles VI's brother Louis, duke of Orléans, was, like his father-in-law Gian Galeazzo Visconti of Milan, an ally of Henry. On 17 June 1399, Henry and Louis sealed an agreement that they would protect and defend each other's life and honour in word and deed.[33] Various men were excluded from the treaty – that is, Henry and Orléans would not defend the other against them; they included 'the most high and illustrious prince, my lord the king of England', Richard's brothers-in-law Václav and Zikmund, Henry's brothers-in-law the kings João of Portugal and Enrique of Castile, and Richard and Henry's mutual uncle Edmund of Langley, duke of York.[34]

The duchess of Orléans, Valentina Visconti, gave Henry a gift of a gold buckle set with rubies, pearls and sapphires.[35] Orléans was Henry of Lancaster's only real ally at the French court; Charles VI and others were committed to the alliance with Richard II and therefore were unwilling to offer Henry any aid against the English king (although relations between the English and French courts had cooled somewhat since the heady days of late 1396). Years later, after Richard's downfall and death, the duke of Orléans claimed – whether accurately or not – that his aid and support of Henry had not included any role in Richard's deposition, or a desire for this to happen.

Henry of Lancaster was not going to sit back and passively accept his disinheritance. He began making plans to return to England, either to claim his rightful inheritance and demand that Richard allow him to return to his homeland permanently, or perhaps even to plot the overthrow of the king himself. The endgame of Richard II's reign was about to begin.

21

'Who Strongly Hath Set Footing in This Land': Henry of Lancaster Returns, 1399

'While the king remained in Ireland attacking the Irish, imagining that he was achieving great things, God suddenly decided to humble his pride and bring succour to the people of England, who were now so miserably oppressed that they had lost all hope of deliverance and relief unless God were to reach forth and help them.'[1] This piously malicious account by Thomas Walsingham puts a typically biased spin on events of 1399. The Dieulacres chronicler, far more sympathetic to Richard II, says that the king's 'preoccupation with Ireland did him little good ... for while he was away various enemies of his, and of the country, made their way stealthily and craftily into England ... although they pretended to talk smoothly of peace, [they] overthrew even the innocent king himself'.[2]

With hindsight it seems utterly astonishing that Richard would leave England at this juncture, though he had probably never imagined that Henry of Lancaster would dare to return without permission or that he had anything to fear from him; Richard seems by now to have imagined that he could do whatever he wished without repercussion. Henry had been joined in Paris by the exiled archbishop Thomas Arundel and Arundel's nephew and namesake Thomas, eighteen-year-old son and heir of the executed earl of Arundel, who had also been banished from England. Henry had only a small number of men with him, yet must have realised that in the king's absence he had a unique opportunity to return to England and fight for his inheritance – and perhaps even more. Henry had, and surely knew that he had, plenty of supporters in England. Walsingham, however, says that Henry had no more than fifteen fighting men with him on the continent and only ten or twelve ships, though the *Vitae et Regni* puts the number of men at about sixty.[3]

Probably on 4 July 1399, Henry of Lancaster and his small band of followers, including Thomas Arundel, sailed from Boulogne and landed at or near Ravenspur in Yorkshire, at the mouth of the Humber.[4] Apparently he sailed along the coast before landing, in order to discover what defences might have been placed against his arrival and whether there was support for his return, and learnt that there was 'great joy among the people' to hear of it and that they believed 'God had sent him in order to release them from their dreadful yoke of servitude'.[5] Henry made his way to his Yorkshire castles of Pickering and Knaresborough, and was soon joined by his mother's first cousin Henry Percy, earl of Northumberland, a man then in his late fifties, and Northumberland's son Henry 'Hotspur' Percy. (Hotspur's wife was Edward III's eldest great-grandchild Elizabeth Mortimer, sister of the late earl of March.) Another man who joined Henry of Lancaster was his brother-in-law Ralph Neville, now earl of Westmorland, husband of his half-sister Joan Beaufort.

Precisely why the two great northern lords Northumberland and Westmorland were willing to join Henry publicly against the king is not entirely clear; presumably they sympathised with him over his disinheritance, though to join him so openly may have meant that they thought he intended to overthrow Richard and assumed that he would be able to do so. At Doncaster and again at Bridlington, Henry of Lancaster swore an oath to the Percys on holy relics that he had only come back to the kingdom to claim his rightful inheritance. Years later, after he had made himself king, Northumberland and Hotspur rebelled against Henry, and both died fighting against him, in 1408 and 1403 respectively. Yet as Michael Bennett has pointed out, the Percys and Ralph Neville would hardly have openly joined Henry against Richard II if they were only concerned with the duke of Lancaster regaining his rightful inheritance.[6]

Henry spent some time travelling around Yorkshire, where his support was at its strongest, awaiting news, testing the waters and deciding what he should do next. He moved south slowly, and on 24 July reached Warwick Castle, which had formerly belonged to the exiled earl of Warwick Thomas Beauchamp and was now held by the king's nephew Thomas Holland, duke of Surrey. A chronicle written in French claims that Thomas Holland had placed a crowned white hart, Richard's emblem, made of stone above the castle gate and that Henry of Lancaster had this knocked down, which has sometimes been taken as an indication that even at this early date he was already intending to usurp the throne.[7]

Richard heard of Henry's landing probably on 10 July, from letters sent by Sir William Scrope on the 4th which urged him to return to England immediately if he did not wish to be driven out of his kingdom.[8] Jean Creton, a French valet who was an eyewitness to events of 1399 and who later wrote a rhyming history about Richard, says that the king's face turned pale with anger (as it so often did) when he heard the news of Henry's arrival, and that he said, 'Come hither, friends. Good lord, this man plans to deprive me of my country.'[9] He first sent John Montacute, earl of Salisbury, across the Irish Sea to Wales to raise troops. Jean Creton states that Edward of York deliberately gave Richard bad and treacherous advice to send John Montacute first and not to hasten back to England himself.[10] On the other hand, for logistical reasons Richard could not immediately return to his kingdom, as it would take time for his fleet to be assembled and ready for him and his retinue to travel.

According to Walsingham, when Richard heard of Henry's landing he shut Henry's son Henry of Monmouth and his cousin Humphrey of Gloucester inside the stronghold of Trim Castle.[11] With the dukes of Albemarle, Exeter and Surrey, the bishops of London, Carlisle and Lincoln (the latter was his cousin Henry Beaufort, Henry of Lancaster's half-brother) and the rest of his retinue, Richard then sped towards his ships. Thomas Walsingham, a fervent supporter of Henry of Lancaster, says that 'it was as if God had ordained that the duke of Lancaster should be allowed to gather his strength and prepare himself' before Richard was able to return to his kingdom and challenge him.[12] The king appointed William Scrope, Sir John Bushy, Sir Henry Green and Sir William Bagot to guard Wallingford Castle, where Queen Isabelle was living, on 12 July. One of the men then living at Wallingford was Richard's distant kinsman Sir Hugh Despenser, brother of the bishop of Norwich; the bishop himself raised arms against Henry of Lancaster in 1399, but Hugh was shortly to join Henry's household.[13]

According to the *Traison et Mort*, John Montacute begged the king to retreat to his birthplace of Bordeaux where he would be well received, but the king's half-brother John Holland suggested instead that they should go to the strong castle of Beaumaris on the island of Anglesey in North Wales and that if Richard went to Bordeaux, it would look to everyone as though he were fleeing. Montacute's advice was sensible as Bordeaux was a centre of anti-Lancastrian feeling, though Holland surely had a point as well.[14] An Italian nobleman named Baldassare degli Ubriachi had been intending to travel to Ireland in July 1399 to meet Richard and present him with a rich navigation map he had commissioned, but was overtaken by events and never met the king.[15]

The regent Edmund of Langley, meanwhile, was making little effort to resist Henry, who was as much as his nephew as Richard was, and with whom he surely sympathised for his disinheritance at the hands of the king. Walsingham even says that Edmund declared publicly that his nephew had been wrongfully disinherited and that he would not attack anyone who came with a just cause.[16] It is doubtful whether the duke would have been able to do much to halt Henry's advance even if he had tried; nonetheless, perhaps unsurprisingly given his usual lethargy and lack of forcefulness and ability, he did little more than dither. On 27 July Edmund met his nephew at Berkeley Castle in Gloucestershire, held by Thomas, Lord Berkeley, then in his mid-forties, one of the great magnates of the west of England and yet another descendant of Edward I.[17] Lord Berkeley, a rival of his kinsman Thomas Despenser, supported Henry of Lancaster, who had with him the two Arundels, plus Henry Percy and Ralph Neville. Richard II must have received the news that his cousin, within a very short space of time, was making himself master of the kingdom, and that his uncle was doing nothing to stop him.[18]

Edmund of Langley and Henry of Lancaster rode together the 20 miles from Berkeley Castle to the important city of Bristol, supposedly with a fighting force of 100,000 men. This number is so huge it sounds like a typical medieval exaggeration or just a suitably large and vague figure, though two chroniclers give it, and the *Traison* says that Henry had to dismiss the greater part of his army as he could not feed them.[19] Even at this early juncture it must have been embarrassingly obvious to everyone that Henry of Lancaster had massive support in England and that the king did not. Jean Froissart says that Edmund of Langley used his influence as keeper of the realm to demand that the city of Bristol open its gates and surrender to Henry of Lancaster.[20] Staying in Bristol Castle at the time were several of Richard II's closest allies: Sir Henry Green, Sir John Bushy and William Scrope, earl of Wiltshire. The three men were accused of committing treason and of evil government of the king and kingdom, and were summarily beheaded on 29 July.[21] The life of another supporter of Richard, Sir John Russell, was spared after he claimed to be insane, a story narrated in the *Vitae et Regni* which sounds implausible but is given credence by an entry on the Patent Roll of 29 August 1399 which speaks of Russell's 'infirmities'.[22]

Henry then travelled north to Shrewsbury, where he arrived on 8 August, having been joined by Edmund Mortimer the elder, brother of the late earl of March.[23] At this point, even Richard II's dog abandoned him. Adam Usk says that Richard adopted a 'greyhound of wonderful nature' which had belonged to his half-brother the earl of Kent on the latter's death in April 1397. For more than two years the animal was his constant companion, 'ever by his side, with grim and lion-like face'. After Richard left his army in South Wales, the dog made its own way from Carmarthen to Shrewsbury, a distance of some 100 miles. It found Henry of Lancaster in the abbey and obediently sat in front of him 'with a look of the purest pleasure on its face'. Pleased at this augury of good fortune for himself and evidently a fan of dogs, Henry adopted the animal and allowed it to sleep on his bed. When the greyhound somewhat later encountered the captive Richard, it did not recognise him, or at least affected not to, which caused Richard much distress. Although this story sounds fabricated, Froissart also gives a version of it and names the dog as Blemach.[24]

Richard II finally returned to his kingdom and arrived at Milford Haven in South Wales, probably on 24 July 1399. Thomas Despenser, earl of Gloucester, was ordered to raise the men of nearby Glamorgan, his own lordship, to Richard's cause, but they refused to obey him, and the duke of Albemarle Edward of York was sent eastwards also to raise troops.[25] As well as York and Despenser, the king was accompanied by his half-brother John Holland, duke of Exeter; nephew Thomas Holland, duke of Surrey; Thomas Percy, earl of Worcester; Thomas Merk, bishop of Carlisle; Sir Stephen Scrope, chamberlain of the royal household since the previous year and brother of the earl of Wiltshire recently executed in Bristol; William Ferriby, a member of the royal council; and Janico Dartasso from Gascony, a squire of Richard's chamber and a good fighter who had 'performed great feats of arms'.[26]

Richard was in Wales when he heard of the fall of Bristol. He made what seems with hindsight to be a peculiar and inexplicable decision to leave his army under the command of Edward of York and the earl of Worcester, while he himself set out during the night with the two Hollands, Thomas Despenser and a handful of others to join John Montacute, earl of Salisbury, and the army Salisbury had raised at Chester. Supposedly the king disguised himself as a Franciscan friar to evade capture.[27] The king and his small company made their way through Wales, via Harlech Castle and on to the great North Wales fortress of Conwy, both built by his ancestor Edward I a century before. Richard was briefly at Caernarfon Castle, where, as he must have been aware, his great-grandfather Edward II had been born, but soon moved on the 20 miles to Conwy, as Caernarfon was not provisioned.

The earl of Salisbury met Richard at Conwy with dire news: he had raised an army of some 40,000 men and kept them in the field for two weeks, but because Richard himself was absent and because Henry of Lancaster was making such astonishing progress throughout the kingdom, the soldiers had grown disheartened and either deserted or went to join Henry.[28] Jean Creton says that both the king and the earl of Salisbury were tearful and distressed at their meeting.[29] At this point John Holland was sent from Conwy Castle, with his nephew Thomas Holland, to negotiate with Henry of Lancaster. John knelt before Henry and, in another excellent example of 'As you know, Bob' dialogue, this time recorded by the author of the *Traison et Mort*, said to him, 'My lord, it is but reasonable that I should show you respect, for your father was the king's son, and moreover my wife is your sister, wherefore I am bound to do so.'[30] Henry asked Holland how Richard was and received the answer that the king was quite well, whereupon the two men drew apart and had a private conversation. Henry subsequently had Holland imprisoned at Chester, and somewhat later he was sent to London with the king.[31]

While John Holland was talking to Henry of Lancaster, Henry Percy, earl of Northumberland, came to meet Richard II at Conwy Castle with only seven attendants, leaving most of his men some distance away concealed 'in ambush between two mountains' or behind some rocks.[32] The earl's series of conferences with the king were fundamental to Richard's subsequent fate. The *Traison* says that Northumberland told the king that what Henry of Lancaster 'most wishes for in this world is to have peace and a good understanding with you, and greatly repents with all his heart of the displeasure he has caused you ... he asks nothing of you in this living world save that you would consider him as your cousin and friend, and that you would please only let him have his land'.[33] Creton says that Northumberland asked Richard to restore Henry of Lancaster to the office of steward of England held by his father John of Gaunt and his ancestors, and to deliver up some of the king's chief allies to stand trial for treason on account of the wrongs they had committed. These men were John and Thomas Holland, John Montacute, Thomas Merk and the royal clerk Thomas Maudelyn, who closely resembled Richard II physically. Duke Henry would act as their judge. The author of the *Traison* also states that Henry wished to be steward of England and to act as the judge of these five men.

Supposedly Northumberland told Richard that Henry 'wants nothing but his land, and whatever belongs to him. He desires nothing that is yours, for you are his immediate and rightful king.' The earl swore on the body of Jesus Christ that 'Duke Henry will most faithfully adhere to everything that I have said'. The Dieulacres chronicle broadly agrees with the *Traison* and Creton, and the Lancastrian narrative of events, the 'Record and Process', is essentially propaganda which states that Richard II told Northumberland and Archbishop Thomas Arundel (apparently not even present) that he would voluntarily relinquish his crown and his royal majesty.[34] It is most unlikely that Richard agreed to abdicate at Conwy, and the earl of Northumberland later claimed that Henry of Lancaster had tricked him.[35] He swore a sacred oath in Richard's presence that everything he had told him from Henry was true, and thus 'perjured himself wickedly and falsely', says the *Traison*.[36]

On Monday 18 August 1399 (the date given in the *Traison*), or more probably some days before, Richard moved onto Flint Castle, 35 miles west of Conwy and only a dozen miles from Chester, where the last great drama of his reign, immortalised later by Shakespeare, would play itself out. With only twelve attendants he travelled with the earl of Northumberland, and realised too late that he had walked into a trap and declared that he had been delivered 'into the hands of wolves'.[37] On the road to Rhuddlan he came to the rocks or hills where the earl of Northumberland's men were concealed, and, astonished at the sight, exclaimed ,'I am betrayed! What can this be? True God of heaven, help me!'[38] He also supposedly said to Northumberland, 'The God upon whom you have sworn, reward you and all your accomplices at the day of judgement!' and to his weeping friends (rather unrealistically), 'Ah, my good and faithful friends, we are all betrayed, and given without cause into the hands of our enemies; for God's sake have patience, and call to mind our Saviour, who was undeservedly sold and given into the hands of His enemies.'[39]

Henry of Lancaster, informed by the earl of Northumberland of the king's arrival, arrived at Flint from Chester the following day, Tuesday 19 August or some days earlier, with a 'large and powerful army' which he 'drew up in awe-inspiring manner in full view of the king'.[40] The author of the *Traison* put the number of Henry's soldiers at 60,000 or 80,000, lined up as if they were going to battle. When the king saw his cousin's forces, he began to tremble and weep and said, 'Alas, now approaches the hour when we shall be delivered into the hands of our mortal enemy.' The earl of Salisbury declared, 'Now I see truly that I am certain to be a dead man, for I know that Duke Henry bears a great hatred towards me.'[41]

Supposedly Richard and Henry's cousin Edward of York, duke of Albemarle, last seen left in charge of the king's army in the south of Wales, appeared at Flint as part of a delegation sent by Henry and wearing Henry's livery. A shame-faced Edward 'said nothing to the king, but kept at as great a distance as he could from him'. Edward's side-switching was to avail him little at first, and he came close to being lynched a few weeks later during Henry's first parliament.[42] If he had ever believed that he was Richard's desired successor as king, the overwhelming support shown to his other cousin Henry must have convinced him that he had no chance of gaining the throne. Thomas Percy, earl of Worcester, had also deserted the king and gone over to the duke of Lancaster, his brother the earl of Northumberland and nephew Hotspur at Chester. Edward of York and Thomas Percy had supposedly told Richard's army at Milford Haven, 'My lads, do the best you can for yourselves; the king has gone away without leaving any orders; get away each of you as well you can.'[43]

The *Traison* gives a moving account of Richard's distress at Flint, and even says that he expected to be beheaded on the orders of his cousin. Crying out to God, the Virgin Mary, John the Baptist (whom he called his 'godfather') and all the saints, Richard said, 'Is it so that I must die, and my companions for my sake? In troth I have never transgressed against the kingdom of England; why should I be thus seized?' He went on to express his sorrow that he would never see his 'dearest sister' little Queen Isabelle again, nor her father Charles VI and his 'dear uncles [the dukes of] Berry and Burgundy', the French author rather betraying his own bias in this account.[44] In an orgy of emotion, 'the earl of Salisbury and the others made extraordinary lamentation, bewailing their wives and children, brothers, mothers and sisters'.[45]

Walsingham says that Richard gave himself up to his cousin at Flint on 20 August, which, as he correctly says, was only the forty-sixth or forty-seventh day after Henry of Lancaster's return to England. 'It was a remarkable feat, in so short a time, to have brought such peace and stability to the whole realm, so much so, indeed, that the sole and universal desire of the inhabitants was now that King Richard should be set aside and Henry duke of Lancaster become their king.'[46] One wonders how and when Walsingham found the time to canvas every single one of the people of England as to their opinion on the matter, or whether he was claiming mental telepathy. Precisely when Henry decided not only to fight for his inheritance but to depose Richard and take his throne cannot be known; equally we cannot know if he had had it in mind all along or genuinely had returned only to claim his inheritance and was swept along by events and his astounding popularity in 1399.

It was agreed that Henry of Lancaster would not enter Flint Castle until after Richard had eaten, and so the king spent a doleful last meal with his few companions while Henry's army outside made such a loud noise 'it seemed as if all would fall down'. Supposedly some of Henry's allies came into the castle and told Richard's companions in English, 'Eat heartily and make good cheer, for by Saint George, your heads will shortly be chopped off!'[47] Henry himself, however, showed the king considerable respect and deference when he came inside the castle, bowing to him from a distance and then bowing again very low to the ground as he approached him, and removing his bonnet from his head.[48] Whatever Richard was feeling, he also remained courteous and removed his hat, and welcomed Henry as his fair cousin of Lancaster. For some reason the king had seen fit to don the clothes of a priest.[49]

Henry said, 'My lord, I am come to help you to govern the kingdom of England, which you have not ruled well these twenty-two years that it has been in your government; and therefore, with the consent of the commons, I will help you to govern it.' Richard's only reply was an oath, according to the *Traison*, or the vastly more compliant statement, 'If it pleases you, fair cousin, it pleases us as well' according to the eyewitness Creton. Creton says at this point in his rhyming chronicle that he heard and understood Richard's words perfectly well, so Richard and Henry must have been speaking French.[50] Henry called, 'Bring out the king's horses', whereupon six rather poor nags were led out from the stables, and Richard and his companions were mounted on them. Around two or three o'clock in the afternoon they set out for Chester, with Richard, according to the *Traison et Mort*, deliberately placed in the custody of his cousin Humphrey of Gloucester and the late earl of Arundel's son Thomas, whose fathers he had put to death.[51]

The king of England was now a captive. Only forty-six days after Henry of Lancaster's return to England and already Richard II was at his cousin's mercy, his allies either having deserted him or also taken prisoner. So easily did the king lose control of his kingdom, and far worse was soon to come.

22

'All Pomp and Majesty I Do Forswear': Deposition, 1399

It is possible that whatever was said in public, privately Richard agreed to name Henry of Lancaster as his heir to the throne, or even to renounce the rule of his kingdom to him, shortly after his capture.[1] At Chester Henry was lauded by the population, but Richard was jeered at. He was housed in a tower of the castle, which he himself had recently had renovated and refurbished.[2] The king was forcibly separated from his companions: the bishop of Carlisle knelt and clasped him round the leg and the earl of Salisbury took his arm, and Richard was so moved by grief he was unable to speak for half an hour. Thomas Despenser, earl of Gloucester, also remained with him until this point. The loyal Gascon squire Janico Dartasso utterly refused to remove Richard's badge of the white hart from his person and was probably the last person to wear it, and may have been put to death.[3] Around this time, Henry of Lancaster's eldest son Henry of Monmouth was reunited with his father, with some grief on the boy's part at having to leave Richard, whom he loved and who had treated him well.[4]

On 19 August writs were sent out summoning a parliament to be held at Westminster on 30 September; they were issued in the king's name and addressed 'Henry duke of Lancastre' and Thomas Arundel as the archbishop of Canterbury among those being summoned, as if they were not responsible for issuing them. Thomas Beauchamp, earl of Warwick, exiled to the Isle of Man two years earlier, was another of those called to parliament.[5] Richard was taken under strict guard south to London, via Lichfield (where he tried unsuccessfully to escape by letting himself down from a tower at night) and Coventry, where they stayed for three days and where a deputation from London met Henry of Lancaster and said to him, 'Dear sire, the commons of London, and all the commons of the realm of England, salute you more than a hundred thousand times, and humbly beseech you to behead King Richard presently, without bringing him any further.' If this truly happened, Henry, to his credit, refused and stated that parliament would decide what should be done with Richard.[6]

According to the *Traison et Mort*, Richard II was taken through London, probably on 1 September 1399, to imprisonment at the Tower. He was riding 'a little horse', his face was covered in tears, and he was accompanied by his captors Humphrey of Gloucester (who died on 2 September) and Thomas Fitzalan. Henry of Lancaster, meanwhile, had visited his father John of Gaunt's tomb at St Paul's Cathedral for the first time, and also cried very much. Henry was greeted as a hero who had rightfully conquered the realm by the London crowd, who played trumpets and other instruments to express their joy, and the bells of churches and monasteries 'rang so merrily that you could not even hear God thundering'.[7] A boy in the London crowd watching the disgraced king being led past exclaimed, possibly sarcastically, that Richard had done great good to the kingdom of England, but others shouted, to general public approval, that they were all well rid of the 'evil bastard' or 'little bastard' who had governed them so badly.[8] The irregular marriage of his parents and Joan of Kent's colourful marital past were, once again, an embarrassment to Richard and a reason to hurl abuse at him and claim that he was illegitimate and therefore not the correct occupant of the throne.

Richard was taken to imprisonment at the Tower – he was allowed to hear mass at Westminster on the morning of 2 September first – and Jean Froissart says that Henry of Lancaster tried to browbeat Richard there with these stories and reminded him that their grandfather Edward III had opposed Richard's parents' marriage. The *Traison* says, though, that when Henry visited Richard in the Tower he greeted his cousin very humbly.[9] Richard was also visited in the Tower by his uncle Edmund of Langley and cousin Edward of York, as part of an effort to wear him down. Furiously, Richard accused them both of treason, cursed them by God and St John the Baptist, and shouted, 'You villain!' at Edmund. He addressed both father and son with the familiar form of 'you', i.e. *tu* in French or *thou* in English, rather than the more distant and courteous form *vous*, though he and Henry of Lancaster continued to use *vous* to each other at this time. Richard even went so far as to claim that his uncle of Gloucester, Thomas of Woodstock, had been put to death thanks to the 'false counsel' of his cousin Edward of York. Edward took off his hat and threw it at Richard's feet in a rage on hearing these words and said that Richard was lying, whereupon the king kicked the hat a few feet away from him. Equally enraged, he shouted that the kingdom of England would be destroyed by the traitor Edward and that neither Edward nor his father was fit to speak to him, and that he would continue as king and be a better lord than ever he was, in spite of all his enemies.[10]

The queen Isabelle de Valois was not allowed to see Richard at this time or indeed ever again, and was now at the mercy of her husband's enemy. When Shakespeare wrote his play about Richard two centuries later he made Isabelle a grown woman, but she was still not even ten years old in August/September 1399. The sudden downfall of her husband, and the realisation that he was loathed by so many of his subjects, can hardly have been anything but distressing for the girl, and she surely feared for her own safety as well.

At first, Henry of Lancaster, Archbishop Thomas Arundel and their allies toyed with the idea of setting up a council which would rule for Richard, who would remain king. It is possible that Richard agreed, at least publicly, to this idea. He had, after all, apparently talked about resigning the crown to his cousin Edward of York the year before. By 10 September 1399, however, this idea was dropped out of necessity. Even the Frenchman Creton, highly sympathetic to Richard's cause, states that Richard declared to his friends that any such concession he made to Henry would not be binding on him, and as soon as he got the chance, he would have his enemies flayed alive.[11] This left Henry and the others with no option: Richard would have to go.

There was a precedent in England for deposing a king, Edward II in January 1327. This, though a revolutionary act the time, passed off without too many problems: Edward was forced to abdicate his throne to his elder son Edward III, who would eventually have become king anyway when Edward II died. Whatever Edward II's feelings on the matter, in public the revolution was presented as the king, of his own free will, abdicating his throne to his son and his subjects accepting his decision. In effect, the succession was 'speeded up', and there was no doubt at all in anyone's mind that Edward III was the true heir to the throne and had been since the moment he was born as the first child of Edward II and Isabella of France in November 1312.

It was by no means clear in 1399, however, that Henry of Lancaster was truly the heir to the throne. The eight-year-old Edmund Mortimer and his uncle, also Edmund Mortimer, the son and younger brother of the late earl of March, might be deemed to have a superior right by descent from Edward III's second son Lionel of Clarence, and Lionel's daughter Philippa. The myth that Henry of Lancaster's great-great-grandfather Edmund, earl of Lancaster (d. 1296), had been the elder son of Henry III and thus had a greater right to the throne than his brother Edward I but had been set aside because of a physical disability was resurrected. The story was absurd but seemingly was considered the best option, and chronicles were searched to ascertain the truth of the matter (which was that Edward I was older than his brother). Henry was advised by his ally Justice William Thirning not to claim the throne by right of conquest. If he could claim it by such a right then so could anyone else, and no future king would be able to sit securely on it; not to mention that it would make men insecure about their property and their right to hold it. Likewise, he had no wish to rest his title on popular election.[12] At least three chronicles state that in 1399 Henry of Lancaster claimed to be the heir male of Henry III, and Henry himself told parliament in a speech made in English that he was 'descended by right line of the blood from the good lord King Henry the third, son of King John'.[13]

Henry of Lancaster and others also harked back 150 years to the papal deposition of the Holy Roman Emperor Frederick II in 1245, which, they said, set a precedent whereby a monarch could be deposed if he had committed major crimes. Richard was thus said to be guilty of sodomy, perjury, sacrilege and other crimes in an official account of the events of September 1399 called the Record and Process. It consisted of thirty-three charges against Richard, and was presented to him at the Tower of London on Monday 29 September 1399.[14]

As one might expect, the charges are exaggerated and distorted, but contain enough kernels of the truth to have made them appear plausible. Probably the most famous of them, often quoted nowadays, is that Richard acted 'as though the laws were in his mouth, or in his breast'. The first accusation was that Richard was 'charged for his evil government' and gave 'the goods and possessions of the crown to unworthy persons', as a result of which he 'had to impose needlessly grievous and intolerable burdens upon the people'. Two charges mentioned the arrest of the three Lords Appellant in 1397, and Richard's faithlessness was a common theme: he borrowed large sums of money but did not pay them back so that many in the kingdom 'regard the king as faithless', and he was 'so variable and dissimulating in both word and letter, and so inconstant in his behaviour ... that virtually no living person who came to know him could or wished to trust him'. Richard, the twenty-fifth charge said, was 'so faithless and deceitful' that he was a scandal not only to the whole of England, 'but above all to foreigners throughout the world who heard about him'.

A document in French called the 'Manner of King Richard's Renunciation' was issued at the Tower of London and at Westminster Abbey between 28 and 30 September 1399. It describes how a deputation was sent to Richard at the Tower on the 28th; this group consisted of the archbishop of York, the bishop of Hereford, the earls of Northumberland and Westmorland, Richard's friend Thomas Despenser (one of the eight men whose safety Richard had asked for at Flint and who had been with him until Chester) and Lord Abergavenny, two knights called Thomas Gray and Thomas Erpingham, two doctors and two notaries. Their task was to ask Richard if he was willing to 'resign all the right that he had to the crown of England'.[15] The king at first, predictably, refused to abdicate; when Henry of Lancaster confronted him in person he agreed in principle to resign his throne to Henry under certain conditions. This also being refused, Richard was given a copy, on parchment, of a document called the Cession and Renunciation, and finally agreed to read it out himself in both Latin and English.[16]

It began with Richard, 'by the grace of God king of England and France and lord of Ireland', absolving all his archbishops, bishops, prelates, dukes, earls, knights and all his other vassals and liegemen from their oath of fealty and homage to him. He also renounced completely all his right to the rule and governance of his dominions, and had to state, 'I confess, acknowledge, recognise, and from my own certain knowledge truly admit that I have been and am entirely inadequate and unequal to the task of ruling and governing the aforesaid kingdoms and dominions, and that, on account of my notorious insufficiencies, I deserve to be deposed from them.' As a visible sign of his renunciation of his throne, he took his signet ring – his personal seal and symbol of his kingship – from his finger and gave it to Henry of Lancaster.[17]

Henry declared, in English, that he was the rightful heir of the good lord Henry III, 'and through that right that God of His grace has sent me, with the help of my kin and friends, to recover it [the realm of England]; which realm was on the point of being undone by default of governance and the undoing of the good laws'.[18] All the lords spiritual and temporal were asked (by the treasurer of England John Norbury and the earl of Northumberland respectively) whether or not they agreed to Henry of Lancaster becoming king, and they all answered in the affirmative. Henry himself spoke to them all: 'My lords spiritual and temporal assembled here, we beg you not simply to speak these words with your mouths if they do not come from your hearts, but to agree to them with your hearts as well as your mouths.' All of them said, 'Yes, yes, yes', and the two archbishops and Henry's uncle the duke of York rose and went to Henry, and kissed his hand. They led him to the throne, and he sat down and made the sign of the cross, and was proclaimed king.[19] According to one Spanish chronicle (though no other source confirms it), an elaborate ceremony to strip Richard of his kingship took place: he was seated in majesty, then his crown, sceptre, orb, sword and finally the throne itself were taken from him.[20]

On 20 September 1399 at Westminster, one of the last orders issued in Richard II's name had been to order the sheriffs of Norfolk and Suffolk to issue a proclamation forbidding the promulgation of opinions contrary to holy doctrine.[21] The following day was the second anniversary of the earl of Arundel's execution, and on 22 September the exiled Thomas Mowbray, presumably unaware of the dramatic events occurring in his native England, died in Venice. Chronicler Adam Usk was permitted to visit Richard in the Tower on the 21st, conducted there by Sir William Beauchamp, and watched the imprisoned king dine. At length, a doleful Richard began to discourse on the cruel fates of his ancestors in his famous, 'My God, this is a wonderful and fickle land, which has exiled, slain, destroyed and ruined so many kings' speech. After hearing it, Usk wrote, 'Seeing therefore the troubles of his soul, and seeing that none of those who had been deputed to wait upon him were in any way bound to him, or used to serving him, but were strangers who had been sent there simply to spy upon him, I departed much moved at heart, reflecting to myself on the glories of his former state and on the fickle fortune of this world.'[22]

Richard was now truly alone, surrounded only by his enemies and by spies who doubtless reported his every word and every move to Henry of Lancaster. Usk also witnessed Richard being bundled onto a boat to be taken to Pontefract Castle 'in the silence of dark midnight'. The former king wept and begged for mercy and declared that he wished he had never been born, but was only told that he should have shown mercy to the earl of Arundel.[23] This was an echo of Richard's supposed words to his uncle the duke of Gloucester in July 1397, when he told him he would receive as much mercy as Simon Burley had in 1388.

Officially the last day of Richard II's reign was 29 September 1399, the feast of Michaelmas in his twenty-third regnal year. Henry of Lancaster was proclaimed king of England on 30 September, and took the regnal number Henry IV; he was the first King Henry of England since the death of his and Richard's great-great-great-grandfather Henry III, who took the throne in October 1216 and died fifty-six years later. On the first day of his reign, Henry IV appointed Henry Percy, earl of Northumberland, as constable of England, and his brother-in-law Ralph Neville, earl of Westmorland as marshal of England, presumably in gratitude for their loyalty and support after he had landed in England with a few followers less than three months previously. The next day, he gave permission to a man called Matthew Danthorp to build a hermitage and a chapel at the place where he had landed at Ravenspur on or around 4 July.[24]

His coronation took place at Westminster Abbey on the feast of St Edward the Confessor on Monday 13 October, which was surely intended to, and no doubt did, cause pain to Richard, given the former king's devotion to that saint. It was also exactly a year since Richard had driven him into exile. On the day before the coronation Henry knighted his three younger sons Thomas, John and Humphrey (born in 1387, 1389 and 1390), supposedly in the presence of Richard, and made his eldest son Henry of Monmouth, born in September 1386 and so just turned thirteen, prince of Wales and duke of Cornwall.[25]

Among those who attended and helped to arrange the coronation was Sir John Holland, Henry's brother-in-law and Richard's half-brother. Holland was then imprisoned in Hertford on 20 October 1399 and on 3 November was tried with other former allies of Richard II, and stripped of his dukedom of Exeter so that he was once again merely earl of Huntingdon. Other supporters of Richard were also downgraded: his half-nephew Thomas Holland was deprived of his dukedom of Surrey and once again became earl of Kent, and Thomas Despenser was deprived of the earldom of Gloucester and was now only lord of Glamorgan and Lord Despenser. Even John Beaufort, Henry IV's half-brother but tainted by his association with Richard, was downgraded from marquis of Dorset to merely earl of Somerset (though thereafter abandoned his support of Richard and remained loyal to the new king). John Montacute, earl of Salisbury, was sent to the Tower of London on 20 October 1399, though was released in December. He and other close friends of the former king immediately began plotting against Henry on Richard's behalf. These men were called before parliament to answer for their actions in appealing the three Appellants Gloucester, Arundel and Warwick of treason. Thomas Despenser denied any involvement in the murder of the royal uncle Thomas of Woodstock, and contemplated leaving the country for a while to go on crusade to Prussia or Rhodes.[26] On the other hand, Henry IV did apparently try to reconcile the two Hollands: uncle and nephew attended meetings of the royal council on 4 and 9 December 1399, witnessed one of Henry's charters on 10 December, and were even invited to the festive jousts at Windsor in early January 1400.[27]

Meanwhile, Richard and Henry's cousin Humphrey of Gloucester, only son of the late Thomas of Woodstock, had died on 2 September 1399 at the age of seventeen, the day after he accompanied Richard through London to imprisonment at the Tower. Humphrey was unmarried and childless, and the duke of Gloucester's heir therefore was his eldest daughter Anne, countess of Stafford. Chronicler Adam Usk claims that Humphrey was poisoned in Ireland by Richard's friend Thomas Despenser, and that Humphrey died on the island of Anglesey after returning to Britain as a result, though no one else even hints at this story and it seems far more likely to be malicious gossip and an attempt at explaining away the sudden death of a royal teenager at the hands of a very unpopular royal favourite.[28] Humphrey's grieving mother Eleanor, *née* de Bohun, dowager duchess of Gloucester, did not long survive him and died on 3 October, still only in her early thirties. Three of Duchess Eleanor's four daughters also died young, though her eldest, Anne, lived into the late 1430s and had families with two of her husbands. Eleanor's mother Joan, *née* Fitzalan, sister of the executed earl of Arundel and the archbishop of Canterbury, and Henry IV's mother-in-law, outlived her daughter and grandson by twenty years and died in April 1419. Duchess Eleanor's will of 1399 mentions numerous books, including a chronicle of France in French and a 'History of the Swan Knight', also in French.[29]

As also happened in 1327 after the forced abdication of Edward II, who became merely Sir Edward of Caernarfon and who was sent to perpetual (albeit comfortable) captivity at Berkeley Castle in Gloucestershire, the presence of Sir Richard of Bordeaux was something of an embarrassment and a worry to his successor. There remained the awkward question of what precisely should be done with a man who had been the crowned and anointed king and was now only a private person, and Richard's continued existence would always be a risk to Henry IV as he would always have supporters who might try to restore him to his lost throne. As Richard was the son-in-law of the king of France, Henry might face enmity and hostility from that quarter one day, perhaps even an attempt by a French army to restore Richard to the throne.

Richard of Bordeaux was still only thirty-two in the autumn of 1399, and might be expected to live for some decades yet; his grandfather Edward III had lived to be sixty-four and his mother to her late fifties, though his father's life had been cut short in his mid-forties by disease. Richard might therefore prove to be a thorn in the new king's side for many years to come. The Tower of London, in the middle of the capital, was deemed too close to too many people and therefore too unsafe for Richard's permanent incarceration. And thus he was sent in late October 1399 to captivity at Pontefract Castle, a rather remote, massive and forbidding fortress in Yorkshire. Supposedly the king was disguised as a forester, first being sent to Leeds Castle in Kent and probably arriving at Pontefract in early December.[30] It may not be a coincidence that Richard was sent to Pontefract specifically: Edward II had had his troublesome Lancastrian first cousin Thomas, elder brother of Henry IV's great-grandfather Henry, beheaded there in March 1322. Both Richard and Henry IV must have been aware of this, and Henry's sending Richard to Pontefract, of all places, was a pointed reminder of how, unlike Thomas of Lancaster, he had won his struggle against the king. Henry may have hoped that Richard would be out of sight, out of mind hundreds of miles away in the north. It did not work.

23

'Treasons Make Me Wish Myself a Beggar': The Epiphany Rising, 1399–1400

The former King Richard II turned thirty-three years old in prison at Pontefract on 6 January 1400, the feast of the Epiphany or the Three Kings. He still had a number of noble supporters: the three earls John Holland, Thomas Holland and John Montacute, and the former earl Thomas Despenser (whose kinsman Hugh Despenser joined the new king's household in November 1399).[1] Henry IV meanwhile had spent Christmas 1399 with his children at Windsor.[2] The four noblemen still loyal to Richard of Bordeaux met on 17 December 1399 in a chamber of the abbot of Westminster's lodging, and determined to free Richard from captivity and (presumably) restore him to the throne, and even to kidnap and kill King Henry and his children. Also involved were the abbot of Westminster, William de Colchester; the bishop of Carlisle, Thomas Merk; Sir Thomas Blount; Ralph, Lord Lumley; Roger Walden; Sir Bernard Brocas; Richard II's physician Master Pol; and the aforementioned Richard Maudelyn, who closely resembled Richard.

Their plot became known as the Epiphany Rising, or the Rising of the Three Earls. Richard and Henry's cousin Edward of York, earl of Rutland, also joined, though whether he took an active role or believed in the objectives at any point is unclear. It was apparently he who would betray the plot to his cousin the king. The plan was to enter Windsor Castle and capture Henry IV, upon which, the plotters hoped, popular uprisings in Richard's favour would take place across the country. Henry had invited John and Thomas Holland to a joust to be held at Windsor at this time, thus bringing the two men, armed, close to himself and his family, a measure of how much he desired to reconcile them and believed – wrongly – that he could trust them. Thomas Despenser had also been invited to attend a meeting of Henry's council on 4 December.[3]

The earls and their allies called on ten-year-old Queen Isabelle at Sonning in Berkshire, a palace of the bishop of Salisbury on the Thames where she was then living, and tore the Lancastrian badges from the clothes of her attendants.[4] On 3 January, it seems that Edward of York betrayed the plot to his father Edmund of Langley, supposedly by leaving a document relating to the plot on a table where his father would see it.[5] William Shakespeare made a dramatic scene of this in his *Richard II*, in which Edward of York is harangued by his mother the duchess (who in fact had died in 1392; the duchess of York in 1400 was Edward's stepmother Joan, *née* Holland, Richard II's half-niece, sister of the earl of Kent who was one of the conspirators and still barely out of her teens). In fairness to Edward of York, he was still only about twenty-five years old and caught between his two first cousins Richard and Henry, and may not have known what to do for the best.

Another chronicle, however, gives an entirely different account of the conspiracy, claiming that a member of Henry IV's household spent the night with a prostitute in London who had previously slept with a man in the retinue of one of the three earls, who told her that the men were 'waiting near Kingston to ambush and kill the king, the archbishop of Canterbury, and all the rest of you when you return from Windsor, and to put King Richard back on the throne'.[6] The same chronicle says Richard of Bordeaux confessed that the plot was devised by him while at Conwy Castle in the summer, and while it is not impossible that some kind of future rescue plan was discussed by the king and his allies before his capture, it seems extremely unlikely that Richard, while in captivity at distant Pontefract, could possibly have organised specific details of the Epiphany Rising.[7] Whether he even knew about it in advance is not clear.

The earls of Kent and Salisbury, Thomas Holland and John Montacute, arrived at Windsor with a force of around 400 men but, finding that the king had already left and sought refuge in the Tower of London, fled towards the west. John Holland, earl of Huntingdon, meanwhile, failed to secure London. Henry IV ordered several sheriffs to arrest Huntingdon and Kent and their adherents as traitors on 5 January.[8] The earls of Salisbury and Kent, with Sir Bernard Brocas, were soon captured in Cirencester, Gloucestershire, where they were staying at the main inn, and their companion Ralph Lumley was summarily beheaded.[9] Another adherent of the earl of Kent, Robert Swalwe, was captured and beheaded in Oxford 35 miles from Cirencester.[10]

The two earls were surrounded by a mob who blocked all the exits out of the town and were handed over to Thomas, Lord Berkeley (and allowed to pray in the abbey and given food), but the next evening, 7 or 8 January 1400, a fire started in the town. Believing that the fire was a diversion by the two men's allies and servants in order to rescue them, as indeed it probably was, the mob took the precaution of beheading Kent and Salisbury in the town square of Cirencester and sending their heads to Henry IV in a basket. Thomas Walsingham states rather sneeringly that John Montacute, widely considered to be a supporter of the heretic followers of the late John Wycliffe, 'ended his miserable life without the sacrament of confession'.[11]

A resident of Cirencester called John Cousyn was granted the large sum of 100 marks yearly on 27 January 1400 for 'manfully resisting' the earl of Kent and 'others who rose in insurrection against the king', and the men of the town were given all the goods and chattels of the earls of Kent and Salisbury left behind in Cirencester with the exception of gold, silver and jewels.[12] Henry IV's knight Sir John Strange was given various items formerly belonging to the late Thomas Holland, earl of Kent, including six chargers (horses), twelve saltcellars, two silver candlesticks and four *houppelandes* (a long and voluminous outer garment with a fur lining) of 'furred golden cloth'.[13] At the same time, Henry IV granted many of the former possessions of the earl of Kent to the released and restored Thomas Beauchamp, earl of Warwick; Kent had stored them at Warwick Castle. These possessions included a bed of red damask embroidered with ostrich feathers and a coverlet and canopy, a second bed of red satin worked with gold roses, three curtains of 'Tartaryn' cloth, six cushions of red damask, another bed canopy embroidered with fawns, and an arras or wall-hanging featuring the legend of Guy of Warwick.[14]

Richard II's half-brother John Holland had taken a sad leave of his wife Elizabeth of Lancaster, reproaching her bitterly for her rejoicing at the accession of her brother Henry and the overthrow of her cousin

Richard.[15] After failing to capture London and on hearing of his allies' deaths, Holland rode to Essex with a knight called Thomas Shelley. He tried to flee from England in a small boat, but was blown back to the Essex coast every time he set sail, 'until, in complete despair of help from Neptune, he gave up this plan'.[16] In desperation Holland sought refuge with the earl of Oxford, Robert de Vere's uncle Aubrey, at Hadley Castle, and then with a sympathiser of Richard II called John Prittlewell at Shoeburyness, but was arrested 'by a crowd of locals' in the latter's house while at dinner and came into the custody of the formidable Joan de Bohun, *née* Fitzalan, dowager countess of Hereford and Henry IV's mother-in-law.

Either she personally, or a mob consisting of 'plebs and mechanics', had Holland beheaded without a trial at Pleshey, Essex on 9 or 10 (or possibly the 15th, according to Thomas Walsingham) January.[17] Holland died on the same spot where Richard II's uncle and Joan's other son-in-law Thomas of Woodstock had been arrested in July 1397. The beheading was carried out in the presence of Joan's nephew Thomas, the new Fitzalan earl of Arundel, whose father Richard had been executed by Richard II in September 1397. John Holland's head was sent to be displayed on London Bridge.

His marriage to Henry IV's sister Elizabeth had not saved him from the king's wrath, and a few months later King Henry gave some items formerly belonging to his brother-in-law to his third son John of Lancaster, future duke of Bedford, born in 1389. These included a bed and canopy made of silk and embroidered with bulls and the arms of the earls of March and Pembroke, eight embroidered cushions and nine matching tapestries, three cloths of gold embroidered with oaks, a 'weak bed' of green silk with three curtains, a rather better bed of silk with a canopy and three blue curtains, a tapestry of red velvet embroidered with stags, five breviaries and a missal (books containing all the liturgical texts for the celebration of Mass throughout the year), and another dozen religious books worth a total of more than £45. These last items would seem to demonstrate that John Holland was rather more conventionally pious than one might imagine from his violent behaviour and his apparent habit of sleeping with married women.

The king's half-brother John Beaufort, earl of Somerset, also benefited, receiving a bed of baudekyn (gold-embroidered silk cloth) with the arms of England and Hainault and matching red curtains and tapestries, ten pillows of red cloth-of-gold 'of which two are long', ten pillows of red velvet, and twelve short pillows of white cloth-of-gold (material shot through with gold thread) formerly of John Holland. A chaplain, confusingly also called John Holland, was appointed to search for the late earl of Huntingdon's jewels, goods, chattels and money in London.[18] Henry IV gave his sister Elizabeth £10 in recompense for a 'black bed' of her husband's which had been confiscated, and allowed her possession of two other silk beds lined with expensive miniver and some costly cloths and silver pots which had also belonged to her husband. He also gave her an allowance of 1,000 marks a year.[19] Apparently a not too disconsolate widow, Elizabeth married her third husband Sir John Cornwall in the summer of 1400, having been impressed by him at a jousting tournament held in York in July that year, barely six months after John Holland's death.[20]

The last remaining noble member of the Epiphany Rising was Thomas, Lord Despenser, brother-in-law of Edward of York, married to Henry IV and Richard II's cousin Constance of York. Despenser supposedly managed to escape from Cirencester by climbing through a window with the clerk Richard Maudelyn, and boarded a ship at Cardiff in his lordship of Glamorgan in South Wales with all his jewels and many other possessions, intending to flee the country. (It seems more plausible that he had not been in Cirencester at all, but remained in or near Cardiff.) Twenty armed men rushed out from below deck and overcame Despenser and his men, and the crew sailed instead to Bristol. Some of the burgesses of the city captured Despenser there in the house of the mayor Thomas Knappe.

Despite the efforts of the mayor to save him and despite messengers Despenser sent to the king pleading for a chance to speak to him, he was dragged out and beheaded by a mob in the marketplace of Bristol on 13 January 1400 and his head sent to London Bridge for display. At the request of his mother he was later given honourable burial at Tewkesbury Abbey in Gloucestershire, in the mausoleum of his family. Despenser was wearing a short *hanselin* (jacket) with silver-gilt spangles and a furred gown of motley velvet and damask when he was captured, which the burgesses confiscated and which Henry IV gave to his servants Ralph Ramsey and William Flaxman some weeks later.[21]

In all, after the failure of the Epiphany Rising, twenty-six men were beheaded in the presence of the king himself at Oxford Castle between 11 and 13 January and in London in early February, and four (Sir Thomas Blount, Sir Benedict Cely, John Walsh and William Baldwin) suffered the full horrors of the traitor's death by hanging, drawing and quartering. Adam Usk gives a grotesquely vivid account of seeing these men's bodies 'chopped up like the carcasses of beasts killed in the chase, partly in sacks and partly on poles slung across pairs of men's shoulders, where they were later salted to preserve them [for public display]'.[22] Richard Maudelyn, the clerk who resembled Richard II and who had been intended to impersonate him, was one of the men executed in London. Sir Bernard Brocas was led on foot to Cheapside in London by four sergeants and beheaded there, in 'such black night' that no one could see it.[23] Henry IV did pardon one man who took part in the Epiphany Rising: John Ferrour of Southwark, who had saved his life in the Tower of London 'in a wonderful and kind manner' during the uprising almost twenty years before.[24] The bishop of Carlisle and the abbot of Westminster remained in prison for the time being, and the bishop, Thomas Merk, was pardoned on 28 November 1400.[25]

And thus so easily did the Epiphany Rising fail; it also sealed Richard of Bordeaux's fate.

24

'Nothing Can We Call Our Own but Death': The End of Richard of Bordeaux, 1400

Curiously, rumours of Richard of Bordeaux's death spread at the French court in early 1400 before he was actually dead. His father-in-law Charles VI (or his advisers) wrote to Henry IV on 29 January 1400, referring to Richard as *nostre tres chier et tres ame Filz Richart n'agueres Roy d'Engleterre, qui Dieux absoille*, 'our very dear and beloved Son Richard, formerly king of England, whom God absolve'; a formulation used only for those who were dead.[1] Yet it seems highly probable that Richard was then still alive, though not for much longer. It is possible that Henry IV thought that Richard would be out of the way and quietly forgotten; he may not have had thoughts of killing him at first. Richard, after all, whatever he had done to Henry and others, was his own cousin and was of royal birth. But after the Epiphany Rising, it became clear that Richard would not simply be forgotten, and that his continued existence would always threaten Henry's position, and his children's.

The date of Richard of Bordeaux's death is often given as St Valentine's Day, 14 February 1400, which may well be correct. There is a persistent story that he starved to death, either voluntarily (by refusing all food in his grief) or involuntarily (because his jailers deprived him of sustenance). Thomas Walsingham reports the rumour that Richard killed himself by voluntary fasting.[2] Adam Usk thought that Sir Thomas Swynford, constable of Pontefract Castle and son of Richard's aunt Katherine Swynford from her first marriage, tormented

Richard to death and deprived him of food.[3] Usk also adds that Richard suffered considerably after learning of the failure of the plot to free him and of the deaths of his supporters, and pined away. The *Vitae et Regni* and the *Traison et Mort* also say that Richard refused food on hearing of the failure of the Epiphany Rising and the death of his half-brother John Holland and the others, and pined away to his death ('declined into such grief, languor and weakness'). The *Vita* adds that some people claimed Richard did not die from lack of food by his own choice, but 'was miserably put to death by starvation'. The *Brut* and Dieulacres chronicles, and a contemporary Londoner, also all said that Richard died of hunger (twelve days without food or drink, according to the Dieulacres chronicle).[4] Jean Creton has Richard giving a dignified speech: 'Make ready, death, and take me; no-one can help me now, for I have lost my friends. Gracious lord who was crucified, deign to have mercy on me, for I can live like this no longer.' He says that Richard was so 'vexed at heart' by news of the failure of the Epiphany Rising that 'from that time onwards he neither ate nor drank; and thus, so they say, it came to pass that he died'.[5]

It would seem to have made things remarkably convenient for Henry IV if Richard did kill himself, and is surely more likely that he was killed in some way by his jailers. The oft-repeated (not least by William Shakespeare) story given in the *Traison* that Richard was attacked by a group of knights led by one Piers or Peter Exton seems virtually certain to be untrue, and Exton apparently never existed; it probably represents a confusion as to the correct name of Henry IV's loyal ally Peter Bukton. Richard's body in Westminster Abbey was examined well over 400 years later, and no marks of violence were found on it.[6] This tends to give credence to the notion that he died of starvation. As with his great-grandfather Edward II, who may have died at Berkeley Castle in Gloucestershire on 21 September 1327 just nine months after his deposition, chroniclers speculated as to the cause of Richard's death. He was only thirty-three and previously in good health and reasonably fit and strong, and under normal circumstances would have expected to live twenty or thirty more years. The many different chroniclers who give starvation as the cause of Richard's demise, however, lead one to conclude that this is indeed the likeliest explanation.

Although for many years afterwards there were rumours that Richard had not died at all and was supposedly seen alive after his presumed death, there is really no reason to doubt that he did die at Pontefract Castle on or around 14 February 1400. The sudden death of a former king, in rather mysterious and secret circumstances, was bound to lead to rumours that he was not actually dead. Richard's fate was discussed by Henry IV's privy council on about 8 February 1400, when it was determined that Richard's body would be displayed in public if he died.[7] Lessons had been learned from 1327, when Edward II's body was not publicly displayed and was apparently not even seen by his close family at or before his funeral in Gloucester in December 1327, and it was widely believed within two years of his death that he was not dead at all.

Richard of Bordeaux was certainly dead by 17 February 1400, when a squire called Richard Pampilion was given 100 marks to bring the former king's body from Pontefract to London, and then on to Langley in Hertfordshire.[8] It was shown in all the towns it passed through on its journey, including at Cheapside in London for two hours, with only the face visible, the rest of the body including the head and hair being encased in lead.[9] Priests received over £16 to celebrate 1,000 masses for Richard's soul.[10] Henry IV and the citizens of London attended a funeral service for Richard at St Paul's Cathedral, and the body was then quickly taken to Langley Priory for burial. In a sparsely attended ceremony at which none of the English magnates were present, the bishop of Chester and the abbots of St Albans and Waltham conducted the service.[11] Richard had had a tomb prepared for himself next to his beloved Anne of Bohemia, but would not be buried in it until after Henry IV's own death.

The *Traison* says that Richard's body was publicly displayed at St Paul's on 18 March 1400, in a chariot covered with black cloths and with four banners above, two of the arms of St George and two of St Edward the Confessor, and with a golden cross. Torches were carried by 100 men dressed all in black. It also says that Richard's body was kept above ground for two days, which was done deliberately so that no one would be in any doubt that he was truly dead.[12] The Frenchman Creton obstinately refused to believe that the dead man really was Richard of Bordeaux, even when his body was displayed at St Paul's: 'I certainly do not believe it was the old king; I think it was [Richard] Maudelyn, his chaplain, whose face, size, height and build were so exactly similar to the king's that everyone firmly believed that it was good King Richard.' Refusing to acknowledge Henry IV as king but instead referring to him as 'Duke Henry', Creton added, 'Nevertheless, they had the body of a dead man carried openly through the city of London, accompanied by the sort of pomp and ceremony that befits a dead king, saying that it was the body of the deceased King Richard.' He was to change his mind some years later when he travelled to Scotland, and discovered that the man there claimed to be 'Richard II' was in fact an impostor.[13]

On 20 March 1400, William Loveday, clerk of Henry IV's great wardrobe, was sent to the castle and town of Pontefract 'on the king's secret affairs' and given £3 6s 8d for his expenses. On the same day a valet of Sir Thomas Swynford was paid £1 6s 8d 'to certify the king's council concerning certain matters for the king's advantage', while another valet, unnamed, was sent from London to Pontefract 'for the protection and safe custody' of Richard's body. Thomas Swynford sent his valet to the king's council in such haste that he was reimbursed for having to hire an extra horse.[14]

Rumours persisted for many years that the former king was still alive and in Scotland, where he had supposedly been taken in great secrecy from Pontefract. An impostor named Thomas Ward of Trumpington established himself in that country in and after 1402 and was recognised at the courts of Robert III and the duke of Albany. In 1416, sixteen years after Richard's death, some years into the reign of Henry IV's son Henry V, a Londoner called Benedict Wolman was hanged because he had attempted to bring 'Thomas Warde, otherwise called Trumpyngtone' to England from Scotland, claiming that he was Richard II and wishing to restore him to the throne.[15] The rumours were taken seriously at the French court at the beginning of the 1400s, if for no other reason than the impact a still-alive Richard II would have on the life of his young French widow Isabelle de Valois. Even in England not everyone was sure that the former king was dead, or at least acted as if they were not sure: letters were sent to Franciscan friars in 1402, supposedly from Richard.[16] Robert de Vere's mother Maud, *née* Ufford, dowager countess of Oxford, also spread rumours throughout Essex that Richard was still alive, and had numerous white hart badges distributed to make it appear that Richard himself was giving them out. She was imprisoned.[17]

Thomas Despenser's widow Constance of York, granddaughter of Edward III, also stood firmly on Richard II's side and against Henry IV. In 1405 she temporarily freed the Mortimers, the children of the late Roger Mortimer, earl of March, from Windsor, presumably with the aim of replacing her cousin Henry on the throne with the eldest Mortimer son, Edmund. Edmund Mortimer, born in 1391, had a good claim to the throne as the male heir of Edward III's second son Lionel of Antwerp, a claim he later passed on to his nephew Richard, duke of York, the father of Edward IV and Richard III. Constance implicated her brother Edward of York in her plot, and Edward was arrested and imprisoned at Pevensey Castle for seventeen weeks.[18] Edward was killed at the battle of Agincourt in 1415, and as he died childless his heir was his nephew Richard of York, only son of Edward and Constance's brother Richard of Conisbrough, earl of Cambridge. Constance was something of a free spirit, and in about 1405 had an affair with Edmund Holland, earl of Kent (Richard II's nephew and brother of the Thomas Holland killed during the Epiphany Rising, but a supporter of Henry IV) who was eight or ten years younger than she, which resulted in an illegitimate daughter, Alianore Holland. Constance and Edward of York's father Edmund of Langley, duke of York and the last surviving child of Edward III, died at his birthplace of Langley in Hertfordshire on 1 August 1402 at the age of sixty-one, and was buried there. His young widow Duchess Joan, one of the sisters of Thomas and Edmund Holland, married again three times.

As for Henry IV, his accession was at first extremely popular in England, though the acclaim did not last long and within months the new king found himself the victim of a strange plot to smear his saddle with a magical ointment which would cause him to swell up and die while still sitting in the saddle before he had ridden 10 miles. A woman in Hertfordshire claimed in March 1402 that since Henry's accession 'there has not been seven days' good and seasonable weather'.[19] Henry killed a king and his own cousin; whatever Richard had done to him, it is hard to see how this is anything but an atrocious act.

Richard of Bordeaux's death left the young queen Isabelle of Valois as a widow while she was still a child. It is easy to feel sympathy for the girl, who was only ten years old when her husband died and who had been deprived of the man who showed her much affection and kindness, left alone in a foreign country and no longer queen but an embarrassment, sent from manor to manor at the whim of her husband's usurper. Isabelle can hardly have wanted to stay in a country ruled by Richard's killer. By late January 1400 false rumours of Richard II's death had reached the French court, and they began to demand the safe return of the young queen and of the treasure she had taken to England with her.

The French refusal to acknowledge Henry IV as king – Charles VI referred to him as 'he who calls himself king of England' – and the English side's reluctance to give up Isabelle's dowry at a time when the treasury was nearly empty proved sticking points. The French also feared that if Isabelle was still in England when she turned twelve in November 1401 she might be forced to accept a marriage with one of Henry IV's sons, and when one of the French envoys managed to secure a private audience with her, he urged her not to accept any English marriage. According to this envoy, Isabelle was desperate to return to France, which may well be true, though he would hardly have reported that she did not want to go back. France was Isabelle's homeland and where her family and her mother were, and was at least a safe haven from Richard's usurper and murderer, though the kingdom was also in chaos. Henry IV saw Isabelle at Sonning, where she was more or less under house arrest, on 27 June 1401. He could not afford to repay the large dowry Isabelle had brought to England with her, and in fact it never was repaid. Henry claimed instead the unpaid ransom money of Isabelle's great-grandfather John II, captured at the battle of Poitiers in 1356 by Richard II's father Edward of Woodstock.[20]

At the beginning of August 1401, Isabelle finally returned to France with an entourage of 500 people and 1,000 marks in cash for her to distribute as largesse during the journey.[21] Henry IV paid over £72 'to restore Isabella, queen of England, to her father, the king of France'.[22] He had ordered two men to provide horses for her passage home as early as 14 October 1400, and a month later asked the chancellor of Oxford University to 'reply to certain questions concerning the restitution of Queen Isabel'.[23] Sadly, King Charles VI was descending more and more into insanity, and the young queen's homeland was torn apart by the power struggle between her uncle the duke of Orléans and her father's cousin the duke of Burgundy. Isabelle's mother Queen Isabeau was pregnant with her tenth child, and a few weeks after Isabelle's return, on 27 October 1401, her little sister Katherine, future queen of England as the wife of Henry IV's son Henry V, was born. Isabelle's brother the future King Charles VII of France followed on 22 February 1403, and in November 1407 Queen Isabeau bore the last of her dozen children, a boy named Philip who died in infancy.

Only three of Isabeau's children outlived her: Charles VII, king of France; Katherine, queen of England; and Marie, a prioress.

On 29 June 1406, when she was sixteen, Isabelle de Valois married her second husband: he was her first cousin Charles of Orléans, count of Angoulême, son and heir of her father's younger brother Louis, duke of Orléans. Charles, born on 24 November 1394, was almost exactly five years Isabelle's junior, and only eleven at the time of their wedding. (Not only did Charles marry his first cousin, his parents Louis of Orléans and Valentina Visconti were also first cousins, both grandchildren of John II of France and Bonne of Bohemia.) Isabelle's father-in-law Louis of Orléans was assassinated in Paris on 23 November 1407, the day before her husband Charles's thirteenth birthday, by their fathers' first cousin John the Fearless, duke of Burgundy. Burgundy publicly accused Orléans at this time of having plotted with Henry of Lancaster to bring about Richard II's downfall.[24] This assassination was part of the increasingly vicious wars that arose in France during the power struggles caused by the king's insanity and inability to rule his kingdom, and John the Fearless himself would be assassinated twelve years later on the orders of Isabelle's brother the future King Charles VII of France.

Evidently Isabelle and Charles of Orléans consummated their marriage more or less as soon as Charles turned fourteen on 24 November 1408, as their daughter Jeanne was born on 13 September 1409. Jeanne's birth killed her mother. Isabelle de Valois, dowager queen of England, duchess of Orléans and countess of Angoulême, died shortly after giving birth at not yet twenty years old, and rather astonishingly, Charles of Orléans had become a father and a widower more than two months before he even turned fifteen. Jeanne of Orléans married Jean II, duke of Alençon, and died on 19 May 1432 childless and only in her early twenties, so there were and are no descendants of Isabelle de Valois, just as there are no descendants of her first husband Richard II or his first wife Anne of Bohemia.

Isabelle's widower Charles, duke of Orléans, was captured at the battle of Agincourt on 25 October 1415, Henry V's great victory over the French, and spent a quarter of a century in captivity in England ('captivity' in the loosest possible sense of the word: he had numerous servants, good food and wine and was allowed to go riding and hunting). He learnt English and wrote poetry in that language as well as in his native French. His second wife Bonne of Armagnac, with whom he had no children, died while he was in England, and in late 1440, after his release, Charles married his third wife Marie of Cleves, who was German. He was forty-six and she fourteen. The marriage remained childless for seventeen years, then curiously produced three offspring in seven years, one of whom was King Louis XII of France, born in 1462, who succeeded his cousin Charles VIII on the French throne in 1498. Charles of Orléans' last child, Anne, an abbess, was born in 1464 shortly before he turned seventy, and was fifty-five years younger than his eldest child with Isabelle de Valois, Jeanne, duchess of Alençon.

As for the late Anne of Bohemia's family, her half-brother Václav was to suffer a great humiliation in 1400 when he was deposed as king of Germany on the grounds of his futility and idleness and was eventually replaced by her younger full brother Zikmund. Václav did continue to reign as king of Bohemia until his death in 1419. Zikmund became Holy Roman Emperor in 1433 and was also king of Germany, Bohemia, Italy, Hungary and Croatia; he died in 1437 in his late sixties. He was made a Knight of the Garter by Henry V in 1415 and visited England in May 1316, more than two decades after the death of the sister he had last seen in 1381 when he was thirteen. Anne of Bohemia's other full brother, Johann von Görlitz, margrave of Moravia and Brandenburg, expelled the Jewish population from his territories in 1396 and died at the monastery of Neuzelle in the same year at the age of only twenty-five, possibly poisoned. Zikmund, Johann and Queen Anne's sister Markéta, burgravine of Nuremberg, each had one child, in all three cases a daughter named Elisabeth after their mother Elżbieta of Pomerania.

Back in England, Henry Percy, earl of Northumberland, and his son Henry Hotspur and brother Thomas seethed at the injustice of Henry of Lancaster making himself king when he had sworn a solemn and sacred oath to them not to do so and at his failing to keep his promise to reward them for their support with lands and money. Their anger exploded into open rebellion, and they faced the king at the battle of Shrewsbury on 21 July 1403. Henry Hotspur was killed during the king's victory, and his uncle Thomas Percy, earl of Worcester, was hanged, drawn and quartered after the battle. Henry Percy, earl of Northumberland, persisted in his opposition to Henry IV, and was killed at the battle of Bramham Moor in February 1408, at the age of sixty-six. Edmund Mortimer, brother of the earl of March who died in 1398, also died in rebellion against Henry.

Henry IV saw no fewer than eight rebellions against his rule in thirteen and a half years and executed an archbishop (Scrope of York) and Thomas Mowbray's eldest son, yet managed against the odds to die peacefully in his bed on 20 March 1413 at the age of not quite forty-six and to pass the throne to the eldest of his four sons, the famous warrior Henry V, of Agincourt fame. Henry V married Isabelle de Valois's youngest sister Katherine in June 1420, and their son Henry VI succeeded him as a baby in 1422 and three months later became king of France as well when the unfortunate Charles VI finally died. The widowed Queen Katherine entered into a romantic liaison with the Welsh squire Owen Tudor and was the grandmother of Henry Tudor, who became King Henry VII of England in 1485, and the great-grandmother of Henry VIII.

In the first year of his reign, Henry V moved Richard II's body from Langley to Westminster Abbey to lie next to Queen Anne. Possibly Henry still regarded Richard, who had treated him kindly, with some affection, and from the perspective of his own self-interest it would also put paid to any rumours of Richard's survival. Thomas Walsingham says that Henry declared at this time that he owed as much veneration to Richard as to his own father.[25] On 8 November 1413, Henry paid £10 in Canterbury for 'diverse banners' to lay on Richard's hearse during its journey from Langley to Westminster. A joiner of London called John Wyddemer was paid £2 for providing a bier 'for the carriage of Richard, late king of England' to Westminster, and 120 torches were purchased to burn around Richard's body.[26]

Henry V also paid £200 for the expenses of his father Henry IV's burial in the Trinity Chapel at Canterbury Cathedral.[27] Rather bizarrely, Henry IV was buried near his uncle Edward of Woodstock, prince of Wales, whose son he had usurped and killed, and the two men lie near each other in Canterbury Cathedral to this day. Henry's second wife Juana of Navarre, queen of England and dowager duchess of Brittany, with whom he had no children, also lies with her husband; she died in 1437 having survived imprisonment by her stepson Henry V on the grounds of witchcraft. Henry IV had six legitimate children yet only one legitimate grandchild, Henry V's son Henry VI of England.

In 1453, Richard, duke of York (b. 1411) claimed the English throne: he was the senior male descendant of Edward III's second son Lionel of Antwerp, duke of Clarence, via his mother Anne Mortimer, and was also the grandson and heir of Edward III's fourth son Edmund of Langley, duke of York (assuming that Richard of York's father Richard of Conisbrough really was Edmund of Langley's son and not John Holland's). Henry VI, meanwhile, was only descended from Edward III's third son John of Gaunt, and Richard of York claimed precedence over his kinsman; the issue arose because of the incapacity of Henry VI, who, although not as seriously affected as his grandfather Charles VI of France, suffered periods of catatonia or schizophrenia and had a major breakdown in 1453/4.

In the second half of the fifteenth century, the descendants of Edward III's sons battled for possession of the English throne in a decades-long series of struggles known later as the Wars of the Roses. This would not have happened if Richard II had not been deposed in 1399, or if he had fathered children, or if he had not been the only surviving legitimate child of his father. The Wars of the Roses ended (more or less) in 1485, when the grandson of Henry V's widow Katherine de Valois, Henry VII, defeated Richard of York's youngest son Richard III at the battle of Bosworth, and ushered in the Tudor dynasty. The unfortunate Henry VI, meanwhile, had been murdered in the Tower of London in 1471. Richard II's deposition thus had important long-term consequences which his cousin Henry of Lancaster could not have foreseen when he took the throne as Henry IV in 1399.

I have previously written a biography of Richard II's great-grandfather Edward II, and Richard interests me for many of the same reasons. The unsuccessful, deeply flawed and deposed kings of England have their fascinations. Edward and Richard, although very different in some ways, were very alike in others, and both were the wrong man in the wrong place at the wrong time. Edward II to a large extent was a man born ahead of his time, a king with the common touch who loved the company of his lowborn subjects and was a fan of exercise who took part in rigorous outdoor pursuits such as digging ditches and thatching roofs. He would arguably have been more at home in the twentieth or twenty-first century than in his own era. Richard II, although he surely would have died before he picked up a spade or jumped into a river in the middle of winter as Edward did, likewise was ahead of his time as well. As historian Michael Bennett has pointed out, Richard II 'must have seemed alarmingly original' to his subjects.[28] Alison McHardy draws attention to the vast difference between Richard the fearless teenager riding out to meet the rebels in 1381 and the frightened figure imprisoned in the Tower eighteen years later, lamenting his fate.[29]

It is hardly surprising that these contradictions have proved endlessly fascinating over the centuries, and they fascinated no less a person than William Shakespeare too. Thomas Walsingham described Richard as inadequate and lacking the intelligence necessary to rule, and there is perhaps something of the spoilt child about him; from early childhood he was thrust into the spotlight, and at the age of only ten he was treated as someone set apart from everyone else, unique, separate and chosen by God to rule over the English. Endlessly told how special he was, knelt and bowed to by everyone from the earliest age, it is probably not surprising if Richard's personality grew a little warped. Like the other unsuccessful kings of England, he is often judged very harshly for his failings and failures, yet it should be remembered that he was born to be king of England and did not choose the position. A hereditary monarchy is bound to throw up both excellent rulers and men who are hopelessly unsuited to ruling.

Richard II had many character flaws, though on the plus side he was capable of loving passionately, most especially his first queen Anne of Bohemia and the nobleman Robert de Vere. Although his love for his wife attracted no criticism, Richard's strong attachment to de Vere, his desire to promote him to a dukedom and favouring him biased advice above others' was politically foolish. Richard never quite grasped, despite his near-obsession with the great-grandfather who had lost his throne in 1327, the necessity of earning his subjects' trust and respect, and demanded loyalty while doing precious little to deserve it.

The king also seemed to lose himself in the late 1390s, and although the assumptions of previous generations of historians that he became insane are overheated and objectionable, something did go wrong in the king's mind in these years, and the intense jockeying for power and lethal factionalism which he created and allowed to flourish brought him down as well. His solution to the problem of his immensely wealthy and powerful Lancastrian cousin was unlawful and brought down the wrath of much of his kingdom on his head, and if he had made more of an effort to make Henry a close and respected ally throughout the years, he could have remained on his throne and lived out his natural lifetime. Whether or not Richard ever did say that the laws of the kingdom were in his own mouth or in his breast, he often behaved as though he believed it to be the case. It is a pity for Richard II's posthumous reputation that he did not die in 1397 at the height of his powers, and whatever he had done, nobody deserves to be starved to death in a forbidding and remote fortress.

Both his contemporaries and posterity have judged Richard II harshly, and much of the criticism of him is warranted: he had his own uncle killed, he unjustly sentenced his cousin to perpetual banishment and deprived him unlawfully of his inheritance, and at least in the last years of his life he ruled tyrannically and greedily and made himself grossly unpopular to the point where his returning cousin was treated with widespread acclaim as a conquering hero. Richard could be, and often was, vindictive, petty, irrational, cruel, prone to overreaction and quick to anger. Yet the deeds of the unsuccessful kings of England are often judged more harshly than those of the more successful rulers. Richard's usurper and murderer Henry IV was, in many ways, no great improvement on Richard, but as Henry managed to survive all the rebellions against him and died peacefully in his bed, his actions (including the execution of an archbishop, extra-judicial executions of friars, and the passing of a law allowing heretics to be burned) tend more often to be glossed over and forgiven.

The contemporary author of the *Historia Vitae et Regni Ricardi Secundi* provides an interesting perspective on Richard II: 'He was prodigal in his gifts, extravagantly ostentatious in his entertainment and dress, and unlucky as well as faint-hearted in foreign warfare. Towards his servants he often displayed great anger; he was also puffed up with pride and consumed by avarice. Yet there were many laudable features in his character: he loved religion and the clergy, he encouraged architecture, he built the church of Westminster almost entirely, and left much property by his will to finish what he had begun.' He also says rather mysteriously that the king 'was much given to luxury, and fond of burning the candle at both ends, sometimes staying up half the night, and at other times right through until morning, drinking and indulging himself in other unmentionable ways'.[30] The contradictions of Richard II's character and of his reign, still frequently brought to new audiences by performances of Shakespeare's wonderful play about him, will continue to fascinate.

Notes

Abbreviations in Notes and Bibliography

Anon: Anonimalle Chronicle
CCR: Calendar of Close Rolls
CChR: Calendar of Charter Rolls
Chron Rev: Chris Given-Wilson, ed., *Chronicles of the Revolution 1397–1400*
CFR: Calendar of Fine Rolls
CIPM: Calendar of Inquisitions Post Mortem
CPL: Calendar of Papal Letters
CPR: Calendar of Patent Rolls
ODNB: Oxford Dictionary of National Biography
PROME: The Parliament Rolls of Medieval England
Reign: A. K. McHardy, ed., *The Reign of Richard II From Minority to Tyranny, 1377–97*
Revolution: Michael Bennett, *Richard II and Revolution of 1399*
Royal Treasure: Jenny Stratford, *Richard II and the English Royal Treasure*
Saul: Nigel Saul, *Richard II*
TNA: The National Archives
Traison: *Chronicque de la Traison et Mort de Richart Deux Roy Dengleterre*

Introduction

1. All the quotations in the chapter headings are taken from William Shakespeare's play about Richard II.
2. *Chronicle of Adam of Usk, 1377–1421*, ed. C. Given-Wilson (Oxford, 1997), 63–5, also cited in *Chron Rev*, 161. In the Latin original: *O Deus! hec est mirabilis terra et inconstans, quia tot reges, tot presules, totque magnates exulavit,interfecit, destruxit, et depredavit, semper discencionibus et discordiis, mutuisque invidiis continue infecta et laborans*. Richard then went on to recite the history of English kings brought down and killed.
3. Cited in Stow, 'Chroniclers Versus Records' in *Documenting the Past*, ed. Hamilton and Bradley, 161.

1 Early Life in Aquitaine, 1367–1371

1. Jean Froissart gives the day of the week correctly, and adds the time of day, in his *Chronicles of Jean Froissart*, 165.
2. Cited in ODNB, 'Richard II'.
3. Barber, *Black Prince*, 189–93; Harvey, *Black Prince*, 107–8.
4. *Historia Anglicana*, I, 302, and *Chronicon Angliae*, 57; Saul, 12 and note 14; Barber, *Black Prince*, 193; Arnd Reitemeier, 'Born to be a Tyrant?', 148.
5. Saul, 12; *Revolution*, 14; citing *Westminster Chronicle*, 22–23.
6. Harvey, *Black Prince*, 104.
7. Cited in Given-Wilson, *Chronicles: The Writing of History in Medieval England*, 74.
8. *Revolution*, 14.
9. Henry III's sons were Edward I and Edmund, named after two Anglo-Saxon saints; Edward I's sons were John, Henry, Alfonso (after his maternal uncle Alfonso X of Castile), Edward II, Thomas and Edmund; Edward II's were Edward III and John; Edward III's were Edward, William, Lionel, John, Edmund, another William and Thomas (both Williams, named after their maternal grandfather Willem, count of Hainault and Holland, died in infancy). Even Richard of Cornwall himself called his sons Henry and Edmund, not Richard, though one of his illegitimate sons bore the name.
10. *CPR 1385–9*, 63. For Richard II's awareness of the Lionheart, see W. M. Ormrod, 'Richard II's Sense of English History' in *Reign of Richard II*, ed. Gwilym Dodd, 103–6. Ormrod points out that Richard II had much in common with his predecessor: they both had older brothers who shared their fathers' Christian names and seemed destined to take the throne but died before accession, and both were childless and their potential successors (Arthur of Brittany and Edmund Mortimer) were no match for the more powerful alternative heirs, King John and Henry IV.
11. *CFR 1319–27*, 68. Edward I and Queen Marguerite also had a daughter Eleanor, born in May 1306 when Edward I was almost sixty-seven. The little girl, Joan of Kent's aunt, died in 1311 when she was five.
12. *CPR 1313–7*, 164; *CIPM 1317–27*, 3; *CFR 1307–19*, 308.
13. *Annales Paulini*, in W. Stubbs, ed., *Chronicles of the Reigns of Edward I and Edward II*, vol. 1, 310, says that Kent married Margaret around the time that his uncle Charles, count of Valois (brother of Philip IV, half-brother of Queen Marguerite and father of Philip VI), died, which was on 16 December 1325. They had received a dispensation to marry from Pope John XXII on 6 October 1325: *CPL 1305–41*, 246.
14. Penny Lawne suggests in her biography of Joan of Kent that Joan's sister Margaret never existed, and that the sole reference to her – when her marriage was being arranged to an Aquitanian lord – really meant Joan, and that her mother Margaret Wake's first name was used in error instead of Joan's. This may well be the case.
15. *CIPM 1352–60*, 41–57. This is the Inquisition Post Mortem of Joan's younger brother John, earl of Kent, taken shortly after he died at the age of twenty-two on 27 December 1352. It says that Joan had turned either twenty-five (according to the Nottinghamshire jurors) or twenty-six (according to the Leicestershire jurors) on the feast of St Michael the previous September,

i.e. September 1352, so she was born on or around 29 September 1326 or 29 September 1327. Joan was not necessarily born exactly on 29 September, the feast of St Michael; this may simply have been the nearest major saint's day to the actual day of her birth. Jurors in other counties in the earl of Kent's IPM were less sure of Joan's date of birth and reported that she was anywhere between 'twenty-two years and more' (it is impossible that she was only twenty-two in 1352) and 'twenty-six years and more' (it is also impossible that she was more than twenty-six in 1352). Such a spread of ages is, however, common in IPMs. No jurors stated specifically that Joan was born on 29 September 1328, the date of her birth almost invariably given in modern works. This seems to be a mathematical error in calculating the date based on her age as given by the jurors of Leicestershire and Nottinghamshire in her brother's IPM, an error which has been repeated numerous times. Joan was at least two years and nine months older than her third husband Edward of Woodstock, and perhaps three years and nine months.

16. *CIPM 1347–52*, 455–6. This is further evidence that Joan was not born in September 1328 as invariably stated; at nineteen months old she would surely have been considered too little for this responsibility. John of Kent's other godparent was John Grenstede, prior of the house of Dominican friars in Arundel.

17. *CPR 1327–30*, 499; *CCR 1330–3*, 14.

18. *CFR 1327–37*, 277, 279.

19. For the 1331 match, *Foedera 1327–44*, 838; *CPR 1330–4*, 157, 224, 273 (the latter two entries name the girl as Joan or Jeanne). For the 1340 match, *Foedera 1327–1344*, 1122, 1140; *CPR 1338–40*, 510, 511; *CPL 1342–62*, 14. The pope's letters to Edward III and Edward of Woodstock name the duke's daughter as Joan or Johanna rather than Margarethe, perhaps by error; Johanna was his eldest daughter and ultimate heir. Duke John III of Brabant was a grandson of Edward I via his mother Margaret, third of the king's five daughters, and therefore Edward III's first cousin.

20. *CPR 1345–8*, 12, 357; Barber, *Black Prince*, 82.

21. F. Royston Fairbank, 'The Last Earl of Warenne and Surrey and the Distribution of his Possessions', *Yorkshire Archaeological Journal*, 19 (1907), 249–50.

22. If Joan of Kent had been born in September 1328, as most modern books wrongly state she was, she would only have been eleven in the spring of 1340. It seems rather incredible, therefore, that her supposed marriage to Holland, then aged about twenty-five, has often been portrayed romantically in fiction.

23. ODNB, 'Joan of Kent'.

24. *CIPM 1352–60*, 552–5.

25. Chris Given-Wilson and Alice Curteis, *The Royal Bastards of Medieval England* (London, 1984), 15–16.

26. Cited in Lawne, *Joan of Kent*.

27. ODNB; *Royal Bastards*, 17.

28. See my article 'The Adherents of Edmund of Woodstock, Earl of Kent, in March 1330', *English Historical Review*, 2011.

29. Michael Bennett, '*Honi soit qui mal y pense*: Adultery and Anxieties about Paternity in Late Medieval England', *The Medieval Python: The Purposive and Provocative Work of Terry Jones*, ed. R. F. Yeager and Toshiyuki Takamiya, 129.

30. A. K. McHardy, 'Richard II: A Personal Portrait', in *Reign of Richard II*, ed. Dodd, 12.
31. McHardy, 'Personal Portrait', 11.
32. *Royal Bastards*, 17, for the rumour.
33. Cited in Bennett, 'Adultery and Anxieties', 127.
34. W. M. Ormrod, *Edward III*, 419.
35. *i eq. voc' Lyard Hobyn emp. eod. die dat. p' d'num Edwardo filiolo suo*: George-Frederick Benz, *Memorials of the Order of the Garter*, 383–4. Edward, prince of Wales, bought numerous other horses at this time, including a palfrey called Bayard Juet for his ten-year-old brother Lionel and a sumpter called Morel Huwet for his mother Queen Philippa.
36. A. E. Prince, 'A Letter of Edward the Black Prince Describing the Battle of Nájera', *English Historical Review*, 11 (1926), 418.
37. George-Frederick Beltz, *Memorials of the Order of the Garter*, 385.
38. Harvey, *Black Prince*, 104.
39. *Anon*, 56.
40. Barber, *Black Prince*, 184; ODNB.
41. Barber, *Black Prince*, 174.
42. *Royal Treasure*, 23.
43. *Calendar of Letter-Books of London 1309–1314*, 310; the letter was recorded on the reverse of the folio on which Isabella of France's announcement of the birth of her son Edward III to the mayor and aldermen in November 1312 was recorded.
44. Ormrod, *Edward III*, 421; *CPR 1364–7*, 180.
45. Barber, *Black Prince*, 184; Frederick Devon, *Issues of the Exchequer*, 184.
46. *Issues of the Exchequer*, 189.
47. Ormrod, *Edward III*, 439, for Galicia; *Issues*, 191, for the horse.
48. Sumption, *Divided Houses*, 115
49. Harvey, *Black Prince*, 112–13.
50. Mortimer, *Fears of Henry IV*, 364–5.
51. *Issues of the Exchequer*, 191.
52. *CPR 1367–70*, 93.
53. Sumption, *Divided Houses*, 82–3.
54. Sumption, 156.
55. Reitemeier, 'Born to be a Tyrant', 148; *CPR 1377–81*, 120, 159, 609; *CCR 1385–9*, 47, 373.
56. *CPR 1385–9*, 115, 553; *CPR 1391–6*, 494; *CPR 1396–9*, 214; *CPR 1401–5*, 386, 453; *CPR 1405–8*, 302.
57. *CPR 1377–81*, 450.
58. Agnes was the wife of a royal squire called William Corby. *CPR 1377–81*, 460, 506, 529; *CPR 1391–6*, 43, 478; *CPR 1389–92*, 175; *CPR 1396–9*, 535. Eliona: *CPR 1391–6*, 595.
59. Michael Bennett, 'Richard II and the Wider Realm' in *Art of Kingship*, ed. Goodman and Gillespie, 189.
60. E. J. Arnould, 'Le Livre de Seyntz Medicines', *Anglo-Norman Texts*, ii (1940), 239: *pur ceo qe jeo sui engleis et n'ai pas moelt hauntee le franceis*.
61. *Chron Rev*, 185–6.
62. See my book *Edward II: The Unconventional King* for examples; for Edward III, Ormrod, *Edward III*, 457ff; Reitemeier, 'Born to be a Tyrant?', 149–50.

63. Reitemeier, 150 note 20.
64. Alfred Thomas, 'Margaret of Teschen's Czech Prayer', 317.
65. *Richard the Redeless* is strongly associated with another poem called *Mum and the Sothsegger* or 'Silence and the Soothsayer' which focuses more on the events of Henry IV's reign.
66. *Fears of Henry IV*, 45–6; Given-Wilson, *Henry IV*, 387–8.
67. V. J. Scattergood, 'Literary Culture at the Court of Richard II' in *English Court Culture in the Later Middle Ages*, ed. V. J. Scattergood and J. W. Sherborne (London: Duckworth, 1983), 34.
68. Gervase Mathew, *Court of Richard II*, 22–3.
69. *Curiosus perscrutator rerum progenitoribus relictarum*, in Walsingham's *Chronica et Annales*, 299, and also *Historia Anglicana*, II, 239.
70. *CPR 1391–6*, 115.
71. *CPR 1385–9*, 162.

2 Arrival in England, 1372–1376

1. Taylor, *English Historical Literature in the 14th Century* (1987), 296.
2. *Issues*, 244, 248.
3. Saul, 15; *CPR 1385–9*, 116, 154, 156.
4. For Guichard, see James L. Gillespie, 'Richard II: Chivalry and Kingship', *Age of Richard II*, ed. Gillespie, 115–6.
5. Saul, 14–15, Reitemeier, 'Born to be a Tyrant?', 150–51.
6. Fletcher, 'Manhood and Politics', 29.
7. Saul, 453.
8. Saul, *Three Richards*, 95
9. Saul, 15, 449; *Issues*, 231, 268–9.
10. *Historia Vitae et Regni*, 166, cited in Taylor, 'Chronicles', in *Art of Kingship*, 28.
11. Froissart, 184; see below for parliament; Creton, *Histoire*, 55, cited in Stow, 'Chronicles versus Records', in *Documenting the Past*, 171.
12. Usk, 1; *Political Poems and Songs*, vol. 1, ed. Thomas Wright, 283, 285; Saul, 452.
13. Cited in *Reign of Richard II*, 53; Saul, 452; *Revolution*, 56.
14. Cited in Saul, 452.
15. This description comes from Eleanor Scheifele, 'Richard II and the Visual Arts' in *Art of Kingship*, 263, and see also Saul 447, 450–52.
16. Fletcher, 'Manhood and Politics', 3–8.
17. Saul, 452.
18. Fletcher, 'Manhood and Politics', 30.
19. *Historia Anglicana*, II, 156.
20. See Stow, 'Handkerchief', 221, for an overview of such comments.
21. Cited in Stow, 'Handkerchief', 223, 226.
22. Stow, 'Handkerchief', 224–6.
23. *CPR 1385–9*, 94.
24. *CPR 1377–81*, 544; *CPR 1385–9*, 538; *CPR 1396–9*, 38, 40, 174, 550.
25. *Issues*, 199–200.
26. *Issues*, 189.
27. Blanche was probably born on 25 March 1342: see her father Duke Henry's Inq. Post Mortem in *CIPM 1361–65*, 92–116. Many modern writers say

that she was born in 1345 or even 1347, which is most unlikely as she would only just have turned thirteen when she bore her first child Philippa in late March 1360. None of the jurors at her father's IPM said that Blanche was born as late as 1347, which seems to be a modern invention. See http://edwardthesecond.blogspot.co.uk/2016/05/the-date-of-birth-of-blanche-duchess-of.html.

28. *Issues*, 187. Her mother was Margarethe of Brabant, proposed as a bride for Edward of Woodstock in 1340.
29. *Issues*, 189.
30. ODNB, 'Edmund of Langley', for the quotation.
31. Saul, 13.
32. Saul, 13.
33. *CPR 1370–74*, 156.
34. *Anon*, 70; ODNB, 'Edmund of Langley'.
35. ODNB, 'Edmund of Langley'.
36. *Issues*, 195.
37. *John of Gaunt's Registers*, vol. 1, 127, 137, 155, 169–70, 248, 256, 261, 276–7.
38. *Anon*, 69.
39. *Anon*, 69; John Pohl and Garry Embleton, *Armies of Castile and Aragon 1370–1516* (2015), 44; Clara Estow, *Pedro the Cruel of Castile: 1350–1369* (2005), 30; Margaretta Jolly, ed., *Encyclopaedia of Life Writing: Autobiographical and Biographical Forms* (2013), 698; Robert Folger, *Generaciones Y Semblanzas: Memory and Genealogy in Medieval Iberian Historiography* (2003), 187.
40. *Anon*, 69 (*furent moult des gentz et des dames et damosels pur veere la beaute de la dite iune dame*), 153.
41. Anya Seton's enormously popular and influential 1950s novel *Katherine*, about Katherine Swynford, also depicts Constanza of Castile as small and skinny with black hair and eyes, a description which could hardly be further from reality and seems to be a simple cliché of how people from the south of Europe are 'meant' to look. Constanza is also depicted in the novel, rather unpleasantly, as a smelly religious fanatic who does not wash often enough and who worships her dead father King Pedro. The novel also has a scene where Katherine Swynford is dancing with Richard II and is said to be several inches taller than he. As Richard was six feet tall, this seems incredibly unlikely.
42. Given-Wilson, *Henry IV*, 31 note 38.
43. Ormrod, *Edward III*, 532.
44. *CPR 1370–74*, 195; *Calendar of Inquisitions Miscellaneous 1348–77*, 323; *CCR 1369–74*, 456, 462, 466; Ian Mortimer, *The Perfect King: A Life of Edward III*, 376–7; Ormrod, *Edward III*, 511–13; Sumption, *Divided Houses*, 135–56.
45. Sumption, *Divided Houses*, 142.
46. Ian Mortimer, *Perfect King*, 376–7.
47. *Foedera*, vol. iii, part ii, 989.
48. *Foedera*, vol. iii, part ii, 983.
49. *Foedera 1373–97*, 508.

3 *The Heir, 1376–1377*

1. Ormrod, *Edward III*, 559.
2. Edward's will is given in full, in English translation, in Harvey, *Black Prince*, 160–65.
3. Bennett, 'Adultery and Anxieties', 127.
4. Ormrod, *Edward III*, 559.
5. *Chronica Maiora 1376–1422*, ed. and trans. David Preest, 27.
6. Ormrod, *Edward III*, 564–5; Bennett, 'Edward III's Entail and the Succession to the Crown', 582.
7. Edward I's younger sons from his second marriage to Marguerite of France, Thomas of Brotherton and Edmund of Woodstock, were not born until 1300 and 1301, and entered the line of succession behind their half-brother the future Edward II. Edward I's brother Edmund of Lancaster was the grandfather of John of Gaunt's father-in-law Duke Henry of Lancaster.
8. Bennett, 'Entail', 584–5. Duke Geoffrey was born in 1158 and died in 1186, and his posthumous son Arthur of Brittany was born in 1187; John was born in 1166.
9. Bennett, 'Entail', 585.
10. Bennett, 'Entail', 592; Ormrod, *Edward III*, 564–5.
11. Bennett, 'Adultery and Anxieties', 126.
12. *Testamenta Vetusta*, vol. 1, 10–12.
13. *CCR 1374–7*, 420–21; *CChR 1341–1417*, 231, 232.
14. *Issues of the Exchequer*, 203.
15. Froissart, *Chronicles*, 205.
16. *CCR 1374–7*, 467, 501–2.
17. Ormrod, *Edward III*, 532–3.
18. Ormrod, *Edward III*, 562.
19. *CCR 1377–81*, 74, gives the time of the king's death.
20. Chris Given-Wilson, 'The Exequies of Edward III and the Royal Funeral Ceremony', 260.
21. *CCR 1377–81*, 74; Saul, 469; Given-Wilson, 'Exequies', 263.
22. *CCR 1377–81*, 74–5.
23. *Foedera 1377–83*, 3, 4. The order for the wax was renewed at regular intervals, on 8 June 1379, 5 July 1382 and 12 July 1384: *Foedera 1377–83*, 63; *CCR 1381–5*, 147, 456.
24. For Edward III's funeral, see Ormrod, *Edward III*, 578–81; Mortimer, *Perfect King*, 392; and Saul, 22–23.

4 *Coronation of a Young King, 1377–1378*

1. *CPR 1377–81*, 2, 4, 5.
2. *Chronicon Angliae 1328–1388*, ed. Maunde Thompson, 154.
3. *Anon*, 107–14; the procession is described on 107–8.
4. *Anon*, 114; *Westminster Chronicle*, 414–6.
5. Saul, 310, 448.
6. *Chron Rev*, 243.
7. *Anon*, 114. The other four appointments are in *CChR 1341–1417*, 235, and *Foedera 1377–83*, 10; *CPR 1377–81*, 372, for Woodstock's income.

The *Anonimalle* chronicle calls Woodstock the earl of 'Herforth' or Hereford by mistake; the late earl of Hereford, Humphrey de Bohun, was Woodstock's father-in-law.

8. *CPR 1381–5*, 78, 161–2, 327.
9. *Anon*, 114; Mortimer, *Fears of Henry IV*, 35.
10. *Anon*, 114.
11. All details of the coronation banquet are from *CCR 1377–81*, 1–5.
12. *Foedera 1377–83*, 28.
13. Saul, 83–4.
14. *Foedera 1377–83*, 90.
15. *Foedera 1377–83*, 10.
16. Numerous examples of the influence of Joan of Kent and Richard's three uncles can be found on the Patent Roll.
17. *CCR 1377–81*, 22–3.
18. *Royal Treasure*, 24, 31.
19. PROME.
20. PROME; Saul, 27.
21. *Royal Treasure*, 51.
22. Saul, 120.
23. Mortimer, *Fears*, 32–3.
24. Mortimer, *Fears*, 36.
25. Anthony Goodman, *Loyal Conspiracy: The Lords Appellant under Richard II*, 153, for the visit to St Albans; Saul, 469.
26. *CPR 1377–81*, 3–4.
27. Saul, 33–4; *CPR 1377–81*, 4.
28. *Foedera 1377–83*, 27.
29. Saul, 39–40.
30. *Foedera 1377–83*, 46, 52.
31. *CPR 1377–81*, 111.
32. *Foedera 1377–83*, 51, 56; *Calendar of Documents Relating to Scotland 1357–1509*, 58, 64.
33. *CPR 1377–81*, 359.
34. Foedera 1377–83, 42 for King Carlos's safe-conduct; for Carloto's visit, *Issues of the Exchequer*, 208, and *Foedera 1377–83*, 55–6. Carloto de Beaumont was the illegitimate son of King Carlos's younger brother Luis, count of Beaumont-le-Roger.
35. *Issues*, 208.
36. *Issues*, 208; *Foedera 1377–83*, 46.
37. Anthony Tuck, 'Richard II and the House of Luxembourg', in *Richard II: The Art of Kingship*, ed. Goodman and Gillespie, 207.
38. *Foedera 1377–83*, 125.
39. Saul, 96ff.
40. *Foedera 1377–83*, 86, 93, 94.
41. *Reign*, 61.
42. *Foedera 1377–83*, 30, 40, 45.
43. Given-Wilson, *Henry IV*, 26 and note 10.
44. *Foedera 1377–83*, 15, 23. Alfonso of Aragon, count of Denia and later duke of Gandia, was born in *c.* 1332 as the son of Pedro, count of Ribagorza, a

younger son of King Jaime II. Alfonso was thus a first cousin of Pedro IV, who was also a grandson of Jaime II.

45. Saul, 36–7; Tuck, *Richard II and the English Nobility*, 41–2; *Reign*, 38–43; *Chronicon Angliae*, 210; http://www.westminster-abbey.org/our-history/people/robert-hauley. The abbot of Westminster at this time was Nicholas Litlington, who may have been an illegitimate son of Edward II's notorious favourite Hugh Despenser the Younger, lord of Glamorgan.
46. *Foedera 1377–83*, 100, 110, 124; *CPR 1377–81*, 546; *CPR 1396–9*, 58, 165; *CPR 1408–13*, 100, 391.
47. *Foedera 1377–83*, 66, 67; Froissart, *Chronicles*, 215–6.
48. Given-Wilson, *Henry IV*, 26.
49. Sumption, *Divided Houses*, 366–7.
50. *CPR 1377–81*, 488, 624.
51. Gillespie, 'Chivalry and Kingship', in *Age of Richard II*, 132.
52. *Issues*, 211–12.
53. *Foedera 1377–83*, 57.
54. *CCR 1377–81*, 160; *CPR 1377–81*, 276, 504.
55. *CPR 1377–81*, 198.
56. Saul, 37–8; *Reign*, 43–5.
57. *Reign*, 44.
58. *Issues*, 188.
59. *Foedera 1377–83*, 69, 71.
60. Cited in *Reign*, 53–4.
61. Cited in ODNB 'Thomas Arundel'.

5 The Great Schism, 1378–1380

1. *CPL 1362–1404*, 228.
2. *Foedera 1377–83*, 84, 164; *Issues*, 222–3.
3. *CPR 1381–5*, 298.
4. Perroy, *Diplomatic Correspondence of Richard II*, 34–5, 197–8; the text of the letters is corrupt and sometimes unintelligible.
5. *Foedera 1377–83*, 60; Saul, 84, for the envoys in Italy.
6. Saul, 87.
7. *Issues*, 224–5; Saul, 87.
8. *Foedera 1377–83*, 104–6; *Issues*, 218.
9. Anthony Tuck, 'Richard II and the House of Luxembourg', in *Art of Kingship*, 218.
10. *Issues*, 212.
11. *Issues*, 213.
12. *Royal Treasure*, 31–2, 51.
13. ODNB, 'Thomas of Woodstock'; *CPR 1374–7*, 337.
14. ODNB; Mortimer, *Fears*, 39–40.
15. ODNB.
16. Mortimer, *Fears*, 41; Given-Wilson, *Henry IV*, 28; *CCR 1377–81*, 439–40; *CPR 1381–5*, 95.
17. Goodman, *Loyal Conspiracy*, 89–90; Given-Wilson, *Henry IV*, 27.
18. Mortimer, *Fears*, 370–71; Given-Wilson, *Henry IV*, 32.

19. *CPR 1381–5*, 95; Given-Wilson, *Henry IV*, 32.
20. Goodman, *Loyal Conspiracy*, 90.
21. *CPR 1381–5*, 88; Alastair Dunn, 'Richard II and the Mortimer Inheritance', 160.
22. *CPR 1381–5*, 111.
23. *CPR 1391–6*, 284, 385, 481.

6 The Great Uprising, 1381

1. Saul, 57.
2. Saul 62, 62–3 note 28.
3. Juliet Barker, *England, Arise*, 214.
4. *Reign*, 66.
5. Saul, 62.
6. *Chronica Maiora*, trans. Preest, 122.
7. *Chronica Maiora*, trans. Preest, 124; *Reign*, 66. The *Anonimalle* gives 50,000 from Kent and 60,000 from Essex, which must be gross exaggerations. Walsingham and the *Vita* also say 100,000 and Froissart says 60,000 in total, which are also surely far too high.
8. Barker, *England, Arise*, 244; Saul, 63.
9. *Chronica Maiora*, 122–6; *Chronicon Angliae*, 291; *Reign*, 64, 66, 75. See ODNB 'Joan of Kent' and W. M. Ormrod, 'In Bed with Joan of Kent'.
10. *Chronica Maiora*, 122, 124 note 5; *Reign*, 66–7; Saul, 63.
11. *Chronica Maiora*, 122; *Reign*, 67; Saul, 64.
12. Saul, 64 note 35.
13. *CPR 1381–5*, 30–31.
14. *CCR 1381–5*, 50.
15. *Reign*, 64–5, 67, 74; Saul, 64–5, 69–70.
16. *CCR 1381–5*, 62.
17. *Chronica Maiora*, 123.
18. *Reign*, 65–7; *Chronica Maiora*, 124.
19. *CCR 1381–5*, 7.
20. *Reign*, 79–83.
21. *Reign*, 67; *Chronica Maiora*, 123.
22. *Reign*, 72–3; Saul, 65.
23. *Chronica Maiora*, 123.
24. ODNB; Saul, 68.
25. Barker, *England, Arise*, 246–7; Saul, 68.
26. *Reign*, 68.
27. Barker, *England, Arise*, 250.
28. Barker, *England, Arise*, 250–57, 373–5.
29. *Chronica Maiora*, 125–6.
30. *Reign*, 68, 75.
31. *CPR 1381–5*, 95; Saul, 73.
32. *Chronica Maiora*, 125–6.
33. ODNB citing TNA E 37/28.
34. *Reign*, 88, citing *Anon*, 152–3. It is at this point that the chronicler calls Constanza a woman of great beauty, as noted above.
35. *CPR 1381–5*, 66, 77.

36. Saul, 70; *Reign*, 69.
37. Saul, 70–71; *Chronica Maiora*, 129; Reign, 65, 69.
38. *Reign*, 69.
39. *Chronica Maiora*, 129–30.
40. Kirkstall chronicle, in *Reign*, 65.
41. Saul, 73–4.
42. *CPR 1381–5*, 30.
43. *Foedera 1377–83*, 126, 128; Barker, *England, Arise*, 385.
44. *Foedera 1377–83*, 127.
45. *CCR 1381–5*, 5.
46. Cited in Barker, *England, Arise*, 374–5.
47. *CPR 1381–5*, 27.
48. Barker, *England, Arise*, 250–51, 372–3; Saul, 76; *Reign*, 86–7.

7 The King Marries the Emperor's Daughter, 1382–1383

1. *Foedera 1377–83*, 113–4, 116.
2. Perroy, *Correspondence*, 15, 190.
3. *Illustrirte Chronik von Böhmen* (Prague, 1854), 131–2; Beltz, *Memorials of the Order of the Garter*, 387.
4. *CPR 1348–50*, 251. Karl had no surviving children from his second marriage to Anna of the Palatinate. Blanche de Valois was a half-sister of Philip VI of France.
5. Barbara Newman, 'The Passion of the Jews of Prague: The Pogrom of 1389 and the Lessons of a Medieval Parody', *American Society of Church History*, 81 (2012), 7. According to other evidence, however, Václav was friendly to the Jews: Alison Coudert and Jeffrey S. Shouson, eds., *Hebraica Veritas?: Christian Hebraists and the Study of Judaism* (2004), 171–2.
6. Heila Lautenschläger, *Begräbniszeremonien und Staatlichkeit am Beispiel Karls IV* (2001), 32; Jörg Gengnagel, Monika Thiel-Horstmann and Gerald Schwedler, eds., *Prozessionen, Wallfahrten, Aufmärsche: Bewegung zwischen Religion und Politik in Europa und Asien seit dem Mittelalter* (2008), 123, 126–8, 142.
7. Henry I's second wife Adeliza of Louvain (d. 1151) came from territory now mostly in Belgium and the Netherlands, though might be considered partly German.
8. For Anne's languages, see Alfred Thomas, *Anne's Bohemia: Czech Literature and Society*, 1; for the English Gospels, Saul, 456; for her New Testament, Susan Groag Bell, 'Medieval Women Book Owners', 760, 764.
9. David Wallace, *Chaucerian Polity* (1997), 359; for Zikmund, see John Jefferson, *The Holy Wars of King Wladislas and Sultan Murad: The Ottoman-Christian Conflict from 1438–1444* (2012), 131.
10. *Prozessionen, Wallfahrten, Aufmärsche*, 128.
11. Malcolm Vale, *The Princely Court: Medieval Courts and Culture in North-West Europe* (2001), 294, 331.
12. *CCR 1381–5*, 97; *Foedera 1377–83*, 136; Saul, 88–9.
13. *Foedera 1377–83*, 136, 140.
14. Saul, 89, citing *Historia Anglicana*, vol. ii, 46.

15. *Issues*, 220–21; Saul, *Three Richards*, 143.
16. Cited in Saul, 342–3.
17. *Foedera 1377–83*, 139. Landgrave, the male form, and landgravine, the female form, were noble titles of the Holy Roman Empire.
18. *CCR 1381–5*, 155.
19. *CPR 1381–5*, 4.
20. Alfred Thomas, 'Margaret of Teschen's Czech Prayer', 313.
21. *Westminster Chronicle*, 24, cited in Saul, 455; *pro tantilla carnis porcione*.
22. *Reign*, 92.
23. Marguerite was a descendant of Edward III's uncle Philip V of France and had been proposed as the wife of Richard's uncle Edmund of Langley in 1365, and in 1369 married Philip the Bold, duke of Burgundy, son of John II of France and youngest brother of Charles V. Richard II was only two years old at the time.
24. *Reign*, 93.
25. As suggested by W. M. Ormrod, 'Richard II's Sense of English History' in *Reign of Richard II*, ed. Dodd, 98.
26. *CPR 1389–92*, 250, and *1391–6*, 185, 496 for Perrin, and for Agnes, see also below; *CPR 1391–6*, 286, and *CPR 1396–9*, 48, for Eliska.
27. Perroy, *Correspondence*, 20.
28. *Historia Anglicana*, vol. ii, 46; *Chronica Majora*, 736: *Anna regina, quam raro uel nunquam lateri suo deesse permisit.*
29. Joachim Leuschner, *Deutschland im Späten Mittelalter* (1980), 174.
30. http://www.history.ac.uk/richardII/anneofb.html
31. An image of it can be seen at http://www.residenz-muenchen.de/englisch/treasury/pic11.htm; see also Cherry, 'Fourteenth-Century Jewellery', 137–8.
32. *Royal Treasure*, 52.
33. See p. 129.
34. Caroline Barron, 'Richard II: Image and Reality', *Making and Meaning. The Wilton Diptych* (1993), 15. Anya Seton in her beloved 1950s novel *Katherine* presents Richard as abnormal and probably incapable of sexual relations with Queen Anne.
35. Saul, 457, suggests probably correctly that either Richard or Anne was infertile.
36. Kristen Geaman discusses this in her article 'Anne of Bohemia's Struggle to Conceive', and see also below, p. 129.
37. *CPR 1381–5*, 192, 263. An entry on the Patent Roll of 30 June 1392 granting a licence to the guild of St John the Baptist in Coventry refers to 'the good estate of the king and queen, the king's uncles the dukes of Lancaster, York and Gloucester, and their children', which might be another reference to Richard and Anne's possible future children, but given the timing eleven and a half years after the royal wedding, might of course simply mean his uncles' children. *CPR 1391–6*, 131.
38. *Historia Anglicana*, vol. ii, 148.
39. Cited in ODNB 'Robert de Vere'.
40. Perroy, *Correspondence*, 21, 35, 38, 95.
41. Saul, 90. The *Liber Regalis* or Royal Book, a fourteenth-century manuscript which details the procedure and order of service for crowning a king, a king and queen or a queen alone which is now held in the library of Westminster

Abbey, may have been compiled in 1382 shortly before Anne's coronation, though it may also belong to 1308 and the coronation of Richard's great-grandparents Edward II and Isabella of France.

42. Given-Wilson, *Henry IV*, 30.
43. A. H. Thomas, *Calendar of Plea and Memoranda Rolls of the City of London 1381–1412*, 3; *CPR 1381–5*, 114.
44. *Issues*, 221–2.
45. *CPR 1381–5*, 119–20.
46. *Calendar of Select Pleas and Memoranda Rolls of the City of London*, 7.
47. *CPR 1381–5*, 384.
48. *Westminster Chronicle*, 20–22; *Anon*, 154–6; Thomas Walsingham's St Albans Chronicle 1376–1394, 566–78, cited in PROME's Introduction to the 1382 parliament.
49. ODNB; K. Towson, 'Hearts Warped by Passion: The Percy-Gaunt Dispute of 1381', *Fourteenth Century England III*, ed. W. M. Ormrod (2004); *Anon*, 152–3; *Reign*, 87–90.
50. *Calendar of Documents Relating to Scotland 1357–1509*, 76.
51. *Foedera 1377–83*, 151, 163; Tuck, 'House of Luxembourg' in *Art of Kingship*, 220.
52. *Foedera 1377–83*, 156.
53. *Reign*, 95–6.
54. *Foedera 1377–83*, 159.
55. PROME; *Reign*, 110–13.
56. *CPR 1381–5*, 263.
57. Geaman, 'Struggle to Conceive', 12–13.
58. Geaman, 'A Personal Letter of Anne of Bohemia', 1086–94, and for the dating and context of the letter especially, 1088; the letter is also mentioned in Perroy, *Correspondence*, 193.
59. Cited in Chris Given-Wilson, *Chronicles: The Writing of History in Medieval England*, 34.
60. *CChR 1341–1417*, 288–9.
61. Saul, 308–9.

8 An Invasion of Scotland and Murder, 1384–1385

1. *Calendar of the Plea and Memoranda Rolls of the City of London 1381–1412*, membrane 14b.
2. Cited in Sumption, *Divided Houses*, 506.
3. *Foedera 1373–97*, 506.
4. PROME, Introduction to the parliament of 13 November to 14 December held at Westminster.
5. *Issues*, 222.
6. Tuck, 'House of Luxembourg', in *Art of Kingship*, 225–6.
7. Cited in ODNB.
8. *Westminster Chronicle*, 66–8; see Taylor, 'Chronicles', in *Art of Kingship*, 28; Saul, 130; *Reign*, 117–8.
9. The younger Richard Fitzalan, born *c.* 1346, married Elizabeth de Bohun, sister of the earl of Hereford (d. 1373) and a great-granddaughter of Edward I, and their son and heir Thomas was born in 1381.

10. *Westminster Chronicle*, 116–17, cited in Stow, 'Chronicles versus Records', in *Documenting the Past*, 157–8.
11. *Reign*, 124.
12. Stow, 'Chronicles versus Records', 160.
13. *Westminster Chronicle*, 68–70, cited in Stow, 'Chronicles versus Records', 157.
14. *Reign*, 116–7, 124; Saul, 131; ODNB, Introduction to the April 1384 parliament.
15. ODNB 'Thomas of Woodstock'.
16. Cited in ODNB 'Robert de Vere'.
17. Richard was at Reading from 18 to 20 August 1384: Saul, 470.
18. Saul, 132–3, citing *Westminster Chronicle*, 92.
19. *CPR 1381–5*, 464; *CPR 1385–9*, 158; *CPR 1389–92*, 297.
20. Saul, 241.
21. *Issues*, 226; Saul, 470, for Richard's itinerary.
22. Mathew, *Court*, 32.
23. Mathew, *Court*, 32–4 and Harvey, *Black Prince*, 144, for the all the preceding.
24. *CPR 1381–5*, 153; *CCR 1381–5*, 140.
25. *CPR 1385–9*, 430.
26. *CPR 1385–9*, 430, 448.
27. *Issues*, 236.
28. *CPR 1391–6*, 8.
29. *CCR 1392–6*, 437–8.
30. Saul, 298–9.
31. See Saul, 301–2.
32. *Issues*, 242.
33. *CPR 1391–6*, 50.
34. Saul, *Three Richards*, 173.
35. *CPR 1385–9*, 194; *CPR 1396–9*, 329.
36. *CCR 1377–81*, 427; *CPR 1381–5*, 241; *CPR 1389–92*, 370; *CPR 1391–6*, 658.
37. *CPR 1381–5*, 562.
38. *CPR 1385–9*, 459.
39. *CPR 1389–92*, 305, 312, 339, 494.
40. *Testamenta Vetusta*, vol. 1, 150–51.
41. *Testamenta Vetusta*, vol. 1, 134–5.
42. *Reign*, 123, 126–7.
43. Sumption, *Divided Houses*, 548–9; *Reign*, 127–8.
44. Sumption, *Divided Houses*, 549.
45. Cited in Ian Mortimer, 'Richard II and the Succession to the Crown', in his *Medieval Intrigue*, 262.
46. *Reign*, 128.
47. *Testamenta Vetusta*, vol. 1, 13–15.
48. *CCR 1381–5*, 553.
49. ODNB 'Joan of Kent'.
50. Saul, 470, for the itinerary; Bennett, 'Adultery and Anxieties', 129.
51. *Foedera 1373–97*, 512.
52. Bennett, 'Adultery and Anxieties', 129 and note 54.

9 The King of Armenia Visits, 1385–1386

1. CPR 1385–9, 114, 368.
2. The appointments are in *CChR 1341–1417*, 300.
3. *Reign*, 134.
4. Walsingham, *Historia Anglicana*, II, 140, cited in Age of *Richard II*, 24 note 69; appointment of de Vere as marquis of 1 December 1385 is in *Rotuli Parliamentorum*, vol. III, 209–11; *CChR 1341–1417*, 301.
5. *Reign*, 134.
6. CPR 1385–9, 11; *CChR 1341–1417*, 281 (made earl of Nottingham on 12 Feb 1383), 301; *CPR 1381–5*, 236.
7. *Issues*, 252.
8. *Westminster Chronicle*, 436–9; Perroy, *Correspondence*, 62–3.
9. *Issues*, 228.
10. *Royal Treasure*, 51.
11. Saul, *Three Richards*, 95.
12. Shelagh Mitchell, 'Richard II and the Broomcod Collar', 173–4 and note 18, citing The National Archives E 101/401/15, mem. 1.
13. *Reign*, 137–9; PROME.
14. PROME.
15. S. Payaslian, *The History of Armenia: From the Origins to the Present* (2008), 100.
16. *Foedera 1373–97*, 509.
17. *Westminster Chronicle*, 130–3, 154–7, cited in Bennett, 'Richard II and the Wider Realm', in *Art of Kingship*, ed. Goodman and Gillespie, 190; Patricia J. Eberle, 'Richard II and the Literary Arts' in *Art of Kingship*, 239–40. The monk was a Benedictine called William Sudbury, who was a doctor of divinity from Oxford.
18. *Issues*, 228–9.
19. *Testamenta Vetusta*, vol. 1, 135; Anthony Goodman, *The Loyal Conspiracy*, 78.
20. *Reign*, 140.
21. *Issues*, 229, 245–6; CPR 1385–9, 310; for the de Vere grant, *CPR 1381–5*, 542.
22. Jacob G. Ghazarian, *The Armenian Kingdom in Cilicia during the Crusades* (2000), 163–4; Mack Chahin, *The Kingdom of Armenia: New Edition* (2013), pp. 257–8.
23. *Revolution*, 25, citing *Historia Anglicana*, vol. II, 142, 151; *Foedera 1373–97*, 510, 523.
24. Perroy, *Correspondence*, 42–3.
25. *Issues*, 229.
26. *Issues*, 230.
27. CPR 1389–92, 251, 261.
28. *Foedera 1373–97*, 511; *Reign*, 143–4.
29. See *Reign*, 140ff.
30. Saul, 243.
31. Saul, 150.
32. *Issues*, 231.
33. *Issues*, 233.
34. CPR 1389–92, 20.

35. Thomas Walsingham, *Rerum Britannicarum Medii Aevi Scriptores*, 160; *Reign*, 171.
36. *Westminster Chronicle 1381–94*, 190–91; *Reign*, 171. *Calendar of Papal Letters 1362–1404* contains only one single indexed reference to a John Ripon or any variant spelling: in 1396 he was said to be a monk of Durham and a papal chaplain and was given permission to hold a benefice; p. 534.
37. *CPR 1399–1401*, 528.
38. *CPR 1391–6*, 5, 716; *CPR 1396–9*, 422, 429, 581; *CPR 1399–1401*, 508, 528; *CCR 1396–9*, 324–5.
39. *CCR 1396–9*, 324–5.
40. *CPR 1389–92*, 117, 151.
41. ODNB 'Agnes Lancecrona' under 'Robert de Vere', citing TNA E 36/66.
42. *CPL 1362–1404* contains no indexed references to either Robert de Vere or Philippa Coucy. Barbara Tuchman, *A Distant Mirror* (1979), 445, says de Vere applied for a divorce on the grounds of 'false testimony' with Richard II's support, and that Pope Urban VI complied as Philippa's father was French and thus the Coucys were of the faction of Clement VII (the Avignon pope or anti-pope). As Robert de Vere and Philippa Coucy were only fifteen and about nine when they married and thus well underage, this might have been a plausible reason for an annulment, yet it is curious that no record of such seems to exist, and Tuchman does not cite a source for her statement. Agnes Strickland's *Lives of the Queens of England*, vol. 2 (1848), 213–4, also claims that de Vere married Launcecrona and that Queen Anne wrote a letter to Urban VI with her own hand asking him to annul the marriage of the earl and countess of Oxford. No source is cited for this claim either.
43. *CPL 1362–1404*, 397.
44. Perroy, *Correspondence*, 38–9.

10 A Threatened Invasion of England, 1386–1387

1. ODNB; PROME; Froissart, *Chronicles*, ed. Brereton.
2. *Reign*, 144.
3. *Reign*, 145.
4. *CPR 1385–9*, 175.
5. *Reign*, 145–6.
6. *CPR 1385–9*, 259; *Issues*, 231–2.
7. *CPR 1385–9*, 135, 160, 174, 175, 176–7, 181, 214, 216, etc.
8. *CPR 1385–9*, 261.
9. *Reign*, 146.
10. ODNB; PROME.
11. Bennett, 'Adultery and Anxieties', 129.
12. *Reign*, 140.
13. Mortimer, *Fears of Henry IV*, 69; Saul, 471; ODNB.
14. *Issues*, 233.
15. *CPR 1385–9*, 316, 372.
16. *CPR 1385–9*, 373.
17. *Reign*, 172–4.

11 The Merciless Lords Appellant, 1387–1388

1. Saul, 181.
2. Goodman, *Loyal Conspiracy*, 77; CPR 1391–6, 13, for Richard's gift to Dodmore.
3. *Reign*, 167–71.
4. ODNB; *Reign*, 175.
5. *Reign*, 183, for this paragraph, citing the *Euologium*, 363–6.
6. *Reign*, 184.
7. *Reign*, 184; Mortimer, *Fears*, 74.
8. Cited in Lynn Staley, *Languages of Power in the Age of Richard II* (2005), 51–2.
9. ODNB 'Robert de Vere'.
10. *Issues*, 234.
11. ODNB 'Michael de la Pole'.
12. *Chronica Maiora*, trans. Preest, 245.
13. Saul, 188–9.
14. From Gloucester's 1397 confession, as recorded in PROME; ODNB.
15. *Reign*, 206.
16. Saul, 189.
17. *CFR 1383–91*, 227.
18. *Issues*, 234–5.
19. *Chronica Maiora*, trans. Preest, 261.
20. *Reign*, 207.
21. *Reign*, 217; PROME, February 1388 parliament.
22. *Reign*, 216, 219–21; ODNB.
23. ODNB 'Alexander Neville'.
24. *Reign*, 225.
25. PROME.
26. Saul, 194.
27. Saul, 194.
28. *Traison*, 133.
29. Saul, 194 note 72.
30. *Reign*, 229.
31. *CPR 1396–9*, 348.
32. *Reign*, 228.
33. *Issues*, 250.
34. Laura A. Hibbard, 'Books of Sir Simon de Burley', 169–71; Scattergood, 'Literary Culture', 35–6.
35. James L. Gillespie, 'Richard II: Chivalry and Kingship' in *The Age of Richard II*, ed. Gillespie, 119–20.
36. See Saul, 195–6.

12 The King Comes of Age, 1389–1390

1. *Reign*, 230.
2. *Calendar of Documents Relating to Scotland 1357–1509*, 87, 93.
3. *Reign*, 253–4; Saul, 198.
4. *CPR 1391–6*, 605–6.

5. *CPR 1391–6*, 8, 28.
6. Thomas Walsingham, *Historia Anglicana*, vol. II, 181, cited in *English Historical Documents*, vol. 4, 160.
7. *Issues*, 239.
8. Bennett, 'Adultery and Anxieties', 129.
9. *Reign*, 264–5.
10. *CPR 1385–9*, 502–3; Saul, 205.
11. *Calendar of Documents Relating to Scotland 1357–1509*, 87–8.
12. See Saul, 207–8.
13. *Foedera 1373–97*, 548.
14. Saul, 241.
15. *Chronica Maiora*, trans. Preest, 268.
16. *CPR 1389–92*, 469.
17. *CPR 1389–92*, 506; *CCR 1392–6*, 318; *CPL 1362–1404*, 391–2.
18. *Testamenta Vetusta*, vol. 1, 129.
19. Given-Wilson, *Chronicles: Writing of History in Medieval England*, 201.
20. Anne was widowed when Thomas Stafford died in July 1392. The third brother William died in 1395, and in 1398 Anne of Gloucester married her former brother-in-law Edmund, the fourth son and ultimate heir, who became earl of Stafford. Their son Humphrey, named after Anne's brother Humphrey of Gloucester and grandfather Humphrey de Bohun, earl of Hereford, became the first duke of Buckingham.
21. Gillespie, 'Chivalry and Kingship', in *Age of Richard II*, ed. Gillespie, 129.
22. *Reign*, 257–8.
23. Bennett, 'Adultery and Anxieties', 126.
24. John M. Bowers, *The Politics of Pearl: Court Poetry in the Age of Richard II* (2001), 174.
25. *CPR 1389–92*, 328; Barker, *England, Arise*, 407.
26. Saul, 241.
27. PROME, January 1394 parliament: ... *qu'il vorroit porter et user un signe de bon amour d'entiere coer entre eux, auxi come il fait des liveres ses autres uncles.*
28. Saul, *Three Richards*, 95.
29. Tuck, 'Richard II and the House of Luxembourg', in *Art of Kingship*, 224. Katharina of Bavaria married Wilhelm, duke of Guelders and Jülich.
30. *Reign*, 258.
31. *Reign*, 261.
32. *Reign*, 258.
33. *Reign*, 259–61; http://faculty.nipissingu.ca/muhlberger/FROISSART/LONDON.HTM.
34. Christopher Fletcher, 'Manhood and Politics in the Reign of Richard II', 29.
35. http://faculty.nipissingu.ca/muhlberger/FROISSART/LONDON.HTM.
36. Mortimer, *Fears of Henry IV*, 89ff; Given-Wilson, *Henry IV*, 63ff.
37. Mortimer, *Fears*, 106–8; ODNB 'Henry IV'; Given-Wilson, *Henry IV*, 74.
38. *CPR 1389–92*, 482.
39. Sumption, *Divided Houses*, 833.
40. Mathew, *Court of Richard II*, 23–5, and http://www.pbm.com/~lindahl/foc/.

13 *Conflict in London, 1391–1393*

1. *Issues*, 244, 263.
2. *Issues*, 247–8.
3. *CPR 1389–92*, 385.
4. *CPR 1391–6*, 45.
5. *Issues*, 247.
6. *CPR 1389–92*, 493.
7. *Royal Treasure*, 60.
8. *Chronica Maiora*, trans. Preest, 283–4.
9. *CPR 1391–6*, 20.
10. *CPR 1381–5*, 441; *CPR 1385–9*, 27; *CPR 1389–92*, 293, 424; *CPR 1391–6*, 207.
11. *Royal Treasure*, 25, 304.
12. *CPR 1377–81*, 139; *CPR 1381–5*, 50, 170.
13. *CPR 1377–81*, 325; *CPR 1385–9*, 540; *CPR 1391–6*, 96.
14. *CPR 1396–9*, 380.
15. *Reign*, 275.
16. Perroy, *Correspondence*, 102.
17. *Foedera 1373–97*, 523; *English Historical Documents*, vol. 4, 160–3.
18. *Foedera 1373–97*, 523–4.
19. *Reign*, 273–5, for the anonymous letter, and see also Alfred Thomas, *A Blessed Shore: England and Bohemia from Chaucer to Shakespeare* (2007), 18.
20. *Reign*, 275; *English Historical Documents*, vol. 4, 160–3; T. Wright, ed., *Political Poems and Songs*, vol. 1 (1859), 282–300.
21. Fletcher, 'Manhood and Politics', 27.
22. *Issues*, 249.
23. ODNB 'Robert de Vere'.
24. See for example *CPR 1396–9*, 581; *CPR 1399–1401*, 528; *CPR 1405–8*, 52.
25. *CPR 1389–92*, 407.
26. *Foedera 1373–97*, 524.
27. *Chronica Maiora*, trans. Preest, 292.
28. *Testamenta Vetusta*, vol. 1, 134–5.
29. *Royal Treasure*, 24.
30. Perroy, *Correspondence*, 118–9.
31. Perroy, *Correspondence*, 122.
32. *CPR 1391–6*, 259.
33. *Issues*, 255.
34. *CCR 1392–6*, 133.
35. *Revolution*, 59.
36. *Revolution*, 59.
37. *CCR 1389–92*, 7.
38. Saul, 92 note 35, citing *Westminster Chronicle*, 516; also Tuck, 'House of Luxembourg', 220; *Revolution*, 59.
39. *Revolution*, 59.

14 *A Tragic Death, 1393–1394*

1. Saul, 242; PROME; *Reign*, 283–4.
2. ODNB 'Edmund of Langley'.

3. *CFR 1391–99*, 150–51.
4. Mortimer, *Fears*, 372; Given-Wilson, *Henry IV*, 421.
5. Geaman, 'Struggle to Conceive', 7–8.
6. Geaman, 'Struggle to Conceive', 10–12.
7. *Revolution*, 62; *Foedera 1373–97*, 525.
8. *Issues*, 255–6.
9. Cited in Christopher Fletcher, *Richard II, Manhood, Youth and Politics*.
10. *Reign*, 285.
11. *Foedera 1373–97*, 526.
12. *Issues*, 265–6.
13. *Issues*, 257.
14. *CChR 1341–1417*, 347–8.
15. *CChR 1341–1417*, 375–80.
16. *Foedera 1373–97*, 526.
17. *Issues*, 258, 264; *Foedera 1373–97*, 527; *Reign*, 305.
18. *Issues*, 262.
19. *Issues*, 263, 265–6.
20. *Issues*, 270.
21. *Reign*, 305.
22. Mathew, *Court*, 34; H. M. Colvin, *A History of the King's Works* (1963), vol. ii, 998; *Reign*, 304.
23. Saul, 456.
24. Stow, 'Chronicles versus Records', in *Documenting the Past*, 163; *Reign*, 304.
25. W. M. Ormrod, 'Richard II's Sense of English History', in *Reign of Richard II*, ed. Dodd, 98.

15 A Second Royal Marriage, 1394–1396

1. *Westminster Chronicle*, 192–4, cited in *Reign*, 174.
2. Given-Wilson, *Chronicles: the Writing of History in Medieval England*, 201.
3. *Foedera 1373–97*, 527.
4. Perroy, *Correspondence*, 161.
5. *Issues*, 253.
6. *Issues*, 253.
7. *Issues*, 257.
8. *Issues*, 259.
9. Mathew, *Court*, 25–8.
10. *Vita*, 134, cited in *Reign*, 285–6.
11. *Vita*, 156, 166, cited in Stow, 'Chronicles versus Records', 159, and *Chron Rev*, 130.
12. W. Paley Baildon, 'A Wardrobe Account of 16–17 Richard II, 1393–94', 498; Stow, 'Chronicles versus Records', 165–6; Rees R. Davies, edited by Brendan Smith, *Lords and Lordship in the British Isles* (2009), 93.
13. *Issues*, 226; *Royal Treasure*, 23.
14. Francis Palgrave, *Antient Kalendars and Inventories of the Treasury of His Majesty's Exchequer*, vol. iii, 358–61.
15. *Royal Treasure*, 24.

16. *Issues*, 257–8.
17. Harvey, *Black Prince*, 149.
18. *Revolution*, 57.
19. *Royal Treasure*, 104.
20. CPR 1377–81, 334; *CPR 1381–5*, 283; *CPR 1389–92*, 72, 199, 228, 237, 244, 332, 456.
21. *Issues*, 258.
22. *CPR 1391–6*, 448; Saul, 279.
23. *Foedera 1373–97*, 527.
24. *Royal Treasure*, 83.
25. Froissart, *Chronicles*, ed. Brereton, 409–17.
26. Cited in Saul, 284–5.
27. *Reign*, 287, and for a lengthy account of Richard's achievements in Ireland, Saul, 279–85.
28. *Issues*, 260.
29. *The Chronicles of Froissart*, ed. Macaulay, 424ff, for his long account of how he met Richard; Saul, 473, for the king's itinerary.
30. *Chronicles of Froissart*, 424, 430.
31. Bennett, 'Adultery and Anxieties', 127.
32. Saul, 461; ODNB.
33. *Chronica Maiora*, trans. Preest, 295.
34. *Chronicles of Froissart*, 436. He also adds the countess of Derby, Gaunt's daughter-in-law Mary de Bohun, but she was dead by then.
35. *Foedera 1373–97*, 530; *CPR 1396–9*, 86; *English Historical Documents*, vol. 4, 164–5; PROME, January 1397 parliament. A *donsel* was a man who did not yet have a title nor had been knighted.
36. *CChR 1341–1417*, 368, for John Beaufort being made earl of Somerset.
37. *Revolution*, 69.
38. Saul, 225–6; Palmer, 'Background of Richard II's Marriage to Isabel of France (1396)', *Bulletin of the Institute of Historical Research*, 1–17; Zita Eva Rohr, *Yolande of Aragon (1381–1442): Family and Power: The Reverse of the Tapestry* (2016), 20–22.
39. *Reign*, 276–8.
40. *Foedera 1373–97*, 529.
41. Perroy, *Correspondence*, 169; *Foedera 1373–97*, 527.
42. Philippa's second husband Sir John Golafre died in November 1396. Her sister Elizabeth had married William Montacute, earl of Salisbury, first husband of Richard II's mother Joan of Kent, as far back as 1349, and so we have the peculiar situation where two sisters born to the same father and mother married men born in 1328 and in 1373/4 respectively, the weddings taking place almost half a century apart. Edward was killed at Agincourt in October 1415 in his early forties, and Philippa outlived him: she died in July 1431, probably in her late seventies or so.
43. Perroy, *Correspondence*, 99, 101, 102, 165, 168, 170.
44. *Reign*, 306–7.
45. Saul, 228.
46. ODNB 'Isabella of France'.

47. *Revolution*, 71–2.
48. *Reign*, 308–9.
49. Tracy Adams, *Life and Afterlife of Isabeau of Bavaria*, 2–4; Sumption, *Divided Houses*, 551–2.
50. Saul, 351–2.
51. G. Daumet and Léon Mirot, *Isabelle de France, reine d'Angleterre, comtesse d'Angoulême, duchesse d'Orléans, 1389–1409*, in *Bibliothèque de l'école des chartes* (1906), tome 67, 273–4.
52. *Revolution*, 57.
53. *Royal Treasure*, 59.
54. *Foedera 1373–97*, 529; *CCR 1396–9*, 32–3; *CPR 1396–9*, 21.
55. Saul, 229.
56. David Wallace, *Chaucerian Polity*, 372; *Reign*, 312; Given-Wilson, *Henry IV*, 99.
57. *Reign*, 311–12.
58. Saul, 230, and *Reign*, 312–3, for all the details in this paragraph.
59. *Royal Treasure*, 63; http://www.history.ac.uk/richardII/vessels.html.
60. *Reign*, 313.
61. Saul, 230; http://www.history.ac.uk/richardII/roll.html.
62. *Revolution*, 81.
63. *Reign*, 313–4.
64. *Reign*, 315.
65. *Royal Treasure*, 68–9.
66. *Reign*, 314; Saul, 230; *Royal Treasure*, 63; *Revolution*, 81.
67. *Royal Treasure*, 63.
68. Walsingham, *Chronica Maiora*, trans. Preest, 297.
69. *Foedera 1373–97*, 529.
70. Goodman, *Loyal Conspiracy*, 86; *Royal Treasure*, 23.
71. *Revolution*, 83.
72. For the new research on Isabeau, see Rachel Gibbons, 'Isabeau of Bavaria, Queen of France (1385–1422): The Creations of an Historical Villainess', and Adams, *Life and Afterlife of Isabeau of Bavaria*, especially 231–3. Rosemary Hawley Jarman's 1978 novel *Crown in Candlelight* provides an excellent example of the older view of Isabeau, neglecting her cold, hungry and dirty children, abusing her insane husband for fun, and sleeping with his brother. For her gifts of books to her daughters, see Susan Groag Bell, 'Medieval Women Book Owners', 756.
73. Adams, *Life and Afterlife*, 232.
74. *Royal Treasure*, 23.
75. http://www.history.ac.uk/richardII/isabelle.html;   http://www.history.ac.uk/richardII/crowns.html; *Royal Treasure*, 23.
76. *Traison*, 203, 205–6.
77. *Chron Rev*, 110.
78. *Chron Rev*, 244.
79. Adams, *Life and Afterlife*, 233.
80. *Revolution*, 11.
81. *Reign*, 310.

16 A Coronation and the Succession, 1396–1397

1. *Issues*, 265.
2. Saul, 454; *Westminster Chronicle*, 230.
3. *Royal Treasure*, 85.
4. CCR 1396–9, 73.
5. *Reign*, 316.
6. Saul, 457 note 101, citing TNA E 403/555 and 556.
7. Saul, 457, citing TNA E 101/411/9 m14; *Issues*, 263; *Royal Treasure*, 84–5.
8. Saul, 457; ODNB.
9. *CPR 1396–9*, 40.
10. *CPR 1396–9*, 136, 188.
11. *Foedera 73–97*, 525; PROME, January 1397 parliament.
12. For the petition, see Alison McHardy, 'Haxey's Case, 1397' in *The Age of Richard II*, ed. Gillespie, 93–114, *Reign*, 317–20, and PROME, January 1397 parliament.
13. McHardy 'Haxey's Case' 102–3. Haxey's pardon is in PROME and *CPR 1396–9*, 141, wrongly given as CCR by McHardy, 'Haxey's Case', 113 note 86. Neither does the Patent Roll entry indicate that the pardon sardonically came at the request of the 'bishops and multitude of ladies', as stated.
14. *Foedera 1373–97*, 528, 530; Mortimer, *Fears of Henry IV*, 137. Edward had been made a Knight of the Garter in 1387.
15. The Godstowe chronicler cited in ODNB 'Edward of York'; I am grateful to Brian Wainwright for bringing this point to my attention.
16. ODNB 'Edward of York' by Horrox.
17. PROME, Appendix to the September 1399 parliament.
18. PROME, Appendix to the September 1399 parliament.
19. For example *CPR 1385–9*, 439, 510; *CPR 1389–92*, 128, 463. Mortimer, *Fears*, 124–5.
20. *Fears*, 114–5.
21. *Reign*, 321.
22. *CFR 1391–9*, 249.
23. ODNB 'John Montague'.
24. *Issues*, 267.
25. *Foedera 1397–1413*, 37.
26. *Revolution*, 90.
27. CPR 1396–9, 25, 247, 577; *Foedera 1373–97*, 530; *Foedera 1397–1413*, 1, 22–3; *Royal Treasure*, 63.
28. *Chron Rev*, 70.
29. *Revolution*, 140.
30. *Revolution*, 140.

17 The King's Strange Behaviour, 1397

1. Cited in Sumption, *Divided Houses*, 837–8.
2. *Chron Rev*, 71.
3. Steel, *Richard II*, 8, 279.
4. *England in the Late Middle Ages*, revised edition, (1965), 21; May McKisack, *The Fourteenth Century 1307–1399* (1959), 497–8; Vivian Green, *The*

Madness of Kings: Personal Trauma and the Fate of Nations (1993), 57–9. For a useful overview of historians' view on the subject, see Stow, 'Stubbs, Steel, and Richard II as Insane', 601–3, and also Saul, 462–4.

5. Saul, 391, 459–61.
6. McHardy, 'Richard II: A Personal Portrait', in *Reign of Richard II*, ed. Dodd, 15–23.
7. Stow, 'Stubbs, Steel, and Richard II as Insane', 602–3 note 9.
8. *Revolution*, 71, and also for the 'heraldic marriage' quotation.
9. Cited in Taylor, 'Richard II in the Chronicles', in *Art of Kingship*, 22; *An English Chronicle of the Reigns of Richard II, Henry IV, Henry V and Henry VI*, ed. J. S. Davies (1856), 12; *Chron Rev*, 68; *English Historical Documents*, vol. 4, 1327–1485, 168.
10. *Anon*, 56.
11. John Taylor, 'Richard II in the Chronicles', in *Richard II: The Art of Kingship*, 22, makes this point; also see Nigel Saul's article 'Kingship of Richard II' in the same volume.
12. Saul, 344–5.
13. Saul, 'Richard II and the Vocabulary of Kingship', 854.
14. Both cited in Roger Mott, 'Richard II and the Crisis of 1397' in *Church and Chronicle in the Middle Ages*, ed. Wood and Loud, 176.
15. Saul, 394.
16. *Chron Rev*, 73–4.
17. Saul, 394.
18. *Chron Rev*, 98.
19. Stow, 'Chronicles versus Records', 158.
20. T. A. Sandquist, 'The Holy Oil of St Thomas of Canterbury', 337–40.
21. Sandqvist, 'Holy Oil', 337.
22. Sandqvist, 'Holy Oil', 338–9.

18 The King's Revenge, 1397

1. *Chronica Maiora*, trans. Preest, 298; *Traison*, 7–8, 127–30; *Chron Rev*, 94–5; ODNB.
2. *Chron Rev*, 54, 96.
3. Saul, 374, for the queen's visit.
4. Saul, 374; *Traison*, 9.
5. *CPR 1396–9*, 241; *CCR 1396–9*, 137–8, 197.
6. *CCR 1396–9*, 208.
7. *CCR 1396–9*, 147–8.
8. Saul 372.
9. Mott, 'Richard II and the Crisis of 1397', 169–71.
10. *Traison, 6.*
11. *CCR 1396–9*, 208.
12. *CCR 1396–9*, 266–7, 324.
13. ODNB 'Thomas of Woodstock'; Saul, 379.
14. *English Historical Documents*, vol. 4, 166–7; *Chron Rev*, 80–2.
15. *Foedera 1397–1413*, 13, 15.
16. PROME, Appendix to the September 1399 parliament.

17. ODNB.
18. *CCR 1396–9*, 149–50, 157; *Foedera 1397–1413*, 19, 20, 24.
19. *Foedera 1397–1413*, 29.
20. PROME, Introduction to the September 1397 parliament.
21. *Foedera 1397–1413*, 15.
22. Saul, 378; *Chron Rev*, 61.
23. Given-Wilson, *Henry IV*, 106 note 31.
24. *CPR 1396–9*, 315.
25. *CPR 1396–9*, 339.
26. Cited in *Revolution*, 136.
27. *Chron Rev*, 58–60; *Revolution*, 101–2.
28. ODNB; Given-Wilson, *Chronicles*, 59; *Revolution*, 102. Thomas Holland, earl of Kent, was the eldest son of Arundel's sister Alice.
29. *Revolution*, 102–3, Given-Wilson, *Henry IV*, 105, citing Adam Usk 30–31.
30. *Chron Rev*, 60; ODNB; *Revolution*, 103.
31. *Revolution*, 103.
32. ODNB; *Revolution*, 103, 112; Given-Wilson, *Chronicles: The Writing of History*, 55.
33. *Testamenta Vetusta*, vol. 1, 130–3.
34. *CCR 1396–9*, 177ff.
35. *Royal Treasure*, 22–3, 30, 31.
36. *CPR 1396–9*, 310; *CFR 1391–9*, 237–9.
37. *CPR 1396–9*, 214.
38. *Chron Rev*, 116.
39. ODNB 'Thomas Arundel'.
40. *Issues*, 264.
41. *CChR 1341–1417*, 369–70. The appointments are also given in *Traison*, 11, whose French author struggled with the spelling of English place-names: *Auorde* for Hereford, *Sudrien* for Surrey, *Noruolt* for Norfolk and *Ontinton* for Huntingdon, for example. He also thought that William Scrope was made earl of the Isle of Man, spelt *Liloman*.
42. *CPR 1396–9*, 211.
43. *Traison*, 11: *ot le pris pour la mieulx dancant*.
44. *Foedera 1397–1413*, 25.
45. *Chron Rev*, 71.
46. *Reign*, 322.
47. Quote from Walsingham's *Annales Ricardi Secundi*, cited in *Chron Rev*, 71.

19 Duel and Exile, 1398

1. *CCR 1396–9*, 291, 292.
2. Saul, 398.
3. Given-Wilson, 'Richard II, Edward II, and the Lancastrian Inheritance', 558.
4. *CPR 1396–9*, 285.
5. Saul, 400. Shakespeare echoed this line in the first scene of his play about Richard, when Henry says 'All the treasons for these eighteen years / Complotted and contrived in this land / Fetch from false Mowbray their first head and spring.'
6. *English Historical Documents*, vol. 4, 170–71.

7. *CCR 1396–9*, 281–2; Foedera 1373–97, 532.
8. *Foedera 1373–97*, 532; Given-Wilson, 'Lancastrian Inheritance', 554.
9. *Foedera 1373–97*, 532.
10. *Usk*, 169, *Traison et Mort*, 148, cited in Saul. 399.
11. *English Historical Documents*, vol. 4, 171; *Chron Rev*, 89.
12. *CCR 1396–9*, 324.
13. *Issues*, 267–8.
14. Gillespie, 'Chivalry and Kingship', in *Age of Richard II*, 120.
15. *Traison*, 18.
16. *Revolution*, 132.
17. *Traison*, 18–19.
18. *Traison*, 17; *Revolution*, 132.
19. *Traison*, 18.
20. *Traison*, 21.
21. Saul, 400–01.
22. *Revolution*, 135, citing TNA E 403/561 membrane 4.
23. *Foedera 1373–97*, 533; *Foedera 1397–1413*, 44; *CPR 1396–9*, 339.
24. *CPR 1396–9*, 420, 422, 439; *Foedera 1397–1413*, 47–8.
25. *Traison*, 22.
26. *CPR 1396–9*, 422.
27. *Foedera 1373–97*, 533; *Foedera 1397–1413*, 47, 51.
28. *Foedera 1373–97*, 533; *Foedera 1397–1413*, 47–8; *CCR 1396–9*, 339; *CPR 1396–9*, 440.
29. Given-Wilson, *Henry IV*, 117.
30. *Issues*, 268.
31. *Issues*, 269.
32. *Chron Rev*, 72.
33. *CPR 1396–9*, 417.
34. *CPR 1396–9*, 425.
35. Given-Wilson, *Henry IV*, 118 note 94, 123 note 21.
36. Froissart, *Chronicles*, ii, 667–8.
37. *Chron Rev*, 105–6.
38. *Chron Rev*, 105.
39. Saul, 405.
40. ODNB 'John Montague'; *Revolution*, 151. Marie of Berry, born around 1375, was widowed for the second time in late 1396 and married her third husband in 1401.
41. Saul, 402–3.
42. *CPR 1396–9*, 418.
43. Given-Wilson and Curteis, *Royal Bastards of Medieval England*, 145–6.
44. *Issues*, 268.
45. *Revolution*, 137.
46. *Foedera 1397–1413*, 39, 51.
47. *CFR 1391–9*, 271–2; *CPR 1396–9*, 408, 431.
48. *CCR 1396–9*, 325; *CPR 1396–9*, 374, 390, 402 etc; Dunn, 'Richard II and the Mortimer Inheritance', 166 citing *Usk*, 40–41.
49. *Royal Treasure*, 30.
50. *CCR 1396–9*, 445, 451, 481; *CPR 1396–9*, 578.

51. *CPR 1399–1401*, 262, 404.
52. *Continuatio Eulogii*, cited in Given-Wilson, 'Lancastrian Inheritance', 558.
53. Given-Wilson, 'Lancastrian Inheritance', 558.

20 Perpetual Banishment, 1398–1399

1. *Revolution*, 139; Gillespie, 'Chivalry and Kingship', in *Age of Richard II*, 129; *Foedera 1397–1413*, 65. The emperor Manuel trusted Doria, and in 1396 had sent him as an envoy to the pope: Joelle Rollo-Koster and Thomas M. Izbicki, ed., *A Companion to the Great Western Schism* (2009), 202.
2. *Issues*, 272.
3. *A Companion to the Great Western Schism*, 202; Sumption, *Divided Houses*, 834.
4. *Chronica Maiora*, trans. Preest, 305.
5. *Revolution*, 110.
6. *English Historical Documents*, vol. 4, 1327–1485, ed. A. R. Myers, 169–70; *Revolution*, 124.
7. *English Historical Documents*, 4, 168.
8. *Revolution*, 123–4; Given-Wilson, *Henry IV*, 122.
9. *Chron Rev*, 75, and the page before the Introduction.
10. Gaunt's will can be read in *Testamenta Vetusta*, vol. 1, 140–45, where it is wrongly dated to 3 February 1397.
11. *Revolution*, 141.
12. *Revolution*, 141, citing TNA E 403/561 membrane 11.
13. *Revolution*, 143.
14. *Issues*, 268–9.
15. *CPR 1396–9*, 425, 490, 502, 563; *CFR 1391–9*, 293–4, 296–7, 303–4.
16. *CPR 1396–9*, 468–9, 470, 499, 501, 502, 514, 517, 534 etc.
17. PROME, Appendix to the September 1399 parliament.
18. John Mowbray's wife Katherine, whom he married in early 1412, was one of the many children of Ralph Neville, first earl of Westmorland and his second wife Joan Beaufort, youngest of the four illegitimate children of John of Gaunt and Katherine Swynford. Katherine Mowbray, *née* Neville, lived long enough to attend the coronation of her nephew Richard III in 1483.
19. *Testamenta Vetusta*, vol. 1, 85.
20. *Revolution*, 145.
21. Richard's will is cited in full, in English translation, in John Harvey's *The Plantagenets*, 219–24, and *Reign*, 322–7; an abridged version is in *Testamenta Vetusta*, vol. 1, 15–17.
22. *Issues*, 270.
23. Bennett, 'Richard II and the Wider Realm', in *Art of Kingship*, ed. Goodman and Gillespie. Humphrey and Henry of Monmouth were first cousins: their mothers Eleanor and Mary de Bohun were sisters.
24. See Alistair Dunn, 'Thomas Holland: Richard II's King of Ireland?', *History Ireland*, vol. 11, no. 1 (Spring 2003), 21–23.
25. *Issues*, 269–70.
26. Saul, 288–90.
27. ODNB; *Traison*, 170 note 1; *Revolution*, 147.

28. *Revolution*, 147; Given-Wilson, *Henry IV*, 125 note 34; *Traison*, 170.
29. *Traison*, 170–71.
30. *Foedera 1397–1413*, 82.
31. *Issues*, 272–3.
32. ODNB 'Thomas Despenser'.
33. *Chron Rev*, 109, 112–4.
34. *Chron Rev*, 112–13; another version of the agreement includes Queen Isabeau and her children, the late Queen Anne's other brother Johann von Görlitz (who in fact was dead by then), and Gian Galeazzo Visconti, duke of Milan.
35. *Revolution*, 152.

21 Henry of Lancaster Returns, 1399
1. Walsingham, *Annales Ricardi Secundi*, 240, cited in *Chron Rev*, 115.
2. *Chron Rev*, 98.
3. *Chron Rev*, 116–7, 126.
4. The *Vitae et Regni* thought Henry arrived in England around 24 June, the Nativity of St John the Baptist: *Chron Rev*, 126.
5. At least according to Walsingham: cited in *Chron Rev*, 117.
6. *Revolution*, 155.
7. *Chron Rev*, 135–6; *Revolution*, 157.
8. *Traison*, 42; *Chron Rev*, 119 note 6.
9. *Chron Rev*, 137.
10. *Chron Rev*, 138.
11. *Chronica Maiora*, trans. Preest, 308; *Chron Rev*, 160.
12. *Chronica Maiora*, trans. Preest, 308; *Chron Rev*, 121.
13. *CPR 1396–9*, 588; *Foedera 1397–1413*, 83.
14. *Traison*, 43–4, 191–2.
15. *Royal Treasure*, 35.
16. *Chron Rev*, 118.
17. *Chron Rev*, 127.
18. *Revolution*, 160.
19. *Chron Rev*, 128, 133; *Revolution*, 158.
20. ODNB 'Edmund of Langley'.
21. *Chron Rev*, 128.
22. *Chron Rev*, 128; *CPR 1396–9*, 589.
23. *Chron Rev*, 128–9.
24. *Revolution*, 162; *Chron Rev*, 242–3.
25. ODNB 'Thomas Despenser'; *Revolution*, 160.
26. *Traison*, 49, 192; *Chron Rev*, 140.
27. *Traison*, 192; *Revolution*, 160.
28. *Revolution*, 160.
29. Saul, 412.
30. *Traison*, 193.
31. ODNB 'John Holland'.
32. *Traison*, 196; Saul, 413; *Chron Rev*, 144.
33. *Traison*, 197–8.
34. *Chron Rev*, 144–5; Saul, 413–4.

35. Given-Wilson, *Henry IV*, 134–5.
36. *Traison*, 199.
37. *Revolution*, 168.
38. *Chron Rev*, 147, citing Jean Creton.
39. *Traison*, 200.
40. *Chron Rev*, 129.
41. *Traison*, 207; *Chron Rev*, 148.
42. ODNB 'Edward of York'.
43. *Traison*, 194–5.
44. *Traison*, 202–6.
45. *Traison*, 206.
46. *Chron Rev*, 123–4.
47. *Traison*, 208–9.
48. *Chron Rev*, 130.
49. *Traison*, 209.
50. *Chron Rev*, 150.
51. *Traison*, 209–10.

22 Deposition, 1399

1. *Revolution*, 169.
2. *Revolution*, 171.
3. *Traison*, 210–11; *Revolution*, 171.
4. *Revolution*, 171.
5. *CCR 1396–9*, 520–21.
6. *Traison*, 212–3; *Revolution*, 172.
7. *Traison*, 63, 214–5.
8. *Traison*, 63–4, 215 (*mauuais bastart*; another manuscript gives *petit bastart*); *Revolution*, 173.
9. *Traison*, 63–4; Given-Wilson, *Henry IV*, 140.
10. *Traison*, 65–6, 216–7. Richard's diatribe was necessarily recorded in French in this French chronicle, though he and the others may well have spoken English.
11. *Revolution*, 174–5.
12. Saul, 419; *Revolution*, 177.
13. Ian Mortimer, 'The Rules Governing Succession to the Crown 1199–1399', in his *Medieval Intrigue*, 298; *Chron Rev*, 166.
14. Given-Wilson, *Henry IV*, 141; *Chron Rev*, 168–89.
15. *Chron Rev*, 162–7.
16. Given-Wilson, *Henry IV*, 142–3.
17. *Chron Rev*, 170–71.
18. *Chron Rev*, 186.
19. *Chron Rev*, 166.
20. *Revolution*, 184.
21. *Foedera 1397–1413*, 87.
22. Given-Wilson, *Chronicles; The Writing of History in Medieval England*, 18; *Chron Rev*, 161.
23. *Chron Rev*, 242.

24. *Foedera 1397–1413*, 89.
25. *Usk*, 70–71, also cited in *Chronica Maiora*, trans. Preest, 311 note 2; *Foedera 1397–1413*, 91.
26. ODNB, 'Thomas Despenser'.
27. Douglas Biggs, 'The Reign of Henry IV' in *Fourteenth Century England I*, 197.
28. *Chron Rev*, 160.
29. *Testamenta Vetusta*, vol. 1, 146–9.
30. *Traison*, 228; Saul, 424.

23 *The Epiphany Rising, 1399–1400*
1. *CPR 1399–1401*, 92.
2. *Revolution*, 189–91; Mortimer, *Fears*, 205–9.
3. Biggs, 'Reign of Henry IV', 197; Martyn Lawrence, 'Too Flattering Sweet to be Substantial' in *Fourteenth Century England IV*, 154.
4. ODNB; *Traison*, lx.
5. *Chron Rev*, 230–1; *Fears*, 206.
6. *Continuatio Eulogii*, 385–6, cited in *Chron Rev*, 235–6.
7. As pointed out by Given-Wilson, *Henry IV*, 163, citing *Continuatio*, 387.
8. *Foedera 1397–1413*, 120.
9. *Revolution*, 191.
10. *CPR 1399–1401*, 220.
11. *Chron Rev*, 226–7; *Fears*, 208; *Revolution*, 141.
12. *CPR 1399–1401*, 183, 225; *Issues*, 277–8.
13. *CPR 1399–1401*, 193.
14. *CPR 1399–1401*, 202.
15. ODNB 'John Holland'.
16. *Chronica Maiora*, trans. Preest, 317; *Chron Rev*, 227.
17. Given-Wilson, *Henry IV*, 162 for the quotation.
18. *CPR 1399–1401*, 180, 387, 394, 435, 439.
19. *Issues*, 278–9; *CPR 1399–1401*, 201, 206, 244.
20. ODNB 'John Cornwall'.
21. *CPR 1399–1401*, 188, 197; *Chron Rev*, 228, 233, 238–9; Lawrence, 'Too Flattering Sweet', 154–5.
22. *Usk*, 89, cited in Given-Wilson, *Henry IV*, 163.
23. *Traison*, 102; *Chronica Maiora*, trans. Preest, 317; *Fears*, 209.
24. ODNB, citing TNA E 37/28.
25. *Foedera 1397–1413*, 156.

24 *The End of Richard of Bordeaux, 1400*
1. *Foedera 1397–1413*, 120.
2. *Chronica Maiora*, trans. Preest, 317.
3. *Chronica Maiora*, trans. Preest, 317; Saul, 426.
4. Mortimer, *Fears*, 212.
5. *Traison*, 104; *Chron Rev*, 241, 243–4.
6. Dillon, 'Remarks on the Manner of the Death of King Richard II'.
7. Saul, 425; *Chronica Maiora*, trans. Preest, 317 note 7.

8. *Issues*, 275, 277; Saul, 426.
9. *Chronica Maiora*, trans. Preest, 318; *Trokelowe*, ed. Riley, 331; *Traison*, lxi.
10. *Issues*, 276.
11. *Chronica Maiora*, trans. Preest, 318.
12. *Traison*, 103.
13. *Chron Rev*, 241–2, 244.
14. *Traison*, lviii.
15. *Chron Rev*, 240.
16. *Revolution*, 206.
17. *Chronica Maiora*, trans. Preest, 332.
18. *Testamenta Vetusta*, vol. 1, 188; Given-Wilson, *Henry IV*, 264–5; ODNB 'Edward of York'.
19. *Revolution*, 203.
20. Mortimer, *Fears*, 241; ODNB.
21. *Royal Treasure*, 116–7, for the negotiations and the queen's journey.
22. *Issues*, 290–91.
23. *Foedera 1397–1413*, 162, 164.
24. *Chron Rev*, 112.
25. *Chronica Maiora*, trans. Preest, 394.
26. *Issues*, 325–7.
27. *Issues*, 326.
28. *Revolution*, 56.
29. McHardy, 'Personal Portrait', in *Reign of Richard II*, ed. Dodd, 15.
30. *Historia Vitae et Regni Ricardi Secundi*, 166, cited in Taylor, 'Chronicles', in *Art of Kingship*, 28, and Stow, 'Chronicles Versus Records', 160; *Chron Rev*, 241.

Bibliography

Primary Sources

Annales Ricardi Secundi et Henrici Quarti, in J. de Trokelowe et Anon., *Chronica et Annales*, ed. H. T. Riley (London, Rolls Series, 1866)

The Anonimalle Chronicle 1333–81, ed. Vivian Hunter Galbraith (Manchester: Manchester University Press, 1927; reprinted with minor corrections 1970)

The Antient Kalendars and Inventories of the Treasury of His Majesty's Exchequer, 3 vols., ed. Francis Palgrave (London, 1836)

The Brut or the Chronicles of England, vol. 2, ed. F. W. D. Brie (London: Early English Text Society, original series, 136, 1908)

Calendar of Charter Rolls 1341–1417, 1 vol. (London: His/Her Majesty's Stationery Office, 1916)

Calendar of Close Rolls 1377–1401, 7 vols. (London: HMSO, 1914–27)

Calendar of Documents Relating to Scotland 1357–1509, 1 vol.

Calendar of Entries in the Papal Registers Relating to Great Britain and Ireland: Papal Letters, volume 4, 1362–1404, ed. W. H. Bliss and J. A. Twemlow (London: HMSO, 1902)

Calendar of Fine Rolls 1377–1399, 3 vols. (London, HMSO, 1926–9)

Calendar of Inquisitions Post Mortem, 11 vols. (London: Public Record Office)

Calendar of Papal Registers, vol. 4, 1362–1404, ed. W. H. Bliss and J. A. Twemlow (London: HMSO, 1902)

Calendar of Patent Rolls 1377–1401, 7 vols. (London: HMSO, 1985–1909)

Calendar of Select Plea and Memoranda Rolls of the City of London, 1381–1412, ed. A. H. Thomas (London: HMSO, 1932)

The Chronica Maiora of Thomas Walsingham, 1376–1422, translated by David Preest (Woodbridge: The Boydell Press, 2005)

The Chronicle of Adam Usk, 1377–1421, ed. Chris Given-Wilson (Oxford: Clarendon Press, 1997)

Sir John Froissart's Chronicles of England, France and the Adjoining Countries, trans. Thomas Johnes, 2 vols. (London: Hafod Press, 1855)

Chronicles of the Revolution, 1397–1400: The Reign of Richard II, ed. Chris Given-Wilson (Manchester: Manchester University Press, 1993)

Chronicque de la Traison et Mort de Richart Deux Roy Dengleterre, ed. Benjamin Williams (London: S. and J. Bentley, Wilson and Fley, 1846)

The Diplomatic Correspondence of Richard II, ed. Edouard Perroy (London, Camden third series, volume 48, 1933)

English Historical Documents, Vol. 4, 1327–1485, ed. A. R. Myers (London: Eyre and Spottiswoode, 1969; reprinted by Routledge, 1996)

Historia Vitae et Regni Ricardi Secundi, ed. George B. Stow (Philadelphia: University of Pennsylvania, 1977)

Jean Froissart: Chronicles, translated and edited by Geoffrey Brereton (London: Penguin, 1968, reprinted with minor corrections 1978)

John of Gaunt's Register, part 1, 1371–1375, ed. Sydney Armitage-Smith (London: Camden third series, volume 20, 1911)

Knighton's Chronicle 1337–1396, ed. Geoffrey Haward Martin (Oxford: Clarendon Press, 1995)

The Parliament Rolls of Medieval England, ed. Brand, Curry, Given-Wilson, Horrox, Martin, Ormrod and Phillips (Scholarly Editions, 2005; online edition)

The Reign of Richard II From Minority to Tyranny 1377–97, ed. A. K. McHardy (Manchester: Manchester University Press, 2012)

Testamenta Vetusta: Being Illustrations From Wills, vol. 1, ed. Nicholas Harris Nicholas (London: Nichols and Son 1826)

Thomae Walsingham, Quondam Monachi S. Albani, Historia Anglicana, ed. Henry Thomas Riley, vol. 2 (London: Longman, Green, 1864)

La Vie du Prince Noir by Chandos Herald, ed. Diana B. Tyson (Tübingen: Max Niemeyer Verlag, 1975)

The Westminster Chronicle 1381–1394, ed. L. C. Hector and B. F. Harvey (Oxford, 1982)

Secondary Sources

Adams, Tracy, *The Life and Afterlife of Isabeau of Bavaria* (Baltimore: Johns Hopkins University Press, 2010)

Ashe, Laura, *Richard II: A Brittle Glory (Penguin Monarchs)* (London: Allen Lane, 2016)

Baildon, W. Paley, 'A Wardrobe Account of 16–17 Richard II, 1393–94', *Archaeologia*, 62 (1911)

Barber, Richard, *Edward, Prince of Wales and Aquitaine: A Biography of the Black Prince* (Woodbridge: The Boydell Press, 1978, reprinted 1996)

Barker, Juliet, *England, Arise: The People, The King and The Great Revolt of 1381* (London: Little, Brown 2014)

Barron, Caroline, 'The Tyranny of Richard II', *Bulletin of the Institute of Historical Research*, 41 (1968)

Barron, Caroline, and Saul, Nigel, eds., *England and the Low Countries in the Late Middle Ages* (Sutton History Paperbacks)

Bell, Susan Groag, 'Medieval Women Book Owners: Arbiters of Lay Piety and Ambassadors of Culture', *Signs*, 7 (1982)

Bennett, Michael, '*Honi soit qui mal y pense*: Adultery and Anxieties about Paternity in Late Medieval England', in *The Medieval Python: The Purposive and Provocative Work of Terry Jones*, ed. R. F. Yeager and Toshiyuki Takamiya (London: Palgrave MacMillan, 2012)

Bennett, Michael, *Richard II and the Revolution of 1399* (Stroud: Sutton Publishing, 1999)

Bennett, Michael, 'Henry of Bolingbroke and the Revolution of 1399', *Henry IV: Establishment of the Regime*, ed. Dodd and Biggs

Bevan, Bryan, *King Richard II* (London: The Rubicon Press, 1990)

Biggs, Douglas, 'The Reign of Henry IV: The Revolution of 1399 and the Establishment of the Lancastrian Regime', *Fourteenth Century England I*, ed. Nigel Saul (Woodbridge: The Boydell Press, 2000)

Burden, Joel, 'How Do You Bury a Deposed King? The Funeral of Richard II and the Establishment of Lancastrian Royal Authority in 1400', *Henry IV: Establishment of the Regime*, ed. Dodd and Biggs

Carlson, David R., ed., 'The Deposition of Richard II: "The Record and Process of the Renunciation and Deposition of Richard II" (1399)' (Toronto Medieval Latin Texts, 29; Toronto, Pontifical Institute of Medieval Studies, 2007)

Cherry, John, 'Late Fourteenth-Century Jewellery: The Inventory of November 1399', *The Burlington Magazine*, vol. 130, no. 1019 (Feb. 1988)

Chrimes, S. B., 'Richard II's Questions to the Judges, 1287', *Law Quarterly Review*, 72 (1956)

Clarke, M. V., 'The Wilton Diptych', *Fourteenth-Century Studies*, ed. L. S. Sutherland and M. McKisack (Oxford: Clarendon Press, 1937)

Davies, Rees, and Smith, Brendan, *Lords and Lordship in the British Isles in the Late Middle Ages* (Oxford: Oxford University Press, 2009)

Dillon, D., 'Remarks on the Manner of the Death of King Richard II', *Archaeologia*, (1840)

Dodd, Gwilym, ed., *The Reign of Richard II* (Stroud: Tempus Publishing, 2000)

Dodd, Gwilym, and Biggs, Douglas, ed., *Henry IV: The Establishment of the Regime, 1399–1406* (Woodbridge, 2003)

Dodd, Gwilym, 'Kingship, Parliament and the Court: the Emergence of 'High Style' in Petitions to the English Crown, *c*. 1350–1405', *English Historical Review*, 129 (2014)

Duls, Louisa DeSaussure, *Richard II in the Early Chronicles* (London: Mouton, 1975)

Dunn, Alastair, 'Richard II and the Mortimer Inheritance', *Fourteenth Century England II*, ed. Chris Given-Wilson (Woodbridge: The Boydell Press, 2002)

Emerson, Barbara, *The Black Prince* (London: Weidenfeld and Nicholson, 1976)

Fletcher, Christopher, 'Manhood and Politics in the Reign of Richard II', *Past and Present*, 89 (2005)

Geaman, Kristen L., 'A Personal Letter Written by Anne of Bohemia', *English Historical Review*, 128 (2013)

Geaman, Kristen L., 'Anne of Bohemia and her Struggle to Conceive', *Social History of Medicine*, 27 (2014)

Gibbons, Rachel, 'Isabeau of Bavaria, Queen of France (1385–1422): The Creations of an Historical Villainess', *Transactions of the Royal Historical Society*, 6th series, 6 (1996)

Gillespie, James L., ed., *The Age of Richard II* (Stroud: Sutton Publishing, 1997)

Given-Wilson, Chris, *The Royal Household and the King's Affinity* (New Haven, 1986)

Given-Wilson, Chris, 'Wealth and Credit, Public and Private: the Earls of Arundel, 1306–1397', *English Historical Review*, 106 (1991)

Given-Wilson, Chris, 'The Manner of King Richard's Renunciation: A "Lancastrian Narrative"?', *English Historical Review*, 108 (1993)

Given-Wilson, Chris, 'Richard II, Edward II, and the Lancastrian Inheritance', *English Historical Review*, 109 (1994)

Given-Wilson, Chris, *Henry IV* (New Haven and London: Yale University Press, 2016)

Goodman, Anthony, *The Loyal Conspiracy: The Lords Appellant Under Richard II* (Coral Gables, Florida: University of Miami Press, 1971)

Goodman, Anthony, and James Gillespie, eds., *Richard II: The Art of Kingship* (Oxford: Clarendon Press, 1999)

Goodman, Anthony, *John of Gaunt: The Exercise of Princely Power in Fourteenth-Century Europe* (London: Longman, 1992)

Green, David, *Edward the Black Prince: Power in Medieval Europe* (London: Longman, 2007)

Gundy, A. K., *Richard II and the Rebel Earl* (Cambridge Studies in Medieval Life and Thought: Fourth Series; Cambridge University Press, 2013)

Gordon, Dillian, 'A New Discovery in the Wilton Diptych', *The Burlington Magazine*, vol. 134, no. 1075 (Oct. 1992)

Harvey, John, *The Black Prince and his Age* (London: B. T. Batsford, 1976)

Hibbard, Laura A., 'The Books of Sir Simon de Burley, 1387', *Modern Language Notes*, 30 (1915)

Jones, Michael, *The Black Prince: The King That Never Was* (Head of Zeus, 2017) (forthcoming)

Jones, Richard, *The Royal Policy of Richard II: Absolutism in the Later Middle Ages* (Oxford: Blackwell, 1968)

Jones, Terry et al, *Who Murdered Chaucer? A Medieval Mystery* (London: Methuen, 2003)

Lawne, Penny, *Joan of Kent: The First Princess of Wales* (Stroud: Amberley Publishing, 2015)

Lawrence, Martyn, 'Too Flattering Sweet to be Substantial'? The Last Months of Thomas, Lord Despenser', *Fourteenth Century England IV*, ed. J. S. Hamilton (Woodbridge: The Boydell Press, 2006)

Mathew, Gervase, *The Court of Richard II* (London: John Murray, 1968)

Mitchell, Shelagh, 'Richard II and the Broomcod Collar: New Evidence from the Issue Rolls', *Fourteenth Century England II*, ed. Chris Given-Wilson (Woodbridge: The Boydell Press, 2002)

Mortimer, Ian, *The Fears of Henry IV: The Life of England's Self-Made King* (London: Vintage, 2008)

Mortimer, Ian, 'Richard II and the Succession to the Crown' in his *Medieval Intrigue: Decoding Royal Conspiracies* (London: Continuum, 2010)

Mortimer, Ian, 'The Rules Governing Succession to the Crown, 1199–1399' in *Medieval Intrigue*

Mott, Roger, 'Richard II and the Crisis of 1397', *Church and Chronicle in the Middle Ages: Essays Presented to John Taylor*, ed. Ian Wood and G. A. Loud (London and Rio Grande: The Hambledon Press, 1991)

Ormrod, W. M., 'In Bed with Joan of Kent: The King's Mother and the Peasants' Revolt' in *Medieval Women: Texts and Contexts in Late Medieval Britain. Essays in Honour of Felicity Riddy*, ed. Jocelyn Wogan-Browne et al (Brepols, 2000)

Ormrod, W. M., *Edward III* (New Haven and London: Yale University Press, 2011)

Palmer, J. J. N., 'The Background of Richard II's Marriage to Isabel of France (1396)', *Bulletin of the Institute of Historical Research*, 44 (1971), 1–17

Reitemeier, Arnd, 'Born to be a Tyrant? The Childhood and Education of Richard II', *Fourteenth Century England II*, ed. Chris Given-Wilson (Woodbridge: The Boydell Press, 2002)

Saul, Nigel, 'Richard II and the Vocabulary of Kingship', *English Historical Review*, 110 (1995)

Saul, Nigel, *Richard II* (New Haven and London: Yale University Press, 1997)

Saul, Nigel, *The Three Richards: Richard I, Richard II and Richard III* (London: Hambeldon, 2005)

Sayles, G. O., 'The Deposition of Richard II: Three Lancastrian Narratives', *Bulletin of the Institute of Historical Research*, 54 (1981)

Scattergood, V. J., 'Literary Culture at the Court of Richard II' in *English Court Culture in the Later Middle Ages*, ed. V. J. Scattergood and J. W. Sherborne (London: Duckworth, 1983)

Staley, Lynn, *Languages of Power in the Age of Richard II* (Pennsylvania State University Press, 2005)

Steel, Anthony, *Richard II* (Cambridge, 1941)

Stow, George B., 'Stubbs, Steel, and Richard II as Insane: The Origin and Evolution of an English Historiographical Myth', *Proceedings of the American Philosophical Society*, 143 (1999)

Stow, George B., 'Richard II and the Invention of the Pocket Handkerchief', *Albion: A Quarterly Journal Concerned with British Studies*, 27 (1995)

Stow, George B., 'Chronicles Versus Records: the Character of Richard II', *Documenting the Past: Essays in Medieval History Presented to George Peddy Cuttino*, ed. J. S. Hamilton and Patricia J. Bradley (Woodbridge and Wolfeboro: The Boydell Press, 1989)

Stratford, Jenny, *Richard II and the English Royal Treasure* (2012)

Sumption, Jonathan, *Divided Houses: The Hundred Years War*, volume III (London: Faber and Faber, 2009)

Taylor, Craig D., 'Weep Thou For Me in France': French Views of the Deposition of Richard II', *Fourteenth Century England III*, ed. W. M. Ormrod (Woodbridge: The Boydell Press, 2004)

Thomas, Alfred, *Anne's Bohemia: Czech Literature and Society, 1310–1420* (Minneapolis: University of Minnesota, 1998)

Thomas, Alfred, 'Margaret of Teschen's Czech Prayer: Transnationalism and Female Literacy in the Later Middle Ages', *Huntingdon Library Quarterly*, 74 (2011)

Wallis, Penelope, 'The Embroidered Binding of the Felbrigge Psalter', *The British Library Journal*, 13 (1987)

Wentersdorf, K. P., 'The Clandestine Marriages of the Fair Maid of Kent', *Journal of Medieval History*, 5 (1979)

Wilkinson, Bertie, 'The Deposition of Richard II and the Accession of Henry IV', *History*, 54 (1939)

Index